Introduction to the Bible

THE OPEN YALE COURSES SERIES is designed to bring the depth and breadth of a Yale education to a wide variety of readers. Based on Yale's Open Yale Courses program (http://oyc.yale.edu), these books bring outstanding lectures by Yale faculty to the curious reader, whether student or adult. Covering a wide variety of topics across disciplines in the social sciences, physical sciences, and humanities, Open Yale Courses books offer accessible introductions at affordable prices.

The production of Open Yale Courses for the Internet was made possible by a grant from the William and Flora Hewlett Foundation.

**RECENT TITLES**

Paul H. Fry, *Theory of Literature*
Christine Hayes, *Introduction to the Bible*
Shelly Kagan, *Death*
Dale B. Martin, *New Testament History and Literature*
Douglas W. Rae, *Capitalism: Success, Crisis, and Reform*
Ian Shapiro, *The Moral Foundations of Politics*
Steven B. Smith, *Political Philosophy*

# Introduction to the Bible

CHRISTINE HAYES

Yale
UNIVERSITY PRESS
New Haven and London

Yale University Press books may be purchased in quantity for educational,
business, or promotional use. For information, please e-mail
sales.press@yale.edu (U.S. office) or sales@yaleup.co.uk (U.K. office).

Set in Minion type by Westchester Book Group
Printed in the United States of America

Biblical verses reprinted from *Tanakh: The Holy Scriptures* by permission
of the University of Nebraska Press. Copyright © 1985 The Jewish
Publication Society, Philadelphia.

Table 3: From *Exploring Exodus: The Heritage of Biblical Israel*, by Nahum
M. Sarna, copyright © 1986 by Nahum M. Sarna, table appears on p. 76.
Used by permission of Schocken Books, a division of Random House, Inc.
For information about this and other Random House, Inc., books and
authors, see the Web site at http://www.randomhouse.com.

Map 6: From *The Old Testament: A Historical and Literary Introduction to
the Hebrew Scriptures*, by Michael Coogan, copyright © 2006 by Oxford
University Press, Inc., map appears on p. 403. Used by permission of
Oxford University Press, Inc.

Library of Congress Cataloging-in-Publication Data

Hayes, Christine Elizabeth.
    Introduction to the Bible / Christine Hayes.
        pages cm — (The open Yale courses series)
    Includes bibliographical references and index.
    ISBN 978-0-300-18179-1 (pbk.)
    1. Bible. O.T.—Introductions.    I. Title.
    BS1140.3.H39 2012
    221.6′1—dc23

                            2012022003

A catalogue record for this book is available from the British Library.

This paper meets the requirements of ANSI/NISO Z39.48-1992
(Permanence of Paper).

undefined

*For my students,*
*real and virtual,*
*past, present, and future*

# Contents

# Preface

This book examines the small library of twenty-four books common to all Jewish and Christian Bibles everywhere[1]—books that preserve the diverse efforts of various writers over a period of nearly a millennium to make sense of both the historical odyssey and the human experience of the ancient Israelite people. Like any library, this ancient collection contains books by many authors writing in many contexts and responding to many crises and questions—political, historical, socioeconomic, cultural, philosophical, religious, and moral—offering an unresolved polyphony that rewards careful reading and reflection.

The great variety and complexity of the many books of the Bible can be daunting to those who wish to understand not only its contents but also its continuing influence through history. This volume guides readers through the complex and polyphonous literature of the twenty-four biblical books that would serve as a foundational pillar of western civilization. Introducing readers to the modern methods of study that have led to deep and powerful insights into the original context and meaning of biblical texts, this book traces the diverse strands of Israelite culture and thought incorporated in the Bible, against the backdrop of their historical and cultural setting in the ancient Near East. It probes the passionate and highly fraught struggle of different biblical writers to understand and represent their nation's historical experience and covenantal relationship with its god.

The twenty-four chapters that constitute the present volume are based on the twenty-four lectures presented in my undergraduate course "Introduction to the Old Testament,"[2] which is widely available online through Yale University's Open Yale Courses project (http://oyc.yale.edu/). This volume is not an exact transcript of those lectures; it revises and adapts them for a written format. At times a different order of presentation is adopted. Repetitions and infelicitous formulations have been deleted, and some new material has been incorporated—in particular, close analysis of primary sources and biblical texts that, in the context of the Yale course, was undertaken by students in small discussion sections.

By their very nature as introductory, the course and the current volume do not represent my own original research. Rather, they draw upon and synthesize a vast body of existing scholarship on the Bible of ancient Israel—especially the writings of Michael Coogan, Moshe Greenberg, Yehezkel Kaufmann, Jonathan Klawans, Jacob Milgrom, Nahum Sarna, and the excellent scholarly essays in *The Jewish Study Bible,* edited by Adele Berlin and Marc Brettler (New York: Oxford University Press, 2004). Readers will also see some correspondences between the present volume and two summary chapters on biblical Israel in my textbook *The Emergence of Judaism: Classical Traditions in Contemporary Perspectives* (Minneapolis, MN: Fortress Press, 2010).

Chapter 1 is a general introduction to the Bible in its ancient Near Eastern context. Chapters 2 through 15 follow the narrative chronology of the Bible, from Genesis through 2 Kings. Readers should be aware that the narrative sequence does not reflect the compositional sequence of the Bible. In other words, and as just one example, most scholars now agree that parts of Genesis were written long after parts of Exodus or Deuteronomy or Isaiah. Many biblical books came into being through the accretion of various materials over the course of centuries. Thus, while following the narrative chronology imposed by the final redactor of Genesis through 2 Kings, we will simultaneously attend to the compositional history of the text, noting the likely provenance of the various units that make up the final redacted biblical text and considering how and why the text acquired the form we see today. Chapters 16 through 19 examine the books of the prophets in historical sequence rather than canonical sequence, and chapters 20 through 24 take a somewhat thematic approach to the books collected in the section of the Hebrew Bible known as the "Writings."

Readers of this volume will derive maximum benefit if they are familiar with the biblical material analyzed in each chapter. Thus, readers are strongly urged to read the relevant biblical passages listed at the beginning of each chapter. However, even readers unable to complete the biblical readings will learn much from the presentations and discussions in this book.

The biblical translation that serves as the basis for both the course and this volume is that of the Jewish Publication Society, particularly as found in *The Jewish Study Bible.* Citations of biblical texts in this volume are taken primarily from *Tanakh: The Holy Scriptures* (Philadelphia: Jewish Publication Society, 1985)[3] but also occasionally from the Revised Standard Version (particularly in the case of well-known passages such as the twenty-third psalm). In both cases, I have modified the translation to more accurately reflect the various modes of reference employed for the Israelite deity. Biblical writings regularly use four distinct terms to refer directly to the Israelite deity (I include here terms of consistent direct address only and not more occasional and descriptive epithets): El, Elohim, Yahweh, and (with less frequency) Adonai. El is the name of the chief god of the Canaanite pantheon. Elohim is a grammatically plural form ("gods"), but in reference to the god of Israel, it takes singular verbs and thus may be understood as another name for this specific god. Yahweh is a divine name attested in archaeological finds from regions to the south of biblical Israel and applied to the Israelite god in biblical writings. Adonai, literally "my lord," is used as a reference to the deity in a few biblical books. Many English translations of the Bible adopt the convention of rendering El and Elohim as "God" (with a capital G) and Yahweh as "the LORD" (in capital letters). The latter rendering is a pious substitution made in deference to a postbiblical reluctance to pronounce the name Yahweh. Unfortunately, all of these renderings are misleading. On the one hand, they obscure the historical connections between Israel's god and the gods of surrounding peoples (specifically the Canaanite deity El and the southern deity Yahweh). On the other hand, the rendering "God" causes readers to confuse the deity of the Hebrew Bible with the deity constructed by the much later tradition of western theology, a deity commonly referred to as "God" (with a capital G). As any astute reader of the Pentateuch will immediately discern, the biblical character El, or Elohim or Yahweh, is not represented by the biblical writer as possessing the attributes attributed to the deity referred to as "God" by the later tradition of western theology (for example, in many narratives he lacks the attributes of omniscience and immutability). It is best that the reader keep these two constructions (the biblical deity and the theologian's "God") distinct in order to fully appreciate the biblical texts. For that reason, the word God with a capital G does not appear in this volume (except when quoting the work of a scholar who does employ the term).[4] In order to provide the most unmediated access to the conceptions of the divine found in ancient Israel, the direct names El, Elohim, and Yahweh will be rendered as they appear in the biblical text.[5]

The terms Hebrew, Israelite, and Judean also require some explanation. "Hebrew" is the name employed in some biblical sources to designate the most ancient ancestors of the Israelite people. It is primarily an ethnic and linguistic term denoting persons who spoke Hebrew, a Canaanite dialect. The Hebrews are thought to have established themselves in the land of Canaan (roughly modern-day Israel) by about 1200 B.C.E. The terms *Israel* and *Israelite* refer to a member of the twelve Hebrew tribes of the Israelite *ethnos* who inhabited Canaan, eventually forming themselves into a united kingdom around 1000 B.C.E. The kingdom of Israel later split into a northern kingdom, Israel, and a southern kingdom, Judah. Although any member of the twelve tribes was a member of the Israelite ethnos, inhabitants of the northern kingdom were Israelites also by virtue of being from the *kingdom* of Israel, while inhabitants of the southern kingdom were (additionally) known as Judeans by virtue of being from the *kingdom* of Judah. However, with the destruction of the northern kingdom in 722, the only Israelites remaining were the Judeans, and thus the terms *Israelite* and *Judean* become somewhat interchangeable (except in contexts that refer clearly to the former inhabitants of the destroyed kingdom of Israel). Falling under Persian rule at the end of the sixth century, the area around Jerusalem was named Yehud and the term *Yehudi* (often translated "Jew" but more properly "Judean") referred to an inhabitant of Yehud/Judea. It would be some centuries before the term *Yehudi* was understood to designate an adherent of the tradition of Judaism (a Jew), rather than an inhabitant of the province of Yehud/Judea (a Judean).

The land in which the kingdoms of Israel and Judah were located is referred to by many biblical writers as "the land of Canaan," and it is that designation that will be adopted in this volume. Finally, throughout this volume, the abbreviations C.E. (Common Era) and B.C.E. (Before the Common Era) will be employed instead of the corresponding abbreviations B.C. (Before Christ) and A.D. (*Anno Domini*).[6]

# Chronology of Significant Events in the History of Ancient Israel

| | |
|---|---|
| 2000–1900 B.C.E. | Third dynasty of Ur in Mesopotamia; XII dynasty in Egypt |
| 1900–1800 B.C.E. | First Babylonian dynasty |
| 1728–1686 B.C.E. | Period of Hammurapi, the historical setting for the patriarchal narratives, spanning four generations from Abraham to the sons of Jacob |
| 1700–1600 B.C.E. | Hyksos invade Egypt; Babylonia declines; possible Hebrew migration into Egypt |
| 1290–1211 B.C.E. | XIX dynasty in Egypt, Pharaohs Ramses II and Merneptah: the historical setting for the story of the Jews' enslavement in Egypt, the rise of Moses, and the Exodus |
| End of thirteenth century B.C.E. | An entity known as Israel is attested in Canaan |
| 1200–1000 B.C.E. | Philistines settle along the coast of Canaan; the historical setting for the events of the book of Judges—Israelite tribes inhabit tribal areas throughout Canaan, at times forming alliances against common enemies under the leadership of "judges" |
| 1100–1000 B.C.E. | Philistine ascendancy in Canaan; the prophet Samuel anoints Saul first king in Israel |
| 1000–961 B.C.E. | King David consolidates the Israelite tribes in a united kingdom and establishes Jerusalem as the national capital |
| 961–922 B.C.E. | King Solomon builds the Temple in Jerusalem |
| 922 B.C.E. | Upon Solomon's death, the ten northern tribes rebel, creating Israel in the north, ruled by Jeroboam I, and Judah in the south, ruled by Rehoboam |
| 876–842 B.C.E. | In Israel: the Omri dynasty; the prophet Elijah (c. 850 B.C.E.) rails against Baal worship under Ahab and his queen, Jezebel. In Judah: Jehoshaphat rules, followed by Jehoram |
| 842 B.C.E. | In Israel: Jehu establishes a dynasty and pays tribute to Assyria. In Judah: Athaliah rules |
| 786–746 B.C.E. | In Israel: Jeroboam II reigns; the prophets Amos and Hosea deliver their oracles |
| 750–730 B.C.E. | Aggressive Assyrian expansion; the prophet Isaiah begins his prophetic career in Judah (c. 742–700 B.C.E.) |
| 732 B.C.E. | Syria falls to the Assyrians; soon after, the prophet Micah delivers oracles in Judah |
| 722 B.C.E. | Assyrians under Shalmaneser V conquer Samaria, the capital of Israel; Sargon II makes Samaria an Assyrian province, marking the end of the northern kingdom; mass Israelite deportation |

*(continued)*

| | |
|---|---|
| 715 B.C.E. | Hezekiah reigns in Judah and initiates religious reforms in line with Deuteronomistic ideology |
| 701 B.C.E. | Sennacherib of Assyria lays siege to Jerusalem; Judah becomes a tributary vassal of Assyria |
| 687–642 B.C.E. | Manasseh reigns in Judah and reintroduces foreign cultic practices |
| 640–609 B.C.E. | Josiah reigns in Judah; initiates religious reforms, centralizing the worship of Yahweh in the Jerusalem Temple; short period of Judean independence |
| 628–622 B.C.E. | Zephaniah delivers his prophecies |
| 626–587 B.C.E. | Jeremiah delivers his prophecies |
| 612 B.C.E. | Babylonians and Medes raze Nineveh, the capital of Assyria; Babylonians soon establish dominance over the ancient Near East |
| 609 B.C.E. | Judean King Josiah killed in the Battle of Megiddo |
| 605 B.C.E. | Habakkuk delivers his prophecies |
| 597 B.C.E. | Nebuchadrezzar of Babylonia attacks Judah; first deportation to Babylonia includes Judah's king Jehoiachin and the prophet Ezekiel |
| 593 B.C.E. | Ezekiel begins to deliver his prophecies in Babylonia |
| 587–586 B.C.E. | Jerusalem falls to the Babylonians; second deportation includes Judah's King Zedekiah; the prophet Jeremiah flees to Egypt |
| 539 B.C.E. | Babylon falls to Cyrus II of Persia; period of the prophecies of Second Isaiah |
| 538 B.C.E. | Cyrus's edict permits Jews to return to Judah and rebuild the Temple; first exiles return under Sheshbazzar |
| 520–515 B.C.E. | Jerusalem Temple is rebuilt; the prophets Haggai and Zechariah are active; Judah (Yehud) is a semiautonomous province of the Persian Empire |
| Fifth century B.C.E. | Malachi delivers his prophecies; a second return under Ezra occurs (date uncertain) |
| 445 B.C.E. | Nehemiah arrives in Judah; rebuilds the walls of Jerusalem |
| 336–323 B.C.E. | Alexander conquers the ancient Near East; Hellenistic period begins |
| 300–200 B.C.E. | Palestine falls under the control of the Ptolemies of Egypt; rise of the Jewish community of Alexandria in Egypt |
| 200 B.C.E. | Palestine falls under the control of the Seleucids of Syria |
| 175–163 B.C.E. | Seleucid King Antiochus IV Epiphanes inflames factional violence in Jerusalem; Judah Maccabee and his sons lead a revolt in 167 B.C.E. |
| 164 B.C.E. | Maccabean victory; the desecrated Temple is rededicated to Yahweh; Judea becomes an independent kingdom under the Hasmoneans |

# CHAPTER 1

# The Legacy of Ancient Israel

In the nineteenth and twentieth centuries, archaeologists unearthed the great civilizations of the ancient Near East: ancient Egypt, Mesopotamia, and the area we refer to as the Fertile Crescent, including Canaan. Scholars have been stunned by the ruins and records of these remarkable cultures and civilizations—massive, complex empires in some cases, many of which had completely disappeared from human memory. Their newly uncovered languages had been long forgotten; their rich literary and legal texts were indecipherable (though that soon changed). Thanks to these discoveries, scholars were soon in a position to appreciate the monumental achievements of these early civilizations.

Many scholars have remarked that it is no small irony that the ancient Near Eastern people with one of the most lasting legacies was not a people that built and inhabited one of the great centers of ancient Near Eastern civilization. It can be argued that the ancient Near Eastern people with the most lasting legacy was a people that had an idea. It was a new idea that broke with the ideas of their neighbors. Those people were the Israelites.

Scholars have come to the realization that despite the Bible's pretensions to the contrary, the Israelites were a small and relatively insignificant group for much of their history. Around the year 1000 B.C.E., they did establish a kingdom in the land that was known in antiquity as Canaan. They probably succeeded in subduing some of their neighbors and collecting tribute (though there is controversy about that), but in approximately 922 B.C.E., this kingdom divided into two smaller kingdoms of lesser importance. The northern kingdom, consisting of ten of the twelve Israelite tribes and retaining the name Israel, was destroyed in 722 B.C.E. by the Assyrians. The southern kingdom, consisting of two of the twelve tribes and known as Judah, managed to survive until the year 586 B.C.E., when the Babylonians conquered it. Jerusalem—the capital—fell, the Temple was destroyed, and large numbers of Judeans were sent into exile.

In antiquity, conquest and exile usually spelled the end of an ethnic national group. Conquered peoples traded their defeated god for the victorious god of their conquerors. Through cultural and religious assimilation, the conquered nation disappeared as a distinctive entity. Indeed, that is what happened to the ten tribes of the northern kingdom of Israel after 722 B.C.E. They were lost to history. But it did not happen to those members of the Israelite nation who lived in the southern kingdom of Judah (the Judeans).[1] Despite the demise of their national political base in 586 B.C.E., the Judeans, alone among the many peoples who have figured in ancient Near Eastern history—Sumerians, Akkadians, Babylonians, Hittites, Phoenicians, Hurrians, Canaanites—emerged after the death of their state, and produced a community and a culture that can be traced, through various twists and turns, transformations and vicissitudes, down to the modern period. And these Judeans carried with them a radical new idea, a sacred Scripture, and a set of traditions that would lay the foundation for the major religions of the western world: Judaism, Christianity, and Islam. So what is this radical new idea that shaped a culture and enabled its survival not only into later antiquity but even into the present day in some form?

## The Israelite Idea

Scholars have postulated that the conception of the universe widespread among ancient peoples was one in which the various natural forces were understood to be imbued with divine power, to be in some sense divinities themselves.[2] The earth was a divinity, the sky was a divinity, the water was a divinity, or possessed divine power. In other words, the gods were *identical with* or *immanent in* the forces of nature. There were thus many gods, and no one single god was all powerful.

There is very good evidence to suggest that most ancient Israelites shared this worldview. They participated, at the earliest stages of their history, in the wider religious and cultic culture of the ancient Near East. Over the course of time, however, some ancient Israelites, not all at once and not unanimously, broke with this view and articulated a different view according to which there was one divine power, one god. More important than this god's singularity was the fact that this god was outside of and above nature. This god was not identified with nature; he transcended nature. This god was not known through nature or natural phenomena; he was known through history and a particular relationship with humankind.

This idea—which seems simple at first and not so very revolutionary—affected every aspect of Israelite culture and in ways that will become clear ensured the survival of the ancient Israelites as an ethnic-religious entity. In various complicated ways, the view of an utterly transcendent god with absolute control over history made it possible for some Israelites to interpret even the most tragic and catastrophic events, such as the destruction of their capital and the exile of the nation not as a defeat of Israel's god or even that god's rejection of them, but as a necessary part of the deity's larger purpose or plan for Israel.

## Goals of the Book

The Israelites bequeathed to later generations the record of their religious and cultural revolution in the writings that are known as the Hebrew Bible. The present book is an introduction to the Hebrew Bible as an expression of the religious life and thought of ancient Israel and as a foundational document of western civilization. The book has several primary goals. First and foremost, this book aims to familiarize readers with the contents of the Hebrew Bible. Second, this book introduces readers to a number of different methodological approaches to the study of the Bible advanced by modern scholars. At times, the approach adopted will be that of a historian, at times it will be that of a literary critic, and at times that of a religious and cultural critic. Third, the book will on occasion provide some insight into the history of biblical interpretation. The Bible's radically new conception of the divine, its revolutionary depiction of the human being as a moral agent, and its riveting saga of the nation of Israel have drawn generations of readers to ponder its meaning and message. As a result, the Bible has become the base of an enormous edifice of interpretation and commentary and debate, not only in traditional settings but also in academic and secular settings. Very occasionally, this book considers how certain biblical passages have been interpreted—sometimes in contradictory ways—over the centuries.

A fourth goal of the book is to explore the culture of ancient Israel against the backdrop of its historical and cultural setting in the ancient Near East. The archaeological discoveries in the ancient Near East referred to above reveal the spiritual and cultural heritage of all of the inhabitants of the region, including the Israelites, and shed light on the background and origin of the materials in the Bible. It is now clear that the traditions in the Bible did not come out of a vacuum. The early chapters of Genesis are an excellent example of this claim. Genesis 1 through 11—known as the "primeval history" (an unfortunate name because these chapters are not best read or understood as history in the conventional sense)—owe a great deal to ancient Near Eastern mythology. The creation story in Genesis 1 echoes themes and motifs found in the Babylonian creation epic known as *Enuma Elish*. The story of the first human pair in the Garden of Eden, found in Genesis 2 and 3, has clear affinities with the *Epic of Gilgamesh*, an ancient Near Eastern epic in which a hero embarks on an exhausting search for immortality. The story of Noah and the flood found in Genesis 6–9 is simply an Israelite version of recently discovered ancient Near Eastern prototypes: a Mesopotamian flood story called the *Epic of Atrahasis* and a flood story incorporated into the *Epic of Gilgamesh*. In short, biblical traditions have roots that stretch deep into earlier times and out into surrounding lands and traditions. The parallels between the biblical stories and ancient Near Eastern stories have been the subject of intense study and will be considered in some depth in this book.

It isn't just the similarity between the biblical materials and the ancient Near Eastern sources that is remarkable. The dissimilarity is also important because it shows us how the biblical writers transformed a common Near Eastern heritage in light of radically new Israelite conceptions of the nature of the deity, of the created world, and of humankind. For example, a Sumerian story dating to the third millennium B.C.E., the story of Ziusudra, is very similar to the Genesis flood story of Noah. In both the Sumerian and the Israelite flood stories, a flood occurs as the result of a deliberate divine decision; one individual is chosen to be rescued; that individual is given very specific instructions regarding the construction of a boat and whom to bring on board; the flood comes and exterminates all living things; the boat comes to rest on a mountaintop; the hero sends out birds to reconnoiter the land; and when he comes out of the ark, he offers a sacrifice to his god. The same narrative elements appear in these two stories, but what is of great significance is that the biblical writer does not simply retell a story that circulated widely in ancient Mesopotamia. The biblical writer *transforms* the story so that it becomes a vehicle for the expression of different values and views. In the Mesopotamian flood stories, for example, the gods act capriciously. In fact, in one of the stories, the gods complain that noisy humans disturb their sleep and decide to wipe them all out indiscriminately with no moral scruple. The gods destroy the helpless but stoical humans who chafe under their tyrannical, unjust, and uncaring rule. But in the biblical story, the details are modified to reflect a moral purpose: It is the deity's uncompromising ethical standard that leads him to bring the flood in an act of divine justice. He is punishing the evil corruption of the human beings he has so lovingly created and whose degradation he cannot bear to witness. Thus, the story provides a very different message in its Israelite version.

Comparing the Bible with the literature of the ancient Near East reveals not only the cultural and literary heritage common to them but also the ideological gulf that separated them. The biblical writers used these stories as a vehicle for the expression of a radically new idea. They drew upon older sources but shaped them in a particular way, creating a critical problem for anyone seeking to reconstruct ancient Israelite religion or culture on the basis of the biblical materials: the conflicting perspectives of the final editors of the text and of the older sources that are incorporated into the Bible. Those who were responsible for the final edited form of the text had a decidedly monotheistic perspective that they attempted to impose on the older source materials. For the most part they were successful. But at times the result of their effort is a deeply conflicted, deeply ambiguous text featuring a cacophony of voices.

In many respects, the Bible represents or expresses a basic discontent with the larger cultural milieu in which it was produced. And yet, many moderns think of the Bible as an emblem of conservatism, an outdated document with outdated ideas. The challenge of the present book is to help readers view the Bible with fresh eyes in order to appreciate it for what it was: a revolutionary cultural critique. To view the Bible with fresh and appreciative eyes, readers must first acknowledge and set aside some of their presuppositions about the Bible.

## Myths and Facts about the Bible

It is impossible not to hold opinions about this text because it is an intimate part of our culture. Even those who have never opened or read the Bible can cite a verse or a phrase, such as "an eye for an eye, a tooth for a tooth" or "the poor will always be with you"—although it is likely they do not know what these phrases really mean in their original context. Verses are quoted or alluded to, whether to be championed and valorized or lampooned and pilloried, and such citations create within us a general impression of the biblical text and its meaning. As a result, people believe they have a rough idea of the Bible and its outlook, when in fact what they have are popular misconceptions that come from the way the Bible has been used or misused. Indeed, many of our cherished presuppositions about the Bible are based on astonishing claims that others have made on behalf of the Bible, claims that the Bible has not made on behalf of itself.

There is value in examining and setting aside some of the more common myths about the Bible. The first common myth is that the Bible is a book. In fact, the Bible is not a book with the characteristic features that such a designation implies. For example, the Bible does not have a uniform style, a single author, or a single message—features conventionally implied by the word *book*. The Bible is a library or an anthology of books written and edited over an extensive period of time by people in very different situations responding to very different issues and stimuli—political, historical, philosophical, religious, and moral stimuli.[3] Moreover, there are many types or genres of material in the Bible. There are narrative texts, and there are legal texts. There are cultic and ritual texts that prescribe how a given ceremony is to be performed. There are records of the messages of prophets. There is lyric poetry and love poetry. There are proverbs, and there are psalms of thanksgiving and lament. In short, there is a tremendous variety of material in this library.

It follows from the fact that the Bible is not a book but an anthology of diverse works that it is also not an ideological monolith. Each book within the biblical collection, or strand of tradition within a biblical book, sounds its own distinctive note in the symphony of reflection that is the Bible. Genesis is concerned to account for the origin of things and wrestles with the existence of evil, idolatry, and suffering in a world created by a good god. The priestly texts in Leviticus and Numbers emphasize the sanctity of all life, the ideal of holiness, and ethical and ritual purity. There are odes to human reason and learning in the wisdom book of Proverbs. Ecclesiastes scoffs at the vanity of all things, including wisdom, and espouses a kind of positive existentialism. The Psalms contain writings that express the full range of emotions experienced by the worshipper toward his or her god. Job challenges conventional religious piety and arrives at the bittersweet conclusion that there is no justice in this world or any other, but that nonetheless we are not excused from the thankless, and perhaps ultimately meaningless, task of righteous living.

One of the most wonderful and fortuitous facts of history is that later Jewish communities chose to put this diverse material in the collection we call the Bible. They chose to include all of these dissonant voices and did not strive to reconcile the conflicts—and nor should modern readers because the Bible isn't a book but a library. Each book, each writer, each voice reflects another thread in the rich tapestry of human experience, human response to life and its puzzles, and human reflection on the sublime and the depraved.

A second myth about the Bible that should be set aside is that biblical narratives are pious parables about saints. Biblical narratives are not simple, pious tales. They are psychologically real literature about realistic people whose actions are not always exemplary and whose lives should not always be models for our own. There *is* a genre of literature that details the lives of saints called hagiography, but that genre emerges later in the Christian era. It is not found in the Hebrew Bible. The Bible abounds with *human*, not superhuman, beings and their behavior can be scandalous, violent, rebellious, outrageous, lewd, and vicious. But at the same time, like real people, biblical characters can turn and act in ways that are loyal and true or above and beyond the call of duty. They can and do change.

Nevertheless, many people open the Bible for the first time and quickly close it in shock and disgust. Jacob is a deceiver! Joseph is an arrogant, spoiled brat! Judah reneges on his obligations to his daughter-in-law and sleeps with a prostitute! Who are these people? Why are they in the Bible? The shock some readers feel comes from their expectation that the heroes of the Bible are perfectly pious people. Such a claim is not made by the Bible itself. Biblical characters are realistically portrayed, with realistic and compelling moral conflicts, ambitions, and desires. They can act shortsightedly and selfishly, but like real people they can learn and grow and change. If we work too hard and too quickly to vindicate biblical characters just because they are in the Bible, or attribute to them pious qualities and characteristics as dictated by later religious traditions, then we miss the moral sophistication and the deep psychological insights that have made these stories of timeless interest.

A third myth to be set aside is that the Bible is suitable for children. The subject matter in the Bible is very adult, particularly in the narrative texts. There are episodes of treachery and incest and murder and rape. Neither is the Bible for naïve optimists. It speaks to those who have the courage to acknowledge that life is rife with pain and conflict, just as it is filled with compassion and joy.

The Bible is not for children in a second sense. Like any literary masterpiece, the Bible is characterized by a sophistication of structure and style and an artistry of theme and metaphor that are often lost even on adult readers. The Bible makes its readers work. It doesn't moralize, or at least it rarely moralizes. It *explores* moral issues and situations; it places its characters in moral dilemmas—but very often the reader must draw the conclusions. There are also paradoxes, subtle puns, and ironies that the careful reader soon learns to appreciate.

The fourth myth to be set aside is that the Bible is a book of theology. The Bible is not a catechism, a book of systematic theology, or a manual of religion, despite the fact that at a much later time, very complex systems of theology would be spun from particular interpretations of biblical passages. There is nothing in the Bible that corresponds to prevailing modern western notions of religion; indeed, there is no word for religion in the language of biblical Hebrew. With the rise of Christianity, western religion came to be defined, to a large degree, in terms of doctrine and belief. The notion of religion as requiring confession of, or intellectual assent to, a catechism of beliefs is entirely alien in biblical times and in the ancient Near East generally. Thus, to become an Israelite, one simply joined the Israelite community, lived an Israelite life, and died an Israelite death; one obeyed Israelite law and custom, revered Israelite lore, and entered into the historical community of Israel by accepting a common fate. The process most resembled what today would be called *naturalization*.

In short, the Hebrew Bible is not a theological textbook. It is not primarily an account of the divine, which is what the word *theology* connotes. It features a great deal of narrative, and its narrative materials provide an account of the odyssey of a *people*, the nation of Israel. To be sure, although the Bible does not contain formal statements of religious belief or systematic theology, it does treat moral and sometimes existential issues that would become central to the later discipline of theology, but it treats them in a very different manner. The Bible's treatment of these issues is indirect and implicit. It uses the language of story and song, poetry, paradox, and metaphor—a language and a style very distant from the language and style of later philosophy and abstract theology.

It is important that readers not import into their reading of the Hebrew Bible their conceptions of a divine being generated by the later discipline of philosophical theology. The character Yahweh of the Hebrew

Bible should not be confused with the god of western theological speculation (generally denoted as "God"). Qualities attributed to the latter by
theologians—such as omniscience and immutability—simply are not attributed to the biblical character Yahweh by the biblical narrators. Yahweh
is often surprised by the actions of humans and is known to change his
mind and adjust his plans in response to what he learns about human nature and behavior. Accordingly, one of the greatest challenges for modern
readers of the Hebrew Bible is to allow the text to mean what it says, when
what it says flies in the face of centuries of theological construction of the
concept "God."

A final myth concerns the Bible's provenance. The Bible itself does not
claim to have been written by a deity.[4] The belief in the Bible's divine
authorship is a religious doctrine of a much later age, though how literally
it was meant is not clear. Similarly, the books of Genesis, Exodus, Leviticus,
Numbers, and Deuteronomy, known as the Pentateuch, nowhere claim to
have been written in their entirety by Moses. Later tradition would refer to
these five books as the Torah (Instruction) of Moses, and eventually the
belief would arise that they were authored by Moses, a view questioned already in the Middle Ages and not accepted by modern scholars. The Bible
was formulated, assembled, edited, modified, censored, and transmitted—
first orally and then in writing—by human beings. There were many contributors over many centuries, and the individual styles and concerns of
those writers and editors, their political and religious motivations, betray
themselves frequently.

## Structure and Contents

The Hebrew Bible is an assemblage of books and writings dating from approximately 1000 B.C.E. (opinions vary on this point) down to the second
century B.C.E. The last book within the Hebrew Bible was written in the
160s B.C.E. Some of these books contain narrative snippets, legal materials,
or oral traditions that may date back even further in time. These materials
may have been transmitted orally but eventually were reduced to written
form. The Bible is written largely in Hebrew (hence the name "Hebrew Bible"), with a few passages in Aramaic (primarily in the books of Daniel and
Ezra).

The biblical writings have had a profound and lasting impact on three
world religions: Judaism, Christianity, and Islam. For the Jewish communities who first compiled these writings in the pre-Christian era, the Bible

was perhaps first and foremost a record of the Israelite god's eternal covenant with the Jewish people. Jews refer to the Bible as the Tanakh, which is
an acronym composed of the initial letters of the three chief divisions of the
Bible: Torah, Nevi'im, and Ketuvim. The first division, Torah, consisting of
Genesis through Deuteronomy, contains a narrative that stretches from
creation to the death of Moses.[5] *Torah* is often translated as "law," but "instruction" or "teaching" better captures the sense of the word in this context.
The name of the second division of the Bible, *Nevi'im*, means "Prophets."
This division is further subdivided into two parts reflecting two different
types of writing. The first part, known as the Former Prophets, continues
the Torah's narrative prose account of the history of Israel from the death
of Moses to the destruction of the kingdom of Judah in 586 B.C.E. Prophets
and kings are central characters in these narratives. The second part,
known as the Latter Prophets, contains poetic and oracular writings that
bear the name of the prophet to whom the writings are ascribed. There are
three major prophets—Isaiah, Jeremiah, and Ezekiel—and twelve minor
prophets (which in the Hebrew Bible are counted together as one book because they were traditionally transmitted on a single scroll). The third and
final division of the Bible is referred to as *Ketuvim*, which simply means
"Writings." This division is a miscellany containing works of various types:
historical fiction, poetry, psalms and liturgical texts, and proverbs, as well as
books that probe some of the fundamental questions of human existence.

The three divisions correspond very roughly to the process of canonization.[6] The Torah probably reached a relatively fixed and authoritative
status first (probably the early fifth century B.C.E.), then the books of the
Prophets (probably the second century B.C.E.), and finally the Writings
(perhaps as late as the second century C.E.). It is likely that by the end of the
second century C.E., the entire collection was organized in a relatively stable form.

Any examination of the Bible runs immediately into the problem of
defining the object of study, because different biblical canons have served
different communities over the centuries (see Table 1). One of the earliest
translations of the Hebrew Bible was a translation into Greek known as the
Septuagint (LXX). The translation was made in the third century B.C.E. for
the benefit of Greek-speaking Jews who lived in Alexandria, Egypt. The
LXX diverges somewhat from the traditional Hebrew text of the Bible (referred to as the Masoretic text, or MT) as we now have it, both in wording
and in the order of the books. The Septuagint's rationale for the order of the
books is temporal: The first section, from Genesis through Esther, tells of

## Table 1. The Canons of the Hebrew Bible/Old Testament with Abbreviations in Brackets

| Jewish | Protestant | Roman Catholic |
|---|---|---|
| *Hebrew Bible (Tanakh)* | *Old Testament* | *Old Testament* |
| **Torah** | **[Pentateuch]** | **[Pentateuch]** |
| Genesis (Bereshit) [Gen] | Genesis | Genesis |
| Exodus (Shemot) [Ex] | Exodus | Exodus |
| Leviticus (Vayiqra) [Lev] | Leviticus | Leviticus |
| Numbers (BaMidbar) [Num] | Numbers | Numbers |
| Deuteronomy (Devarim) [Deut] | Deuteronomy | Deuteronomy |
| **Prophets (Nevi'im)** | **[Historical Books]** | **[Historical Books]** |
| *Former Prophets* (Nevi'im Rishonim) | Joshua | Joshua |
| Joshua (Yehoshua) [Josh] | Judges | Judges |
| Judges (Shophetim) [Jud] | Ruth | Ruth |
| 1 & 2 Samuel (Shmuel) [1 Sam; 2 Sam] | 1 & 2 Samuel | 1 & 2 Samuel |
| 1 & 2 Kings (Melakhim) [1 Kgs; 2 Kgs] | 1 & 2 Kings | 1 & 2 Kings |
| *Latter Prophets* (Nevi'im Aharonim) | 1 & 2 Chronicles | 1 & 2 Chronicles |
| Isaiah (Yeshayahu) [Isa] | Ezra | Ezra |
| Jeremiah (Yirmiyahu) [Jer] | Nehemiah | Nehemiah |
| Ezekiel (Yehezqel) [Ezek] | Esther | Tobit |
| *The Twelve* (Tere Asar) | | Judith |
| Hosea (Hoshea) [Hos] | | Esther |
| Joel (Yoel) [Joel] | | 1 Maccabees |
| Amos (Amos) [Amos] | | 2 Maccabees |
| Obadiah (Ovadyah) [Obad] | **[Poetical Books]** | **[Poetical Books]** |
| Jonah (Yonah) [Jon] | Job | Job |
| Micah (Mikhah) [Mic] | Psalms | Psalms |
| Nahum (Nahum) [Nah] | Proverbs | Proverbs |
| Habakkuk (Havakkuk) [Hab] | Ecclesiastes | Ecclesiastes |
| Zephaniah (Tsephanyah) [Zeph] | Song of Solomon | Song of Solomon |
| Haggai (Haggai) [Hag] | | Wisdom of Solomon |
| Zechariah (Zekharyah) [Zech] | | Sirach (Ecclesiasticus) |
| Malachi (Malakhi) [Mal] | **[Prophets]** | **[Prophets]** |
| **Writings (Ketuvim)** | Isaiah | Isaiah |
| Psalms (Tehillim) [Pss] | Jeremiah | Jeremiah |
| Proverbs (Mishle) [Prov] | Lamentations | Lamentations |
| Job (Iyyov) [Job] | | Baruch |

*(continued)*

Table 1. (continued)

| Jewish | Protestant | Roman Catholic |
|---|---|---|
| *Five Scrolls* | Ezekiel | Ezekiel |
| Song of Songs (Shir haShirim) [Song] | Daniel | Daniel |
| Ruth (Rut) [Ruth] | | Additions to Daniel |
| Lamentations (Ekhah) [Lam] | Hosea | Hosea |
| Ecclesiastes (Qohelet) [Eccl] | Joel | Joel |
| Esther (Ester) [Est] | Amos | Amos |
| Daniel (Daniel) [Dan] | Obadiah | Obadiah |
| Ezra-Nehemiah (Ezra-Nehemyah) [Ezra; Neh] | Jonah | Jonah |
| 1 & 2 Chronicles (Divre haYamim) [1 Chron; 2 Chron] | Micah | Micah |
| | Nahum | Nahum |
| | Habakkuk | Habakkuk |
| | Zephaniah | Zephaniah |
| | Haggai | Haggai |
| | Zechariah | Zechariah |
| | Malachi | Malachi |

things past; the second section, from Job through the Song of Songs (also known as the Song of Solomon), contains wisdom that applies to the present; and the third section, the prophetic books from Isaiah through Malachi, tells of future things. In the Christian Bible, the prophetic books come immediately before the New Testament to support the doctrine that the former foretell the events of the latter rather than conveying a message specific to their historical context. Some copies of the Septuagint contain books not included in the Hebrew canon but accepted in the early Christian canon.

The Septuagint translation of the Hebrew Bible became the Bible of Christianity (most early Christians spoke Greek), or more precisely, it became the "Old Testament" of the Christian Bible when, in an effort to associate itself with an old and respected tradition, the church adopted these writings as the "precursor" to its Hellenistic gospels. The Christian Old Testament contains some material not included in the Hebrew Bible. Some of these works are referred to as Apocrypha (from a Greek term meaning "hidden away," though there is little evidence that they were hidden away). These writings were composed between approximately 200 B.C.E. and 100 C.E.

Although they were widely used by Jews of the period, Jews did not consider them to be of the same authoritative status as the twenty-four books that became the Hebrew Bible. They did, however, become part of the canon of Catholic Christianity. During the Renaissance and the Reformation, some Christians became interested in the Hebrew version of the Bible rather than the ancient Greek version. In the sixteenth century, the Protestant church denied canonical status to the non-Hebrew books (the books of the Apocrypha). Although deemed important for pious instruction, these works were excluded from the Protestant canon proper, with the result that the Protestant Old Testament and the Jewish Tanakh contain the same books but in a different order. In the same century, the canonical status of the apocryphal books was confirmed for the Catholic Church. Other writings from roughly the same period and known as the Pseudepigrapha (because they are attributed to ancient heroes who did not in fact author them) were never part of the Jewish or the Catholic canon, but some eastern Christian groups include them in their biblical canon.

In short, there have been many sacred canons cherished by many religious communities, all of which are designated "Bibles." In this volume, our primary concern is the Bible of the ancient Israelite and Jewish community— the twenty-four books grouped in the Torah, Prophets, and Writings—that are common to all Bibles, Jewish or Christian, everywhere and at all times. Because the term *Old Testament* is theologically loaded (emerging from the dogma that the New Testament has somehow fulfilled, surpassed, or antiquated the Bible of ancient Israel), this book employs the more neutral terms *Hebrew Bible* or *Tanakh* to refer to the twenty-four books that are the subject of our study, in contrast to more expanded canons. For the sake of convenience, however, the unqualified term *Bible* should also be understood as referring to this common base of twenty-four books found in all Bibles, Jewish and Christian.[7]

Not only has there been some variety in the scope of the biblical canon cherished by different communities, there has also been some fluidity in the actual text itself. We do not, of course, possess "original" copies of any biblical materials—indeed, the very notion of original copies is anachronistic because texts circulated in multiple versions in antiquity. Before the mid-twentieth century, our oldest Hebrew manuscripts of the Bible— the Aleppo Codex and the Leningrad Codex—dated to the years 920 and 1008 C.E., respectively. These and other manuscripts stand at a great chronological distance from the events described in the writings, raising all sorts of questions about the transmission and preservation of the biblical text over time. The exciting discovery of the Dead Sea Scrolls in the middle of the twentieth century brought about a dramatic change in our Hebrew manuscript evidence and in the state of our knowledge of the biblical text. The Dead Sea Scrolls, found in caves at Qumran near the Dead Sea in the Judean desert, are widely believed to have been the library of a small sectarian community.[8] The scrolls contain many Hebrew Bible manuscripts. Most are partial manuscripts, except for the famous scroll of Isaiah. Every book of the Bible except Esther is represented among the scrolls, and some of the manuscripts date back to perhaps the third or second century B.C.E. The importance of this discovery lies in the fact that it provides evidence for the biblical text significantly older than the evidence of medieval manuscripts—more than a thousand years older. Although there are certainly differences between the Qumran fragments and the later manuscripts, there is nevertheless a remarkable degree of correspondence. It is possible, therefore, to speak of a relatively stable textual tradition despite some textual fluidity.

## CHAPTER 2
# Understanding Biblical Monotheism

As noted in Chapter 1, this volume will examine the biblical corpus from a variety of different viewpoints, adopting a variety of approaches—historical, literary, religious, and cultural. In this chapter, we begin our appraisal of the first division of the Bible (the Torah or Pentateuch) as the product of a religious and cultural revolution.

The Bible is the product of minds that were exposed to, influenced by, and reacting to the ambient ideas and cultures of their day. Thus, comparative study of the literature of the ancient Near East and the Hebrew Bible reveals a shared cultural and literary heritage at the same time as it reveals great differences between the two. In the literature of the Bible some members of Israelite society—probably a cultural, religious, and literary elite—broke radically with the prevailing norms of the day. Those responsible for the editing of the Bible, much of which may have occurred between the sixth and fourth centuries B.C.E., mounted a critique of prevailing norms. Moreover, they had a specific worldview that they imposed upon older traditions and stories incorporated in the Bible. That radical and new worldview was monotheism.

Why should the idea of one god, instead of many gods, be so radical? What is so different about asserting the existence of one god instead of a pantheon of gods headed by a superior god? In short, what is so new and revolutionary about monotheism?

According to one school of thought, there *isn't* anything particularly revolutionary about monotheism. The classical account of the rise of

15

monotheism argues that in every society there is a natural progression from polytheism (the belief in many gods who are usually personifications of natural forces) to henotheism or monolatry (the worship of one god as supreme over other gods) and finally monotheism (the belief in the reality of only one god). In the eighteenth and nineteenth centuries this progression was viewed as an advance—unsurprisingly, since the theory was espoused by scholars who were themselves western monotheists. These scholars maintained that biblical religion contained elements of "pure" religion, religion evolved to its highest form and no longer "tainted" by the pagan and polytheistic traits of Canaanite religion. Applying an evolutionary model to religion implied a clear value judgment. Polytheism was understood as an inferior and primitive form of religion; monolatry was an improvement, but monotheism was judged to be the best and purest form of religion.

At first, the great archaeological discoveries of the nineteenth century were adduced in support of the claim that Israelite monotheism had evolved from ancient Near Eastern polytheism. Once deciphered, cuneiform tablets inscribed with the great literature of Mesopotamian civilizations shed astonishing light on biblical religion. These discoveries led to a kind of "parallelomania" with scholars feverishly pointing out the parallels in theme, language, plot, and structure between biblical stories and ancient Near Eastern stories. For example, more than a thousand years before the Israelite legend of Noah and the ark, Mesopotamians told the story of Ziusudra, or in some versions Utnapishtim, who survived a great flood by building an ark on the instruction of a deity. As noted in Chapter 1, there are great similarities with the biblical flood story, even at the level of small detail. With parallels like these, it was argued, it is fair to assume that the religion of the ancient Israelites was not so very different from that of their polytheistic neighbors. Both had a creation story. Both had a flood story. Both performed animal sacrifice. Both observed purity taboos. Israelite religion was one more ancient Near Eastern religion differing only in the number of gods worshipped: one versus many. It was, in essence, a more refined, more highly evolved, version of ancient Near Eastern religion.

The evolutionary view of the development of monotheism was challenged by Yehezkel Kaufmann in the 1930s. Kaufmann argued that monotheism does not and cannot evolve from polytheism because the two are based on radically divergent worldviews, radically divergent intuitions about reality. In a multivolume work, *The Religion of Israel* (later abridged and translated into English by Moshe Greenberg), Kaufmann asserted that the monotheism of Israel was not and could not be the natural outgrowth of the polytheism of an earlier age. Monotheism, he argued, was a cultural and religious discontinuity, a polemic against polytheism and the pagan worldview. This polemic is implicit, according to Kaufmann, throughout the biblical text. Kaufmann replaces the evolutionary model for the rise of monotheism with a *revolutionary* model.

One advantage of Kaufmann's model is that it avoids the pejorative assessment of polytheism as a primitive stage of religion inferior to monotheism. The model simply posits the existence of two distinct orientations, two divergent worldviews. This is not to say that Kaufmann was not judgmental of polytheisms—clearly he felt monotheism was the better option. However, the model itself at least has the potential to represent monotheism and polytheism as simple alternatives, each with its own particular strengths and explanatory power and each with its own weaknesses and explanatory deficiencies.

In Kaufmann's view, the similarities between biblical and ancient Near Eastern religion and culture should be understood, in the end, as similarities in form and external structure rather than essential meaning or function. All of the cultures of the ancient Near East practiced animal sacrifice and followed ritual purity laws. They all told stories about creation and a worldwide flood and preserved legends of heroes. But the biblical writings adopted and transformed these cultural forms into vehicles for the conveyance of a monotheistic worldview. For this reason, a similarity in form is no guarantee of a similarity in meaning or function. In this respect, Kaufmann anticipated arguments made by later anthropologists: The ritual cult of the Israelites may look like that of Israel's neighbors, but its purpose and function were very different from that of Israel's neighbors. The Israelites may have set up a king over themselves like other ancient Near Eastern peoples, but Israelite monarchy differed from Canaanite monarchy in significant ways. These differences are due to Israelite monotheism. The meaning and function of Israel's cult, of Israel's king, of its creation stories and legends derive from their place within the larger cultural framework or worldview of Israel. That larger framework or worldview is one of basic monotheism.

## Kaufmann on "Pagan" Religion

How does Kaufmann describe the fundamental distinction between the polytheistic worldview and the revolutionary monotheistic worldview that took root in Israel? According to Kaufmann, the fundamental idea of "pagan" religion (to adopt Kaufmann's terminology) is "the idea that there exists a realm of being prior to the gods and above them, upon which the gods depend, and whose decrees they must obey."[1] He refers to this realm as the metadivine realm. It is the realm of supreme and ultimate power that transcends even the deities. The deities emerge from, and are therefore subject to the laws and forces of, the metadivine realm. The nature of this realm will be represented differently from culture to culture. It might be water, it might be darkness, it might be spirit, or, as in ancient Greek religion, it might be fate.

Kaufmann argues that positing a primordial metadivine realm beyond or beside the gods has several important consequences. First, the gods are automatically limited by this realm whose decrees they must obey. The gods are not the source of all but are bound by, and subservient to, this metadivine realm. There can be, therefore, no supreme, absolute, or sovereign divine will because the will of any one god can be countered by the will of another, and the will of all the gods collectively can be thwarted by the decrees of the primordial metadivine realm. Not only are the gods limited in power, but they are limited in wisdom. No god is all knowing or all wise because the metadivine realm is ultimately mysterious and unpredictable. Individual gods might be very wise or skilled in a particular craft or science, such as healing. But no god possesses wisdom as an unqualified and essential attribute.

Kaufmann asserts that mythology is basic to pagan religions. Mythology tells of the lives and exploits of the gods. In pagan mythologies, the gods are born and live lives very similar to human lives but on a grand scale. They also die and may be reborn, too. Pagan religions contain theogonies (= accounts of the birth of a god) as well as cosmogonies (= accounts of the birth of the world). In these theogonies and cosmogonies, everything emerges from the impersonal primordial realm because this realm contains the seeds of all being. The creative process usually begins with the emergence of the gods—as sexually differentiated divine beings. Subsequently the natural world and its inhabitants (humans and animals) are generated from the primordial realm in some way. In short, the metadivine realm is the primordial womb for everything mundane and divine—the gods, humans, and the natural world.

What that means, Kaufmann asserts, is that in pagan religion there is a fluid boundary between the divine, the human, and the natural worlds. Because they all emerge from the same primordial world stuff, the distinctions between them are soft. Thus, the gods are often identified with powerful natural forces and entities. The sky is a god, the fire is a god, fertility—a natural process—is a god, and there is no real distinction between the worship of gods and the worship of nature. Moreover, because humans also emerge ultimately from this primordial realm there is often a "confusion" of the boundary between the divine and the human. Thus, pagan religions may feature (sexual) unions between divine beings and human beings, and "the continuity of the divine and human realm is the basis of the pagan belief in apotheosis" (p. 36)—the process by which humans become gods. This may happen after death through the acquisition of immortality, for example, or it may happen to a king when he ascends the throne.

According to Kaufmann, in pagan religions power is materially conceived. Whatever power the gods have is derivative, because the metadivine realm that transcends the gods is the source of all power; indeed, the stuff of which it is made is what has ultimate power. Power is thus material because it inheres in certain substances—particularly substances akin to the primordial world stuff. If the metadivine realm is conceived of as water or blood, then actual water or blood will be thought to be imbued with the power of the metadivine realm. Gods have power only insofar as they are connected with the primordial substance or its physical cognates.

The material conception of power—the idea that power inheres in certain natural substances akin to the primordial substance—creates the possibility of magic. Magic involves the manipulation of inherently powerful material substances to release or harness their power. By manipulating these substances, humans can tap into the primordial power. The human magician is a kind of technician who accesses and harnesses the powerful forces of the metadivine realm in order to coerce the gods to do his will and even to influence the "decrees" of the metadivine realm itself. Magic, Kaufmann claims, accesses the power of the primordial metadivine realm in order to get around or circumvent the capricious will of the gods and demons, to influence the gods in a particular way, or to protect oneself against the gods. Likewise, divination is an attempt to discern the future that, once again, aims at the source of all power and knowledge. It is not directed at the gods (unless the gods are a medium through which one gains access to the metadivine realm), but at the metadivine realm itself in an effort to reveal its secrets. Discerning the will of the gods would be of little use, because the will of any god can be thwarted by other gods and by the decrees of the metadivine realm.

The material conception of power informs the pagan cult as well. Kaufmann claims that the pagan cult is a system of rites that involves the manipulation of substances (such as blood, animal flesh, human flesh, or precious metals) believed to have inherent power because of their connection to the primordial world substance of the metadivine realm. The pagan cult is inherently magical as it seeks, through the manipulation of material substances, to tap into a primordial power that can coerce the gods (to be propitiated or appeased, to bestow favor or protection, and so on). Some cultic acts are defensive, ensuring that the god will not harm the worshipper, and some are prophylactic, ensuring that a demon will not harm the god. Cultic festivals are tied to mythology, the stories of the lives of the gods. Many cultic festivals consist of reenactments of events in the life of a god such as a battle in which the god is killed, only to rise again. Winter festivals may reenact the death of the god who is resurrected with the return of life in the spring. It is believed that these reenactment festivals harness magical powers that ensure and maintain the cycles of nature.

A further and very important implication of the ascription of all power and life to the metadivine realm is the idea that the primordial realm is the source of both good and evil. Just as there are good gods who aid and protect human beings, there are evil gods who seek to destroy both humans and other gods. Death and disease belong to the realm of these evil demons or impure spirits, but they are nevertheless siblings with the good gods. Human beings are essentially powerless, according to Kaufmann, in the continual cosmic struggle between the good gods and the evil demons— unless they can utilize magic to tap into the powers of the metadivine realm and circumvent the gods who make their lives miserable. Most important, according to Kaufmann, is that evil in the pagan worldview stems from *an autonomous demonic realm,* as primary and real as the realm of the holy or good gods. Evil is a metaphysical reality, built into the structure of the universe. The primordial metadivine realm that spawned the universe gave birth to forces of good and evil locked in a perpetual cosmic struggle.

On this view, according to Kaufmann, salvation is the concern of humans, not the gods. The gods aren't interested in human salvation from the capricious forces at work in the world because they are busy trying to save themselves. The good gods are attacked by evil gods, and their desires are thwarted by the powers and decrees of the metadivine realm. Salvation is attained through magic or gnosis (secret knowledge that can liberate one from prevailing powers). Tapping into primordial power or secret knowledge to escape the reach of the demons and the capricious gods who make life on earth a misery—that is the path to salvation in a polytheistic system.

According to Kaufmann, the pagan worldview is of an amoral universe—not an *im*moral universe, but a morally neutral or *a*moral universe. While some gods are legislators and guardians of social order and justice, their laws aren't absolute and can be leveled by the activity of demons and the operation of the supreme metadivine realm. The knowledge and wisdom of each god is limited. If morality is defined as what a particular god likes or desires, then there can be no absolute morality. It is that picture of the universe, Kaufmann wants to argue, that is challenged by the monotheistic revolution as exemplified by biblical religion.

## Kaufmann on Israelite Monotheism

Kaufmann argues that the fundamental idea of ancient Israel, which receives no systematic formulation but permeates the entire Bible, is a radically new conception of a god who is himself the source of all being—and not subject to a metadivine realm. The universe knows no metadivine realm or power. This god does not emerge from some preexisting realm, and he is therefore free of all of the limitations of mythology and magic. Unchallenged by any other power, this god's will is absolute and sovereign. What follows from the Israelite elimination of a metadivine realm? First, biblical literature contains no theogony and no mythology (no account of the birth or life history of the deity). Israel's god is not born of a primordial womb, and he does not have a life story. There is no realm prior to him; there is no realm that is the source of his power and wisdom. In the opening chapters of Genesis, the deity simply is. He doesn't grow, he doesn't age, he doesn't mature, he doesn't have a female consort, and he doesn't die. For the first time in history, Kaufmann claims, we encounter in the Hebrew Bible an unlimited god who is timeless and ageless, nonphysical and eternal.

The biblical god is not akin to nature—he transcends nature. As the sovereign of all nature, this god is not identifiable as a force of nature. Nature becomes the stage upon which this god expresses his will and purpose in human history but nature isn't itself divine. Likewise, this god is not akin to humans in any way. The boundary between humans and the divine is not soft but hard, according to Kaufmann. For this reason the Hebrew Bible rejects the idea of apotheosis as well as the idea of life after death. There is no instance of humans becoming gods or gods becoming human.

The Hebrew Bible lacks magic and represents magic actions as useless. The lack of a primordial metadivine realm of power means that power is not materially conceived and the possibility of magical manipulation of inherently powerful substances is eliminated. Israel's god cannot be coerced by magical rituals or secret knowledge. Indeed, magic is sin or rebellion against the deity because it is predicated on a mistaken notion of his power as limited by other powers. To be sure, Kaufmann acknowledges that there are magical-looking actions throughout the Bible. But he argues that the editors of the stories in which these actions occur take pains to emphasize that the actions themselves effect nothing. Nothing occurs as a result of the magician's artifices, nothing occurs that is independent of the will of Israel's god. According to Kaufmann, magic in the Bible is stripped of its autonomous potency and recast as a witness to the deity's sovereignty and power.

Divination also cannot be assimilated to the monotheistic idea, according to Kaufmann, because it, too, falsely presupposes the existence of a metadivine realm of knowledge and power. Divination, which attempts to reveal the god's secrets, is predicated on a mistake. While it is permitted to make inquiries of Israel's god through oracular devices, he conveys information only as he wills. There is no ritual, no incantation, no material substance, says Kaufmann, that can coerce a revelation from the deity. Magic, divination, oracles, dream revelations, and prophecy appear in the pagan world and in ancient Israel. But according to Kaufmann, any similarity is a similarity in form only. Each of these phenomena is fundamentally transformed by the Israelite idea of a supreme, transcendent god whose will is absolute and uncoerced. There is no recourse to a separate science, body of knowledge, or magical craft that summons forces independent of and transcending the deity.

By the same token, the cult in Israel does not harness independent powers and does not work automatically. Nor does it protect or service the material needs of the deity. The cult does not affect his life and vitality through reenactment rituals. No events in the deity's life are celebrated. The mythological rationales that motivate the cultic activities of Israel's neighbors are often replaced in Israel by historical rationales commemorating an event in the history of the nation. This historicization of festivals and cultic practices will be discussed in Chapter 8.

In a monotheistic system there are no evil agents that oppose the deity as equal rivals; there is no divine evil agent. If Israel's god is the source of all being, then there cannot be a realm of supernatural beings that does battle with him, no divine antagonist of the one supreme god. According to Kaufmann, in the Hebrew Bible sin and evil are demythologized and dedivinized. The Bible does not conceive of evil as the work of an independent evil power or sin as the result of demon possession necessitating coercive and magical acts of exorcism. In the Hebrew Bible, evil results from the clash of the will of the deity and the will of humans who have the freedom to defy him, the power to sin. There is nothing inherently supernatural about sin in a monotheistic system. In the biblical worldview, Kaufmann asserts, evil was transferred from the metaphysical realm to the moral realm. Evil is not a force or a power built into the structure of the universe, and it has no concrete independent reality. It is a moral, not a metaphysical, reality. This means that human beings and only human beings are the potential source of evil in the world. Responsibility for the reign of evil or goodness lies in the hands of humanity.

Because the biblical god is a creator god capable of imposing order on the cosmos rather than a created god, the pagan picture of an amoral universe of competing good and evil powers is replaced by the picture of a moral cosmos. The highest law is the will of the deity, who imposes not merely an order but a morality upon the universe. Israel posits about its god not merely that he is a single transcendent power but that he is a morally *good* power. In the biblical system, absolute standards of justice and morality are possible. The deity is just, he is compassionate, and humans who would be good must conform their actions to his will. Those who defy him commit a sin and bring evil into the world.

We may summarize Kaufmann's argument this way: Biblical religion conceived of the divine in an entirely new way. The biblical god differed from the pagan gods in his essential nature. The pagan gods were natural gods, associated with the blind forces of nature and possessing no intrinsic moral character. The biblical god was understood to transcend nature. His will was not only absolute, it was absolutely good and moral (unlike the morally neutral metadivine realm). The biblical god is demythologized, but he is not rendered completely impersonal. He is spoken of in anthropomorphic terms, in order to express his interaction with human beings. Those interactions happen not in the realm of nature but in the realm of history. This god is known not through natural forces and phenomena but through one-time actions that occur in historical (rather than mythic) time and that affect the lives of people.

Concerning the conceptual abyss that separates monotheism and polytheism, Kaufmann wrote that it would be

> a mistake to think that a merely arithmetic difference sets off Israel's religion from paganism. The pagan idea does not approach Israelite monotheism as it diminishes the number of its gods. The Israelite conception of their deity's unity entails His sovereign transcendence over all. It rejects the pagan idea of a

realm beyond the deity, the source of mythology and magic. The
affirmation that the will of God is supreme and absolutely free is
a new and non-pagan category of thought.[2]

Kaufmann admits that this affirmation is not stated explicitly in the He-
brew Bible, but, he argues, it pervades Israelite creativity and biblical texts.
He also asserts that the idea underwent some development and evolution.
Its latent possibilities were realized only over time.

## Evolution, Revolution, or Civil War?

We have seen two models for understanding the rise of biblical monotheism. One model claims that biblical monotheism evolves from and is in
many ways essentially continuous with ancient Near Eastern polytheism,
merely limiting the number of gods worshipped to one, but housing that
god in a temple, propitiating him with sacrifices and purity practices, as in
any ancient Near Eastern culture. The other model, Kaufmann's model,
claims that biblical religion, culture, thought, and practice is a radical break
from that of the cultures of the ancient Near East.

The value of Kaufmann's work lies in the important insight that
monotheism and polytheism *in the abstract* are predicated on divergent
intuitions and describe very different worlds, that the difference between
Israel's god and the gods of her neighbors was not merely quantitative but
qualitative. However, it is clear that Kaufmann must often force his evidence and force it rather badly. It is simply a fact that practices and ideas
that are not strictly or even strongly monotheistic on his description appear
in the Bible. Perhaps those scholars who stress the continuity between Israel and its environment are right after all?

This impasse can be resolved when we realize that there is likely a
distinction between the *actual* religious practices and beliefs of the *actual*
inhabitants of Israel and Judah (which we may call Israelite-Judean religion) and the monotheism promoted by the later writers and editors who
tell the story of these people (which we may call biblical religion)—a distinction featured in a helpful article by Stephen Geller.[3] What second-
millennium Hebrews and early-first-millennium Israelites and Judeans
actually believed or did is not always retrievable to us. In all likelihood,
Hebrews of the patriarchal period (second millennium B.C.E.) as well as
most first-millennium Israelites and Judeans were not markedly different

from many of their polytheistic neighbors. In early sources incorporated into the Bible and in the archaeological record, there is evidence of popular religious practices that were not monotheistic (the worship of household idols and local fertility deities, for example). Most scholars conjecture that ancient Israelite-Judean religion (the practices and beliefs of the actual inhabitants of the kingdoms of Israel and Judah in the first millennium B.C.E.) was at most monolatrous (promoting the worship of one god, Yahweh, without denying the existence of other gods) rather than monotheistic (asserting the reality of one god only).

Moreover, Yahweh was in many respects similar to the gods of Canaanite religion, especially the sky god El and the storm god Baal (indeed the names El and Baal are both explicitly applied to or associated with the Israelite god in certain biblical passages; see Chapter 8 especially). Continuities with Canaanite and ancient Near Eastern polytheisms are apparent in the worship practices and cult objects of ancient Israel and Judah, as described in biblical stories and attested in archaeological finds. Moreover, the Hebrew Bible contains numerous passages that exhibit features of contemporary polytheisms. In Genesis 6, divine beings (Nefilim) descend to earth to mate with female humans (Gen 6:1–4). In many passages, Yahweh is represented as presiding over a council of gods (Gen 3:22, Ps 82, Job 1:6–12). Some poetic passages contain mythological representations of Israel's deity doing battle with monstrous forces in order to establish his dominion, as the Babylonian god Marduk did (Ps 74:12–14, 89:9–11, Isa 51:9–10). Other passages assume the existence of other gods worshipped by other nations (Num 21:29; Deut 4:19, 29:25; Jud 16:23–24), suggesting an early Israelite henotheism.

Nevertheless, Kaufmann is correct to point out that the most strongly monotheistic sources of the Bible posit a god that is qualitatively different from the gods that populated the mythology of Israel's neighbors and Israelite-Judean religion. In these sources of what we may call biblical religion found in certain passages of the Torah and especially in the Prophets, Israel's deity is alone the source of all being. Because he does not emerge from a preexisting realm and has no divine siblings, this god's will is absolute and sovereign. Moreover, biblical monotheism assumes that this god is inherently good, just, and compassionate and that human morality consists in conformity to his will. Because certain texts of the Bible posit an absolutely good god who places absolute moral demands upon humankind, biblical monotheism is often referred to as *ethical monotheism*.

Beginning perhaps as early as the eighth century B.C.E. and continuing for several centuries, literate and decidedly monotheistic circles within Israelite society put a monotheistic framework and veneer on the ancient stories and traditions of the nation. Older sources that reflect traditions of Israelite-Judean religion were altered or reframed to reflect the monotheistic viewpoint of later editors. In this way, older sources were molded into a foundation myth that was to shape Israelite/Jewish self-understanding and identity in a profound way. Monotheizing editors projected their monotheism onto an earlier time, onto the nation's most ancient ancestors, though historically speaking this is most unlikely. Israelite monotheism is represented in some biblical passages as beginning with Abraham, but in historical terms, it began much later—as a minority movement that grew to prominence over centuries. This later monotheism projected back over Israel's long history by the final editors of the Bible is the biblical religion that Kaufmann describes, and it is this that most closely resembles Kaufmann's portrait of monotheism.

So the biblical record incorporates two conflicting sets of sources—one set reflects religious practices and views that are not strictly monotheistic and the other reflects religious practices and views that are. The later sources of "biblical religion" break not only with ancient Near Eastern religious conceptions but also with much Israelite-Judean religion. Thus, biblical monotheism as Kaufmann describes it was not simply a revolution of Israel against the nations, but a civil war of Israel against itself.

In this respect, Israel is not unique. A similar cultural struggle is evidenced in ancient Egypt. Creation texts dating to the Old Kingdom (2575–2134 B.C.E.) describe the sun-god Ra (later Atum) worshipped at Heliopolis as creator and ruler. Ra's creative activity involves sexual generation.

> I planned a multitude of living creatures,
>> All were in my heart, and their children and their
>> grandchildren.
> Then I copulated with my own fist.
>> I masturbated with my own hand.
>> I ejaculated into my own mouth.
> I exhaled Shu the wind.
>> I spat Tefnut the rain.
> Old Man Nun the sea reared them,
>> Eye the overseer looked after them. . . .[4]

But in a text from Memphis (originating possibly in the Old Kingdom but preserved in an eighth-century copy), Atum's method of creation is ridiculed. This work, known as the Hymn to Ptah, contrasts Atum (= Ra), the god of Heliopolis, with Ptah, the god of Memphis. Like a physical laborer, Atum works with material substances and engages in lower body (sexual) activities in order to create. By contrast, Ptah creates through upper body or intellectual functions—thought and speech—to create each member of the Ennead, that is, the nine deities worshipped at Heliopolis and including Atum. This text seeks to assert the preeminence of the new capital, Memphis, and its deity, Ptah, and does so by asserting the latter's precedence over the gods of Heliopolis: The creator god Atum was *himself* created by the god Ptah, and the latter employed an entirely intellectual method of creation.

> Ptah gave life to every member of the Ennead and to the soul (Egyptian: ka) of each. Each came into being through the thoughts in his heart and the words on his tongue. Horus came forth, and Thoth came forth from the thoughts in the heart of Ptah and the words on the tongue of Ptah. The thoughts of the heart of Ptah and the words of the tongue of Ptah guide all the thoughts and all the words of the Ennead, and all the thoughts and all the words of humans, and of all life. Ptah creates the Ennead with only teeth and lips. Atum must create with hands and semen. Atum had to masturbate to bring forth the Ennead. Ptah had only to speak, and the Ennead came forth. Ptah called the names of Shu the wind and Tefnut the rain, who gave birth to Geb the earth and Nut the sky. Just as all the sense of sight, of hearing and of smell all report to the heart, and just as the heart is the source of all knowledge, and the tongue speaks what the heart desires, so all the members of the Ennead came forth . . . according to the thoughts of the heart of Ptah and the words of the tongue of Ptah. . . .[5]

The polemic, the internal cultural critique, could not be more explicit. Ancient Egypt and ancient Israel—like all cultures before and since, including our own—were complex and messy entities often at war with themselves.

The differences between the god of the monotheizing sources of the Bible and the gods of both surrounding Mesopotamian literature and Israelite-Judean culture are apparent from the very first chapter of Genesis—a creation story added to the Pentateuch in one of the last rounds of editing, perhaps in the sixth century B.C.E. Genesis 1 is a strongly monotheistic opening to the primeval myths contained in the first eleven chapters of Genesis. Chapter 3 examines Gen 1–3, reading these chapters with an eye to Israel's adaptation of Near Eastern motifs and themes to express a new conception of the deity, the world, and humankind.

## CHAPTER 3

# Genesis 1–3

## The Biblical Creation Stories

*Readings:* Genesis 1–3

This chapter examines the opening chapters of Genesis. Our goal is to illustrate the way in which biblical writers (later we will be more precise about who these writers probably were and when they may have lived) drew upon the cultural and religious legacy of the ancient Near East (its stories, imagery, motifs) even as they transformed what they borrowed so as to align it with a new vision of a nonmythological god. The scholar who has written extensively and eloquently on the adaptation of ancient Near Eastern material by the composers of the book of Genesis is Nahum Sarna. This chapter draws heavily upon his work.[1] Sarna and others have shown that the comparison of biblical and ancient Near Eastern stories reveals the features they share as well as the chasm that divides them so deeply.

A study of Genesis 1–2 requires familiarity with the Babylonian epic known by its opening words *"Enuma Elish,"* meaning "when on high." This epic begins prior to the formation of heaven and earth, when nothing existed except water in two forms. The primeval freshwater ocean is identified with the male god Apsu; the primeval saltwater ocean is identified with the female goddess Tiamat. Tiamat is also represented as a fierce dragonlike monster.

When on high the heaven had not been named,
Firm ground below had not been called by name,
Naught but primordial Apsu, their begetter,
(And) Mummu-Tiamat, she who bore them all,
Their waters co-mingling as a single body;
No reed hut had been matted, no marsh land had appeared,
When no gods whatever had been brought into being,
Uncalled by name, their destinies undetermined—
Then it was that the gods were formed within them.
    (I, pp. 60–61)[2]

The sexual union of Apsu and Tiamat begins a process of generation producing first demons and monsters and eventually gods. In time, however, Tiamat and Apsu are disturbed by the din and tumult of the younger gods.

The divine brothers banded together,
They disturbed Tiamat as they surged back and forth,
Yea, they troubled the mood of Tiamat
By their hilarity in the Abode of Heaven.
. . . . . . . . . . . . . . . . . . .  . . .
Apsu, opening his mouth,
Said unto resplendent Tiamat:
"Their ways are verily loathsome unto me.
By day I find no relief, nor repose by night.
I will destroy, I will wreck their ways,
That quiet may be restored. Let us have rest."
. . . . . . . . . . . . . . . . . . . . . .
Then answered Mummu, [Mummu Tiamat] giving counsel to
    Apsu;
[Ill-wishing] and ungracious was Mummu's advice:
"Do destroy, my father, the mutinous ways.
Then shalt thou have relief by day and rest by night."

When Apsu heard this, his face grew radiant
Because of the evil he planned against the gods, his sons.
    (I, p. 61)

Apsu decides to destroy the gods, but he is killed by Ea, the earth-water god. Tiamat is bent on revenge and makes plans to attack all the gods with her assembled forces. The gods need a leader and turn to Marduk, who agrees to lead them in battle against Tiamat and her general, Kingu, but only on condition that he be made sovereign when the battle is over.

> His heart exulting, he said to his father:
> "Creator of the gods, destiny of the great gods,
> If I indeed, as your avenger,
> Am to vanquish Tiamat and save your lives,
> Set up the Assembly, proclaim supreme my destiny!
> . . . Let my word, instead of you, determine the fates.
> Unalterable shall be what I may bring into being,
> Neither recalled nor changed shall be the command of my
>     lips." (III, p. 65)

The agreement is struck. Marduk is successful in the fierce battle that follows and in a memorable passage, he fells Tiamat.

> In fury, Tiamat cried out aloud,
> To the roots her legs shook both together.
> . . . Then joined issue, Tiamat and Marduk . . . ,
> They strove in single combat, locked in battle.
> The lord [Marduk] spread out his net to enfold her,
> The Evil Wind, which followed behind, he let loose in her face.
> When Tiamat opened her mouth to consume him,
> He drove in the Evil Wind that she close not her lips.
> As the fierce winds charged her belly,
> Her body was distended and her mouth was wide open.
>
> He released the arrow, it tore her belly,
> It cut through her insides, splitting the heart.
> Having thus subdued her, he extinguished her life.
> He cast down her carcass to stand upon it. (IV, p. 67)

What does one do with the carcass of a ferocious monster? One builds a world. Marduk slices the carcass into two halves and with one half he creates the heaven and with the other half he creates the earth.

> He split her like a shellfish into two parts.
> Half of her he set up and ceiled it as sky,

Pulled down the bar and posted guards.
He bade them to allow not her waters to escape. (IV, p. 67)

Marduk has used the upper half of Tiamat's body to press back her waters
on high. This is the sky or firmament, which is understood to be a physical
expanse that holds back the upper waters. Rain occurs when openings are
made in this physical barrier. With the bottom half of Tiamat's body, Marduk forms the land, which presses down and holds back the monster's
lower waters. These waters emerge in the form of springs and rivers, seas
and lakes.

Marduk doesn't stop with the creation of the earth. He goes on to create various heavenly bodies.

He constructed stations for the great gods
Fixing their astral likenesses as constellations.
He determined the year by designating the zones;
He set up three constellations for each of the twelve months.
. . . The moon he caused to shine, the night to him entrusting.
   (V, p. 67)

Immediately, the complaints roll in. The gods are unhappy that they have
been assigned duties in the maintenance of the cosmos. For example, the
moon god must come up and shine each night—a tedious fate. They want
relief from laboring at their stations, and Marduk accedes to this demand.
He takes blood from the slain general Kingu, the leader of Tiamat's army,
and fashions a human being—with the express purpose of freeing the gods
from menial labor.

Blood I will mass and cause bones to be.
I will establish a savage, "man" shall be his name,
Verily, savage man I will create.
He shall be charged with the service of the gods
That they might be at ease. (VI, p. 68)
. . . . . . . . . . . . . . . . . .
"It was Kingu who contrived the uprising,
And made Tiamat rebel, and joined battle."
[So] They bound him, holding him before Ea.
. . . . [And] Out of [Kingu's] blood they fashioned mankind
[And] Ea imposed the service and let free the gods. (VI, p. 69)

The grateful gods recognize the sovereignty of Marduk. They build him a magnificent shrine in Babylon ("Bab-el," which means "gateway of the god"). A banquet follows in which Marduk is praised and his kingship confirmed.

*Enuma Elish* was the great national epic of Babylon, recited during the all-important New Year Festival. Nahum Sarna (*Genesis*, 7–8) points out the four main functions of the epic. First, it had a theogonic function describing how the generations of the gods came into being. Second, it had a cosmological function explaining the origins of cosmic phenomena. Its third function was sociopolitical. The portrait of the created universe in the epic corresponded to and legitimated the structural forms of Babylonian society. The position and function of the humans in the scheme of creation paralleled precisely the status of the slave in Mesopotamia, while Marduk's position paralleled that of the Babylonian ruler. The epic also both mirrored and legitimated Marduk's rise from an obscure city-god to a position at the head of the Babylonian pantheon and Babylon's rise as one of the greatest cities of the region. Finally, the epic served a cultic function. According to Sarna and other scholars, the conflict of Tiamat and Marduk symbolized the conflict between the forces of chaos and the forces of cosmic order, a perpetual conflict repeated each year in the cycle of the seasons. The epic served as a kind of script for the reenactment of the primeval battle in a cultic setting. This reenactment of the victory of the forces of cosmos over the forces of chaos was believed to play a critical role in the renewal of nature each spring.

Recalling now the theories of Kaufmann, the worldview expressed in *Enuma Elish* might be described this way. First, the gods are amoral and limited. They emerge from an indifferent primal realm (water) that is the source of all being and ultimate power. The gods age, mature, fight and harm one another, and die. They are not wholly good, and they are not wholly evil. Their will is not absolute. Second, humans are unimportant menials. They are the slaves of the gods, who have little reciprocal interest in or concern for them. The gods create humans to do the hard work of running the world and look down upon them as slaves and pawns. Third, the world is morally neutral, which means that for humans it can be a difficult and hostile place. One's best bet is to serve the god of the day (i.e., the god who is ascendant) as best one can so as to earn his favor, but even that god has limited powers and abilities and may turn on his devotees if he so desires.

If the creation story of Gen 1:1–2:4 is read in light of these same three categories, a different picture emerges.[3]

## The Divine

The god of the first biblical creation story is supreme and unlimited. There is a corresponding lack of mythology in Gen 1 (or rather, as we shall see, a suppression of mythology). Mythology refers to stories that deal with the birth and life events of the gods, demigods, and legendary heroes of a particular people. The biblical creation account is nonmythological because there is no story about the deity—he simply is. There is no theogony—that is, no account of the birth of the god—and no biography. The deity is preexistent, and there is no realm of power beyond him. In the Mesopotamian account, the gods themselves are created (there is a theogony), and their generation is sexual. Indeed, the first beings to emerge from the union of the primeval waters are demons and monsters, and the gods appear only after several generations. The god of creation (Marduk) is born rather late in the process.

The absence of mythology in Genesis is not to be understood as an absence of myth. Mythology and myth are quite distinct. In contrast to mythology, which deals with the lives of gods, a myth is generally defined as a traditional story—often fanciful and imaginative—that relates events in historical time, usually in order to explain a custom, institution, natural phenomenon, religious rite, or belief. It is a story invented as a veiled explanation of truth, a parable or allegory. The Bible may not present stories of the births, lives, and deaths of gods (mythology), but it certainly does contain myths—traditional stories and legends that attempt to explain how and why something is as it is.

To return to Gen 1, the absence of theogony and mythology means the absence of a metadivine or primordial realm from which the biblical god emerges. It also means the absence of the idea that this god is immanent in nature, natural substances, or phenomena. Therefore, the biblical god's powers and knowledge are not limited by the existence of any superior power or substance. Nature is not divine. The created world is not divine. It is not the physical manifestation of various deities. There is no intrinsic, material connection between the deity and creation. The line of demarcation is clear.

In short, and as Sarna notes (*Genesis*, 12), Gen 1 reflects the view that there is one supreme god who is creator and sovereign of the world. He simply exists. He appears to be incorporeal, and the realm of nature is subservient to him. He has no life story (mythology), and his will is absolute. This god creates through the simple expression of his will. "Elohim said, 'Let there be light' and there was light" (Gen 1:3). The deity expresses his will, and it comes to be—so different from ancient Near Eastern cosmogonies in which creation is always a form of procreation, the combination of male and female principles.

## Humans

In Gen 1, humans are said to be created in the divine image (Gen 1:27). Being created in the divine image implies that human life is unique, sacred, and deserving of special care and protection. Thus, in Gen 9:6 we read, "Whoever sheds the blood of man, in exchange for that man shall his blood be shed, for in the image of Elohim was man created."[4] This verse suggests that because human life is sacred, there is no way to compensate for murder. Murder requires the forfeiture of the murderer's own life.

The concept of the divine image in humans is a clear break with other ancient conceptions of the human. For example, as Sarna points out (*Genesis*, 15), in Gen 1, humans are not the menials of the gods. In fact, Genesis expresses the antithesis of this idea: It is the creator who cares for his creatures. The creator's first communication is concern for the physical needs of his creatures as well as their continued growth and welfare. "Elohim blessed them and Elohim said to them, 'Be fertile and increase, fill the earth and master it; and rule the fish of the sea, the birds of the sky, and all the living things that creep on earth'" (Gen 1:28–29); and "Yahweh Elohim commanded the man, saying, 'Of every tree of the garden you are free to eat'" (Gen 2:16). Humans in Genesis are not presented as the helpless victims of the blind forces of nature, the playthings of capricious gods. On the contrary, they are creatures of majesty and dignity, of central importance and value to the god who has created them.

At the same time and in line with the assertion that humans are made in the divine *image*, humans are not said to actually *be* gods or even the kin of gods. In the biblical view, humans are still creatures—in the sense of "created things"—dependent on a higher power. And so in the second creation story, which begins in Gen 2:4, the first human is formed when the god fashions it from the dust of the earth, or clay. There are numerous ancient Near Eastern stories of gods fashioning humans from clay (Sarna, *Genesis*, 14; Coogan, *The Old Testament*, 14). Even so, the biblical account, while borrowing this motif, takes pains to distinguish and elevate the human. First, the fashioning of the human from clay is a dramatic moment in the story (though the final and climactic creative act is the creation of gender by means of the separation of the female from the male). Second, and significantly, the deity himself blows the breath of life into the *adam's* nostrils (2:7). Thus, in the second creation story, just as in the first, there is a sacred imprint of some kind that distinguishes the human from other creatures. The idea of the human as a being that is molded from clay yet enlivened by the divine breath conveys the paradoxical mix of earthly and divine traits—of dependence and freedom—that mark humans as unique.

In the first creation account, there is no implication that man and woman are in an unequal relationship before the deity. The Hebrew word designating the creature—the *adam*—is a generic term meaning simply "the human," or more literally "the earthling" since the word *adam* derives from *adamah,* meaning "earth," and thus denotes something made from the earth. Genesis 1:27 describes the creation of the *adam* this way: "And Elohim created the *adam* [the earthling] in his own image, in the image of Elohim he created it; male and female he created them."[5] This line, with its definite article ("*the* earthling"), its reference to both genders, and its switch to a plural object in the final clause, has vexed commentators for centuries. Contrary to popular belief, the verse seems to tell of the creation not of a single man with the personal name of Adam, but of a species of earthlings consisting of males and females, together and all at once. Moreover, this earthling that includes both male and female is said to be created in the divine image, suggesting that the ancient Israelites did not conceive of their god as gendered male or female. Even in the second creation account, where the woman is built from a rib taken from the sleeping man, it is not clear that the woman is subordinate to the man. Medieval Jewish commentators hint at this when they playfully suggest that the woman was not made from the man's head—lest she rule over him—or from his foot—lest she be subservient to him—but from his side so that she might be a companion to him. Indeed, the creation of woman is the *climactic* creative act in the second Genesis account. With the emergence of woman, creation is finally complete.

Thus, the biblical creation stories individually and jointly present a portrait of humans as the pinnacle and purpose of creation, godlike in some way and in possession of distinctive faculties and character traits that equip them, male and female, for stewardship over the created world.

## The World

In the Gen 1 creation story, there is an emphasis on the essential goodness of the created world and a rejection of the principle of a primordial evil. Kaufmann asserted that in polytheistic systems, evil is a permanent necessity built into the cosmic order because the primordial realm spawns both gods and demons, locked in eternal conflict. Consequently, the universe is not essentially good. By contrast, in the first biblical creation story, each act of creation is followed by the declaration that "it is good" (Gen 1:4, 10, 12, 18, 21, 25). After the creation of living things, the text states that the creator found all that he made to be "very good." There are seven occurrences of the word *good* in Genesis. The sevenfold or tenfold repetition of a word (a *leitwort*) is a favorite literary technique of the biblical author to emphasize an idea. Genesis 1 creates in its reader a tremendous rush of optimism. The world is good; humans are important; they have purpose and dignity. The biblical writer rejects the concept of an inherent primordial evil, a concept found in the literature of the ancient Near East. For the biblical writer, evil is not a metaphysical reality built into the structure of the universe. Hence all signs of a cosmic battle—between the forces of chaos and evil and the forces of cosmos and good—are eliminated. In *Enuma Elish,* cosmic order is achieved only after a violent struggle with hostile forces. In Genesis, creation is not the result of a struggle between antagonists. The biblical god imposes order or cosmos on the demythologized and inert elements of chaos. A closer examination of Gen 1 will show this to be the case.

The chapter begins with a temporal clause often translated "In the beginning." This translation implies that what follows is an account of the ultimate origins of the universe. The reader of such a translation expects to hear of the first act in time: "In the beginning, X happened as the first act in time." Thus many English translations read: "In the beginning, Elohim created the heaven and earth." This is, however, a poor translation of the Hebrew. The Hebrew phrase in question is similar to the opening phrase in other Near Eastern cosmologies and is best translated "when Elohim began creating the heavens and the earth," just as *Enuma Elish*'s opening phrase is best translated as "when on high." This more accurate translation suggests that the story is concerned not to depict the ultimate origin of everything, but rather to explain why and how the world is the way it is. The full translation of verses 1–2 is: "When Elohim began to create heaven and earth (the earth being unformed and void and darkness on the face of the deep and the wind of Elohim hovering over the face of the water) Elohim said, "Let there be light" (Hayes's translation).

Thus when the story opens, we find that the physical elements exist but have no shape or form. Creation in Gen 1 is described not as a process of making something of nothing (creation ex nihilo) but as a process of organizing preexisting materials, of imposing order on chaos. The story begins with an existing chaotic mass and "the *ruah* of Elohim" (sometimes translated anachronistically as the "spirit" of the deity, but better as his "wind" or breath) sweeps over the deep. It will be recalled that in *Enuma Elish*, creation followed upon a cosmic battle in which Marduk the god of the storm released his wind against Tiamat—a divine monster, the primeval sea or "deep" who represents the forces of chaos. The similarities here are immediately apparent. Our story opens with a temporal clause and a wind that sweeps over the chaotic waters or deep (like the wind of Marduk released against the chaotic waters of Tiamat). The Hebrew word for "deep" is *Tehom,* the Hebrew equivalent of *Tiamat.* In fact, a better translation of verse 2 might read "darkness was on the face of Deep," without a definite article and capitalized almost as if *deep* were a proper name.

The storyteller has set the stage for a retelling of the cosmic battle story, a story near and dear to the hearts of any ancient Near Eastern listener. All the elements are there—wind, a primeval chaotic watery mass or deep. But then—surprise! There is no battle. There is only a word. The ancient Near Eastern listener would prick up his ears. Where's the battle, the violence, the gore? Something new and different is being communicated in this story.

It cannot be argued that the biblical writers were unfamiliar with the motif of creation as a sequel to a cosmic battle. Many poetic passages of the Bible contain clear and explicit allusions to the myth of a cosmic battle preceding creation, suggesting that it was a well-known motif in ancient Israel.

> O Elohim, my king from of old, who brings deliverance
>     throughout the land;
> it was you who drove back the sea with your might, who
>     smashed the heads of the monsters in the waters;
> it was you who crushed the heads of Leviathan [a sea monster].
>     (Ps 74:12–17)

And again:

> It was you that hacked Rahab [the name of a primeval monster]
> in pieces, that pierced the Dragon. It was you that dried up the
> Sea, the waters of the great deep. . . . (Isa 51:9–10)

In a similar vein, Job 26:12–14; Ps 74:12–17; 89:10–11; and Ps 104 all depict the Israelite deity engaged in a primeval battle. Clearly, cosmic battle stories at the dawn of creation—stories of a god who violently slays the forces of chaos, represented as watery dragons, as a prelude to creation—were known and recounted in Israel. The rejection of this idea in Genesis 1's demythologized creation account therefore appears to be pointed and purposeful. The Genesis account establishes a single uncontested god who by the power of his word or will creates cosmos out of chaos. He follows this initial ordering by establishing the celestial bodies, which are not themselves divinities but merely his creations.

After felling Tiamat with his wind and dividing her carcass like a shellfish, Marduk separates her waters above and below, posting guards so that they cannot escape. Similarly, according to the biblical conception, the world consists of a space (an air bubble) between water above and water below. The water above is held up by a thin firmament. The firmament seems to be a beaten sheet inverted like a bowl over the earth (the Hebrew word for *firmament* means "beaten flat," invoking the image of metal beaten into a thin sheet). By opening windows in this firmament, the deity lets in water as rain, as we will see in the story of the flood.

The first biblical creation story takes place over a period of seven days. There is a logical and parallel structure in the description of the six days of actual creation. The deity's actions on Days 1, 2, and 3 create the necessary conditions, physical spaces, or habitats for the natural phenomena and creatures created on Days 4, 5, and 6, respectively. Thus, on Day 1, light and darkness are separated—the necessary condition for the creation of the heavenly bodies that give off light, on Day 4. On Day 2, the firmament is established by assigning water to its appropriate place and opening up the space of the sky and, on Day 5, the inhabitants of sky and water are created (the birds of the air and the fish of the sea). On Day 3, the land is separated from the sea, and on Day 6, the inhabitants of the land are created—land animals. But Days 3 and 6 each have an additional element, and the pairing of the other elements suggests that these excess elements are also to be paired. On Day 3, vegetation is created, and on Day 6, humans are created. The implication is that the vegetation is for the humans, and indeed it is expressly stated by the deity that humans are given every fruit-bearing tree and seed-bearing plant for food (1:29). No mention is made of animals as food. Moreover, in Gen 1:30 animals are given the green plants (grass, herbs) so that there is no competition between humans and animals for food, and thus no excuse to live in anything but a peaceful coexistence. In short, in the biblical creation story, humans are created vegetarian, and in every respect the original creation is imagined as free of bloodshed and violence of any kind.

On the seventh day, the creator is said to rest from his labors, and for this reason he blessed the seventh day and declared it holy, that is, belonging to the deity. Part of the purpose of the Gen 1 creation story, then, is to explain the origin of the observance of the Sabbath and the seven-day weekly cycle.

The Israelite accounts of creation contain clear allusions to and resonances of ancient Near Eastern cosmogonies, but they are best characterized as a demythologization of what was a common cultural heritage. There is a clear tendency toward monotheism in this myth and a pointed transformation of widely known stories so as to express a monotheistic worldview and to deny the presence of a primordial evil. Genesis 1–3 rivals and implicitly polemicizes against the myths of Israel's neighbors, rejecting certain elements while incorporating and demythologizing others.

## Whence Evil?

Kaufmann argued that in the Hebrew Bible, evil has no independent existence. Yet evil and suffering are experienced as a condition of human existence, a reality of life. How can this state of affairs be explained? The Garden of Eden story seeks to answer that question, asserting ultimately that evil stems not from the activity of an independent demonic force but from the exercise of human free will in defiance of the creator. The created world is a good world; humans, however, in the exercise of their moral autonomy, have the power to corrupt the good. According to Kaufmann, the Garden of Eden story communicates this basic idea of the monotheistic worldview: Evil is not a metaphysical reality; it is a moral reality. Ultimately, this means that evil lacks inevitability. It lies within the realm of human responsibility and control.

Nahum Sarna (*Genesis*, 26) points out that there is a very important distinction between the Garden of Eden story and its ancient Near Eastern parallels. The motif of a tree or plant of life is widespread in ancient Near Eastern literature, myth, and ritual. The quest for such a plant and the immortality it promises is a primary theme of the Mesopotamian *Epic of Gilgamesh*. By contrast, we know of no parallel in ancient Near Eastern literature to the biblical tree of the knowledge of good and evil.[6]

What is the significance of the fact that the Bible mentions both trees only to then focus on the tree of the knowledge of good and evil while virtually ignoring the tree of life so central to the myths of other ancient Near Eastern cultures? Sarna argues that the subordinate role of the tree of life in this story signals the biblical writer's dissociation from the ancient world's preoccupation with immortality (*Genesis*, 27). The biblical writer insists that the central concern of life is not mortality but morality. The drama of human life revolves not around the search for eternal life, but around the moral conflict and tension between a good god's design for creation and the free will of humans that can corrupt that design.

The serpent tells Eve that if she eats the fruit of the tree of the knowledge of good and evil, she will become like the deity. His words are both true and false. The humans will become like gods knowing good and evil, not because of some magical property of the fruit itself. By choosing to eat of the forbidden fruit, the humans learn that they have the power to disobey the deity, that they have moral freedom to conform their actions to the divine will or to defy it. To know good and evil, to know that one has moral freedom, is no guarantee that one will choose or incline toward the good. This is what the serpent omits in his speech. The serpent implies that it is the power of moral choice alone that is godlike. But true godliness is not simply the power to choose good and evil (Sarna, *Genesis*, 27). True godliness—imitation of the deity—is the exercise of one's power and free will in a manner that is good and life-affirming. For it is the biblical writer's contention that the god of Israel is not only morally free but also essentially and necessarily good.

According to Sarna (*Genesis*, 27–28), the Garden of Eden story conveys an idea central to Kaufmann's description of the monotheistic worldview: that

> evil is a product of human behavior, not a principle inherent in the cosmos. Man's disobedience is the cause of the human predicament. Human freedom can be at one and the same time an omen of disaster and a challenge and opportunity.

The humans learn that the concomitant of their freedom is responsibility. Their first act of defiance is punished harshly, teaching that the moral choices and actions of humans have consequences that must be borne by the perpetrator. One of these consequences is the loss of access to the tree of life. Prior to the discovery of their moral freedom, humans—it is implied—could eat freely from the tree and live forever. But Gen 3:22 makes it clear that humans cannot have both immortality and the capacity for evil. The deity must retain the upper hand against the agents of evil if his creation is to survive. Were humans to add immortality to their newly discovered capacity for evil, they would be true rivals to their creator. And so he expels the first human pair from the garden and blocks access to the tree of life. Human moral freedom is therefore gained at the cost of eternal life; human mortality is a necessary concomitant of moral freedom.

The Garden of Eden story in Gen 2–3 attempts to account for the paradoxical and problematic existence of evil and suffering in a world that, according to Genesis 1, was created and is governed by an essentially good god. But other perspectives on this story are possible—as will be seen in the next chapter.

## CHAPTER 4

# Doublets and Contradictions

*Readings:* Genesis 4–9

## The Second Creation Story

Genesis 1–3 presents two distinct creation myths side by side differing in general character and in small detail,[1] and in this chapter we will examine the second creation myth in isolation from the first account and in the light of an important ancient Near Eastern parallel: the *Epic of Gilgamesh.* Here again, the work of Nahum Sarna (*Genesis*) and other scholars (especially Michael Coogan, *The Old Testament*) who have devoted themselves to the study of these textual parallels will be of central importance.

The *Epic of Gilgamesh* is a magnificent Mesopotamian epic relating the exploits of the Sumerian king Gilgamesh of Uruk (see Figure 1). The epic as we now have it was composed between 2000 and 1800 B.C.E. Although Gilgamesh was apparently a historical character and king of Uruk, this story of his adventures and great journey has fantastic, legendary elements. A full text of the epic was found in Assurbanipal's library, from the seventh century B.C.E. However, fragments have been uncovered in Iraq that date to the eighteenth century B.C.E.; there are even older prototypes for certain portions of the epic.

The story opens with a description of Gilgamesh as a most unpopular king. He is tyrannical, undisciplined, and oversexed. The citizens cry out to

Fig. 1. A tablet of the *Epic of Gilgamesh*. Erich Lessing /
Art Resource, NY.

the gods for relief from his arrogance and abuses—citing in particular his
behavior with the young women of the city. The god Aruru is told to deal
with Gilgamesh. Aruru fashions a noble savage named Enkidu who is to be
a match for Gilgamesh. Enkidu, like the biblical human in Gen 2, is fashioned from clay. He appears as an unclothed and innocent primitive, living
a free and peaceful life in full harmony with nature and the beasts, racing
across the steppes with the gazelles. Before he can enter the city to meet and
subdue Gilgamesh, he must be "tamed." A woman is sent to Enkidu to provide the sexual initiation that will tame and civilize him.

For six days and seven nights Enkidu comes forth,
   mating with the lass.
After he had had (his) fill of her charms,
He set his face toward his wild beasts.
On seeing him, Enkidu, the gazelles ran off,
The wild beasts of the steppe drew away from his body.
Startled was Enkidu, as his body became taut.
His knees were motionless—for his wild beasts had gone.
Enkidu had to slacken his pace—it was not as before;
But he now had [wi]sdom, [br]oader understanding.
Returning, he sits at the feet of the harlot.
He looks up at the face of the harlot,
His ears attentive, as the harlot speaks;
[The harlot] says to him, to Enkidu:
"Thou art [wi]se, Enkidu, art become like a god!
Why with the wild creatures dost though roam over the steppe?
Come, let me lead thee [to] ramparted Uruk,
To the holy Temple, abode of Anu and Ishtar,
Where lives Gilgamesh, accomplished in strength
And like a wild ox lords it over the folk."
As she speaks to him, her words find favor,
His heart enlightened, he yearns for a friend.
Enkidu says to her, to the harlot:
"Up lass, escort thou me (to Gilgamesh) . . .
I will challenge him [and will bo]ldly address him."[2]

Through sexual experience, Enkidu becomes wise, growing in mental and spiritual stature. He is said to be like a god, but there has been a concomitant loss of innocence. Enkidu's harmonious unity with nature is broken. He clothes himself, and his old friends, the gazelles, run from him. He will never again roam free with the animals.

As one reads the *Epic*, one senses a deep ambivalence regarding the relative virtues and evils of civilized life. On the one hand, it is held to be good that humans rise above the animals, build cities, wear clothing, pursue the arts of civilization, and develop bonds of love, duty, and friendship as animals do not. These are the very things that make humans like the gods. But on the other hand, these advances come at a cost, and one senses a deep longing for the freedom of life in the wild, the innocent, simple, uncomplicated life lived day to day, without plans and toil, and in harmony with nature.

There are obvious parallels between this portion of the *Epic* and our second creation story. Enkidu like the *adam* is fashioned from clay, a noble savage, an innocent primitive. He lives in peaceful coexistence with the animals. Nature yields its fruits to him without hard labor, and he is unaware of and unattracted by the benefits of civilization—clothing, cities, and their labor. Just as Enkidu gains wisdom, becomes like a god, and loses his oneness with nature, so the *adam* and the woman after eating the fruit of the knowledge of good and evil are said to have become like gods and lose their harmonious relationship with nature. To the snake, Yahweh[3] says,

> I will put enmity
> Between you and the woman,
> And between your offspring and hers;
> They shall strike at your head,
> And you shall strike at their heel. (Gen 3:15)

Banished from the garden that yielded its fruits without labor, the human must now toil for food, the earth yielding its fruit only stintingly. To the *adam*, Yahweh says,

> "Cursed be the ground because of you;
> By toil shall you eat of it
> All the days of your life:
> Thorns and thistles shall it sprout for you.
> But your food shall be the grasses of the field;
> By the sweat of your brow
> Shall you get bread to eat."

Moral freedom, it seems, comes at a high price.

But there are some important differences between the *Epic of Gilgamesh* and the biblical Garden of Eden story. The most important difference has to do with the nature of the act that leads to the transformation of the human characters. In the *Epic of Gilgamesh* it is Enkidu's sexual experience that makes him wise and godlike, at the cost of his life with the beasts. To be sure, there has been a long tradition of interpreting the sin of the first biblical human pair as sexual, and there are some hints in the text that might support such a view. The earthling and the woman eat from the tree of the knowledge of good and evil, in violation of Yahweh's command and eating can be a metaphor for sex. Knowledge of good and evil can be understood in sexual terms since the verb *to know* in biblical Hebrew can mean to have sexual intercourse. Snakes are symbols of renewed life and fertility in the east (because they shed their skins), and they are also phallic symbols. The woman says that the snake seduced her. Do all of these sexual overtones suggest that in the biblical view the fall of the *adam* and the woman came about through sex? Is sex therefore a negative act forbidden by Yahweh? That seems unlikely, given that the deity's first command to the first couple was to be fruitful and multiply. Admittedly, that command appears in the first creation story (Gen 1:28). Nevertheless, the second creation story's account of the creation of woman refers to the fact that man and woman become one flesh. This suggests that sex was part of the plan for humans even at creation. Further, it is only after their defiance of Yahweh's command that the humans become aware of and ashamed by their nakedness.

Perhaps, then, Gen 2–3 is yet another example of an Israelite adaptation of familiar stories and motifs to express something new. For the biblical writer, the earthling's transformation occurs after an act of disobedience, not after a seven-day sexual encounter. This disobedience comes about in a somewhat indirect way. Yahweh tells the *adam,* before the creation of the woman, that he is not to eat of the tree of the knowledge of good and evil (Gen 2:16) on pain of death. The woman does not hear this command directly. Genesis 3 introduces the clever serpent, and although much later Hellenistic Jewish texts and the New Testament will identify him as Satan, there is clearly no such creature in this earthy fable or, indeed, in the Hebrew Bible.[4] The snake of Eden is simply a talking animal, a standard literary device of myths and fables such as the stories of Aesop. The woman responds to the serpent's queries by saying that eating and even touching the tree is forbidden on pain of death. But whence the addition of touching? Did the *adam* convey Yahweh's command to the woman with an emphasis of his own: "Don't even touch that tree, or it's all over for us!"? Or did the woman mishear in a tragic version of the telephone game? The serpent tells her that she will not die if she eats the fruit; in fact, he adds, the fruit will bring wisdom, making the humans like gods who know good and bad. This much, at least, is certainly true.

Genesis 3:7 is a critical verse that is rarely properly translated. Most translations read: "She took of its fruit and ate. She also gave some to her husband and he ate." The implication is that the woman acts alone, then goes to find her husband and give him of the fruit. But in fact the Hebrew literally reads "She took of its fruit and ate and gave also to her husband *with her* and he ate"—implying that at that fateful moment of taking and eating the fruit, the man and woman stood at the tree together. Although only the serpent and the woman speak, at the time of eating the fruit, the *adam* was present with the woman and accepted the fruit that she handed him. In short, he was fully complicitous and he, arguably, should have known better since he heard the deity's original instructions. Indeed Yahweh holds him responsible. He reproaches the *adam,* who tries to dodge responsibility by claiming, "The woman that you gave to be with me, she gave to me from the tree and I ate." For her part, the woman explains that the serpent tricked her. Yahweh vents his fury on each of the three in ascending order: first the snake for his trickery, then the woman, and finally, the man.

Just as the harlot tells Enkidu after his sexual awakening and humanization that he has become like a god, so the *adam* and the woman after eating the forbidden fruit are said to be like divine beings. Why? As suggested in Chapter 3, they become wise and like divine beings because they learn that they have moral choice, that they have free will and can defy the good god and his good plans for them, in a way that animals and natural phenomena cannot. But there is a serious danger here. In Gen 3:22, Yahweh says, "Now that the man has become like one of us, knowing good and evil, what if he should stretch out his hand and take also from the tree of life and eat, and live forever?" It is the threat of an immortal antagonist that must be avoided, and thus Yahweh banishes the humans from the garden, stationing cherubim and a fiery, ever-turning sword to guard the way back to the tree of life.

The acceptance of mortality as an inescapable part of the human condition is also a theme of the *Epic of Gilgamesh.* Enkidu earns Gilgamesh's respect and deep love—the first time that this rapacious tyrant has respected or loved anyone—and his character is reformed. The rest of the epic contains the adventures of these two close friends. When Enkidu dies, Gilgamesh is devastated, stunned with grief over his beloved Enkidu. He becomes obsessed with his own mortality and so begins his exhausting quest for immortality. He leaves the city and travels far and wide, crossing primeval seas and the waters of death. Weary, filthy, ragged, he finally finds Utnapishtim, the only mortal to have been granted immortality, but the latter cannot assist him. Gilgamesh learns the whereabouts of a plant of eternal youth, which at least will keep him young, but in a moment of carelessness Gilgamesh loses the plant to a thieving snake—explaining why snakes shed their skins so as to be forever young. Exhausted by his travels, Gilgamesh returns to Uruk. As he gazes at the city, he takes comfort in the thought that although humans are finite and frail and doomed to die, their accomplishments and great works secure their foothold in human memory.

As Sarna emphasizes (*Genesis,* 26–27), the quest for immortality that is so central in the *Epic of Gilgamesh* is deflected in the biblical story. The tree of life is mentioned with the definite article—"with THE tree of life in the middle of the garden" (Gen 2:9)—as if it is a familiar motif, but it is then forgotten. The snake associated with the plant of eternal youth in Gilgamesh is here associated with the tree of the knowledge of good and evil instead, which is the focus of the narrative. Only at the end of the Garden of Eden story does the tree appear again in a passage that emphasizes its sudden and permanent inaccessibility. Two conclusions might be drawn from this. First, it may be that the humans had access to this tree as long as their will conformed to that of Yahweh, but once they discovered their moral freedom, once they discovered that they could thwart Yahweh and work evil in the world, abuse and corrupt all that the deity had created, Yahweh could not afford to allow them access to the tree of life. This would be tantamount to creating immortal divine enemies. The deity maintains the upper hand in his struggle with humans in this: Eventually humans must die. Second, the motif of guards blocking access to the tree of life suggests that humans have no access to immortality and that the pursuit of immortality is futile. One might say then that Yahweh spoke the truth after all—the fruit did bring death, not immediately to those who ate it, but to humankind in general by forcing Yahweh to block the humans' access to the tree of life.

The opening chapters of Genesis have been subjected to centuries of theological interpretation generating, for example, the doctrine of original sin—the idea that humans after Adam[5] are born into a state of sinfulness from which they cannot free themselves. As many interpreters—ancient and modern—have already observed, however, the actions of Adam and Eve[6] are said to bring death to the human race, not a state of utter and unredeemed sinfulness from which they are powerless to escape. On the contrary, for centuries the story was read as affirming, and explaining the origin of, the moral *freedom* of humans.

The Garden of Eden story is primarily etiological rather than prescriptive or normative. At its base lie certain observable features of the human condition: As humans grow, they emerge from innocent childhood to self-conscious adulthood; survival is a difficult endeavor in a world that can seem harshly hostile; women are often desirous of and emotionally bonded to the very persons who establish the conditions of their subordination. The story explains how these odd conditions of life came to be as they are—which is not to say that they are ideal or that they represent the divine will for humankind. (Indeed, these features of human life seem to be the result of a rupture, or *failure,* in the original plan.) They are etiological fables—and best read as such.

The Garden of Eden story contains a narrative feature that will recur in the Pentateuch: Yahweh's recalibrations in the light of human activity. Following the creation, Yahweh has to punt a bit. He modifies his plans for the first couple—barring access to the tree of life in response to their unforeseen disobedience. Despite their new mortality, humans are nevertheless a force to be reckoned with—unpredictable to the very god who created them. This, then, is the one limitation to which the Israelite god Yahweh is subject—the free will of humans. Yahweh's plans and desires can be thwarted not by the decrees of a metadivine realm that lies beyond him, not by other divine beings who reign beside him, but by the human creature who purchased moral freedom at a high price. Those who confuse the biblical character Yahweh with the "God" constructed by classical western theology may be troubled by the fact that Yahweh is presented in his interactions with humans in the Pentateuch as neither omniscient nor omnipotent. Unacquainted with the god constructed by western theology many centuries later, the biblical narrator(s) felt no such confusion, asserting the great power of Yahweh on the one hand and the absolute freedom of humankind on the other.

## Genesis 4: Cain and Abel

Genesis 4 relates the story of the first murder. In this story, Cain, the firstborn of Adam and Eve, kills his brother Abel because Yahweh preferred Abel's offering from the flock over Cain's offering from the soil. Cain sets upon Abel when they are alone in the field, despite Yahweh's warning to Cain that it is possible to master the urge to violence by an act of will: "Sin crouches at the door; its urge is toward you, yet you can be its master" (Gen 4:7). As Sarna notes (*Genesis,* 30), the term *brother* recurs throughout this short story, climaxing in Yahweh's question "Where is your brother Abel?" and Cain's response "I do not know; am I my brother's keeper?" Ironically, one senses that what Cain intends as a rhetorical question is hardly rhetorical at all. Yes, he is—we all are—our brother's keeper, and the strong implication of this story is, as Sarna states, that all homicide is in fact fratricide (*Genesis*, 31). Sarna further notes that the culpability of Cain rests on the unexpressed assumption of the existence of a universal moral law (*Genesis*, 31): the divinely endowed sanctity of human life. What the deity has created with loving care and attention in his own image must not be destroyed wantonly.

The story of Cain and Abel has been cited as evidence of the tension between settled, civilized areas and the unsettled desert areas of the nomads in biblical culture. Abel, the keeper of sheep, represents the nomadic pastoralist while Cain, the tiller of the soil, represents settled urban life. When Yahweh prefers the offering of Abel, Cain is distressed and jealous to the point of murder. Yahweh's preference for the offering of Abel valorizes the free life of the nomadic pastoralist over urban existence.[7] Even after the Israelite settlement in the land of Canaan, the life of the desert pastoralist remained a romantic vision.

This terse story contains some oddities that should not pass unnoticed. First, we may ask why Cain expresses fear that all who meet him will try to kill him. At this point in the narrative chronology, there are precisely three human beings: Adam, Eve, and Cain. Who, then, does Cain fear he will encounter in his restless wandering on the earth? Second, in response to Cain's fear, Yahweh promises to take sevenfold vengeance on anyone who kills Cain. The deity's words imply multiple "killers of Cain," all of whom will be punished. But surely, one man can only be killed once. Third, after departing the presence of Yahweh, Cain and his wife bear a child. Who is Cain's wife?

These curious narrative gaps point to a primary compositional feature of the biblical text—the incorporation of previously independent sources. Scholars concur that the story of Cain and Abel was originally an independent story, probably an etiological tale about the nomadic Kenite people, descended from Cain. It was incorporated into the national narrative and linked by an editor to the Garden of Eden story by the addition of Gen 4:1–2, establishing Cain and Abel as the sons of Adam and Eve. But the narrative discontinuities created by the story's incorporation into the early history were not smoothed over.

Similarly, the biblical account of the flood features numerous literary oddities (repetitions and contradictions) that have helped scholars trace the composite structure and compositional techniques of the biblical text.

## Genesis 6–9: The Flood Story

The murder of Abel and exile of Cain are followed by genealogical lists that provide continuity between the tales and relate ancient lore concerning the origins of the civilized arts, such as building, metalwork, and music. But in Gen 6:5 we read that "every plan devised by his [the human] mind was nothing but evil all the time," and the stage is set for the story of a worldwide flood.

Here again the Bible makes use of ancient traditions it adapts for its own purposes, including a third-millennium B.C.E. Sumerian flood story whose hero is Ziusudra and a second-millennium B.C.E. Semitic work known as the *Epic of Atrahasis*. The most detailed flood story is on the eleventh tablet of the lengthy *Epic of Gilgamesh*. As we have seen, Gilgamesh's desire for immortality leads him to Utnapishtim, who had obtained eternal life. Gilgamesh begs for the secret of eternal life, only to learn that Utnapishtim and his wife gained their immortality by a twist of circumstances: They were the sole survivors of a great flood, in consequence of which the gods graciously decided to bring the couple into their ranks.

The Sumerian story of Ziusudra is similar to the Genesis account. In both, the flood is the deliberate result of a divine decision, and one individual is chosen to be saved and is told to build a boat as a means of survival. In both, instructions are given as to who and what shall board, the flood exterminates all living things, the boat comes to rest on a mountaintop, and the hero sends out birds to reconnoiter the ground. In both, the emerging hero erects an altar, offers a sacrifice, and is blessed.

But there are significant contrasts between the Mesopotamian stories and their Israelite adaptation. In the *Epic of Gilgamesh*, no motive is mentioned for the divine destruction. It seems to be a divine act of pure capriciousness. The *Epic of Atrahasis* suggests a reason. The text states:

> The land became wide and the people became numerous; the land bellowed like wild oxen. The god was disturbed by their uproar. Enlil heard the clamor and said to the gods, "Oppressive has become the clamor of humankind. By their uproar they prevent sleep."

It seems that humankind is to be destroyed because the gods are irritated by their tumult and noise. In the *Epic of Gilgamesh*, Ea asks Enlil how he could have brought on the flood so senselessly. "Lay upon the sinner the sin, lay upon the transgressor his transgression." Pure capriciousness was the cause. The Bible rejects this portrait by providing a moral rationale for the deity's actions. The earth is destroyed because of *hamas* (literally, "violence and bloodshed" but including all kinds of injustice and oppression), and Noah is saved because of his righteousness. In this story, Israel's god does not act capriciously but according to clear standards of justice.[8]

Moreover, in the Mesopotamian flood story, the gods do not appear to be in control. Enlil wanted to destroy all humankind, but the god Ea thwarts that plan by dropping hints of the impending disaster to Utnapishtim. When the flood comes, the gods themselves are terrified and cower, as the text says, "like dogs crouched against the outer wall; Ishtar cried out like a woman in travail." Moreover, the flood deprives the gods of food and drink. Famished, they crowd around Utnapishtim's sacrifice like flies. By contrast, in the biblical flood story Yahweh does not need Noah's postdiluvian sacrifice as food. He is unthreatened by the forces of nature that he unleashes. He makes the decision to punish humans because the world has corrupted itself through bloodshed and violence. He selects Noah to survive because of his righteousness and issues a direct command to him to build an ark. Yahweh has a clear purpose and retains control throughout the story.

According to Sarna, the flood story—like the story of Cain and Abel before it and the story of Sodom and Gomorrah after it—presupposes the existence of a universal moral law governing the world, for the infraction of which the supreme judge will bring humans to account. If the will of the sole, unchallenged deity is understood to be moral, then morality can become an absolute value subject to punishment. Further, the message of the flood story seems to be that when humans destroy the moral basis of society, they endanger the very existence of that society, of all civilization (Sarna, *Genesis,* 52). Corruption, injustice, and lawlessness inevitably bring about destruction. Moreover, like Kaufmann, Sarna stresses (*Genesis,* 53) that humankind is not, in this story, punished for violations of religious sins, that is, for idolatry or failure to worship the god of Israel. It is the view of the Torah books that each nation worships its gods in its own way, and only Israel is obligated to worship the god of Israel.[9] The other nations are not held accountable for idolatry in the Torah as Israel will be. But all peoples, Israelites and non-Israelites alike, by virtue of having been created by the one god and in his image—even though they may not know or worship that god—are bound to a basic moral law that precludes murder and all forms of physical and social violence. What better way to drive home the point that inhumanity and violence undermine the very foundations of society than to describe a situation in which a cosmic catastrophe is the result of human corruption and violence! This idea runs through the entire Bible and much of later Jewish, Christian, and Muslim thought. The Psalmist makes use of this motif when he denounces the exploitation of the poor, the fatherless, the afflicted, and the destitute, for through such wicked deeds, he says, "all the foundations of the earth are moved" (Ps 82:5).

The Noah story ends with the ushering in of a new era, a second creation. This time, Yahweh realizes that he must make a concession to human weakness and the human desire to kill, and rectify the circumstances that made his destruction of the earth necessary (another divine recalibration). He establishes a covenant with Noah. Humankind thus receives its first laws, and they are universal in scope according to the biblical narrative. In other words, these laws apply to all humanity, not just Israel, because Noah is the progenitor of all humanity. These few laws, often referred to as the Noahide covenant, explicitly prohibit the spilling of human blood. Blood is the biblical symbol for life (see Lev 17), and life is sacred. Following the flood, however, Yahweh makes a concession to the human appetite for power and violence (another example of divine recalibration, as the deity learns more about the unpredictable earthling he has created). Previously humans were to be vegetarian (Gen 1:29–30), but now Yahweh concedes that humans may kill animals to eat them. Even so, the animal's life is to be treated with reverence. The blood, which is the life essence, is to be poured out on the ground, returned to Yahweh. The animal may be eaten to satisfy the human hunger for flesh, but the life essence itself is sacred and belongs to Yahweh. Moreover, the absolute ban on human blood (previously implied) is stated explicitly for the first time. Thus Gen 9:4–6 reads:

> But you shall not eat flesh with its life, that is, its blood. For your lifeblood I will surely require a reckoning; of every beast I will require it and of humans, of every person's fellow I will require the life of the person. Whoever sheds the blood of a person in exchange for that person shall his blood be shed, for Elohim made humans in his own image.[10]

All life, human and animal, is sacred to the deity. Human blood cannot be spilled without forfeiting one's own blood in exchange. As a concession, animals may be killed, but their blood may not be appropriated. It must be returned in reverence to its true owner. The covenant also entails Yahweh's promise to restore the rhythm of life and nature and never again destroy the earth. Yahweh sets the rainbow in the sky (like a bowman hanging up his weapon) as a symbol of this promise, a token of eternal reconciliation between the divine and human realms. The notion of a god who can make and keep an eternal covenant is only possible on the view that that god's word and will are not susceptible to nullification by superior powers.

## Doublets and Contradictions

Readers of the flood story in Genesis 6–9 are often struck by the odd literary style, the repetitiveness, and the doublets that can make the story hard to follow and even self-contradictory. In the first place, two designations for Israel's god are used: the sacred tetragrammaton "Yahweh," a personal name for the deity usually rendered in English with the pious substitution "the LORD" (6:5–8, 7:1–5, 7:17), and "Elohim" (6:9–22, 7:16—P), a generic term meaning "deity" and usually rendered in English as "God." Twice the divine being looks upon his creation and is displeased; twice he determines to destroy all living things (Gen 6:5–8 and 6:9–13). Twice the deity issues instructions to Noah, but they are contradictory. In Gen 7:1–5, Yahweh tells Moses to take seven pairs of all clean animals, one pair of unclean animals, and seven pairs of the birds of the heaven. But in Gen 6:14–22, Elohim instructs Noah to take two of each sort of living thing—animals, birds, and creeping things. In Gen 7:17, we learn that the flood was on the earth forty days, but in Gen 7:24, the waters prevail for 150 days. There are subtler contradictions throughout also. At times the flood appears to be the result of heavy rain, but at times the picture is one of a cosmic upheaval in which the waters placed above the firmament at creation and the waters placed below the dry land are released into the bubble of sky and earth, returning the universe to its chaotic and watery state before the creation. In keeping with the idea of a return to chaos, Noah is represented as the beginning of a new creation. Like the first human pair at the first creation, Noah is told to be fruitful and multiply and is also given rule over everything—extending now to the taking of animal life.

The Bible in general contains a great deal of repetition and contradiction. Sometimes repetition and contradiction occur within one passage, as in the flood story, while at other times they occur in stories or passages that are separate from one another, such as the two creation accounts of Gen 1 and Gen 2–3. There are many significant differences between these two stories. The two differ greatly in style. Genesis 1 is highly formalized and abstract, while Gen 2–3 is more dramatic, more earthy. The first contains no puns or wordplays, while the second abounds in them: the *adam* is made from the earth (*adamah*); the earthling and the woman are naked (*arum*) and not ashamed, while the serpent is also *arum* (= "clever, shrewd"). There are differences in terminology. Where Gen 1 uses the terms *male* and *female,* Gen 2 uses the terms *man* and *woman.* Genesis 1 refers to the deity as Elohim and depicts him as remote and transcendent, creating effortlessly through his word and will alone. Genesis 2–3 refers to the deity as Yahweh Elohim and depicts him as more down-to-earth, forming the human like a potter working with clay. He talks to himself, plants a garden, and strolls in it in the cool of the evening. He makes clothes for the humans and is generally spoken of in anthropomorphic terms. In short, the first several chapters of Genesis contain two creation stories with distinctive styles, themes, vocabularies, and substantive details placed side by side. And in Gen 6–9, there are two flood stories with distinctive styles, themes, vocabularies, and substantive details but interwoven, rather than placed side by side. There are many such doublets in the Bible. At times, whole books repeat the same material. The historical saga recorded in Gen–2 Kgs (from creation to Israel's defeat and exile to Babylon) is repeated with significant differences and modifications in 1 and 2 Chronicles.

What are we to make of the repetitions and contradictions here and elsewhere in the Bible? What are the implications for the text's authorship and manner of composition?

These textual features are evidence of the composite structure and multiple authorship of the biblical writings. As early as the Middle Ages, scholars noticed anachronisms, contradictions, repetitions, and other features that are evidence of composite structure and multiple authorship. This evidence presented a challenge, of course, to traditional religious convictions regarding the Mosaic authorship of the first five books of the Bible. The idea that Moses may not have written the Pentateuch grew incrementally. Medieval commentators, noting that Deut 34 describes the death and burial of Moses, suggested that at the very least Moses could not have written that chapter. Certain anachronisms led to the same conclusion. A famous example is Gen 13:7. In the midst of a story describing the division of land between Lot and Abram, the narrator interjects that "the Canaanites and Perizzites were then dwelling in the land." The sentence was clearly written by someone living *after* the time of the Canaanites' and Perizzites' residence in the land, someone who could look back to "the days of the Canaanites and Perizzites" as a thing of the past. Such a person could not be

Moses: During his entire lifetime, Canaanites lived in the land of Canaan. But these were only the first steps in what would be a radical revision of traditional beliefs about the Bible.

The next chapter reviews the emergence of the modern critical study of the Bible in light of the internal literary evidence and explores leading theories regarding the Bible's sources, composition, and authorship.

## CHAPTER 5

# The Modern Critical Study of the Bible

*Readings:* Genesis 10–11

## The Bible's Sources and the Documentary Hypothesis

With the rise of rationalism in the modern period, traditional notions of the divine and Mosaic authorship of the Pentateuch were called into question. The modern critical study of the Bible is often said to have begun with the seventeenth-century philosopher Baruch Spinoza, who first suggested that the Bible should be studied and examined like any other book, without presuppositions as to its divine origin or deference to any other dogmatic claim. But it was a Catholic priest, Richard Simon, who first argued that Moses did not write the Torah and that it contained many anachronisms and errors.

In the mid-eighteenth century, Jean Astruc first noticed that some biblical passages used the name Yahweh to refer to the deity while others used Elohim. On this basis he identified what were to become known as the J (Yahwist) and E (Elohist) sources. He happened to maintain the idea of Mosaic authorship but argued that Moses drew upon two long and distinct documents that used different names for the deity. In the next century, his work would be expanded by Germans who identified other sources making up the Pentateuch. In 1878 the classic statement of biblical source theory was published by Julius Wellhausen. In his *History of Israel*,[1] Wellhausen presented what is known as the Documentary Hypothesis. According to this hypothesis, the historical narrative section of the Bible—Genesis to 2

Kings—is composed of four identifiable source documents. Wellhausen argued that these documents date to different historical periods and reflect different interests and concerns. These four prior documents were woven together by a person or group of persons to form the narrative core of the Bible. Wellhausen argued that these sources tell us not so much about the times or situations they purport to describe but about the beliefs and practices of Israelites in the period in which they were written. Thus, although the sources talk about events from creation forward, they actually reflect the beliefs and religion of Israel from the tenth century and later, the period in which they were written. Wellhausen's work created a sensation because it undermined traditional claims about the divinely inspired Mosaic authorship of the Bible. It is still disputed by conservative groups and Roman Catholic authorities, though not by Roman Catholic scholars.

The four sources identified in Wellhausen's hypothesis are: J (Yahwist source because the phoneme *y* is represented in German by the letter *J*), E (Elohist source), P (Priestly source), and D (most of Deuteronomy).

The first two sources are identified by the name for the deity that they employ. According to J, knowledge of the proper or personal name of Israel's god—Yahweh—begins in the lifetime of Adam ("And to Seth also there was born a son; and he called his name Enosh; then men began to call upon the name of Yahweh"—Gen 4:26). However, according to P and E, Yahweh's name is not known until he reveals it to Moses at the time of the Exodus. In Ex 6:2–3, which is assigned to the P source, the deity appears to Moses and tells him that his name is Yahweh. He then says, "I appeared to Abraham, Isaac, and Jacob as El Shaddai, but I did not make myself known to them by my name Yahweh." (Similarly, Ex 3:13–16, which is assigned to E, places the revelation of the name Yahweh at the time of the Exodus.) Once the J and E sources were separated by the name of the deity, they could be analyzed to identify their characteristic styles and terminology.

The main characteristics of the J source, which begins with the creation story of Gen 2:4b, are identified by scholars as follows: In addition to using the personal name Yahweh (translated in English as "the LORD"), the J source has a vivid and concrete writing style. Yahweh is described anthropomorphically. So, for example, in the J source Yahweh shuts the door of the ark behind Noah (Gen 7:16), he smells the sacrifice Noah offers after the flood (Gen 8:21), he bargains with Abraham (Gen 18:22–32), and he meets with Moses and tries to kill him (Ex 4:24). The J source refers to the place where Moses and the Israelites conclude their covenant with Yahweh as Mt. Sinai. As for provenance, source critics (the term for scholars who analyze literary details of the biblical text in order to identify its distinct sources) felt that a clue to dating could be found in J's description of the land promised to Israel. In the J material, Yahweh's promise of land extends from the river of Egypt to the Euphrates. These are the borders of Israel in the time of kings David and Solomon in the tenth century. Thus, according to classical source theory, J most likely dates to the tenth century. The writer of J sought to justify Israel's possession of its kingdom by presenting it as a fulfillment of Yahweh's promises to her ancestors in ancient times. Moreover, J seems to reflect the interests of the southern kingdom of Judah (regarding the division of Israel into a northern and a southern kingdom after the death of Solomon in 922, see chapter 14), and so it was concluded that the J source was probably composed in the tenth century, in the southern kingdom.

The E source, which seems to occur first in Gen 15, is the most fragmentary and difficult source to isolate, but source critics have also identified its primary characteristics: The E source uses the term *Elohim* to refer to Israel's god. The word *Elohim* is plural in form (and as such would mean "divine powers" or "deities"), but it is always used with a singular verb when referring to Israel's god and is usually translated into English as "God."[2] The E source is more abstract and less picturesque than J. It has a less anthropomorphic view of Israel's deity, who is depicted as more remote than he is in J. In E, there are no direct face-to-face revelations—only indirect communications from the divine by means of messengers and dreams. Also, E emphasizes the role of prophets and describes both Moses and Miriam as prophets. The E source refers to the place where Moses and the Israelites conclude their covenant with their deity as Mt. Horeb. As for provenance, because the E source is concerned primarily with the northern tribes, classical source theory hypothesized that it was composed in the northern kingdom in the ninth century B.C.E.

According to the documentary hypothesis, J and E were combined, probably in the eighth century, into JE, forming the backbone of the Pentateuchal narrative. This narrative includes the creation and early history of humankind and Israel's early ancestors (the patriarchs and matriarchs) in Genesis, the story of Moses and the Exodus from Egypt in the book of Exodus, and the wanderings of the Israelites in the wilderness in Numbers. The anonymous scribe or editor who combined these sources did not remove contradictory or redundant material, as we have seen.

The Documentary Hypothesis of Julius Wellhausen posits two additional sources: D and P. D is essentially the book of Deuteronomy, which purports to be three speeches delivered by Moses as the Israelites are poised to enter the Promised Land. The book of Deuteronomy clearly reflects the interests of a settled agrarian life and thus postdates the period of Moses' life. The main characteristic of D that assisted early scholars in fixing its date is its insistence that only one central sanctuary is acceptable to Yahweh. According to D, Israel's god cannot be worshipped through sacrifices at a local altar or sanctuary. Now, centralization of the cult was a key part of the religious reform of King Josiah in 622 B.C.E. For that reason, source critics date D in its final form no later than the late seventh century. However, D also reflects northern traditions. Since the northern kingdom was destroyed in 722, source critics concluded that D was originally composed in the north in the eighth century. With the fall of the northern kingdom, it was brought to Jerusalem and stored in the Temple, where it was rediscovered and championed in the late seventh century.

P designates the "priestly source," which is found mostly in Leviticus and much of Numbers. The major characteristics of P are a concern with religious institutions, the sacrificial system, the sabbath and holidays, circumcision, the Passover, dietary restrictions (*kashrut*), the system of ritual purity and impurity, and ethical and cultic holiness. The deity is more transcendent and remote in P than in J, being concealed in his *Kavod,* a term that is translated as "glory" but refers to a sort of light-filled cloud that travels with the Israelites. The P source is also interested in covenants, censuses, and genealogies. It contains many prescriptive ritual texts and legal texts, but it also includes narratives, such as the creation story in Gen 1 and much of the flood story. Because P sources often appear in introductory and concluding statements, many source critics believe that priestly writers were responsible for the final editing of the Pentateuch. Wellhausen dated P to the sixth century, after the destruction of Israel and its exile into Babylon.

The Documentary Hypothesis holds that P, J, and E are continuous parallel accounts of the history of the world from creation to the death of Moses. Each has a uniform style, vocabulary, set of themes, and chronological framework.

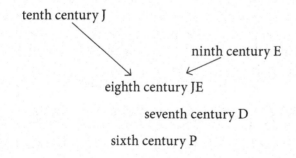

tenth century J

ninth century E

eighth century JE

seventh century D

sixth century P

According to Wellhausen, the priestly school drew all the old material together, added some of its own editorial material to form a narrative frame, and inserted the large priestly documents of Leviticus and much of Numbers. So the Torah is the result of five centuries of religious and literary activity. What a different portrait from traditional claims about the authorship of the Pentateuch by one man—Moses—in approximately the fourteenth century B.C.E.!

There are several terms used to describe the modern critical study of the Bible in the late nineteenth century. It is called *literary criticism* because it proceeds by means of close analysis of the literary features of the text— terminology, style, motifs, and the like. However, insofar as the goal of this literary analysis is the identification and isolation of sources, it is also called *source criticism*. Since the term *literary criticism* today has a slightly different connotation, the term *source criticism* is to be preferred. Further, because the purpose of identifying sources in the biblical text was to ascertain as far as possible their relative dates and so enable the work of historical reconstruction to proceed (primarily the history of the religion of Israel and the historical situation of the authors of the various sources), this type of study was also called *historical criticism*. Hence *literary criticism = source criticism = historical criticism*.[3]

In a nutshell, the Documentary Hypothesis is an effort to explain the contradictions, doublets, and other literary peculiarities in the Bible by means of hypothetical source documents. The theory posits hypothetical sources, traditions, and documents to explain the current shape of the Torah. As a next step, the sources are assigned either relative or absolute dates and then analyzed to reveal the different stages of Israel's religious history. Source criticism is known as historical criticism because it is a tool for accessing the history of the text and ultimately the history of Israelite religion.

Wellhausen's Documentary Hypothesis was subtle and brilliant, but it did reflect certain biases of nineteenth-century German scholarship— specifically a belief in the superiority of Christianity over Judaism and in the superiority of Protestant Christianity over Catholicism. Wellhausen characterized Judaism at the end of the biblical period as a dead tree, twisted and perverted, and he harbored a particular distaste for priests, cult, and ritual (features of ancient Israelite religion shared by contemporary Catholicism). These biases are apparent in his dating of the sources and in his description of the evolutionary stages of Israel's religion. For example, scholars before Wellhausen thought P was an early source attesting to ancient ritual practices that find parallels in the ritual practices of Israel's neighbors in the ancient Near East, but Wellhausen asserted that P had to be the latest source (late sixth to fifth century B.C.E.) because its "obsession" with cult and ritual represented a degenerate and guilt-ridden devolution of Israelite religion. Wellhausen's conclusions are driven in no small measure by his view of postexilic Judaism as a degraded form of religion devoid of genuine spiritual content and his view of priest-led rituals and cultic activities as the same. Thus the priestly source had to date to the time of Judaism's lowest spiritual ebb—the postexilic period. This dating is one of the most controversial aspects of Wellhausen's theory.[4] We shall return to this debate and to a consideration of what is at stake in the dating of P in the chapters dealing with Leviticus and Numbers. It should be remembered, however, that the historical-critical method and the Documentary Hypothesis in particular are not inherently biased theories—they are simply analytical tools that can be applied fairly to the text, even if some source critics have ideological axes to grind.

The Documentary Hypothesis is, after all, a hypothesis. None of the sources posited by critical scholars—J, E, P, or D—has been found independently, and thus the reconstructions of source critics must be continually reevaluated and revised as new information comes to light. For example, some of the criteria invoked by early source critics to separate sources were later shown to be based on an ignorance of ancient literary conventions: Repetition can serve a rhetorical function, and variant terms may be a literary and aesthetic choice. If so, then not every repetition and variant is necessarily a sign of multiple sources.

Nevertheless, the Documentary Hypothesis works well in explaining parallel accounts and combined doublets (see Table 2). It works less well in passages in which the hypothesized sources are closely interwoven. Often, picking apart the sources becomes a dry and mechanical task that can destroy the power and drama of a biblical story. While it is an important and worthwhile project to analyze the Bible's component sources and examine their specific concerns and contribution, it is important to remember that at some point the sources were woven together with great skill and care by a final redactor or redactors in order to be read as a unity. Today we are in a position to read the Bible analytically and synthetically, combining an awareness of origins and sources with a sensitivity to the final composition.

While most biblical scholars today accept some version of Wellhausen's theory, there are doubts about specific aspects of it. Some doubt the existence of E, others defend the antiquity of P, and still others argue that almost everything in the Pentateuch is postexilic. Many Scandinavian

Table 2. Flood Story with Source Analysis

6 (5) The LORD saw how great was man's wickedness on earth, and how every plan devised by his mind was nothing but evil all the time. (6) And the LORD regretted that He had made man on earth, and His heart was saddened. (7) The LORD said, "I will blot out from the earth the men whom I created—men together with beasts, creeping things, and birds of the sky; for I regret that I made them." (8) But Noah found favor with the LORD.

   (9) This is the line of Noah.—Noah was a righteous man; he was blameless in his age; Noah walked with God.—(10) Noah begot three sons: Shem, Ham, and Japheth.

   (11) The earth became corrupt before God; the earth was filled with lawlessness. (12) When God saw how corrupt the earth was, for all flesh had corrupted its ways on earth, (13) God said to Noah, "I have decided to put an end to all flesh, for the earth is filled with lawlessness because of them: I am about to destroy them with the earth. (14) Make yourself an ark of *gopher* wood; make it an ark with compartments, and cover it inside and out with pitch. (15) This is how you shall make it: the length of the ark shall be three hundred cubits, its width fifty cubits, and its height thirty cubits. (16) Make an opening for daylight in the ark, and terminate it within a cubit of the top. Put the entrance to the ark in its side; make it with bottom, second, and third decks.

   (17) For My part, I am about to bring the Flood—waters upon the earth—to destroy all flesh under the sky in which there is breath of life; everything on earth shall perish. (18) But I will establish My covenant with you, and you shall enter the ark, with your sons, your wife, and your sons' wives. (19) And of all that lives, of all flesh, you shall take two of each into the ark to keep alive with you; they shall be male and female. (20) From birds of every kind, cattle of every kind, every kind of creeping thing on earth, two of each shall come to you to stay alive. (21) For your part, take everything that is eaten and store it away, to serve as food for you and for them." (22) Noah did so; just as God commanded him, so he did.

7 Then the LORD said to Noah, "Go into the ark, with all your household, for you alone have I found righteous before Me in this generation. (2) Of every pure animal you shall take seven pairs, males and their mates, and of every animal that is not pure, two, a male and its mate; (3) of the birds of the sky also, seven pairs, male and female, to keep seed alive upon all the earth. (4) For in seven days' time I will make a rain upon the earth, forty days and forty nights, and I will blot out from the earth all existence that I created." (5) And Noah did just as the LORD commanded him.

*(continued)*

## Table 2. (continued)

---

(6) *Noah was six hundred years old when the Flood came, waters upon the earth.* **(7) Noah, with his sons, his wife, and his sons' wives, went into the ark because of the waters of the Flood.** (8) Of the pure animals, of the animals that are not pure, of the birds, and of everything that creeps on the ground, (9) two of each, male and female, came to Noah into the ark, as God had commanded Noah. (10) And on the seventh day the waters of the Flood came upon the earth.

(11) In the six hundredth year of Noah's life, in the second month, on the seventeenth day of that month, on that day

All the fountains of the great deep burst apart,

And the floodgates of the sky broke open.

(12) (The rain fell on the earth forty days and forty nights.) (13) That same day Noah and Noah's sons, Shem, Ham, and Japheth, went into the ark, with Noah's wife and the three wives of his sons—(14) they and all beasts of every kind, all cattle of every kind, all creatures of every kind that creep on the earth, and all birds of every kind, every bird, every winged thing. (15) They all came to Noah into the ark, two each of all flesh in which there was breath of life. (16) Thus they that entered comprised male and female of all flesh, as God had commanded him. **And the LORD shut him in.**

**(17) The Flood continued forty days on the earth, and the waters increased and raised the ark so that it rose above the earth. (18) The waters swelled and increased greatly upon the earth, and the ark drifted upon the waters. (19) When the waters had swelled much more upon the earth, all the highest mountains everywhere under the sky were covered. (20) Fifteen cubits higher did the waters swell, as the mountains were covered.** (21) And all flesh that stirred on earth perished—birds, cattle, beasts, and all the things that swarmed upon the earth, and all mankind. **(22) All in whose nostrils was the merest breath of life, all that was on dry land, died. (23) All existence on earth was blotted out—man, cattle, creeping things, and the birds of the sky; they were blotted out from the earth. Only Noah was left, and those with him in the ark.** (24) And when the waters swelled on the earth one hundred and fifty days. . . .

---

J    P    <u>Redactor of JE</u>    *Other*

Source analysis based on Michael Coogan, *The Old Testament: A Historical Literary Introduction to the Hebrew Scriptures.* New York: Oxford University Press, 2006, p. 24.

scholars are not enthusiastic about source criticism generally and prefer to view the Bible as consisting of a basic oral narrative that was subject to supplementation and accretion over time. In the last few decades, source criticism in the conventional sense of the analysis of the documentary sources that constitute the Bible has given way to other new and exciting methodologies in the study of the Bible, as we shall see. However, insofar as these alternative methodologies often presuppose the four hypothesized sources, it is clear that they owe much to the Documentary Hypothesis.

## Genesis 10–11: The Tower of Babel

Returning to the biblical text, the story of Noah and the flood is followed by a genealogical table of nations (Gen 10) in which the peoples of various lands are portrayed as having descended from a common ancestor—Noah— through his three sons Japheth, Ham, and Shem. S(h)emites are said to descend from Noah's son Shem. The story that follows in Genesis 11 is an etiological tale that explains the diversification of languages and the spread of distinct ethnic-linguistic groups throughout the lands of the earth. As such, the story acts as a bridge carrying us from the universal focus of the first ten chapters of Genesis to the particular focus—a focus on one group and one land—that will begin in Gen 12. Kaufmann argues that with the Tower of Babel story, the biblical narrator expresses his view of idolatry (221, 294–295). Up to this point, the Bible assumes that knowledge of the one deity was characteristic of the earliest humans. Only with the rise of various nations, languages, and imperialism does the worship of other "manufactured" gods arise.

Babel (pronounced "Bavel") is the name of ancient "Babylon." The tower in the story is identified by scholars as the famous tower or ziggurat of Marduk in Babylon. The Bible's hostility to Babylon and its imperialism is clear in this satirical story. Although the word means "gate of the god," it is made the basis of a mocking pun in Hebrew. The substitution of one letter creates *balal*, meaning "confusion." Thus, this mighty tower, which was the pride of Babylon, is represented by the biblical author as the occasion for the confusion of human language.

Why is the construction of Marduk's ziggurat represented as displeasing to Yahweh? According to some interpreters, the tower builders seek to elevate themselves, and perhaps storm heaven, by building a tower with its top in the sky. But Sarna (*Genesis*, 67, 72) sees the tower builders as defying the deity's explicit desire that humans be fruitful and multiply and fill all the earth. Their goal is to congregate in one place, so Yahweh frustrates their plans for self-monumentalizing and scatters them over the face of the earth. He makes it more difficult for them to join together again by confusing their tongues. For other interpreters, the story represents a rejection of civilization, monumental architecture, and empire building. Such ambitions are viewed negatively as leading to human self-aggrandizement, arrogant self-reliance, and a forgetting of god. Humans worship the work of their own hands—which is a turn toward idolatry.

Sarna argues that the Tower of Babel story presents the biblical writer's view that idolatry was not the original state of affairs; it was the result of a forgetting of the deity, an obsession with self-worship and power (*Genesis*, 77). If so, then, idolatry is here represented as coincident with urbanization and as the consequence rather than the cause of sin, since sin is rebellion against, or turning away from, Israel's god (*Genesis*, 77).

The first eleven chapters of Genesis provide a cosmic and universal setting for the history of Israel. These chapters cover 2,500 years. The rest of Genesis (chapters 12–50) covers just four generations, the generations of the patriarchs and matriarchs: Abraham and Sarah, Isaac and Rebekah, Jacob and Rachel and Leah, and their twelve sons and daughter. The focus of the narrative has shifted dramatically. Why?

By the end of the universal history of Gen 1–11, things are not going well. Although Yahweh created the earth as an intrinsically good paradise and humans in the divine image, those very humans have put their moral freedom to poor use. While ancient Near Eastern mythologies feature the struggle between good and evil cosmic powers, the myths of the opening chapters of the Bible recount the struggle between the will of the creator and rebellious humans (Kaufmann, 65, 295). In the stories of the first human pair, Cain, the generation of the flood, and finally the builders of the Tower of Babel, the deity is repeatedly spurned. The stage is thus set for Yahweh to show graciousness to one small group. And so Gen 12, which begins the second stage of the Bible's historical narrative, opens with Yahweh's call to Abram, son of Terah, to leave the land of his fathers and travel to a land that he will show him.

## Genesis 12–50: The Patriarchal Narratives and Historical Methodologies

The stories contained in Gen 12–50 differ from the stories in the preceding eleven chapters. These stories lack some of the fanciful and exaggerated elements characteristic of the genre of myth (no talking snakes, no tree of life, no worldwide flood) and purport to record events in the lives of the Hebrew ancestors of the Israelite nation—the patriarchs and matriarchs. Modern scholars ask: To what extent is it justified to view these materials as "historical" or to employ tools of historical analysis when studying these texts?

The first part of this chapter reviewed the main tenets of source criticism and the Documentary Hypothesis. The source critical method focuses on the hypothetical period of the compilation of the four sources that constitute the Torah. But subsequent scholarship began to delve into the question of the *prehistory* of the four sources. What were the sources' sources, and do these older sources provide us with older historical information?

The question was an important and controversial one. Source critics had concluded that the sources J, E, P, and D were written in the tenth to fifth centuries and that despite the fact that these sources purport to describe events from an earlier period (the patriarchal stories and the Exodus of the Israelites from Egypt are said to take place in the second millennium B.C.E.), they are not reliable for those periods and represent the retrojections of a much later time. Thus we cannot know anything of Israel's history and religion before the tenth century.

This was a somewhat dissatisfying conclusion to many people. After all, the writers of J, E, P, and D probably did not sit down and invent their documents—the narratives, legal traditions, cultic and ritual practices—out of whole cloth like a modern-day novelist. It is far more likely that they drew on older traditions, stories, customs, laws, and ritual practices that had developed and been transmitted over centuries. Scholars soon became interested in the following questions: What materials did the compiler or compilers of J and E, for example, draw upon in the composition of J and E? Did they use ancient materials? Did those ancient materials contain reliable traditions? If so, then perhaps we do have access to information regarding the history and religion of the ancient Israelites in an even earlier age, a time before the composition of J, E, P, and D.

The idea that the Bible's four sources drew on even older sources finds support in the Bible itself. At various times, biblical writers name some of their earlier sources explicitly, sources for which we unfortunately have no copies. For example, Num 21:14 contains a brief poetic excerpt concerning the boundaries between Moab and the Amorites. The excerpt is attributed to the Book of the Wars of Yahweh, which is mentioned as if it would be a source familiar to the reader. Joshua 10:13 contains a poetic snippet that is attributed to the Book of Yashar, the same book referenced in 2 Sam 1:18, when David laments the deaths of Saul and Jonathan by reciting an epic poem about ancient Israelite heroes. It seems entirely reasonable in light of the practices of other peoples and the explicit citation of earlier sources in a few instances in the Bible itself to suppose that the four primary literary documents hypothesized by the source critics are themselves compilations of older source materials from even earlier periods.

Some of these early sources may have been transmitted in oral rather than written form. One of the leading scholars to devote himself to this question was Hermann Gunkel. Gunkel's great knowledge of the oral literature of other nations led him to ask whether one might further analyze the four literary source documents of the Bible so as to uncover the preliterary stages of their development, that is, the stages of their oral transmission. Gunkel focused on small units found within the four primary source documents and was able to identify certain specific genres or forms (*gattungen*). The name given to this approach is thus *form criticism*. Gunkel believed that he was identifying older, preliterary forms that had been taken up and incorporated in the literary sources J, E, P, and D that constitute the biblical text. Examples of the *gattungen*, or forms, identified by Gunkel are hymns, laws, rituals, proverbs, folk stories, poems, legends, songs, and fragments of mythologies. An example of the last may be found in Gen 6:1–4:

> When men began to increase on earth and daughters were born to them, the divine beings saw how beautiful the daughters of men were and took wives from among them that pleased them. Yahweh said, "My breath shall not abide in man forever, since he too is flesh; let the days allowed him be one hundred and twenty years." It was then, and later too, that the Nephilim appeared on earth—when the divine beings cohabited with the daughters of men, who bore them offspring. They were the heroes of old, the men of renown.

Another form commonly found in the Bible is the etiological story (a legend that explains the origin of a name, ritual, institution, or the like). Gunkel described various types of etiological stories: *Ethnological* legends explain the origin of a people; *etymological* legends explain the origin of a name; *ceremonial* legends explain the origins of a ritual.

These various forms were probably older oral traditions adopted by the biblical writers. They may preserve historical reminiscences, but Gunkel maintained that more important than the actual events that might lie behind a particular form is the function of that particular form—its setting in life (or *sitz-im-leben*)—and what that might tell us about ancient Israelite history and culture. If, for example, it could be determined that a particular genre functioned in a liturgical context or a judicial context, we might learn from it something about biblical religion or law. Thus, form criticism was not content with merely identifying the various genres of the basic units that constitute the biblical text. Rather, it was concerned with the particular function, the cultural context, the *sitz-im-leben* of that literary unit as a window onto the history and culture of ancient Israel.

Growing out of form criticism is another modern critical method for analyzing the biblical text: *tradition criticism* (or traditio-historical criticism). Tradition criticism focuses on the history of the transmission of ancient traditions (through oral and literary stages) until they reach their final or present form. The present text of the Pentateuch unquestionably rests upon a long history of oral recitation and transmission, just like the epic poetry of Homer's *The Odyssey* and *The Iliad*. Tradition criticism examines the way people receive traditional material and creatively rework it before transmitting it, adapting it to their own purposes and context. This process is sometimes reflected within the Bible itself. Traditions in one part of the Bible are taken up and modified in later parts of the Bible. The book of Deuteronomy, for example, recounts events in the book of Exodus but modifies them or adds different emphases in the process. First and second Chronicles rework the traditions recorded in the historical narrative of Gen–2 Kgs. Legal material in one part of the Pentateuch is subject to reinterpretation, expansion, and modification in other parts of the Pentateuch. Tradition criticism aims at uncovering the early form of a tradition and the various stages in the transmission and transformation of that tradition—a process that is central to the project of historical reconstruction.

The schools of form criticism and tradition criticism emphasized the real-life, historical setting of the materials that constitute the biblical sources and their relationship to the wider culture—something almost entirely lacking in earlier source criticism. All of these analytical modes of examining the Bible, developed primarily by German scholars, can be contrasted with a North American tradition of scholarship that emphasized the correlation of biblical and archaeological data. W. F. Albright was a leading scholar of this American school of biblical studies. He was an expert in the areas of Palestinian archaeology and Assyriology and focused on illustrating the Bible with the ancient Near Eastern sources newly coming to light and with nonliterary archaeological findings. He argued that archaeology supported the basic historicity of the biblical tradition.

But how historical is the biblical text? To begin with, there are definite problems with chronology in much of the biblical material. It is often hard to pin down exact dates for many of the events mentioned; sometimes more than one date is given in the text. The Bible tends to use ideal numbers (e.g., multiples of 5 or multiples of 5 plus 7), which casts doubt on its dating of events. For example, ten generations pass from Adam to Noah and ten more from Noah to Abram. Moreover, there are suspicious repetitions of particular motifs for two or more of the patriarchs. As an example, twice Abraham enters foreign territory and to protect himself passes off his wife as his sister; Isaac also does this once. Are these three versions of one basic tradition, or do they "record" three separate incidents? What is the likelihood of three such incidents occurring—is it historically reasonable to suppose that they would?

For these and other reasons, we may agree with Sarna, who concludes that the biblical chronologies of the patriarchal period are not accurate historical records (*Genesis*, 84). Yet, in the twentieth century scholars of the Albright school argued that many of the traditions of the book of Genesis, beginning with the patriarchal narratives, contained authentic reflections of the second millennium B.C.E. and were not merely the retrojected fabrications of a much later age. Sarna also is among those scholars who point to internal biblical evidence for the authenticity and antiquity of the patriarchal stories. He advances the following arguments: First, representing Abraham, Isaac, and Jacob as foreigners and strangers in Canaan is hardly a convenient tradition for a people seeking to establish a claim to Canaan as its homeland (*Genesis*, 86). If this myth of origins were the fabrication of a later writer, surely that writer would have provided the nation with a less tenuous connection to the land. Second, Sarna notes (*Genesis*, 87) that the patriarchal stories contain many details that would have been offensive to later sensibilities and stand in direct contradiction to later Israelite law (such as Jacob's marriage to two sisters simultaneously, a violation of Lev 18:18; the establishment of cultic pillars at various points throughout the land in violation of the later principle of the centralization of worship in one sanctuary). Surely a later writer would have cleaned up the ancestral record to agree with later Israelite tradition and law. Finally, Sarna notes that the representation of interethnic relationships conflicts with the reality of a later period. For example, the Aramaeans are depicted as close kin in the patriarchal stories, but in the period of the monarchy when these stories were presumably put into writing, the Aramaeans were bitter enemies of the Israelites. Why would a biblical author portray the hated Aramaeans as close kin unless he had an old and established tradition that reflected that fact (*Genesis*, 89)? According to scholars like Sarna, these inconsistencies and more suggest that the patriarchal traditions are not entirely the fabrications and retrojections of a later period, the period of the monarchy. He argues that the stories contain authentic memories of an earlier historic situation that were incorporated by later composers of the biblical text.

On the other extreme, works from the 1970s by authors such as Thomas Thompson and John Van Seters take the position that the confused chronologies and numerous anachronisms in the patriarchal stories are the rule rather than the exception and point to a very late date of composition. They view the entire Pentateuch as a postexilic fabrication.

These two extremes are mirrored in the development of the discipline of archaeology. In its early stages, archaeology of the region tended toward credulity, evidenced by the fact that the discipline was referred to as "biblical archaeology." In other words, archaeologists saw themselves as searching for evidence to verify the details of the biblical text. W. F. Albright is representative of those archaeologists who believed archaeological findings often provided important external evidence for the basic historicity and authenticity of the patriarchal stories. Maintaining this view sometimes required that discrepancies between the biblical and archaeological evidence be explained away. Nevertheless, some archaeological findings seemed quite remarkable. Scholars of the Albright school pointed to texts and clay tablets discovered at second-millennium Nuzi and Mari in Mesopotamia (near the area identified in the Bible as the ancestral home of the patriarchs) as illuminating biblical customs and institutions. The Nuzi texts attest to the custom of adoption for purposes of inheritance—particularly the adoption of a slave in the absence of offspring. Biblical scholars excitedly point to the biblical passage in which Abraham expresses the fear that his servant Eliezer, and not his own flesh and blood, will inherit Yahweh's promise (Gen 15:2–4). Also according to the Nuzi texts, a barren wife is to provide a maidservant as a substitute to bear her husband's child. This scenario occurs with three of the four matriarchs: Sarah, Rachel, and Leah (Gen 16:2, Gen 30:3–13). Other parallels in family and marriage law uncovered by archaeologists correlate with biblical details. In addition, the eighteenth-century B.C.E. Mari texts contain names that correspond to Israelite names such as Benjamin, Laban, and Ishmael.

Biblical scholars, buoyed by the correlations between such texts and biblical stories, asserted that the patriarchs were real persons whose customs, legal practices, and social institutions could be verified against the backdrop of the second millennium as revealed by archaeological findings. Thus it has been argued that the mode of life described in the period fits the premonarchic (pre-1000 B.C.E.) period quite well, even though it is hard to pinpoint the time of the patriarchs. Correspondences between personal and place names used in the Hebrew Bible and in cuneiform tablets discovered at Ebla, an ancient trading city destroyed about 2250 B.C.E., led some scholars to suggest that the patriarchs lived in the Early Bronze Age (before 2150 B.C.E.). Because some biblical customs are paralleled in the materials discovered in the royal archives at Mari, dating to the eighteenth century, some scholars argued for the Middle Bronze Age (2150–1550 B.C.E.). These dates seem highly improbable to many other scholars, who identify the setting of these stories as the Late Bronze Age (1550–1200 B.C.E.). The patriarchs are said to come from areas in northern Syria, which is Aramaean territory, and Aramaeans are dated to this time. Moreover, the patriarchs are depicted as seminomads living in tents, wandering in search of seasonal pasture for their flocks, sometimes going as far as Mesopotamia and Egypt. This seminomadic lifestyle, as well as various details of language, customs, laws, and cultic practice, are believed to fit the Late Bronze Age.

However, even if we were to conclude—and this is far from certain—that the stories reflect the circumstances of, or were handed down from, the Late Bronze Age, the question must still be asked: Were the patriarchs actual historical figures, chieftains of seminomadic clans? And even if we assume that the patriarchs, or figures who were the basis for the stories about the patriarchs, lived sometime between 1550 and 1200, the very earliest date hypothesized for the literary composition of the patriarchal stories is the tenth to ninth century if not later—creating a gap of many centuries in which oral transmission, elaboration, and development undoubtedly occurred.

Certainly, some degree of skepticism is in order, and it has been argued that some of the ancient sources have been misread or misinterpreted in a zealous effort to find parallels with biblical institutions. But the degree to which skepticism is warranted is hotly debated. Extreme skeptics like Thompson and Van Seters point out that many of the biblical customs paralleled in very old ancient Near Eastern sources were alive and well in the first millennium also. Stories that refer to these customs could therefore derive from anytime in the second or first millennium. Given the many late features that appear in biblical stories—such as references to Philistines who did not inhabit the region until late in the second millennium—it is more reasonable to suppose a later date of composition.

Over time it became apparent that discrepancies between the archaeological record and the biblical text could not be explained away easily. Increasingly, practitioners of what would now be termed "Palestinian

Archaeology" or "Ancient Near Eastern Archaeology" or "Archaeology of the Levant" rather than "Biblical Archaeology" grew uninterested in pointing out correlations between archaeological data and biblical stories and focused on the best possible reconstruction of the history of the region on the basis of the archaeological evidence alone—regardless of whether the results would confirm the biblical account. This reconstruction often directly contradicted biblical claims (see Chapter 13, which compares the story of Israel's lightning invasion of the land of Canaan as presented in the biblical book of Joshua with archaeological data).

On the other hand, Marc Brettler has warned recently against a "creeping skepticism"—according to which legitimate doubts about the antiquity and historicity of certain elements of the Bible have led to the wholesale discrediting of the Bible as a source for historical reconstruction.[5] He also warns against a "negative fundamentalism," according to which the Bible is deemed historically useless until proven otherwise—an inversion of an older positive fundamentalism, according to which the Bible was historically reliable until proven otherwise. Brettler points out that the Bible is in many ways no different from other ancient sources that—though marred by anachronism, revision, and ideological presentation—can still be used with caution and in conjunction with other extratextual data in the reconstruction of history (Brettler, 21).

The historicity of biblical materials continues to be the subject of controversy. One reason for this is clear: Many people cling to the idea of the Bible as a historically accurate document, out of ideological necessity. Many fear that if the historical information of the Bible isn't true, then the Bible is unreliable as a source of religious instruction and inspiration. This is an unfortunate and heavy burden to place upon this fascinating library of writings from antiquity. People who equate truth with historical fact will certainly end up viewing the Bible dismissively—as a naïve and unsophisticated web of lies—since it is replete with fantastic elements and contradictions that simply cannot be literally true. But to view it this way is to make a genre mistake. Shakespeare's *Hamlet*, while set in Denmark, an actual place, is not historical fact, but that doesn't make it a naïve and unsophisticated web of lies. We accept when we read or watch the play that it is not a work of historiography (writing about history) but a work of literature. In deference to that genre and its conventions, we know and accept that the truths it conveys are not those of historical fact but are social, political, ethical, and existential truths. The Bible deserves at least the same courteous attention to its genre.

The Bible doesn't pretend to be and shouldn't be read as what might be called "objective history"—a bare narration of events. To be sure, we do find that some events mentioned in the Bible correlate to events known from sources outside the Bible. For example, Pharaoh Shishak's invasion of Palestine in 924 is mentioned in both Egyptian sources and the biblical text; the destruction of the northern kingdom in 722, the capture of Jerusalem in 597, and the destruction of the southern kingdom in 586 are recorded in Assyrian and Babylonian records, as are some other events from the time of the monarchy. As a consequence, most scholars are willing to accept the general biblical chronology of the monarchic period starting around 1000 B.C.E. (the sequence of kings and battles and so on). But ultimately, it is a mistake to read the Bible as a historical record. The Bible's composition is shaped by nonhistorical goals as well as literary conventions and forms.

It is a commonplace that there is no such thing as purely objective history. We never have direct access to past events—only mediated access, in material remains that yield information only after a process of interpretation, or in texts that are already an interpretation of those events. The biblical narrative is an interpretation of events that were held by centuries-long tradition to be meaningful in the life of the people. To the biblical narrators these events, known perhaps from ancient oral traditions, pointed to a divine purpose, and the narrative is told to illustrate that basic proposition. The biblical narrators did not try to write history as a modern historian might try to do. They were concerned to show us what they believed to be the finger of their god in the events and experiences of the Israelite people. As Brettler has noted, in the Bible the past is refracted through a theological lens if not a partisan political-ideological lens (22–23). But then all ancient historical narrative is written this way. With due caution, we may learn something of Israel's history from biblical sources, just as classical historians have learned much about classical history from the tendentious, partisan, and ideologically motivated work of classical writers.

The discussion of the patriarchal stories in the next chapter adopts this perspective. We will not ask whether the patriarchal stories are historically accurate; we will assume they are not, if only because they are not historiographic in nature. Ridding ourselves of the burden of historicity, we are free to appreciate the stories for what they are: powerful narratives that must be read against the literary conventions of their time and whose truths are social, political, moral, and existential. We begin by identifying the major themes of these stories.

## CHAPTER 6

# Biblical Narrative

## The Stories of the Patriarchs (Genesis 12–36)

*Readings:* Genesis 12–36

### The Threefold Promise

The first eleven chapters of Genesis provide a cosmic and universal introduction to the story of Israel. According to these chapters, the creator god has been spurned and all but forgotten by the humans he created. Repeatedly, humans have turned their moral freedom to evil use. In Gen 12, Yahweh narrows his focus, singling out one family—indeed one individual—to whom he issues a command and makes a promise. The story of Terah's son Abram (later Abraham) and his family, prefaced by a genealogical table in Gen 11, is marked by this dual theme of divine command and divine promise. The biblical writer represents the emigration of Terah's son Abram as divinely commanded, the first step in a journey that will lead ultimately to the formation of a nation in covenant with Yahweh. First, we meet our cast of characters.

> Now this is the line of Terah: Terah begot Abram, Nahor, and Haran; and Haran begot Lot. Haran died in the lifetime of his father Terah, in his native land, Ur of the Chaldeans. Abram and Nahor took to themselves wives, the name of Abram's wife being Sarai [who will become Sarah]; and that of Nahor's wife Milcah. . . . 30 Now Sarai was barren, she had no child.

Terah took his son Abram, his grandson Lot the son of Haran, and his daughter in law Sarai, the wife of his son Abram,
and they set out together from Ur of the Chaldeans for the land
of Canaan; but when they had come as far as Haran, they settled
there.

The days of Terah came to 205 years; and Terah died in
Haran. (Gen 11:27–32)

Yahweh said to Abram, "Go from your native land and from
your father's house, to the land that I will show you.

I will make of you a great nation,
And I will bless you;
I will make your name great
And you shall be a blessing.
I will bless those who bless you
And curse him that curses you;
And all the families of the earth
Shall bless themselves by you." (Gen 12:1–3)

Abram is commanded to go forth from his home and family to a location
that remains for now unspecified, a fact that has led commentators over the
centuries to praise Abram for his faith—a virtue associated with Abraham
in later religious tradition.

The divine command is coupled with a promise: "I will make of you,"
Yahweh says, "a great nation and I will bless you" (12:1). When Abram, his
wife Sarai, his nephew Lot, and those traveling with them reach Canaan,
Yahweh makes an additional promise: "I will assign this land to your offspring" (12:7). Thus, in just a few short verses, the writer has established the
threefold promise that underpins the biblical drama that is about to unfold.
The promise of progeny, blessing, and land establishes a narrative tension for
the stories of the patriarchs but also for the story of the nation of Israel in
subsequent books. In the patriarchal stories, there is a suspenseful vacilla-
tion between episodes that threaten to extinguish Yahweh's promise and
episodes that reaffirm them. For example, Israelite matriarchs seemed to be
a singularly infertile group, and lines of succession defy our expectations. In
short, the process by which the promise is fulfilled is halting and tortuous.

The promise is affirmed in two important encounters between Yahweh and Abraham. In Gen 15, Yahweh's promise to Abraham is formalized in a ritual ceremony. Yahweh and Abraham are said to "cut a

covenant." Covenant is a central biblical concept. The Hebrew word for covenant, *"brit,"* refers to a promise, vow, contract, agreement, or pact. Ancient Near Eastern parallels to the biblical covenant have been pointed out by historians. In suzerainty covenants, a superior party dictates the terms of a political treaty, and an inferior party obeys them. The arrangement serves primarily the interests of the suzerain, or superior party. In parity covenants, two equal parties agree to observe the provisions of a treaty.

There are four major covenants in the Hebrew Bible initiated by Yahweh, as expressions of divine favor and graciousness. Two of these appear in Genesis: the Noahide covenant and the Abrahamic (or patriarchal) covenant. The Noahide covenant in Gen 9:1–17 is universal in scope, encompassing all life on earth. The covenant stresses the sanctity of life, and Yahweh promises never to destroy all life again. By contrast, the Abrahamic covenant is a covenant with a single individual and so resembles an ancient Near Eastern suzerainty covenant. Yahweh appears as a suzerain making a land grant to a favored subject. An ancient ritual ratifies the oath—the parties to the oath pass between the split carcass of a sacrificial animal, symbolically signaling their agreement to suffer a like fate should they violate the covenant. In Gen 15, Abraham cuts several sacrificial animals in two. Yahweh, and only Yahweh, passes between the two halves. Thus, the striking thing about the Abrahamic covenant is its unilateral character. Only Yahweh is obligated by the covenant, obligated to fulfill the promise he has made. Abraham does not appear to have any obligation in return. Thus, it is the subject—Abraham—and not the suzerain—Yahweh—who is benefited by this covenant, a reversal of the reader's expectations.

Moreover, the biblical writer goes out of his way to provide a moral justification for the grant of this land to Israel. In the biblical writer's view, Yahweh is the owner of the land, empowered to establish residency requirements for those who would live in it. The current inhabitants were polluting the land with bloodshed and idolatry. When the land is completely polluted, it will spew out its inhabitants. Until this expulsion, the descendants of Abraham will have to wait, "for the iniquity of the Amorites is not yet complete" (15:16). Here, and even more explicitly in Deuteronomy 9:5, the Bible makes it clear that Yahweh's covenant with Israel is not due to any special merit or favoritism. Rather, Yahweh seeks replacement tenants who, unlike the previous tenants, will follow the rules of residence that he has established for his land.

Genesis 17 appears to be a second version of the same covenant—this time by the priestly writer. There are some notable differences between the two accounts. First, the deity refers to himself as El Shaddai.[1] Second, the promise is extended to include a line of kings that will come forth from Abraham. Moreover, the deity requires that Abraham and his male descendants be circumcised as a perpetual sign of the covenant:

> And throughout the generations, every male among you shall be
> circumcised at the age of eight days. . . . Thus shall my covenant
> be marked in your flesh as an everlasting pact. (Gen 17:12–13)

Failure to circumcise on the eighth day is tantamount to breaking the covenant.

Circumcision is known in many cultures of the ancient Near East, generally as a rite of passage at the time of puberty; circumcision timed to the eighth day after birth appears to be a uniquely biblical institution. As is the case with so many biblical rituals, laws, and institutions, whatever its original meaning or significance in the ancient world or among Israel's earliest ancestors, circumcision is here infused with new meaning—the rite loses its direct association with sexual maturation and fertility and becomes instead a sign of Yahweh's eternal covenant with Abraham and his seed.

## Abraham: A Man of Faith?

Despite the affirmations of Yahweh's promise in Gen 15 and Gen 17, the story of Abraham is peppered with episodes in which the realization of the promise and blessing is threatened. Ironically, a careful reading of the text suggests that Abraham himself poses one of the greatest threats to the fulfillment of Yahweh's plan and calls into question the traditional characterization of Abraham as an exemplar of faith. Consider the following evidence that emerges from a literary analysis of this brilliantly crafted tale.

The genealogical table in Gen 11 introduces us to Abram's family and contains a seemingly irrelevant detail, buried among the list of names—the infertility of Abram's wife Sarai.

> 29 Abram and Nahor took to themselves wives, the name of
> Abram's wife being Sarai and that of Nahor's wife Milcah, the

daughter of Haran, the father of Milcah and Iscah. 30 Now Sarai
was barren, she had no child.

A few verses after this announcement of Sarai's barren state, the narrator
details Yahweh's promise to make of Abram a great nation (Gen 12:2). In
retrospect, the reader understands that the seemingly irrelevant datum of
Sarai's infertility establishes a dramatic tension that will run through the
remainder of the Abra(ha)m story—for Abram doesn't seem to understand
that the promise will be realized through Sarai. Why should he (or the
reader) think otherwise? Yahweh wasn't specific. He simply says, "I will
make of *you* [masculine singular] a great nation" and he says nothing of
Sarai, who is, after all, barren. Abram very likely assumes some other mate
awaits him.

In the episode immediately following Yahweh's promise, Abram travels to Egypt, where he plans to pass Sarai off as his sister in order to advance
his position among the Egyptians. In so doing he creates the conditions for
Sarai's entry into the palace of Pharaoh. While the narrator gives no direct
indication of Sarai's reaction to Abram's treatment of her, the sense of bitterness and rejection that she expresses on future occasions (Gen 16:5, 18:12,
21:10) may have been fueled by incidents like this. Yahweh punishes Pharaoh, and when Pharaoh learns that he is being punished for taking another man's wife, he is furious with Abram. It seems that Pharaoh's moral
compass is more intact that Abram's.

In Gen 15, Abram seems to have given up hope of an heir, saying,
"Since you have granted me no offspring, my steward will be my heir" (Gen
15:5). Yahweh repeats to Abram his promise of countless offspring and reassures him that his heir will be his own biological child. Abram trusts Yahweh (Gen 15:6), although he remains in the dark as to the identity of the
mother. This time the promise is sealed in a solemn covenant ritual.

In Gen 16, Sarai—still childless—swallows her pride and offers Abram
her Egyptian slave, Hagar, in an ancient Near Eastern form of surrogacy:
The child that she will bear will be credited to Sarai ("perhaps I shall have a
son through her," Gen 16:2). Abram willingly accepts the offer. But when
Hagar becomes pregnant, she does not play the humble surrogate role as
expected. Rather, she acts arrogantly toward Sarah ("her mistress was lowered in her esteem," Gen 16:4). Sarai's sense of failure and humiliation
become even more acute. That Abram does nothing to curb Hagar as he
should is suggested by Sarai's anguished cry: "The wrong done me is your
fault! I myself put my maid in your bosom; now that she sees that she is

pregnant, I am lowered in her esteem. May Yahweh decide between you and me!" (Gen 16:5). In this speech, Sarai points out that she was cooperative in finding a means to supply an heir—she should not be humiliated or displaced in her own household after such a deed! Abram shows a distinct lack of initiative in the face of this domestic disturbance. He does not curb Hagar, nor does he address Sarai's pain, and Sarai's subsequent harsh treatment of Hagar causes the latter to run away.

In the wilderness, Yahweh promises Hagar offspring too numerous to count (Gen 16:9), suggestively echoing the promise of countless offspring to Abram in Gen 15:5 so that the reader wonders whether Hagar will indeed bear the heir. Yahweh tells Hagar to return home, for she will have a son and she will call him Ishmael. That Hagar shares this wondrous news with Abram upon her return is suggested by the fact that Abram himself names the child Ishmael, the name that Yahweh had revealed only to Hagar. Surely to Abram and Hagar—and presumably to Sarai, usurped and humiliated in her own home—it must have seemed that the child who would inherit the covenantal promise had arrived. Any reader unfamiliar with the story's ending may be excused for drawing the same conclusion at this point in the narrative.

The last verse of Genesis 16 tells us that Abram was eighty-six years old when Ishmael was born; the first verse of Gen 17 tells us that Abram was ninety-nine years old when Yahweh appears to him to reestablish the covenant. Thus thirteen years have passed—thirteen years in which Abram and Hagar (and probably Sarai) have believed that their beloved Ishmael was the child of the promise. But Abram's hopes for Ishmael begin to unravel as a result of two important developments in chapter 17. First, in reaffirming the covenant, the deity commands circumcision on the eighth day as a sign of the covenant. Ishmael is, of course, thirteen years old and thus unable to fulfill the requirement of eighth-day, or covenantal, circumcision. Second, in Gen 17 Yahweh is finally explicit about his plan. It is *Sarah* (as she is now to be known) who will bear the child of the promise:

> As for your wife . . . Sarah. I will bless her; indeed, I will give you a son by her. I will bless her so that she shall give rise to nations; rulers of peoples shall issue from her. (Gen 17:15–16)

Abraham (as he is now known) is incredulous. "Can Sarah bear a child at ninety?" he says, mocking the idea (Gen 17:17). But the deity remains silent in the face of Abraham's disbelief and—we may say—disappointment. In that silence, Abraham seems to experience a moment of realization—Yahweh is entirely serious. He intends to carry out this plan—a plan that Abraham himself has actively jeopardized on occasion. Abraham protests vigorously: "O, that Ishmael might live by your favor!" (Gen 17:18). But the deity insists,

> Nevertheless, Sarah your wife shall bear you a son, and you shall name him Isaac, and I will maintain My covenant with him as an everlasting covenant for his offspring to come. (Gen 17:19)

Sensing Abraham's distress over the rejection of Ishmael, Yahweh relents a little but not on the main point at issue:

> As for Ishmael, I have heeded you. I hereby bless him. I will make him fertile and exceedingly numerous. He shall be the father of twelve chieftains, and I will make of him a great nation. But my covenant I will maintain with Isaac, whom Sarah shall bear to you at this season next year. (Gen 17:20–21)

Tradition characterizes Abraham as a man of faith, trusting in Yahweh's promises and obedient to his plan, but certain textual details suggest otherwise. Indeed, there are hints that even after the announcement about Sarah in Gen 17, Abraham continues to resist and even seeks to thwart Yahweh's plan, presumably because of his love for Ishmael. The first hint is found in Gen 17:23–27. Following the deity's designation of circumcision as the sign of the covenant, Abraham immediately takes Ishmael and circumcises him. We may see in this act a desperate attempt to win Yahweh's approval of Ishmael—desperate because it is physically impossible for Ishmael to meet the requirement of *covenantal* (i.e., eighth-day) circumcision due to his advanced age.

The second indication that Abraham resists Yahweh's plan is revealed in Gen 18. Here we learn that Abraham has withheld from Sarah the divine plan revealed to him in Gen 17! Sarah clearly does not know that she will bear the heir to the covenantal promise. Sarah only learns of Yahweh's plan by overhearing the three divine visitors speaking outside the tent (18:10). When she hears that she is to have a son, Sarah "laughs" (ṣ.ḥ.q.)—not a joyful laugh but a bitter laugh of disbelief that her husband would even wish to be intimate with her in her aged and withered condition.[2] Sarah's reaction may reflect the humiliating and uncaring treatment she has received at the hands of Abraham on at least two previous occasions (Gen 12:12–13; 16:5).

The third indication that Abraham resists Yahweh's plan to forgo Ishmael in favor of a child from Sarah occurs in Genesis 20, when Abraham—now in full knowledge of Yahweh's plans for Sarah—allows Sarah to be taken into the household of King Abimelech of Gerar. If Abraham thinks that he can thwart Yahweh's plan by ridding himself of Sarah, he is mistaken. The deity intervenes to restore Sarah to her home.

In chapter 21, a child is indeed born to Sarah. Abraham names him Isaac (*yitshaq*, from the same Hebrew root *ṣ.ḥ.q*.) and circumcises him on the eighth day (thus Isaac is the first Israelite to receive covenantal circumcision as stipulated in Gen 17). Again, the name Isaac may reflect not joy so much as Abraham's bitter sense that Yahweh has played a trick on him. Certainly, Sarah feels anxiety that onlookers will mock her for bearing a child at the age of ninety. Sarah's words in Gen 21:6 may be read as follows: "Elohim has brought me laughter; everyone who hears will *mock* me!" And indeed, at the feast that is held at Isaac's weaning, Sarah sees Ishmael (presumably seventeen or eighteen years old by now) "mocking" (*ṣ.ḥ.q*.)—precisely what she most feared (Gen 21:6). Wounded by years of feeling mocked and humiliated by Ishmael's mother, Sarah's pent-up jealousy and bitterness lead her to demand the expulsion of Ishmael lest he usurp Isaac as his mother nearly usurped Sarah:

> Cast out that slave-woman and her son, for the son of that slave
> shall not share in the inheritance with my son Isaac. (Gen 21:10)[3]

Abraham is distressed (another sign of his underlying loyalty to Ishmael) but follows the directive of the deity to heed Sarah's wishes.

A challenge for modern readers of the Bible is to read as if one doesn't know the end of the story. The interpretation of Gen 12–21 presented above is an attempt at just such a "naïve" reading. Reading the story as if we are encountering it for the very first time, and freed from traditional assertions about the faithful and obedient character of Abraham, we understand it in a radically new light. Such a reading also reveals the literary artistry of the biblical narrator, who carefully raises certain expectations only to dramatically subvert them. Finally, it should be noted that the entire narrative tension that runs through Gen 12–21—the tug-of-war between Abraham, Hagar, and Sarah, between Ishmael and Isaac—is initiated by a brief and seemingly irrelevant line in 11:30, a throwaway datum that one might easily gloss over: "And Sarai was barren; she had no child." Such is the power and genius of biblical narrative.

## The Binding of Isaac

If there is indeed a case to be made for Abraham's devotion to Ishmael, despite Yahweh's plan to establish his covenant with the son of Sarah, we must ask about the meaning of Genesis 22, the story of the binding of Isaac. Here, Yahweh is said to "test" Abraham with the most horrible of demands. The child of the promise—Isaac, born miraculously to Sarah when she was no longer of childbearing age—is to be sacrificed by Abraham's own hand. When the story opens, we wonder: What precisely is Yahweh testing? Does he seek to discover whether Abraham has finally understood that the covenant lies with Isaac, not Ishmael? Does he hope that Abraham will object violently to the sacrifice of the heir to the promise and thus finally prove his acceptance of and love for Isaac? If so, then Abraham fails the test the moment he saddles his ass and begins his journey with Isaac toward the site of sacrifice. Or is Yahweh testing Abraham's obedience? Has Abraham come to realize that Yahweh's plans cannot be thwarted? Does Yahweh hope that Abraham will demonstrate the obedience he lacked earlier and follow Yahweh's plan unquestioningly, even if what Yahweh demands is that Abraham annihilate the promise itself? If so, then Abraham passes the test when he raises the knife over his bound son. For this reason, Yahweh declares in verse 12,

> Do not raise your hand against the boy, or do anything to him.
> For now I know that you fear Elohim, since you have not withheld your son, your favored one, from Me.

The story of the binding of Isaac is one of the most powerful and riveting stories not only in the Bible but, some have claimed, in world literature. The story is also a marvelous example of the biblical narrator's literary skill and artistry, as described by Robert Alter in his groundbreaking work, *The Art of Biblical Narrative.*[4] Alter underscores the extreme economy of biblical narratives, in their description of physical setting and character, as well as speech (Alter, 24, 42, 68). Rarely does the narrator comment upon or explain a character's thought or motives, and there is only the barest minimum of dialogue. On the few occasions that the Bible violates this norm of verbal economy, for example, when two characters converse at length, the violation is significant.

The biblical narrator's concealing of details and the motives of all the characters—Yahweh, Abraham, and Isaac—leads to ambiguity and the possibility of many interpretations. Indeed, this is a striking characteristic of biblical prose—its suppression of detail, its terse, laconic style that makes the little that is given so powerful and, in the words of Erich Auerbach, so fraught with background.[5]

The ambiguities and indeterminacy of this story make it one of the most interpreted texts of all time. Why is the deity testing Abraham?[6] Does he really desire such a sacrifice? What is Abraham thinking and feeling as he walks—for three days already—with his son, bearing the wood and the fire for the sacrifice? Does he fully intend to obey this command, to annul the covenantal promise with his own hand, or does he trust in Elohim to intervene? Or is this a paradox of faith: Does Abraham intend, faithfully, to obey, all the while trusting, faithfully, that the divine promise will nevertheless be fulfilled? What is Isaac thinking? Does *he* understand what is happening? Is he prepared to be slaughtered? He sees the wood and firestone in his father's hand. Clearly a sacrifice is planned. He asks his father, "Where is the sheep for the burnt offering?" (v 7)—but does he know the answer even as he asks? Does he hear the double entendre in his father's simple and solemn reply, which in the unpunctuated Hebrew might be read: "Yahweh will provide the sheep for the offering: my son"? Does he struggle as he is bound; does he acquiesce? The beauty of this narrative is its sheer economy. It offers so little that we as readers are forced to imagine the innumerable possibilities. We play out the drama in countless ways—with an Abraham who is reluctant and an Isaac who is ignorant, or an Abraham eager to serve his god to the point of sacrificing his own son and an Isaac who willingly bares his neck to the knife.

The story of the binding of Isaac can be contextualized in a number of different ways. Read in the context of Yahweh's promise to make Abraham the father of a great people through his son Isaac, the story has a searing power and pathos. Read in the context of Abraham's devotion to Ishmael (as presented above), the story is a test of obedience. One can also read the story in the historical context of child sacrifice in the ancient Near East. Although child sacrifice was adamantly condemned in later layers of the Bible, some scholars argue that it was practiced in some quarters throughout the period of the monarchy, thus necessitating the prohibitions of Lev 18:21, 20:3, Deut 12:30–31, and 18:19.[7] Does Gen 22 assume or reject the practice of child sacrifice? Some scholars argue that an original story tolerant of child sacrifice has been edited to serve as a polemic against child sacrifice.

Abraham's silent obedience in the face of the commandment to kill his innocent son can be contrasted with his spirited defense of the sinful inhabitants of the towns of Sodom and Gomorrah in Gen 18–19. The inhabitants of Sodom and Gomorrah stand condemned before Yahweh by the outcry of those they have violated and harmed.

> Then Yahweh said, "The outrage of Sodom and Gomorrah is so great, and their sin so grave! I will go down to see whether they have acted altogether according to the outcry that has reached me. . . . (Gen 18:21a)

However, Abraham challenges Yahweh's decision to destroy all of the people of Sodom: "Will you sweep away the innocent along with the guilty? Shall not the judge of all the earth deal justly?" (18:23–25). The question is, of course, rhetorical. Abraham is evidently quite confident that Yahweh would not act unjustly, destroying the innocent along with the wicked. Indeed, Abraham is counting on the fact that Yahweh is merciful and will overlook evil for the sake of righteous individuals. And so Abraham haggles with Yahweh for the lives of the innocent:

> ". . . Shall not the judge of all the earth deal justly?" And Yahweh answered, "If I find within the city of Sodom fifty innocent ones, I will forgive the whole place for their sake." Abraham spoke up, saying, "Here I venture to speak to my lord, I who am but dust and ashes: What if the fifty innocent should lack five? Will you destroy the whole city for want of the five?" And he answered, "I will not destroy if I find forty-five there." But he spoke to him again, and said, "What if forty should be found there?" And he answered, "I will not do it, for the sake of the forty." And he said, "Let not my lord be angry if I go on: What if thirty should be found there?" (Gen 18:25b–30a)

In this way Abraham finally whittles the number down to ten, and Yahweh answers: "I will not destroy for the sake of ten men."

There is a delicious irony in Abraham's negotiations with Yahweh over the fate of Sodom. Yahweh shared his plans for Sodom and Gomorrah with Abraham for the following reason: "For I have singled him out, that he may instruct his children and his posterity to keep the way of Yahweh by doing what is just and right" (Gen 18:19a). Yahweh intends to school Abraham in the ways of justice so that he may instruct others. And yet Abraham's first pupil, a mere four verses later, is not his biological offspring but Yahweh

himself! "Shall not the judge of all the earth deal justly?" Abraham pointedly asks, after learning of Yahweh's plans for Sodom.

At first glance it would appear that Abraham invokes a principle of
justice that is independent of Yahweh and that Yahweh is expected to conform his decrees and interactions with humanity to this self-operating
principle. Were this the case, one might be able to speak of a robust principle of natural law in the Hebrew Bible. However, verse 19a makes it clear
that "doing what is just and right" is in fact identical to "the way of Yahweh." Moreover, despite his question "Shall not the judge of all the earth
deal justly?" Abraham does not call upon Yahweh to observe justice. Justice
demands that the guilty be punished and the innocent spared, but Abraham is asking that the guilty be spared for the sake of the righteous. His
goal is not, in fact, to convince Yahweh to do justice; he *assumes* that
Yahweh is a god of justice ("Shall not the judge of all the earth deal
justly?"—Of course, he shall!). His aim is to convince Yahweh to *transcend* justice and forgive the guilty altogether ("forgive it [the city] for the
sake of the innocent fifty who are in it"). It may be Abraham's vocation to
teach *justice* to his offspring, but evidently it is also his vocation to teach
*mercy* to his god.

But not even ten righteous men are found in Sodom. As the narrator
takes great pains to point out, the mob that comes to gang-rape the two
divine visitors includes "all the people to the last man." And so Sodom and
its four sister cities of the plain around the Dead Sea are destroyed. Out of
consideration for Abraham, Abraham's nephew Lot is saved ("Elohim was
mindful of Abraham and removed Lot from the midst of the upheaval"
Gen 19:29). This is the first biblical instance of the doctrine of the merit of
the righteous (the idea that an unrighteous person might be spared for the
sake of, or on account of, the accrued merit of a righteous person). Lot is no
prize himself, but he is saved from destruction on Abraham's account.

In this story, we see Abraham rising to the defense of a thoroughly
wicked and reprehensible group of people, arguing pointedly that the innocent should never be wantonly destroyed. Can this be the same Abraham who, a few chapters later, when told to slaughter his own perfectly
innocent son, not only makes no objection but rises early to get started on
the long journey to the sacrificial site? What are we to make of the juxtaposition of these two stories? Which represents behavior more desirable to
Israel's god? Or are the stories incommensurable since Gen 22 describes an
act of cultic sacrifice for which an unblemished and innocent victim is required?

The story of Sodom and Gomorrah has often been cited as a condemnation of homosexuality, the assumption being that the Sodomites were destroyed for homosexual intercourse with the divine visitors. The very terms *sodomy* and *sodomize* represent such an interpretation. But the idea that the fundamental sin of Sodom was its homosexual nature is not at all clear in the Hebrew Bible (it is suggested in later interpretations found in the Christian New Testament such as James 7 and 2 Peter 2:6–10 and subsequent texts). The Sodomites are guilty of gang rape, and the gender of the victims is hardly relevant. The Sodomites, like the generation of the flood, stand condemned by the "outcry" against them, a Hebrew term generally associated with the appeal of victims of violence, bloodshed, and oppressive injustice (Sarna, *Genesis,* 144–146). The Sodomites' violation of the unwritten desert law of hospitality to strangers, their violent desire to abuse the strangers they should have been sheltering, is evidently merely one instance of their violent brutality.

### Isaac, Rebekah, and Jacob

Isaac, the child of Yahweh's promise to Abraham, is often described as the most invisible of the patriarchs. Perhaps his passive acceptance of his father's effort to sacrifice him serves as the key to the biblical narrator's perception of his character. By contrast, Israel's wife Rebekah is often described as the most determined and energetic of the matriarchs. She runs to extend hospitality to a stranger, draws water for him quickly, and equally quickly draws water for all his camels—little knowing that the man she greets is the servant of Abraham, come to seek a wife for his master's son Isaac. Rebekah herself accepts the offer of an unknown bridegroom in a faraway land, overriding the urgings of her mother and brother to delay her departure. In a moving conclusion to this betrothal story, we read in 24:67 that Isaac brought Rebekah "into the tent of his mother Sarah, and he took Rebekah as his wife. Isaac loved her, and thus found comfort after his mother's death."

But like the other matriarchs, Rebekah is barren. Isaac pleads with Yahweh for a child on her behalf, and Rebekah becomes pregnant with twins—the older child is Esau, the father of the Edomites, and the younger is Jacob, the father of the Israelites.

Jacob is the most fully developed, colorful, and complex of the patriarchs. Jacob has long been identified by commentators as the classic trickster. Marc Brettler (*How to Read the Bible,* 50) has described the Jacob stories as a kind of morality tale, the main message of which is "trick and you shall be tricked." Jacob tricks his brother out of his birthright and in turn is tricked by his brother-in-law, his wife, and his sons. The reader wonders how much of Jacob's trickery is really necessary. After all, Rebekah, who suffers tremendous pain during her pregnancy, is told by Yahweh that the twins fighting and struggling in her womb for priority will become two nations, the older of which shall serve the younger:

> Two nations are in your womb,
> Two separate peoples shall issue from your body;
> One people shall be mightier than the other,
> And the older shall serve the younger. (Gen 25:23)[8]

Nahum Sarna (*Genesis,* 183) argues that this announcement is the narrator's way of establishing for the reader that the younger child, Jacob, is the son who will inherit the divine blessing—a fact that raises serious questions about Rebekah and Jacob's morally problematic efforts to wrest the birthright and blessing from Esau. Is the reader to conclude that it is all right to fulfill a divine plan by any means, fair or foul? Or are we to conclude, as Sarna suggests (*Genesis,* 183), that Jacob's possession of the birthright was predetermined and disengaged from his acts of trickery? Perhaps then, Jacob's efforts indicate a deceitful and narcissistic personality: On one occasion he exploits Esau's hunger and barters a pot of lentil stew for the birthright; on another, he and Rebekah plot to deceive Isaac into bestowing the blessing of the firstborn on Jacob. Perhaps by informing us that Jacob has been chosen from the womb, the narrator is able to paint a portrait of Jacob at this stage in his life as grasping and faithless—a great contrast to his grandfather Abraham, who, unaware of Yahweh's plans, followed Him from his home to an unknown land.[9]

Jacob's treatment of Esau earns him the latter's enmity, and Jacob finds it expedient to leave Canaan for the home of his mother's brother Laban. On his way east to Haran in Mesopotamia, where Laban resides, Jacob has an encounter with Yahweh. At a place called Luz, Jacob lies down to sleep resting his head on a stone. He has a dream in which he sees a "ladder" reaching from earth to heaven. Angels are ascending and descending on the ladder. In the dream Yahweh appears to Jacob and reaffirms the Abrahamic or patriarchal covenant, promising land, posterity, and, in addition,

Jacob's own personal safety until his return to the land of Canaan. Jacob is stunned, as we read in Gen 28:16–17:

> Jacob awoke from his sleep and said, "Surely Yahweh is present in this place, and I did not know it!" Shaken, he said, "How awesome is this place! This is none other than the abode of Elohim, and that is the gateway to heaven."

The stone that served as his pillow Jacob sets up as a cultic pillar, sanctifying it with oil and renaming the site Bethel—"house of El." However, it is significant that despite this direct vision, Jacob is still reluctant to rely on Yahweh and his promise. He makes a conditional vow (v. 20):

> If Elohim remains with me, if he protects me on this journey that I am making, and gives me bread to eat and clothing to wear, and if I return safe to my father's house—Yahweh shall be my god. And this stone, which I have set up as a pillar shall be Elohim's abode; and of all that you give me, I will set aside a tithe for you.

Where once Yahweh had tested Abraham, it seems now that Jacob is testing Yahweh.

## Jacob Becomes Israel

Jacob spends some fourteen years in the household of his mother's brother Laban. Jacob meets Laban's two daughters, Leah the elder and Rachel the younger, and soon loves Rachel. He agrees to serve Laban seven years for the hand of the younger daughter, Rachel. When the seven years pass, Laban deceives Jacob and gives him the elder daughter, Leah. Jacob the trickster is furious at having himself been tricked, but he is willing to give an additional seven years of service for Rachel. Rachel, Leah, and two handmaidens will conceive one daughter and twelve sons from whom will come the twelve tribes of Israel. But the two sons of Rachel—Joseph and Benjamin— are the most beloved to Jacob.

Jacob determines to leave Laban to return to Canaan. One final remarkable incident in Jacob's life occurs on his return journey—an incident that most readers associate with a significant transformation in his character (Gen 32:23–33). This incident is Jacob's nighttime struggle with a mysterious figure who is in some way representative of Israel's deity. The two wrestle all night in the dark (darkness is mentioned four times in this short passage). The struggle occurs as Jacob is about to cross the river Jabbok and reconcile himself with his former rival and enemy Esau. Jacob has sent everyone on ahead—his wives, children, household, and possessions—and he stands alone at the river where

> a man wrestled with him until the break of dawn. When he saw that he had not prevailed against him, he wrenched Jacob's hip at its socket, so that the socket of his hip was strained as he wrestled with him. Then he said, "Let me go, for dawn is breaking." But he answered, "I will not let you go, unless you bless me." Said the other, "What is your name?" He replied, "Jacob." Said he, "Your name shall no longer be Jacob, but Yisrael (Israel) for you have striven with Elohim and men, and have prevailed." Jacob asked, "Pray tell me your name." But he said, "You must not ask my name!" And he took leave of him there. So Jacob named the place Peniel, meaning, "I have seen a divine being face to face, yet my life has been preserved." The sun rose upon him as he passed Penuel, limping on his hip. (Gen 32:25–32)

Michael Coogan[10] and other scholars see this story as an Israelite adaptation of popular stories of rivergods, or trolls and ogres who guard river crossings and must be defeated by a hero before the river or bridge is safe to cross. In its Israelite version, the story is historicized and serves an etiological function: we learn why Israelites abstain from eating the sciatic nerve "to this day" and we learn how Peniel and Israel got their names.

Names are an important theme of the story. In the biblical context, names seem to encapsulate the essence of their bearer. Naming something or knowing the name of something gives one power over it. This is why the stranger will not reveal his name—it would give Jacob power over him. As for Jacob's name, it is the occasion for several puns in this story. His name (based on the root letters $y.'.q.b.$) means to supplant or uproot. He emerges from the womb grasping his brother's heel ($'.q.b.$) in an effort to supplant him at birth, and he continues the effort through much of his early life. The writer makes this explicit for us when Esau cries out in Gen 27:36: "Was he, then, named Jacob that he might supplant me these two times?" The answer would appear to be yes! And in chapter 32, Jacob wrestles (*y.ʿ.b.q.*) with the mysterious divine being at the Jabbuk River (*y.b.q.*). Jacob's very name, therefore, hints at and foreshadows the struggling, wrestling, and trickery that are the major themes of his life. But Jacob's striving reaches a climax in chapter 32, and so the angel names him Israel (Yisrael), meaning "he who has striven with El," for indeed as the stranger says, Jacob has striven and wrestled all his life with men—particularly his brother—and now with the deity. ("El" is the name for the chief god of the Semitic pantheon and is the name applied to the patron deity of Abraham, Isaac, and Jacob in the patriarchal narratives.)

Many commentators observe the change in character or essence that accompanies this change in name. Sarna (*Genesis,* 206) states that the struggle with the angel is the final purging of those unsavory qualities of character that marked Jacob's past career (206). Although he appears to be almost an antihero—he literally limps into the land of promise—Jacob is a new and honest man. We see this immediately in his reunion with Esau. He greets his former rival and enemy with these words:

> "If you would do me this favor, accept from me this gift, for to see your face is like seeing the face of Elohim, and you have received me favorably. Please accept my present which has been brought to you, for Elohim has favored me and I have plenty." And when he urged him, he accepted. (Gen 33:10–11)

With Jacob, Yahweh seems finally to have found the working relationship with humans that he has been seeking since their creation. Yahweh learned immediately after creating this unique creature that he will exercise his free will against the deity. Yahweh sees that he must limit the life span of humans or risk creating an enemy nearly equal to him, so he casts humans out of the garden and blocks access to the tree of life. But humans continue their violent and evil ways, and in desperation Yahweh wipes them out and starts again. This second creation proves to be no better, forgets Yahweh, and builds a tower of self-aggrandizement toward the heavens. Having promised never to destroy all humankind again, Yahweh starts again with a single individual. After some false starts, Abraham ultimately proves himself to be obedient to Yahweh in a way that no one else has been up to this point—but perhaps ultimately the model of blind obedience is rejected, too. When Abraham prepares to slaughter his own son, perhaps the deity sees that blind faith can be as destructive and evil as disobedience. So Yahweh relinquishes his demands for blind obedience by stopping Abraham himself. The only relationship with humans that will work is one in which a balance between unchecked independence and blind obedience is achieved, and Yahweh finds such a relationship with Jacob. The metaphor for this relationship is the metaphor of struggle—Yahweh and humans lock in an eternal struggle, neither prevailing yet both forever changed by their encounter one with the other.

## CHAPTER 7

# Israel in Egypt

## Moses and the Beginning of Yahwism

*Readings:* Genesis 37–Exodus 4

### Joseph Story

The rest of Genesis (Gen 37–50) relates the story of Joseph and his brothers (the twelve sons of Jacob) and contains one of the most magnificent psychological dramas in the Bible. The story is intensely human, focusing on familial relationships and jealousies with little reference to a divine perspective. Scholars divide over the authenticity of the Egyptian elements in the story—some point to the presence of Egyptian names, customs, religious beliefs, and laws as a sign of historical memory; others point to anachronisms and a general lack of specificity as a sign of relatively late composition. The art of dream interpretation plays an important role in the story. Dream interpretation was a developed science in ancient Egypt and Mesopotamia. Although Joseph is known for his ability to interpret dreams, the monotheizing biblical narrator describes him as reporting what the deity reveals to him rather than relying on an occult science of interpretation (Gen 41:39).

Joseph's brothers are jealous of Jacob's partiality to Joseph (Gen 37:4), and they conspire to be rid of him. At the last moment Judah convinces the brothers that if instead of killing Joseph, they sell him to traders traveling to Egypt, they can at least make a little profit for their trouble (Gen 37:26–27).

Joseph is sold to the household of Pharaoh, where various adventures prove his meritorious character. He rises to a position of great power when he correctly interprets Pharaoh's dreams regarding an impending famine (Gen 41). With Joseph as governor of the country in control of the grain supply, Egypt successfully weathers seven years of famine (Gen 41:47–57).

The famine, which strikes Canaan as well, drives Joseph's brothers to Egypt in search of food. Joseph does not reveal himself to his brothers but puts them to the test—are they the same men who so callously broke their father's heart by selling his favorite son, Joseph, many years ago? In the climactic moment, Joseph tests his frightened brothers by demanding that they leave Benjamin as a pledge in Egypt. Joseph knows it would overwhelm Jacob to lose Rachel's only remaining son, but he seeks to know whether his brothers have reformed since the day they sold him into slavery. And, indeed, Judah—the very one who had figured so prominently in the sale of Joseph that had crushed his father Jacob—now offers himself instead of Benjamin, knowing that his father would be devastated to lose his beloved Rachel's second son (Gen 44:33–34). The brothers having proven their new integrity, Joseph weeps and reveals his identity in a moving scene, and the family is relocated to and reunited in Egypt, where they live peacefully and prosperously for some generations.

One important theme of these stories is divine providence. Jacob's sons, their petty jealousies and murderous conspiracy, and Joseph himself are the unwitting instruments of a larger divine plan. As Joseph says to his brothers in Gen 50:20, "As for you, you meant evil against me; but Elohim meant it for good, to bring it about that many people should be kept alive, as they are today." Joseph's betrayal by his brothers and descent into Egypt set the stage not only for the reformation of his brothers' characters, but for the descent of all the Israelites into Egypt so as to survive widespread famine—yet another threat to the promise overcome. Significantly, the deity says to Jacob in Gen 46:4: "I myself will go down with you to Egypt and I myself will also bring you back"—in short, there seems to be a plan afoot.

Israel's descent into Egypt sets the stage for the rise of a Pharaoh who did not know Joseph and all he had done for Egypt. This new Pharaoh will enslave the Israelites and so embitter their lives that their cry will rise up to heaven. Thus begins the book of Exodus, which will lead the Hebrews from Egypt to Sinai.

Most of the narrative account in Gen 12–50, with the notable exception of the Joseph story, is assigned to the J source. Certain themes emerge from the J narrative. The first is that Yahweh's promises are sure but the manner and timing of their fulfillment are unpredictable. For example, the land never does belong to the patriarchs to whom it is promised. Their descendants will take possession of it but only after much struggle. In other ways Yahweh's methods are curious. Why does he go against the traditional ancient Near Eastern practice of primogeniture (inheritance by the firstborn) and choose Isaac over Ishmael, and Jacob—a liar and cheat in his early life—over the elder Esau? Why does he choose young Joseph, a spoiled, arrogant brat who provokes his older brothers with his delusions of grandeur? The law of primogeniture as stated in Deut 21:15–17 would dictate differently:

> If a man has two wives, one loved and the other unloved, and both the loved and the unloved have borne him sons, but the first-born is the son of the unloved one—when he wills his property to his sons, he may not treat as first-born the son of the loved one in disregard of the son of the unloved one who is older.

Yet is this not what happens to Ishmael, to Esau, to all of Joseph's brothers born before him? There is no explanation for these seemingly arbitrary choices. Nevertheless, despite the false starts and trials, the years of famine and childlessness, the seed of Abraham survives and the promise is reiterated: "I myself will go down with you to Egypt and I myself will also bring you back." Ultimately, J would appear to assert, Yahweh does control history, and all tends toward his purpose even if the path is unpredictable and tortuous.

## Exodus

The Exodus story has been described as follows:

> Israel's history had its true beginning in a crucial historical experience that made her a self-conscious historical community—an event so decisive that earlier happenings and subsequent experiences were seen in its light. This decisive event—the great watershed of Israel's history—was the Exodus from Egypt. Even today the Jewish people understand their vocation and destiny in the light of this revealing event which made them a people and became their undying memory.[1]

The Exodus has also been described as the pivotal event in the Bible connecting past, present, and future generations. A myth of national origins, it obligates each present generation and serves as a model for future redemptions and liberations.

The book of Exodus is a true sequel to Genesis. Despite the deity's promise of land and blessing, the book of Genesis closes with the Israelites residing in Egypt, having managed to procure no more than a burial plot in the Promised Land. Even the deity has left the land, descending with the Israelites into Egypt. The threefold promise seems remote. The book of Exodus relates the beginning of the process by which the promises will be fulfilled.

The structure of the book is as follows:

1–15:21—The story of Israel in Egypt; the rise of a new Pharaoh who did not know Joseph; the oppression of the Israelites (their enslavement in a state labor force and the killing of all firstborn Hebrew males); the birth, early life, and call of Moses; the struggle for freedom (Moses pleads with Pharaoh to let his people go and worship their god in the wilderness); and the final liberation when Yahweh drives back the waters of the reed sea so that the Israelites can pass, leaving the heavy Egyptian chariotry to flounder in the mud.

15:22–18—The journey toward Sinai and the people's complaints that they will starve, to which Yahweh responds with quail, manna, and water.

19–24—The theophany and covenant at Sinai and Yahweh's revelation of his Torah (teaching) to Moses and the Israelites.

25–40—Instructions for the erection of the Tabernacle and the report of its subsequent construction, interrupted by the incident of Israel's apostasy with the golden calf in Ex 32.

Source critical scholars believe that J supplies the main narrative in Exodus, supplemented by excerpts from E and the addition of considerable genealogical, legal, and ritual material from P.

The historical value of the story of the Exodus has fascinated scholars and laypeople for generations. Could the Exodus really have happened and, if so, when? Is there any evidence for the story in external sources?

## Historical Considerations

A victory hymn on a stele erected about 1204 B.C.E. by a pharaoh Merneptah mentions his recent victory over various groups in Canaan; one of the groups mentioned is Israel (see Figure 2). The stele reads:

> The rulers of my enemies now lie prostrate before me and beg for peace. Not one of my enemies raises his head in revolt. I have devastated Tehenu and put down a revolt against the great king of Hatti. I have plundered Canaan from one end to the other, taken slaves from the city of Ashkelon, and conquered the city of Gezer. I have razed Yanoam to the ground. I have decimated the people of Israel and put their children to death. Hurru is a widow. All Canaan has been pacified. Every rebel is now prostrate before Merneptah, pharaoh of Upper and Lower Egypt, the divine presence of Amon Ra, beloved of the divine assembly, who dawns each day like Amon Ra the sun.[2]

Despite its exaggerated claims, this is a fabulously important inscription because it is the earliest known reference to the people of Israel outside the Bible. The inscription attests to the fact that a people known as Israel was settled in the land of Canaan by the end of the thirteenth century B.C.E. Whether they arrived after an exodus from Egypt is not, of course, indicated. Indeed, there is no evidence of a large group entering the land of Canaan at this time. The archaeological record shows a steady cultural continuum rather than a disruption of the type caused by the influx of a new people. If for the sake of argument, we assume one generation was needed to enter the land, we might date Israel's entry into Canaan to 1225 B.C.E. at the latest, and if we assume forty years of journeying from Egypt to the land, that takes us to 1265 as a date for the Exodus. In 1265, the eighteenth dynasty's most illustrious pharaoh occupied the throne, Ramses II—famous for his building projects. According to the biblical record, the Hebrews were set to work on urban building projects in the Nile Delta, in the cities of Pithom and Ramses. Most biblical scholars who accept that there is a historical kernel to the Exodus story identify Ramses as pharaoh of the exodus event (Coogan, *Old Testament*, 99).

Now the Bible states that Israel was in Egypt for 430 years, which would put the descent of Joseph and his brothers into Egypt around 1700. There is a certain appeal to this scenario. In the 1720s B.C.E., Egypt was in-

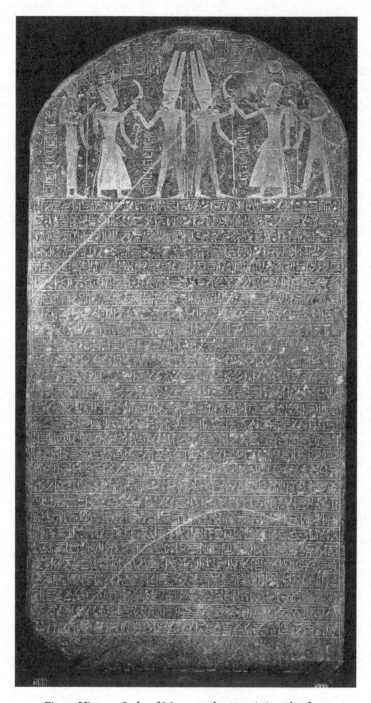

Fig. 2. Victory Stele of Merneptah, containing the first
extrabiblical reference to Israel (late thirteenth century B.C.E.).
Cairo Museum. Courtesy of Jürgen Liepe.

vaded and conquered by a Semitic people known as the Hyksos. They established a dynasty of rulers, centered in the north of Egypt in an area known as Goshen. It has been suggested that the pharaohs of the Hyksos dynasty might have favored other Semites, allowing them to enter in times of famine to dwell in the land of Goshen, as the Bible says the Israelites did (Gen 47:27). That Joseph, a Semitic foreigner, could be elevated to the important post of governor is less surprising if we suppose a Semitic regime. In the sixteenth century B.C.E., the native Egyptians, who had smoldered under the humiliating foreign rule of the hated Hyksos, finally succeeded in driving them out and reestablishing a native Egyptian dynasty. Some scholars have speculated that this is the event behind the statement in Ex 1:18 that a new pharaoh who knew nothing of Joseph began to oppress the Hebrews. The establishment of a new native Egyptian dynasty might have led to the enslavement of any remaining Semitic outsiders, including the Hebrews. In all probability, anyone associated with the hated occupying regime would be treated poorly by the new one. It all seems to fit.

Unfortunately, there are problems with this theory of a late-eighteenth-century descent into Egypt. The Bible itself contains contradictory statements regarding the length of the Israelites' sojourn in Egypt. Exodus 6:16–20 states that the Israelites lived there for only four generations (from Levi to Moses) and not 430 years, which would mean an arrival in Egypt long after the Hyksos. It is not even clear whether migration occurred in the Hyksos period, so ultimately all we have is a hypothesis with little solid support.

Even so, scholars have pointed to some interesting circumstantial evidence for the general historicity of the Exodus event. We do know that Semites were engaged in building projects in the thirteenth century B.C.E. We know that the fortified city of Pi-Ramesse was rebuilt in the early thirteenth century on the site of the old Hyksos capital of Avaris in the area of Goshen, and that the city was reoccupied in the time of the Pharaoh Ramses II in the thirteenth century B.C.E. We know that Egyptian officials allowed hungry nomads to enter the Delta region for food, and we know that Semitic slaves are well attested in Egypt at this time. Specifically, we know of peoples called Habiru or Apiru (some scholars have suggested a connection with the word Hebrew) who worked on building the capital city of Ramses II. One thirteenth-century B.C.E. Egyptian papyrus describes Egypt's tight control of its borders; another reports the pursuit of runaway slaves escaping into the desert. The Exodus story has many Egyptian elements; for example, the names Moses, Aaron, Pinhas, and more are all Egyptian. Of course, none of this corroborates the specific details of the biblical story—there is no Egyptian record of a man named Moses, or of plagues, or of the defeat of pharaoh's army. And yet some would argue that the circumstantial evidence just named lends plausibility to a story of slaves working on building projects who may have escaped as a small group from Egypt at this time. Thus, if there is any historical basis to the Exodus, the most plausible backdrop is the thirteenth century B.C.E.

Some scholars assume some historical memory behind the elaborate and dramatic story of a miraculous redemption by Yahweh (why invent a national hero with an entirely Egyptian identity and name—Moses—and cast the ignominy of slavery upon one's ancestors?). Nevertheless, as noted earlier in connection with the patriarchal stories, in the end we are dealing with sacred history, a myth of origins for the nation of Israel. More important than historical verifiability is the conviction of the ancient Israelites who received, embellished, transmitted, and venerated these traditions that Yahweh had once acted on their behalf, rescuing them from bondage and binding them to himself in an eternal covenant.

## The Enslavement of Israel and the Birth and Life of Moses

According to the biblical narrative, the Israelites had multiplied and filled the land of Goshen given to them during Joseph's period in office (Ex 1:7). A new pharaoh who did not know Joseph feared the foreign presence and attempted to curb their growth, pressing all adult males into slavery, "harsh labor at mortar and brick" (1:14). However, "the more they were oppressed, the more they increased and spread out" (Ex 1:12). The pharaoh resorted to more drastic measures, decreeing the murder of all newborn Israelite males at the hands of Egyptian midwives (Ex 1:15–17).

Thwarted by the midwives, who allow the male infants to live, the pharaoh enlists all the people to annihilate the Israelites by drowning all newborn males in the Nile River (Ex 1:22). This leads to the account of the birth of Moses and his exposure to the Nile River. Born to a Levite (priestly) family, Moses is hidden away for three months and then placed in a wicker basket lined with bitumen and set among the bulrushes at the edge of the Nile, where Pharaoh's daughter will eventually discover him. With his own mother as a nurse, the infant is eventually adopted by Pharaoh's daughter who names him Moses (an Egyptian name).

Scholars note that this story is full of irony and puns (Sarna, *Exodus*, 28). The rescue of Moses who will foil Pharaoh is effected by the daughter of

Pharaoh, and Moses is sheltered in Pharaoh's own palace. Further, the future significance of Moses is hinted at through literary allusion. Moses' basket is called an ark (*tevah*). This word is used precisely twice in the entire Hebrew Bible—here and in the story of Noah's ark. Sarna notes that in both cases the ark/*tevah* "is the instrument of salvation through perilous waters" (*Exodus*, 28)—waters that threaten to capsize it and so blot out Yahweh's hopes and plans for his creatures. Further, the child is placed among reeds (Hebrew *suf*), an allusion to the fact that Moses will lead the Israelites through a reed sea (*yam suf*).

This legendary birth story has important parallels in ancient Near Eastern and other literature. It is common to find tales of extraordinary events surrounding the birth of one who was later to become great (Cyrus of Persia, Oedipus, Jesus, and others). Indeed, the birth story of Moses echoes details of the birth story of the great Akkadian king Sargon (2300 B.C.E.):

> Sargon, the mighty king, king of Agade, am I.
> My mother was a changeling [or priestess?], my father I
>     knew not.
> The brother(s) of my father loved the hills.
> My city is Azupiranu, which is situated on the banks of the
>     Euphrates.
> My changeling mother conceived me, in secret she bore me.
> She set me in a basket of rushes, with bitumen she sealed
>     my lid.
> She cast me into the river which rose not (over) me,
> The river bore me up and carried me to Akki, the drawer
>     of water.
> Akki, the drawer of water lifted me out as he dipped his e[w]er.
> Akki, the drawer of water, [took me] as his son (and)
>     reared me.[3]

From the concealment of the infant after conception to the bitumen-lined basket placed in the river, the stories are strikingly similar, a fact that underscores the degree to which biblical narratives are shaped by literary convention.

Nothing is said of Moses' childhood, but we learn of his growing awareness of his Israelite identity in the following passage:

Some time after that, when Moses had grown up, he went out to his kinsfolk and witnessed their labors. He saw an Egyptian beating a Hebrew, one of his kinsmen. He turned this way and that and seeing no one about, he struck down the Egyptian and hid him in the sand. When he went out the next day, he found two Hebrews fighting so he said to the offender, "Why do you strike your fellow?" He retorted, "Who made you chief and ruler over us? Do you mean to kill me as you killed the Egyptian?" Moses was frightened, and thought: Then the matter is known! When Pharaoh learned of the matter he sought to kill Moses; but Moses fled from Pharaoh. He arrived in the land of Midian and sat down beside a well. (Ex 2:11–15)

Coming to the aid of an oppressed kinsman, Moses kills an Egyptian and must flee to the territory of Midian. There at a well he again acts to defend the defenseless—a key to his character.

The priest of Midian had seven daughters. They came to draw water and filled the troughs to water their father's flock; but shepherds came and drove them off. Moses rose to their defense and he watered their flock. (2:16–17)

Moses will marry Zipporah, one of the women, and live as a shepherd in Midian for forty years. But the situation of the Israelites in Egypt remains bitter.

The Israelites were groaning under the bondage and cried out; and their cry for help from the bondage rose up to Elohim. Elohim heard their moaning, and Elohim remembered his covenant with Abraham and Isaac and Jacob. (Ex 2:23–24)

One day in the wilderness at a mountain called Horeb (also Sinai), Moses sees a flame in a bush that does not consume it. He then hears a voice saying: "I am the Elohim of your father, the Elohim of Abraham, the Elohim of Isaac, and the Elohim of Jacob" (Ex 3:6). Moses hides his face in fear, but the god continues. He has a job for Moses:

I have marked well the plight of my people in Egypt and have heeded their outcry because of their taskmaster; yes, I am

mindful of their sufferings. I have come down to rescue them
from the Egyptians and to bring them out of that land to a good
and spacious land, a land flowing with milk and honey, the region of the Canaanites, the Hittites, the Amorites, the Perizzites, the Hivites and the Jebusites. Now the cry of the Israelites
has reached me; moreover, I have seen how the Egyptians oppress them. Come, therefore, I will send you to Pharaoh and you
shall free my people the Israelites from Egypt. (Ex 3:7–10)

Moses demurs and suggests his brother Aaron, a much better public
speaker. But as we have already seen in Genesis, Israel's god selects whom
he selects, and his reasons cannot always be fathomed.

## The Divine Name and the History of Israelite Religion

When Moses asks who he shall say sent him, the deity replies, "Ehyeh asher
ehyeh" ("I am who I am" or "I will be who I will be").[4] Moses converts this to
a third-person formula: "Yahweh asher yahweh" ("he is who he is" or "he
will be who he will be"). This sentence is then shortened to its first word—
Yahweh—and comes to be understood as the personal name of the deity.[5]
Some have argued that the name Yahweh expresses the quality of dynamic
being. This god is the god who brings new things into being—a cosmos from
chaos, and now a new nation from a band of runaway slaves. But it could
well be that the sentence uttered by this god is simply his way of *not* an-
swering Moses' question: Who am I? I am who I am, and never you mind!

There are certain important and unique features of this burning bush
dialogue. First, the deity identifies himself to Moses as the god (Elohim) of
Abraham, Isaac, and Jacob. As numerous commentators have pointed out,
in so doing, the writer establishes an unbroken historic continuity between
the present revelation to Moses and the revelations and promises received
by Israel's forefathers, the patriarchs. And yet, paradoxically, the very assertion of continuity only serves to underscore a fundamental discontinuity. For even as the deity asserts that he is the god of the patriarchs, he
reveals to Moses a new name, Yahweh, so that Yahwism and the Yahweh
cult can be said to begin with Moses.

As discussed in Chapter 5 the biblical sources differ on this point. According to the J source in Genesis 4:26, the earliest humans worshipped
Yahweh as Yahweh. The name was always known to humankind. J seeks to
assert a direct continuity between the god of the patriarchs and the god of

the Exodus. The P and E sources, however, tell a different story. In Ex 6:2–4, assigned to P, the deity says, "I am Yahweh. I appeared to Abraham, Isaac, and Jacob as El Shaddai but I did not make myself known to them by My name Yahweh"—which contradicts the J source. Many scholars suggest that P and E preserve a memory of a time when Israel worshipped the Canaanite god El.[6] P and E wish to claim that the god who covenanted with the patriarchs is the god of the Exodus, but with a new name. They, too, assert a continuity, but they do so in a manner that precisely draws attention to an underlying discontinuity and a new beginning. To understand this new beginning requires an examination of differences between patriarchal religion and Mosaic Yahwism.[7]

In the patriarchal traditions of Genesis, the deity is six times called El Shaddai (Gen 17:1, 28:3, 35:11, 43:14, 48:3, 49:25, Ex 6:3). Other names are El Elyon (Gen 14:18–22, Ps 78:35), El Olam (Gen 21:33), El Roi (Gen 16:13), and El Bethel (Gen 31:13, 35:7). The common denominator in all of these is "El." El is the proper name of the head of the Canaanite pantheon, as revealed in literary works discovered in 1928 by a peasant at Ras Shamra (ancient Ugarit) in Syria (see Figure 3). A tomb excavated by the French was found to contain a cuneiform tablet library, written in a language very close to Biblical Hebrew. The narratives in these texts report the exploits of the gods of Canaanite religion. These gods include the sky god El, the father of various gods and humans; El's wife Asherah, a mother goddess; their daughter Anat, goddess of love and war; and a storm god, Baal, who is depicted in mythological literature as defeating both the chaotic sea god, Yam, and the god of death, Mot.

There are striking resemblances between the biblical god of the patriarchs and the Canaanite god El. El is the head of the council of gods. He is said to have a long, white beard. He dwells on a mountaintop in a tent. His epithets include "father of all creatures," "bull," and "king." He is also a protector of patriarchal figures—a "god of the father of the clan"—guiding them, protecting them, and promising them descendants. Likewise, many biblical passages depict Israel's deity as the head of a council of divine beings, and he is occasionally described with the epithets associated with the Canaanite El (father of all creatures; bull in Gen 49:24, Ps 132:2, 5, Isa 49:26, 60:16; king). In the patriarchal narratives, Israel's god refers to himself as the "god of the father," guiding, protecting, and making promises to Abraham and his heirs (Gen 26:24, 28:13, 32:9, 43:23, 46:1, 3, Ex 3:15). Many personal and place names in these narratives are compounds in which one element is El (Israel, Ishmael, Bethel). By contrast, after the time of Moses,

Fig. 3. The Canaanite god El enthroned with worshipper
(thirteenth century B.C.E., Ugarit). Erich Lessing /
Art Resource, NY.

Israelite names are formed from Yah or Yahu (short for Yahweh), such as
Eliyahu and Adoniyah.

Other biblical texts describe Israel's god in terms reminiscent of the
storm god Baal, who, according to Canaanite mythology, defeated El and
assumed his position as head of the Canaanite pantheon. Thus, like Baal,
Yahweh is said to ride on the clouds (Ps 68:4), and his revelations are accompanied by thunder, storms, and earthquakes. Poetic fragments allude

to Yahweh's victory over a watery foe (Ex 15, Ps 114, Isa 51:9–11), a motif associated with Baal (see Figure 4). Finally, the influence of ancient Near Eastern holy war traditions may be discerned in descriptions of Yahweh as a warrior leading his hosts in battle, armed with spear, bow, and arrows.

The worship practices of ancient Israel and Judah resemble Canaanite and ancient Near Eastern worship practices. Canaanite religious rituals took place in small temples housing cultic statues, stone pillars (symbols of the gods or memorials to the dead), and altars for animal, cereal, and liquid sacrifices. Similarly, Israel's god was worshipped at various "high places"—shrines with altars, cultic pillars, and wooden poles (called *asherot*, singular *asherah*). These shrines may have been associated with some kind of contact with ancestors or a cult of the dead. Worship at various local altars runs counter to Deuteronomy 12, which insists that all worship must occur at one central sanctuary and decrees the destruction of all outlying altars and high places. The patriarchal stories are clearly not the work of the Deuteronomist. Yet these stories must have had a long-standing traditional authority if they were adopted without serious modification by the Deuteronomistic redactor.

What are we to make of the remarkable similarity between the deity and cult of Israel and the deities and cults of her neighbors? How are we to understand the rise of Israel's god and cultic practices? In Chapter 2, two models for understanding the rise of biblical monotheism were outlined: First, the classic evolutionary model: From polytheism's worship of many gods, there is a natural evolution to henotheism's elevation of one god to a supreme position, to monotheism's denial of all gods but one. Second, Kaufmann's model: Monotheism and polytheism are so radically distinct that the former could not have evolved from the latter. There is surely an element of truth in both models. The evolutionary model responds to the fact that in many respects, Yahweh resembles the gods of Israel's neighbors. To be blunt, the patriarchs appear to have worshipped El, the Canaanite god. But the evolutionary model doesn't account for the fiercely polemical relationship that would develop between Israel's religion and that of her neighbors. By contrast, Kaufmann's revolutionary model focuses almost exclusively on the dissimilarities and polemical relationship between Yahwism and Canaanite polytheism. But the revolutionary model fails to fully acknowledge the many areas of contact and similarity.

A third model for understanding the rise of biblical monotheism has emerged recently, one that seeks to avoid the polytheism-monotheism dichotomy. Instead of viewing Israelite religion as an evolution from and re-

Fig. 4. The Canaanite storm god Baal with lightning
rod in hand (mid-second millennium, Ugarit).
Erich Lessing / Art Resource, NY.

finement of Canaanite religion or as a radical break with Canaanite religion, biblical scholar Mark Smith examines the cultural and ideological negotiations that gave rise to Israelite monotheism. He describes the origin and development of Israelite religion as a process of convergence and differentiation. He writes: "Convergence involved the coalescence of various deities and/or some of their features into the figure of Yahweh."[8] By contrast, differentiation is the process whereby Israel came to reject its Canaanite roots and create a separate identity.

On Smith's model, the Canaanite roots of Israel's ancestors are clear. The Hebrew language itself is a Canaanite dialect. The Canaanite god El was the god of Israel's earliest ancestors. Through a process of convergence, the god Yahweh, originally from a region further to the south (in Sinai or Edom perhaps), came to take on the characteristics of other deities—first El and then, as Baal replaced El in the Canaanite pantheon (see below in Chapter 8), Baal (see Figure 5 for an eighth-century depiction of Yahweh with his Asherah). Later, certain aspects of this convergence would be polemicized against and rejected, as a Yahweh-only party sought to differentiate itself from those now labeled "Canaanites." Smith's model of convergence and divergence has great explanatory power: It explains the deep similarity of Israel's deity and the deities of her neighbors, and it explains the vehement

Fig. 5. Yahweh and his Asherah, jar drawing from Kuntillet 'Ajrud, Israel (early eighth century B.C.E.). Courtesy of Zeev Meshel, site excavator.

biblical polemic against Canaanite religion and Baal worship in particular. It avoids unhelpful dichotomies (Israel is either like or unlike her neighbors) and helps us understand Israel's god as the end product of familiar cultural processes—the processes of convergence and differentiation.

When and why did this differentiation occur? When and why did some Israelites adopt a "Yahweh-only" position and seek to differentiate pure Yahwism from the cult of Baal, for example? The debate over this question is fierce, and it is one that will be taken up in Chapter 11.

To sum up: It is clear that the biblical patriarchs and matriarchs are not strict Yahwists. The P and E sources preserve that insight in their insistence that the patriarchs worshipped a god named El, but at the time of the Exodus, that god revealed himself as Yahweh. In Josh 24:14–15, Joshua, the successor to Moses, presents the Israelites with the following choice:

> Now, therefore, revere Yahweh and serve Him with undivided loyalty; put away the gods that your forefathers served beyond the Euphrates and in Egypt, and serve Yahweh. . . . Choose this day which ones you are going to serve . . . but I and my household will serve Yahweh.

This passage preserves a memory of the people's ancestors worshipping many gods (perhaps El, Baal, and others in the Canaanite pantheon). Only later would a Yahweh-only party polemicize against and seek to suppress certain undesirable elements of Israelite-Judean religion. Those elements would be labeled "Canaanite" as part of a process of Israelite differentiation. Thus, what appears in the Bible as a battle between Israelites and Canaanites may be better understood as a civil war between Yahweh-only Israelites and Israelites participating in the cult of their ancestors.

## CHAPTER 8

# From Egypt to Sinai

*Readings:* Exodus 5–24, 32; Numbers 11–14, 16, 20, 25

## The Exodus from Egypt

Following the theophany at the burning bush, Moses returns to Egypt to free Yahweh's people from slavery, but Pharaoh refuses to let the Israelites go, initiating what will become a battle of wills between Yahweh and Pharaoh. The story has high drama and some folkloric elements, including the contest between Moses and Aaron on the one hand and the magicians of Egypt on the other. Moses announces ten plagues against the Egyptians: a bloody pollution of the Nile, swarms of frogs, lice, insects, affliction of livestock, boils on humans and animals, lightning and hail, locusts, total darkness—all climaxing in the death of the firstborn males of Egypt in one night. The Egyptian magicians—initially able to mimic the plagues sent by Yahweh—are quickly bested, and Yahweh's defeat of the magicians is tantamount to a defeat of the gods of Egypt.

Source critics view the account of the plagues as a complex interweaving of diverse sources that preserve different traditions on the number and nature of the plagues as well as the principal actors in the drama. According to source critics, no single source contains all ten plagues. J has eight, E has three, and P has five. Some are unique to one source, others are found in more than one source, but the merging of the three lists has resulted in ten. Nevertheless, an examination of the larger contours of the account shows the artistic hand of the final editor. Sarna (*Exodus*, 76) has noted that this editor has organized the plagues in three sets of three followed by a climactic tenth plague (again, three and ten are ideal numbers in our biblical texts). Each set of three shares certain structural and literary features: The first and second plague in each set are forewarned, and the third is not. The first plague in each set is accompanied by the same divine instruction to Moses: "Present yourself" before Pharaoh "in the morning." The second plague in each set is introduced with the divine instruction: "Go to Pharaoh" while the third plague has no introduction. This structural repetition creates a crescendo leading to the final and most devastating plague (see Table 3): the slaughter of the Egyptian firstborn sons, which may be understood as measure-for-measure punishment for the Egyptians' earlier killing of Hebrew infants but is represented in the text as retaliation for Egypt's treatment of Israel, the firstborn son of Yahweh. In Ex 4:22, Yahweh tells Moses to say to Pharaoh:

> Thus says Yahweh: Israel is my first-born son. I have said to you,
> "Let my son go, that he may worship me," yet you refuse to let
> him go. Now I will slay your first-born son.

In this last plague, the deity (or his angel of death; compare Ex 12:12–13 and Ex 12:23) passes over Egypt at midnight, slaying every Egyptian firstborn male (Ex 12:29). Moses orders each Israelite family to perform a ritual action to protect themselves from the slaughter. The ritual consists of two parts: First, each family is to eat unleavened bread. In addition, each family is told to sacrifice a lamb that will then be eaten as a family meal, to smear some of the blood on their doorposts, and to remain indoors until morning.

> For that night I will go through the land of Egypt and strike down
> every first-born in the land of Egypt, both man and beast; and I
> will mete out punishments to all the gods of Egypt, I Yahweh.
> And the blood on the houses where you are staying shall be a sign
> for you: when I see the blood I will pass over you, so that no plague
> will destroy you when I strike the land of Egypt. (Ex 12:12–13)

This Passover ritual, established on Israel's last night of slavery, is to be observed as an institution for all time (Ex 12:24).

This story attests to a phenomenon long noted by scholars: the Israelite historicization of preexisting ritual practices, in this case two separate

Table 3. The Literary Structure of the Plagues Narrative

| Plague | Exodus source | Forewarning | Time indication of warning | Instruction formula | Agent |
|---|---|---|---|---|---|
| **First series** | | | | | |
| 1. Blood | 7:14-24 | Yes | "In the morning" | "Station yourself" | Aaron |
| 2. Frogs | 7:25-8: 11 | Yes | None | "Go to Pharaoh" | Aaron |
| 3. Lice | 8:12-15 | None | None | None | Aaron |
| **Second series** | | | | | |
| 4. Insects | 8:16-28 | Yes | "In the morning" | "Station yourself" | God |
| 5. Pestilence | 9:1-7 | Yes | None | "Go to Pharaoh" | God |
| 6. Boils | 9:8-12 | None | None | None | Moses |
| **Third series** | | | | | |
| 7. Hail | 9:13-35 | Yes | "In the morning" | "Station yourself" | Moses |
| 8. Locusts | 10:1-20 | Yes | None | "Go to Pharaoh" | Moses |
| 9. Darkness | 10:21-23 | None | None | None | Moses |
| **Climax** | | | | | |
| 10. Death of Egyptian firstborn | 11:4-7, 12:29-30 | Yes | None | None | God |

From Nahum M. Sarna, *Exploring Exodus: The Heritage of Biblical Israel*. New York: Shocken Books, 1986, p. 76.

and older springtime rituals (Sarna, *Exodus,* 89). One ritual—the sacrifice of the first lamb of spring to procure favor from a deity—is characteristic of seminomadic pastoralists, and the other—the offering of the first barley harvested in spring and quickly ground into fresh flour free of fermentation—is characteristic of agriculturalists. If Israel was formed from the merging of diverse groups in Canaan, including farmers and shepherds (we will return to this point in Chapter 12), it is likely that the rituals of these various groups were retained but linked to the story of the enslavement and liberation of the Hebrews. The association of older nature festivals with events in the life of the new nation may be seen as part of a process of differentiation from Israel's neighbors. Thus, the blood of the sacrificial lamb was said to have protected the Hebrews from the slaughter of the firstborn, and the bread was said to have been consumed in unleavened form because the escaping Hebrews had no time to allow the dough to rise.

Following the last plague, Pharaoh finally allows the Israelites to go into the desert to worship their god. But he quickly changes his mind, sending his infantry and charioteers in pursuit of the Israelites, who soon find themselves trapped between the Egyptians and a reed sea (not the huge Red Sea, as is sometimes mistakenly thought). Some want to surrender.

> Was it for want of graves in Egypt that you brought us to die in
> the wilderness? What have you done to us, taking us out of Egypt?
> Is this not the very thing we told you in Egypt, saying, "Let us
> be, and we will serve the Egyptians, for it is better for us to serve
> the Egyptians than to die in the wilderness?" (Ex 14:11–12)

But Moses rallies the frightened people, and at the moment of crisis, Yahweh intervenes on Israel's behalf.

Once again, source critics see in the account of the parting of the reed sea in Ex 14–15 three versions of events—though it must be stressed that scholars differ quite a bit on where J, E, and P begin and end. The very name Yam Suf (reed sea) implies a marshlike setting rather than the open sea, yet images of the sea prevail in the poetic fragment in Ex 15:1–12, 18, which is widely considered to be the oldest unit in these two chapters. Verse 5 portrays the Egyptian army and officers sinking and drowning in the Yam Suf as if caught in a storm at sea. Verse 8 describes a blast of wind from Yahweh's nostrils that causes the waters to stand straight like a wall, while a second blast causes the sea to cover the Egyptians so that they sink like lead in the majestic waters. The fragment does not specifically refer to people crossing on dry land.

John Collins points out that the image of sinking in deep waters is found elsewhere in Hebrew poetry—in the Psalms particularly—as a metaphor for distress.[1] In Ps 69, the psalmist asks Elohim to save him:

> for the waters have reached my neck;
> I am sinking into the slimy deep
> and find no foothold;
> I have come into the watery depths;
> the flood sweeps me away. (vv. 1–2)

A few verses later it is apparent that the poet is not really drowning but that he is using this language as a metaphor for his straitened situation.

> More numerous than the hairs of my head
> are those who hate me without reason;
> many are those who would destroy me,
> my treacherous enemies. (v. 5)

Collins suggests that the poem in Ex 15 celebrates and preserves a historical memory of an escape from or defeat of Pharaoh and that the drowning imagery is used metaphorically to describe the Egyptians' humiliation and defeat. Later writers filled out the allusions to drowning in this ancient song, composing the prose accounts in Ex 14 in which the metaphor is literalized. According to these prose accounts, Pharaoh's army was *literally* drowned in water. But even in the prose account, source critics see a composite of two intertwined versions. In P's account (often identified as Ex 14:1–4, 15–18, 22–23, 26–29), Moses is depicted as stretching out his staff first to divide the waters, which stand like a wall so that the Israelites can cross on dry land, and then to bring the waters crashing down upon the Egyptians. However, according to Ex 14:24–25 (attributed to J by some scholars), the Egyptians are stymied by their own chariots. As the Israelites work their way on foot through the marsh, the Egyptians' chariot wheels get stuck in the mud, forcing them to give up the chase. Despite the tensions and internal contradictions, the final narrative that emerges from this long process of transmission, interweaving, and literary embellishment reiterates a motif we have seen before—the threatened destruction of Yahweh's

creation or Yahweh's people by chaotic waters and divine salvation from
that threat.

## El, Baal, and Yahweh

In the "Song of the Sea"—the poem in Ex 15—the Hebrews adopt the language of Canaanite myth and apply it to Yahweh. Yahweh appears here in
the manner of a storm god, heaping up the waters with a blast of wind. This
portrait of Yahweh is reminiscent of the Canaanite storm god Baal, who
rode on the clouds and was accompanied by wind and rain. At the beginning of rainy season, Baal opens a slit in the clouds and thunders, shaking
the earth. In one central legend, he defeats an adversary known as Prince
Sea or Judge River. After vanquishing his watery foe, he is acclaimed king
of the gods and men and is housed in a cedar home on top of a mountain.

Ancient Hebrew descriptions of Yahweh employ similar language in
poetic passages. Psalm 68:5 reads "extol Him who rides the clouds, Yahweh
is His name"—as if to correct the record and establish Yahweh, not Baal, as
the god of the storm. Psalm 29 also employs the language of a storm god,
and some scholars believe the psalm was originally a psalm about Baal:

> The voice of Yahweh is over the waters;
> the El of glory thunders,
> Yahweh over the mighty waters. (Ps 29:3)

Images of Israel's god engaged in a battle with some form of watery monster appear also in Ps 74:12–15:

> it was you who drove back the sea with your might,
> who smashed the heads of the monsters in the waters.

What are we to make of the biblical representation of Yahweh in terms
reminiscent of Baal? Coogan notes that Baal is the key figure in a change in
Canaanite religion that occurred between 1500 and 1200 B.C.E.—the traditional time of the Exodus and the introduction of Israelite Yahwism
(Coogan, *The Old Testament*, 101–103). At this time, there was a transfer of
power in the Canaanite pantheon from the older gods to the younger generation of gods. The old sky god El was replaced by the storm god Baal by
virtue of the latter's defeat of Prince Sea. Coogan notes that at about the
same time a similar change occurred in many of the major traditions of the

region—a younger storm god usurped power from an older god by virtue of a victory over a water god. In *Enuma Elish,* as we have seen, the young storm god Marduk defeats Tiamat, the watery deep, and so establishes his claim to rule instead of the old sky god An[u]. In India, the storm god Indra assumes power in place of Dyaus. In Greece, Zeus—who is associated with the storm, thunder, and lightning—replaces Chronos as head of the pantheon. And here in Exodus we find that just as the nation of Israel is said to come into existence, just as the Israelites make the transition from a nomadic existence to a settled way of life in their own land, there is a collective memory of a similar change in her religion. Like the storm gods, who ascended to a position of dominance in the myths of Israel's neighbors, Yahweh heaps up the waters of the reed sea and wins a stunning victory, establishing himself as the god of the Israelites in place of El, the old god of Israel's patriarchs. And like the Canaanite god Baal who overthrows the Canaanite god El, Yahweh will eventually come to rest in a cedar-lined house on a mountaintop—the sanctuary atop Mt. Zion in Jerusalem.[2]

There are, of course, important ways in which Israel's use of the storm god motif diverges from that of other ancient Near Eastern societies. The most important is that Yahweh's battle is a historical battle rather than a mythic battle. The sea is not Yahweh's opponent, nor is Yahweh's enemy another god. Yahweh does battle with a human foe, the Egyptian Pharaoh and his army; the sea is but a weapon in the divine arsenal deployed on behalf of Israel. In short, Yahweh is represented as transcending nature, using forces of nature for his historical purpose, and acting in history to deliver his people and create a new nation—Israel. Just as in Genesis 1 the universe is created when the wind of the deity parts the primeval waters, so in Ex 14–15 a new nation is created when the wind of Yahweh parts the waters of the reed sea. But to describe what was understood to be a historical event, the ancient Israelites employed language and images drawn from the traditions and myths of their broader cultural context.

As has long been noted, the Exodus event became the paradigm of Yahweh's salvation of his people—not in the later Christian sense of personal salvation from sin that is so often anachronistically read back into the Hebrew Bible. Salvation in the Hebrew Bible does not refer to the individual's deliverance from a sinful nature; it refers instead to collective, communal salvation from national suffering and oppression, particularly in the form of foreign rule or enslavement. When biblical writers speak of Yahweh as Israel's redeemer and savior, they are referring to Yahweh's *physical* deliverance of the *nation* from the hands of her foes.

It would be a mistake to view the Exodus event as the climax of the preceding narrative. The physical redemption of the Israelites is not the end of the story that began in Genesis. It is only a dramatic way station in a story that reaches its climax in the covenant concluded at Sinai. As many sensitive readers of the Bible have noted, the road from Egypt leads not to the other side of the reed sea but on to Sinai. Yahweh's redemption of the Israelites is a redemption *for a purpose*, a purpose that becomes clear at Sinai. For at Sinai, the Israelites will become Yahweh's people, bound by a covenant.

## The Sinaitic Covenant

And so the story continues: In the third month after the Exodus, the Israelites arrive at the wilderness of Sinai and encamp at the mountain where Moses was first called by Yahweh. The covenant concluded at Sinai is referred to as the Mosaic covenant, and it differs radically from the Noahide and Abrahamic (or patriarchal) covenants that we have already seen. Here, Yahweh promises to be the patron and protector of the Israelites whom he has chosen to live in his land, but he sets terms in this covenant requiring obedience to a variety of laws and commandments. Thus the Mosaic covenant is neither unilateral nor unconditional. It involves mutual obligations for both Yahweh and the Israelites; if the Israelites do not meet their obligations, then Israel can be expelled from the land. Israel must fulfill her obligation by obeying Yahweh's Torah (instruction) and living in accordance with his will as expressed through this instruction. Only then will Yahweh fulfill his obligations of protection and blessing toward Israel.

The biblical scholar Jon Levenson maintains that historical-critical scholarship has been unkind to biblical Israel because of a pervasive bias against the two foci of the religion of ancient Israel—Torah (instruction, but commonly translated as "law") and Temple.[3] On the one hand, negative Christian stereotypes, rooted in Paul's condemnation of the Mosaic Law as a deadening curse from which belief in Jesus offers liberation, color scholarly accounts of the giving of the Torah. On the other hand, a Protestant distaste for priest-centered cultic ritual colors scholarly accounts of the Temple and its meaning in ancient Israel. These biases permeate the work of even secular scholars of the Bible. A negative view of the Law has contributed to scholarly emphasis on the deliverance from Egypt as the high point in the Exodus narrative rather than the more natural literary climax— the conclusion of the covenant at Mount Sinai, the delivery of the Torah, the construction of the tabernacle, and Yahweh's descent to dwell in the tabernacle among the Israelites. In his book *Sinai and Zion,* Levenson tries to correct this prejudicial treatment and give the two central institutions of Torah and Temple "a fair hearing" (4). He explores the two great mountain traditions that express these central concepts: the tradition of Mt. Sinai, where Israel received the Torah and entered into a defining covenantal relationship with Yahweh, and the tradition of Mt. Zion, the future site of the nation's holy Temple and its attendant cult. In this chapter, we consider Levenson's analysis of the Sinai tradition as an entrée into the Israelite conception of Torah and the covenant bond.

Levenson stresses the importance of the covenant formulary. There are ancient Near Eastern parallels to the covenant of the Bible, especially Hittite treaties (1500–1200 B.C.E.) and Assyrian treaties (eighth century B.C.E.) between suzerain and vassal. Levenson (*Sinai*, 27–30) details the following six elements characteristic of Hittite treaties:[4] (1) a preamble in which the suzerain identifies himself; (2) an account of the historical circumstances leading to the treaty (historical prologue); (3) the stipulations and requirements; (4) arrangements for public reading of the treaty and its safekeeping in a shrine; (5) a concluding invocation of the gods as witness to the binding covenantal oath; and (6) a list of blessings for the party who obeys and of curses for the party that violates the pact (the curses are emphasized in Assyrian treaties). Levenson then identifies many of these elements in Yahweh's first speech to Moses upon the Israelites' arrival at Sinai. The speech, in Ex 19:3–6, reads as follows:

> 3. Yahweh called to him from the mountain, saying, "Thus shall you say to the house of Jacob and declare to the children of Israel: 4. 'You have seen what I did to the Egyptians, how I bore you on eagles' wings and brought you to me. 5. Now then, if you will obey me faithfully and keep my covenant, you shall be my treasured possession among all the peoples. Indeed, all the earth is mine, 6. but you shall be to me a kingdom of priests and a holy nation.' These are the words that you shall speak to the children of Israel." 7. Moses came and summoned the elders of the people and put before them all that Yahweh had commanded him. All the people answered as one, saying, 8. "All that Yahweh has spoken we will do!" and Moses brought back the people's words to Yahweh.

Drawing on the work of previous scholars, Levenson (*Sinai*, 30–32) finds several of the main elements of the Hittite suzerainty treaty in this speech. Verse 4 serves as the historical prologue. Verse 5 contains Yahweh's stipulation in the form of a very general conditional that will be fully articulated in the detailed stipulations to follow. Verses 5b–6 contain the reward: Yahweh confers on Israel the status of royalty. Thus, the passage contains three of the main elements of a treaty. In verse 8, the people solemnly undertake to fulfill the terms of the covenant.

If we take a broader view of the full biblical account of Israel's covenant with Yahweh, all six elements may be identified, though scattered throughout the text (Levenson, *Sinai*, 32–35). The preamble and historical background to the covenant may be seen in Yahweh's summary introduction to the people in Ex 20: "I am Yahweh who brought you out of the land of Egypt"—this fact presumably establishes Yahweh's claim to sovereignty. The terms of the treaty are stipulated at length in the instructions and laws of Ex 20–23. Moses reads the book of the Covenant publicly (Ex 24:7a), and in Deuteronomy it is deposited in a special ark (Deut 10:5). The Israelites vow to obey (Ex 24:3, 7b), and the covenant is sealed with a formal sacrifice (Ex 24:8). In a monotheistic system, other gods are not available as witnesses, but in Deut 4:26, 30:19, and 31:28, heaven and earth (i.e., the inhabitants thereof) are called upon as witnesses. As for blessings and curses, long lists of each are found in Lev 26 and Deut 28. (Some of these curses bear a great resemblance to curses in a treaty concluded by the Assyrian king Esarhaddon in about 677 B.C.E.) So while no one passage contains all the elements of the Hittite treaty form, there are enough of them scattered around to suggest it as one model.

According to Levenson, the use of the suzerainty treaty as a model for Israel's relationship to Yahweh expresses several key ideas. First, the historical prologue that is so central to the suzerainty treaty grounds the obligations of Israel to Yahweh in the history of his acts on her behalf (Levenson, *Sinai*, 37). Second, the historical prologue bridges the gap between generations—Israel's past, present, and future generations form a collective entity that collectively assents to the covenant. Even today, at Passover ceremonies the world over, Jews are reminded of the obligation to see themselves as if they personally came out of Egypt and covenanted with Yahweh. Third, the historical prologue explains why Israel accepts her place in the suzerain-vassal relationship. Israel's acceptance of a relationship with Yahweh does not stem from mystical introspection or philosophical speculation, Levenson argues. Instead, the Israelites affirm their identity and relationship with Yahweh by telling a story whose moral is that Israel can rely on Yahweh as a vassal can rely on his suzerain (*Sinai*, 39).

But the goal is not ultimately the affirmation of Yahweh's suzerainty in a mere verbal acclamation. As Levenson astutely points out, the affirmation of Yahweh's suzerainty is rendered in the form of obedience to command-ments (*Sinai*, 43). Observance of Yahweh's commandments is, as Levenson puts it, the teleological end of history (*Sinai*, 44). Why is this important? Unless we recognize that the road from Egypt leads inextricably to Sinai, that the story of national liberation issues in and is subordinate to the obli-gation to Yahweh's covenantal stipulations and observance of his laws, we run the risk of doing what has been done for centuries: reading Exodus as first and foremost a story of miraculous deliverance rather than a story of a relationship expressed through obligations to the observance of specific commandments.

The suzerain-vassal model has further implications underscored by Levenson and other scholars. Just as ancient Near Eastern suzerainty treaties specify that vassals are to treat each other as vassals of the same suzerain, so the Israelites are bound to one another as vassals of the same suzerain. Thus covenant in Israel is the basis of social ethics and the reason for Yahweh's in-structions regarding the treatment of one's fellow Israelites (*Sinai*, 54).

Finally, just as a vassal cannot serve two suzerains, the covenant with Yahweh entails the notion of Israel's exclusive service of Yahweh (Leven-son, *Sinai*, 68). The assertion is not that there is no other god, but that Israel will have no other god before Yahweh. The jealousy of the suzerain is the motivation for prohibitions against certain intimate contacts with non-Yahweh peoples, for such alliances will entail recognition of the gods of those peoples. The covenant with Yahweh will also preclude alliances with other human competitors (as will become apparent later). If Israel serves a divine king, she cannot, for example, serve a human king—an idea that will find expression in passages opposing the creation of a monarchy in Is-rael or the formation of alliances with, or subservience to, foreign kings—whether of Egypt, Assyria, or Babylon. Subservience to human kings is a rejection of the exclusive kingship of Yahweh and a breach of the covenant (Levenson, *Sinai*, 72).

Ancient Near Eastern suzerainty models speak repeatedly of the vas-sal's love for the suzerain, an element that is not absent in the biblical texts dealing with the covenant bond. The Israelites' promise to serve and love Yahweh is thus an additional theme associated with the covenant—one that will be taken up in greater detail in Chapter 11. But for now, we may accept

Levenson's claim that Sinai represents an intersection of law and love (*Sinai,* 75–80).

The covenant concept is critical to the Bible's portrayal and understanding of the relation between Israel and her god. The entire history of Israel as portrayed by the biblical writers is governed by this one outstanding reality of covenant. Israel's fortunes are seen to ride on its degree of faithfulness to the covenant.

Once the covenant between Yahweh and Israel has been consummated, the social and legal spheres of life regulated, and the judicial system established, all that remains is the organization of the cult—the complex of rites, ceremonies, practices, symbols, institutions, and personnel giving outward expression to the concepts that underlie Israel's understanding of its deity. Through the erection of the tabernacle, the experience with the divine presence that occurred at Sinai could be extended as a living reality. At the divine behest, Moses ascends the mountain alone and receives from Yahweh the elaborately detailed and lengthy instructions for the construction of the tabernacle. The tabernacle is not the permanent abode of the transcendent deity but a temporary structure symbolic of his dwelling in the midst of his people. In aniconic Israel, the tangible symbol of the deity housed in the tabernacle was not a statue but the tablets of the covenant.

Exodus closes with the construction of the sanctuary. When it is completed, the "Presence of Yahweh" fills the tabernacle as a sign of divine approval (Ex 40:34). But the receipt of the instructions for the tabernacle and the actual construction of it in Ex 25–40 are interrupted by the account of the apostasy of Israel with the golden calf. The moment of Israel's greatest glory is to be the moment of her greatest shame, for as Moses receives Yahweh's covenant on Mt. Sinai, the Israelites encamped at the foot of the mountain grow restless and rebellious. They demand of Aaron a god, since they do not know what has become of Moses (Ex 32:1). Aaron makes them a golden calf, and the people bow down to it, declaring, "This is your Elohim, O Israel, who brought you out of the Land of Egypt." An enraged Yahweh tells Moses to descend from the mountain, for the people are sinning and Yahweh in his fury wishes to destroy them all and start a new nation with Moses. Moses placates the deity momentarily, then turns to face the people. Approaching the camp, he is stunned by what he sees and smashes the tablets of the covenant, before halting the activities and punishing the perpetrators. This temporary alienation from Yahweh is repaired through Moses' prayer and intercession. A renewal of the covenant occurs, and another set of stone tablets is given.

This embarrassing episode is just the beginning in a series of embarrassing events that occur as the Israelites move from Egypt to the Promised Land. Most of these occur in the book of Numbers and involve the rebellion of the people, Yahweh's fury, Moses' intervention, and Yahweh's appeasement.

## Numbers

The book of Numbers recounts the itinerary of the Israelites throughout the forty years of their wanderings (see Map 1) and encampments around the sacred tabernacle. It contains a complex mix of materials of varying genres: laws, ritual texts, poetic folk traditions, and rich narrative. The narratives tell of Yahweh's provision for his people, but also the Israelites' constant complaints and rebellion. Even Miriam, Aaron, and Moses experience moments of frustration, discord, and rebellion (leading to Yahweh's surprising decree that Moses and Aaron will not enter the Promised Land; Num 20:12), but the primary focus is on individual Israelites or the collective community, murmuring and rebelling against both Moses and Yahweh, and longing for Egypt. Several times Yahweh threatens to exterminate them, but Moses dissuades him. In Numbers 14, when the Israelites complain again, Yahweh is determined to destroy them. Moses' intervention leads to a compromise. Yahweh swears that none of the adults who witnessed the Exodus—with the exception of Caleb and Joshua, who had not joined in the rebellion—would see the fulfillment of Yahweh's salvation and enter the Promised Land. The Israelites will wander forty years in the desert until all those who left Egypt as adults have passed away, leaving the new generation to enter the land.

### The Coparenting of Moses and Yahweh

The book of Numbers is remarkable for the relationship it describes between Moses and Yahweh. That relationship is an intimate one, and the two work as partners to preserve the Israelites and ready them for life in Yahweh's land as Yahweh's people. They alternate in losing patience with the Israelites and wishing to throw them over, but each time one convinces the other to be forbearing. Two examples of the way Moses and Yahweh act as a check upon one another will illustrate this point. The first example is from Num 14 and shows Moses' ability to placate the wrath of Yahweh. In this story the Israelites express great fear after hearing the report of a

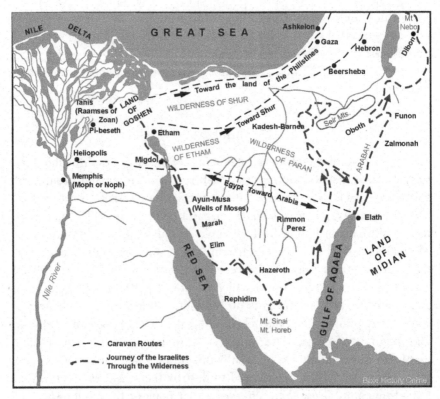

Map 1. Map of the Exodus route. Courtesy of Bible History Online.

reconnaissance team that their chances of conquering the Promised Land
are slim:

> The whole community broke into loud cries, and the people
> wept that night. All the Israelites railed against Moses and
> Aaron. "If only we had died in the land of Egypt," the whole
> community shouted at them, "or if only we might die in this
> wilderness! Why is Yahweh taking us to that land to fall by the
> sword? Our wives and children will be carried off! It would be
> better for us to go back to Egypt!" And they said to one another,
> "Let us head back for Egypt." (Num 14:1–4)

> The Presence of Yahweh appeared in the Tent of Meeting to all
> the Israelites. And Yahweh said to Moses, "How long will this

people spurn me, and how long will they have no faith in me despite all the signs that I have performed in their midst? I will strike them with pestilence and disown them, and I will make of you a nation far more numerous than they!" But Moses said to Yahweh, "When the Egyptians, from whose midst you brought up this people in your might, hear the news, they will tell it to the inhabitants of that land. . . . If then you slay this people to a man, the nations who have heard your fame will say, 'It must be because Yahweh was powerless to bring that people into the land he had promised them on oath that he slaughtered them in the wilderness.' Therefore, I pray, let my lord's forbearance be great, as you have declared, saying, "Yahweh! Slow to anger and abounding in kindness. . . . Pardon, I pray, the iniquity of this people according to your great kindness, as you have forgiven this people ever since Egypt."

And Yahweh said, "I pardon, as you have asked." (Num 14:10b–14a, 15–20)

In his fury, Yahweh offers to destroy Israel and start all over again with Moses. Readers will recognize a pattern in this god's behavior: He created humans with high hopes, but as they corrupted their path, he destroyed them with a flood, saving one individual as a fresh start. But humans continue to frustrate his plans for them, seeking aggrandizement instead of filling the earth as commanded. Having promised never to destroy creation again, Yahweh responds by frustrating their plans, scattering them far and wide, and once again pinning his hopes on a single individual—Abraham. And now the children of Abraham have disappointed him with their faithlessness and corruption, and once again, as if by reflex, Yahweh's first thought is to abandon them and start afresh with Moses. But Moses draws the line. He refuses to accept the offer and advances a line of argument that appeals primarily to Yahweh's vanity: What will the neighbors think if you destroy them? They will think you couldn't fulfill your promise. They will think you are not the powerful god of history. No, you have covenanted with Israel forever and there will be no more fresh starts. They are your people and you are their god, and so it will ever be. Here as before, Moses averts the Israelites' destruction.

But the roles are reversed in the following passage. This time Moses is impatient with the Israelites' constant complaints and lack of faith and is ready to throw in the towel. In Num 11, Yahweh consoles him and reconciles him to the daunting task he faces:

> The riffraff in their midst felt a gluttonous craving; and then the Israelites wept and said, "If only we had meat to eat! We remember the fish that we used to eat free in Egypt, the cucumbers, the melons, the leeks, the onions, and the garlic. Now our gullets are shriveled. There is nothing at all! Nothing but this manna to look at!" (Num 11:4–6)

> Moses heard the people weeping, every clan apart, each person at the entrance. "Why have You dealt ill with your servant [me], and why have I not enjoyed your favor, that you have laid the burden of all this people upon me? Did I conceive all this people, did I bear them, that you should say to me, 'Carry them in your bosom as a nurse carries an infant,' to the land that you have promised on oath to their fathers? Where am I to get meat to give to all this people, when they whine before me and say, 'Give us meat to eat!' I cannot carry all this people by myself, for it is too much for me. If you would deal thus with me, kill me rather, I beg you, and let me see no more of my wretchedness!" Then Yahweh said to Moses, "Gather for me seventy of Israel's elders of whom you have experience as elders and officers of the people, and bring them to the Tent of Meeting and let them take their place there with you. I will come down and speak with you there, and I will draw upon the spirit that is on you and put it upon them; they shall share the burden of the people with you, and you shall not bear it alone." (Num 11:10–17)

In many ways Moses sets the paradigm for the classical prophet, performing the double duty of chastising and upbraiding the Israelites for their rebellion and failures but at the same time consoling the people when they fear they have driven Yahweh away irreparably, defending them before Yahweh, and pleading for mercy even when they deserve punishment. At times, he expresses frustration with the difficulty of his task and resentment that it has been assigned to him. But he never yields to Yahweh's suggestions to abandon Israel and start a new nation from Moses' offspring. Indeed, it is Moses who brokers and secures Yahweh's eternal commitment to Israel.

## CHAPTER 9

# Biblical Law

*Readings:* Exodus 18–20, 24:10–23, 25; Leviticus 17, 25; Numbers 35; Deuteronomy 15, 17, 19, 22, 25

The covenant ceremony at Sinai included Yahweh's announcement of and Israel's agreement to certain covenantal stipulations. Exodus 24:3–4 describes this agreement as follows:

> Moses went and repeated to the people all the commands of Yahweh and all the rules, and all the people answered with one voice, saying "All the things that Yahweh has commanded we will do!" Moses then wrote down all the commands of Yahweh.

The covenant concluded at Sinai is the climactic moment in the Pentateuchal narrative. The conclusion of biblical scholarship is that a number of separate bodies of law have gravitated to the story of the forty-year period of Israel's formation into a people—the period of the covenant at Mt. Sinai and the journey toward the Promised Land. Because this period was viewed as the moment when Yahweh articulated his instruction (Torah) to Israel, later editors inserted law collections from various periods and authorships into the narrative at this juncture. Thus, all Israelite law is represented in the biblical account as having issued from that time of intimate contact between Yahweh and Israel at Sinai—a claim that imbued the nation's legal traditions with an air of high antiquity and conferred upon them divine sponsorship.

Modern source theory assigns the varied bodies of legal material found in the Pentateuch to the main biblical sources as follows: Laws found in the JE source occur in Exodus and are believed to have been formulated in writing from earlier oral traditions in the tenth to ninth century B.C.E.; laws of the P source are found in Exodus, Leviticus, and Numbers and are believed to have been formulated in writing from earlier oral traditions in the eighth to sixth century B.C.E; finally, laws of the D source are found in Deuteronomy and are believed to have been formulated in writing from earlier (primarily northern) traditions in the eighth to sixth century B.C.E. In all cases, it is supposed that the sources drew upon much older oral traditions; some individual laws are believed to be quite ancient, resembling ancient Near Eastern legal materials that date back to the second millennium B.C.E.

Regardless of their actual origins, the Bible represents these materials as having been given at Sinai or in the forty-year period afterward. According to the biblical narrative, the laws given at Sinai include:

| | |
|---|---|
| 1. The Decalogue or ten commandments | Ex 20:1–17 |
| 2. The Covenant Code (civil and religious law) | Ex 20:22–23:33 |
| 3. A Ritual decalogue | Ex 34:10–26 |
| 4. Cultic instructions | Ex 25–31 (fulfilled in Ex 35–40) |
| 5. Laws of sacrifice and ritual purity | Lev 1–18, 27 |
| 6. The Holiness Code | Lev 19–26 |
| 7. Priestly supplements (miscellany) | Num 1–10 |

According to the biblical narrative, the following materials were given in the forty years after Sinai as the Israelites encamped in the wilderness on their journey toward the land of Canaan.

| | |
|---|---|
| 8. Priestly supplements (miscellany) | Num 28–31, 33–36 |
| 9. Deuteronomic Code | Deut 12–26 |
| 10. Laws sanctioned by a curse | Deut 27 |

## The Decalogue

The twentieth-century biblical scholar Albrecht Alt noticed two general forms of biblical law: conditional or case law and absolute or apodictic law. Conditional law is the common form employed in ancient Near Eastern legal collections (as exemplified by the laws of Hammurapi) and features a characteristic if-then pattern: If a person does X, or if X happens, then Y will be the legal consequence. Casuistic law can be complex and very specific in its formulation: If X happens, Y is the consequence, but if X happens under these different circumstances, then Z is the consequence. Absolute or apodictic law by contrast is an unconditional statement of prohibition or command and tends to be general and somewhat undifferentiated: You shall not murder. You shall love Yahweh your god. The apodictic formulation of law is not unknown in other ancient Near Eastern cultures (especially in curses and covenant stipulations). The two literary forms are mixed in the biblical corpus (as in the Hittite laws). The provisions of the Decalogue (known in English as the Ten Commandments, a translation of the Hebrew "Ten words" or "Ten utterances") are in the absolute or apodictic form.

The Decalogue is the only part of Yahweh's revelation that is disclosed directly to all Israel at Sinai without an intermediary.[1] Its directives are couched in the masculine singular and thus appear to address Israelite males as the legal subjects of the community or Israel as a single collective entity. The Decalogue sets out Yahweh's most basic and unconditional covenant demands. The division into ten is questionable (see Table 4) and should probably be seen as an ideal biblical number since there are in fact thirteen or fourteen separate statements in the Decalogue.[2] The first five statements have traditionally been interpreted as defining Israel's relationship with her suzerain: She is to be exclusively faithful to Yahweh and is not to bow down to any man-made image; she may not use Yahweh's name in a false oath; she is to honor Yahweh's Sabbath and honor parental authority, arguably an extension of Yahweh's authority. The remaining statements concern Israel's relationship with her fellow vassals. These statements prohibit murder, adultery, robbery, false testimony, and covetousness.

The Pentateuch contains three versions of the Decalogue, and there are differences among them. The Exodus 20 Decalogue is repeated in Deuteronomy 5 with minor variations: Deuteronomy prohibits vain testimony (Deut 5:16) while Exodus prohibits false testimony (Ex 20:12); Israel is to "keep" the Sabbath day (Deut 5:16) rather than "remember" it (Ex 20:7); the rationale for observing the Sabbath is different (cf. Deut 5:14 and Ex 20:10);

Table 4. Ten Commandments by Tradition: Exodus 20:1–14

| Most Protestant, Eastern Orthodox | Catholic, Anglican, Lutheran | Jewish | Exodus 20 |
|---|---|---|---|
| – | – | 1 | (1) God spoke all these words, saying: |
| Preface | – | 1 | (2) I the LORD am your God who brought you out of the land of Egypt, the house of bondage: |
| 1 | 1 | 2 | (3) You shall have no other gods besides Me. |
| 2 | 1 | 2 | (4) You shall not make for yourself a sculptured image, or any likeness of what is in the heavens above, or on the earth below, or in the waters under the earth. (5) You shall not bow down to them or serve them. For I the LORD your God am an impassioned God, visiting the guilt of the parents upon the children, upon the third and upon the fourth generations of those who reject Me, (6) but showing kindness to the thousandth generation of those who love Me and keep My commandments. |
| 3 | 2 | 3 | (7) You shall not swear falsely by the name of the LORD your God; for the LORD will not clear the one who swears falsely by His name. |
| 4 | 3 | 4 | (8) Remember the Sabbath day and keep it holy. (9) Six days you shall labor and do all your work, (10) but the seventh day is a Sabbath of the LORD your God: you shall not do any work—you, your son or daughter, your male or female slave, or your cattle, or the stranger who is within your settlements. (11) For in six days the LORD made heaven and earth and sea, and all that is in them, and He rested on the seventh day; therefore the LORD blessed the Sabbath day and hallowed it. |
| 5 | 4 | 5 | (12) Honor your father and your mother, that you may long endure on the land that the LORD your God is assigning to you. |
| 6 | 5 | 6 | (13) You shall not murder. |
| 7 | 6 | 7 | You shall not commit adultery. |
| 8 | 7 | 8 | You shall not steal. |
| 9 | 8 | 9 | You shall not bear false witness against your neighbor. |
| 10 | 9 | 10 | (14) You shall not covet your neighbor's house: |
| 10 | 10 | 10 | you shall not covet your neighbor's wife, or his male or female slave, or his ox or his ass, or anything that is your neighbor's. |

and the final commandment singles out the neighbor's wife before listing other entities that must not be coveted (Deut 5:17; cf. Ex 20:13). What are we to make of these variations in the description of what was deemed to be a climactic moment of divine revelation?

Marc Brettler has noted that the variations in these accounts of the Decalogue may tell us something about the way ancient Israel preserved and transmitted important texts.[3] Ancient cultures generally did not strive for verbatim preservation, and biblical editors did not employ mechanical cut-and-paste methods in the composition of the biblical text. Sources were modified in the course of their transmission—even a text like the Decalogue that is represented as the unmediated word of Yahweh.

A more surprising variation occurs in Ex 34. After smashing the first set of tablets inscribed with the Decalogue of Ex 20, Moses is given a second set of tablets. The biblical writer emphasizes that Yahweh wrote on the tablets the words that were on the former tablets that had been broken (Ex 34:1). We expect, therefore, a verbatim repetition of Ex 20. Yet the Decalogue that follows has very little overlap with the earlier Decalogue, and even where there is some overlap in substance, the wording is entirely different. This Decalogue, often called the Ritual Decalogue, bans intermarriage with Canaanites lest they entice Israelites into worship of their gods. Other terms prescribe the observance of various festivals, the dedication of firstfruits and firstborn animals to Yahweh, observance of the Sabbath, and so on. Evidently different traditions regarding the contents of the Decalogue circulated in ancient Israel. The story of the golden calf and Moses' destruction of the first tablets is a brilliant narrative strategy for introducing and presenting one of these alternative Decalogue traditions.

Also surprising is the fact that the Decalogue in Exodus 20 does not stand completely unchallenged. Exodus 20:5–6 states explicitly the principle of intergenerational punishment—Yahweh is said to show kindness to the thousandth generation of those who love and obey him and to spread punishment for sin over three or four generations. In context, this passage is intended to signal the deity's great mercy in that he lightens the punishment of the sinner by spreading it to other generations *and* he limits the distribution of punishment to *only* three or four generations; by contrast, he spreads his kindness to the thousandth generation. However, the notion of intergenerational punishment is explicitly rejected in Deut 7:9–10.

> Know, therefore, that only Yahweh your god is god [Elohim], the steadfast god [El] who keeps his covenant faithfully to the thou-

sandth generation of those who love him and keep his commandments, but who instantly requites with destruction those
who reject him—never slow with those who reject him, but re-
quiting them instantly.

According to this text, Yahweh punishes the sinner only and not subsequent generations, and he does so instantly. Ezekiel and Jeremiah will also
reject the idea of intergenerational punishment (Jer 31:27–30, Ezek 18:20).

What are we to make of this contradiction? Brettler concludes that
the Decalogue (or Decalogues) did not originally possess the absolute nature that is so often claimed for it even today. Later religious traditions have
elevated the Decalogue to a position of absolute and inflexible authority, a
position not completely justified, given the Bible's own fluid treatment of
the Decalogue's text and content, and later modification of at least one of its
terms. In short, the claim that Yahweh's revelation of the Decalogue was
fixed in form (the exact words we see in Ex 20, for example) and immutable
in substance is not a claim that is native to or justified by the biblical
text—it is a later ideological imposition upon the text.

## Biblical Law in Its Ancient Near Eastern Context

Biblical law shares in the legal patrimony of the ancient Near East, even if it
is sometimes clearly reforming it. It is therefore helpful and instructive to
compare it with other important ancient collections. In doing so, we find
that certain key features distinguish Israelite law from other ancient law
collections.

The main ancient law collections of the ancient Near East[4] uncovered
by archaeologists are:

- The laws of Ur-Nammu (UN). 2112–2095 B.C.E., founder of
  the third dynasty of Ur. Sumerian language, known from
  scribal copies dating to 1800–1700. Prologue but no preserved
  epilogue.
- The laws of Lipit-Ishtar (LI). 1980–1970 B.C.E, fifth ruler of Isin
  Dynasty. Sumerian language. Originally on stele but preserved
  in seven clay tablets. Prologue and epilogue.
- Laws of Eshnunna (LE). Early second millennium, 1900 B.C.E.?
  Amorite-controlled state. Akkadian language. No prologue or
  epilogue.

- Laws of Hammurapi (CH). 1792–1750 B.C.E., sixth of eleven kings of the Old Babylonian (Amorite) Dynasty. Akkadian language. On diorite stele with bas-relief showing Hammurapi receiving commission to write the law code from the god of justice, the sungod Shamash. Carried to Susa by Elamite raiders; prologue and epilogue. These laws were copied by Mesopotamian scribes for centuries.
- Hittite Laws (HL). Second-millennium B.C.E. Hittite language in cuneiform. Two tablets in a series, though there may have been a third. Contains revisions, no prologue or epilogue.
- Middle Assyrian Laws (MAL). May go back to the eighteenth century B.C.E. Akkadian language, preserved in clay tablets, some badly broken and dating to the time of Tiglath-pileser in the twelfth century B.C.E. May have had short introduction.

These materials are law *collections* rather than law *codes*. Law codes are generally systematic and exhaustive and intended for use by courts. These collections are not exhaustive and do not exhibit much system or order. Nor is it known precisely how these materials were used, but scholars are increasingly convinced that they were not intended for use by courts.

In an important article written in 1960, biblical scholar Moshe Greenberg argued that a comparison of biblical law with other ancient Near Eastern law collections reveals the central postulates or values that undergird biblical law.[5] The following discussion of biblical law tracks Greenberg's persuasive essay quite closely.[6]

There is an immediate and critically important difference between the ancient Near Eastern codes and the Israelite laws as presented by the biblical narrator—a difference in authorship. The prologues and epilogues of ancient Near Eastern law collections, where they exist, make it clear that the laws are issued by the human king. Certainly the king's authority is underwritten by the gods—they often grant the king a just and discerning mind, or they install him in the kingship. But the laws themselves issue from the king. Thus, An and Enlil are said to give kingship to Ur-Nammu, Lipit-Ishtar, and Hammurapi, but the kings themselves are said to establish the laws (UN A i 31–42, iii 104–113, Roth 15; LI i 20–55, Roth 25; CH prologue I 27–49, v 14–24, Roth 76, 80–81). Hammurapi receives the principles of justice from Shamash (CH epilogue, Roth 135), but the laws are the handiwork of Hammurapi himself (see Figure 6): "When the god Marduk commanded me to provide just ways for the people of the land (in order to attain) appropriate

Fig. 6. The Stele of Hammurapi (eighteenth century B.C.E.).
Erich Lessing / Art Resource, NY.

behavior, I established truth and justice as the declaration of the land (CH prologue v 14–24, Roth 80–81). Hammurapi refers to the laws as "*my* judgments," "*my* pronouncements," "*my* achievements," "*my* inscribed stela" (CH epilogue, Roth 136). By contrast, the biblical narrative takes pains to ascribe authorship of the laws to Yahweh, rather than Moses.

> Moses went and repeated to the people all the commands of Yahweh and all the rules; and all the people answered with one voice, saying "All the things that Yahweh has commanded we will do!" Moses then wrote down all the commands of Yahweh. (Ex 24:3–4)

> When he [Yahweh] finished speaking with him on Mount Sinai, he gave Moses the two tablets of the Pact, stone tablets inscribed with the finger of Elohim. (Ex 31:18)

Greenberg argues that the principle of divine authorship has several important implications. First, it has a significant effect on the scope of the law. Ancient Near Eastern and biblical law differ as to the areas of human life and activity that fall within the scope of the laws' concern. Biblical law contains more than the rules and provisions generally recognized as falling within the scope of the coercive power of the state and the jurisdiction of law courts. Biblical law is holistic and contains social, ethical, moral, and religious prescriptions. It is not unusual for laws of this description to be couched in an authoritative, apodictic style. By contrast, the extrabiblical law collections deal almost entirely with matters that are enforceable by the state and not with matters of conscience, moral rectitude, or compassion. There is nothing in these collections that is truly parallel to the following biblical prescriptions.

> When you encounter your enemy's ox or ass wandering, you must take it back to him. When you see the ass of your enemy lying under its burden and you would refrain from raising it, you must nevertheless raise it with him. (Ex 23:4–5)

> You shall not hate your kinsfolk in your heart. Reprove your kinsman but incur no guilt because of him. You shall not take vengeance or bear a grudge against your countrymen. Love your fellow as yourself. I am Yahweh. (Lev 19:17–18)

These ethical norms, whose enforcement is necessarily a matter of individual conscience, are represented as stemming from the divine will, as are rules of buying and selling, damages, and criminal law. The indiscriminate mixing of what moderns would identify as legal norms and ethical norms raises all norms to the same level of importance and obligation grounded in the divine will. This holistic approach to normativity explains the inclusion, within a single extended passage, of laws regarding oppression, Sabbath observance, civil damages, incest, idolatry, and ritual offerings.

A second and related implication of divine authorship, according to Greenberg, is the deep and essential connection between law and morality. Technically, in the biblical legal framework, every crime is also a sin, since the laws and norms of the covenant express the moral will of the deity. Thus, what is illegal is also immoral and vice versa. This is quite different from the modern conceptual distinction between law and morality. All offenses are (also) religious offenses (sins) because all are infractions of the divine will (Greenberg, "Some Postulates," 22).

The fusion of morality and law is the reason that biblical law not only expresses but also legislates a concern for the poor and disadvantaged members of society—orphans, widows, strangers—as well as respect for the aged (see Lev 19:32: "You shall rise before the aged and show deference to the old; you shall fear your god: I am Yahweh"). The extrabiblical codes contain rhetorical expressions of concern for the rights of the poor in their prologues, but they do not prescribe charity and compassion. This is not to say that ethical expectations of charity and compassion were absent in other ancient Near Eastern cultures; it is simply to say that charity and compassion fell largely outside the domain and jurisdiction of the courts and were not subject to legal formulation (just as they are not in contemporary American society). In biblical legal literature, by contrast, nothing falls beyond the jurisdiction of the divine lawgiver, and so we read:

> When you reap the harvest of your land, you shall not reap all the way to the edges of your field, or gather the gleanings of your harvest. You shall not pick your vineyard bare, or gather the fallen fruit of your vineyard. You shall leave them for the poor and the stranger: I, Yahweh, am your god. (Lev 19:9–10)

> You shall not insult the deaf, or place a stumbling block before the blind. You shall fear your Elohim: I am Yahweh. (Lev 19:14)

Love your fellow as yourself. I am Yahweh. (Lev 19:18)

When a stranger resides with you in your land, you shall not
wrong him. The stranger who resides with you shall be to you as
one of your citizens; you shall love him as yourself, for you were
strangers in the land of Egypt: I, Yahweh, am your god. (Lev
19:33–34)

If, along the road, you chance upon a bird's nest, in any tree or on
the ground, with fledglings or eggs and the mother sitting over
the fledglings or on the eggs, do not take the mother together
with her young. Let the mother go, and take only the young, in
order that you may fare well and have a long life. (Deut 22:6)

Furthermore, Greenberg argues, the fact that every crime is also a sin lays
the ground for certain acts to be viewed as absolute wrongs that transcend
the power of humans to pardon. This idea comes to expression in the biblical treatment of adultery and murder.

If a man is found lying with another man's wife, both of them—
the man and the woman with whom he lay—shall die. Thus you
will sweep away evil from Israel. (Deut 22:22)

Likewise,

The murderer must be put to death. . . . You may not accept a
ransom for the life of a murderer who is guilty of a capital crime;
he must be put to death. (Num 35:16, 31)

These texts suggest that adultery and murder are absolutely wrong and
must always be punished, regardless of the desire of the offended parties. A
husband cannot ask that his adulterous wife be spared punishment, nor
can the relatives of a murdered person request that the life of the murderer be spared. These crimes, as infractions of Yahweh's will expressed
in Yahweh's law, are always wrong and will be punished regardless of the
disposition of human actors. By contrast, adultery is conceived as a private
offense in ancient Near Eastern legal collections (as in contemporary
American law).

If a man's[7] wife should be seized lying with another male, they shall bind them and cast them into the water; if the wife's master allows his wife to live, then the king shall allow his subject (i.e., the other male) to live. (CH 129)

The Middle Assyrian laws frame adultery as a crime against the property of the husband and thus within his power to prosecute or not.

If a man should fornicate with another man's wife either in an inn or in the main thoroughfare, knowing that she is the wife of a man, they shall treat the fornicator as the man declares he wishes his wife to be treated. If he should fornicate with her without knowing that she is the wife of a man, the fornicator is clear; the man shall prove the charges against his wife and he shall treat her as he wishes.

If a man should seize another man upon his wife and they prove the charges against him and find him guilty, they shall kill both of them; there is no liability for him [i.e., the husband]. If . . . they prove the charges against him and find him guilty—if the woman's husband kills his wife, then he shall also kill the man; if he cuts off his wife's nose, he shall turn the man into a eunuch and they shall lacerate his entire face; but if [he wishes to release] his wife, he shall [release] the man. (MAL A14–15)

Likewise in the Hittite laws, the husband may decide to spare his wife.

If he brings them to the palace gate (i.e., the royal court) and says: "My wife shall not die," he can spare his wife's life, but he must also spare the lover and "clothe his head." If he says, "Both of them shall die," they shall "roll the wheel." The king may have them killed or he may spare them. (HL II 197–198)

Another consequence of the principle of divine authorship, according to Greenberg ("Some Postulates," 22), is that the purpose of the law in Israelite society is different from its purpose in other societies. In non-Israelite society, the purpose of the law is to secure certain sociopolitical benefits like those listed in the preamble of the U.S. Constitution, where the purpose of law is to establish justice, ensure domestic tranquility, provide for the common defense, promote the general welfare, and secure the blessings of liberty. In the prologue to the laws of Ur-Nammu, we read that the purpose of the laws is to establish equity, protect the underprivileged, and promote the common weal and welfare. In the prologue to the laws of Lipit-Ishtar, we read that the purpose of the law is to establish justice, banish complaints, bring well-being, and promote the common weal and welfare. Similarly, the prologue to Hammurapi's laws refers to promoting the welfare of the people, good government, the right way, and prosperity.

But for biblical Israel, Greenberg asserts, the law is not limited to these material benefits. The law aims at sanctifying—rendering holy or like the deity—those who abide by its terms. The laws of the Holiness Code open with Yahweh's exhortation to holiness, followed by an enumeration of various laws by means of which one may achieve that status:

> You shall be holy, for I, Yahweh your god, am holy. You shall each revere his mother and his father, and keep My Sabbaths [etc.]. (Lev 19:2–3)

Being holy in imitation of Yahweh is emphasized repeatedly as the very purpose of the civil, criminal, moral, and ritual laws detailed in the Holiness Code (Lev 17–26). Indeed, the biblical narrator introduces the theme of holiness at the very inception of the covenant. When Israel is assembled at Mt. Sinai, Yahweh says,

> Now then, if you will obey me faithfully and keep my covenant, you shall be my treasured possession among all the peoples. Indeed, all the earth is mine, but you shall be to me a kingdom of priests and a holy nation. (Ex. 19:5–6)

Greenberg also points to formal and stylistic differences between ancient Near Eastern and biblical law, differences all the more striking for the fact that these materials contain numerous general and specific similarities and parallels (for example, laws concerning goring oxen and laws about pregnant women who miscarry after being accidentally struck by men in a brawl were apparently common elements of a larger ancient Near Eastern scribal tradition, since they appear in many of these collections). A distinguishing formal feature of Israelite law is the addition of a rationale or motive clause for certain laws, particularly the humanitarian laws. One of the most common rationales appeals to Israel's experience in Egypt and addresses the Israelites as persons of intelligence and compassion, capable of moral reasoning. Biblical passages expressing the idea that Israel's experience of alien status, slavery, and liberation should be an impetus for moral action include:

> You shall not wrong a stranger or oppress him, for you were strangers in the land of Egypt. (Ex 22:20)

> You shall not oppress a stranger for you know the feelings of the stranger, having yourselves been strangers in the land of Egypt. (Ex 23:9)

> When a stranger resides with you in your land, you shall not wrong him. The stranger who resides with you shall be to you as one of your citizens; you shall love him as yourself, for you were strangers in the land of Egypt. (Lev 19:33–34)

> Six days you shall labor and do all your work, but the seventh day is a sabbath of Yahweh your god: you shall not do any work—you, your son or your daughter, your male or female slave, your ox or your ass, or any of your cattle, or the stranger in your settlements, so that your male and female slave may rest as you do. Remember that you were a slave in the land of Egypt and Yahweh your god freed you from there. (Deut 5:12–15)

> For Yahweh your god is god [Elohim] supreme and lord supreme, the great, the mighty, and the awesome god [El] who shows no favor and takes no bribe, but upholds the cause of the fatherless and the widow, and befriends the stranger, providing him with food and clothing. You too must befriend the stranger, for you were strangers in the land of Egypt. (Deut 10:17–19)

> You shall not subvert the rights of the stranger or the fatherless; you shall not take a widow's garment in pawn. Remember that you were a slave in Egypt and that Yahweh your god redeemed you from there; therefore do I enjoin you to observe this commandment. (Deut 24:17–22)

> If a fellow Hebrew, man or woman, is sold to you, he shall serve you six years and in the seventh year you shall set him free. When you set him free, do not let him go empty-handed. Furnish him

out of the flock, threshing floor, and vat, with which Yahweh your god has blessed you. Bear in mind that you were slaves in the land of Egypt and Yahweh your god redeemed you; therefore I enjoin this commandment upon you today. (Deut 15:12)

You shall not abhor an Egyptian, for you were a stranger in his land. (Deut 23:7)

When you beat down the fruit of your olive trees, do not go over them again; that [which remains on the tree] shall go to the stranger, the fatherless, and the widow. . . . Always remember that you were a slave in the land of Egypt; therefore do I enjoin you to observe this commandment. (Deut 24:20, 22)

Sarna compares ancient Near Eastern and biblical law in terms of the elimination of social class distinctions (*Exodus*, 166, 178), concrete provisions for the disadvantaged (172–173, 177), and a trend toward humanitarianism. He notes that while many of the extrabiblical collections pay homage to the notion of justice for all persons in their prologues, they retain laws that clearly serve the interests of the upper class. By contrast, the biblical concern for the disadvantaged of society finds concrete expression in various legal provisions. Specifically, the biblical laws do not contain the same distinctions of social class among free persons that may be found in the contemporary laws of Eshnunna and Hammurapi, which distinguish between punishments for crimes committed against upper-class and lower-class persons, not to mention slaves. From the Collection of Hammurapi:[8]

196. If an *awīlu* should blind the eye of another *awīlu*, they should blind his eye.

197. If he should break the bone of another *awīlu*, they shall break his bone.

198. If he should blind the eye of a commoner or break the bone of a commoner, he shall weigh and deliver 60 shekels of silver.

199. If he should blind the eye of an *awīlu*'s slave or break the bone of an *awīlu*'s slave, he shall weigh and deliver one-half of his value (in silver).

200. If an *awīlu* should knock out the tooth of another *awīlu* of his own rank, they shall knock out his tooth.

201. If he should knock out the tooth of a commoner, he shall weigh and deliver 20 shekels of silver.

202. If an *awīlu* should strike the cheek of an *awīlu* who is of status higher than his own, he shall be flogged in the public assembly with 60 stripes of an ox whip.

203. If a member of the *awīlu*-class should strike the cheek of another member of the *awīlu*-class who is his equal, he shall weigh and deliver 60 shekels of silver.

204. If a commoner should strike the cheek of another commoner, he shall weigh and deliver 10 shekels of silver.

205. If an *awīlu*'s slave should strike the cheek of a member of the *awīlu*-class, they shall cut off his ear. (CH xl 45–xli 3)

In these laws, even free persons are not deemed to be of equal value (Sarna, *Exodus*, 166), and punishments are determined by the social class of both the aggressor and the victim. In the continuation of this passage, compensation for an assault that causes a miscarriage or the death of a pregnant woman is greater when the victim is an upper-class woman and when the assailant is of lower rank than the victim (CH 209–214). The same class distinctions may be seen in the Hittite laws (95, 99) and the Middle Assyrian laws. By contrast, the personal liability laws in Lev 24:17–22 contain a clear and explicit statement to the effect that there shall be one standard for citizen and stranger alike:

> If anyone maims his fellow, as he has done so shall it be done to him: fracture for fracture, eye for eye, tooth for tooth. The injury he inflicted on another shall be inflicted on him. . . . You shall have one standard for stranger and citizen alike: for I am Yahweh, your god.

The principle articulated here is the (in)famous principle of talion. As Greenberg points out (24), the biblical "eye for an eye" is often cited as an example of the allegedly harsh and cruel standards of the Old Testament deity, a primitive archaic reflex of the vendetta principle. But when seen in a comparative light against the backdrop of the class-differential distribution of justice in the ancient Near East, this biblical principle may be appreciated for what it was—a somewhat astonishing and probably polemical assertion of the equality of all citizens before the law.[9] The slogan "an eye for an eye" expresses the idea that the punishment should fit the crime—no more and no less—for all free persons regardless of the social class of the perpetrator or the victim. All free citizens who injure are treated equally before the law—neither let off with something less than the injury caused nor punished in excess of the injury caused (see also Sarna, *Exodus,* 182–189). An example of excessive punishment may be found in the Middle Assyrian laws (A21 and F1) in the cases of inducing a miscarriage (the guilty party pays two talents and thirty minas of lead, is flogged fifty times, and performs state labor for a month) and sheep stealing (the guilty party is flogged 100 times, his hair is pulled out, he performs state labor for a month, and he is subject to a monetary fine). Are these ideas—that punishments should be neither too little nor too much but should match the crime, that all (free) persons are equal before the law, and that one standard of justice should apply regardless of the social status of either the victim or the perpetrator—"primitive" legal concepts?

In addition to asserting basic equality before the law for all free citizens, the Bible mandates concern for the disenfranchised and the needy. As noted above, Lev 19:9–10 states that some produce should be left in the fields and orchards so that the poor and the stranger might glean. Deuteronomy is a little less generous, substituting "the widow, the orphan, and the stranger" for Leviticus's "poor."

> When you beat down the fruit of your olive trees [or gather the grapes of your vineyard], do not go over them again; that [which remains on the tree] shall go to the stranger, the fatherless, and the widow. Always remember that you were a slave in the land of Egypt; therefore do I enjoin you to observe this commandment. (Deut 24:20–22)

Leviticus supports outright charity for the poor in the form of gleanings, but Deuteronomy is less clear. Deuteronomy envisages a class of working poor, assisted by loans on generous terms.

> If there is among you a poor man, one of your brethren . . . you shall not harden your heart or shut your hand against your poor brother, but you shall open your hand to him and lend him sufficient for his need, whatever it may be. Beware lest you harbor the base thought "the seventh year, the year of debt release is approaching," so that you are mean to your poor kinsman and give him nothing. You shall give to him freely and your heart

shall not be grudging when you give to him . . . for the poor will
never cease out of the land; therefore I command you, you shall
open wide your hand to your brother, to the needy and to the
poor in the land. (Deut 15:7–11)

Deuteronomy exhorts the Israelite to lend money to the poor even if it
means potential loss because of the universal release of debts required every
seven years. Loans to the poor must be made under all circumstances for
the simple reason that poverty is a terrible and persistent problem.

   While there is much in the biblical legal corpus that deeply offends
modern western sensibilities—including the legalization of slavery (Ex 21:2–
6, Deut 15:12–18, Lev 25:44–46), the imposition of the death penalty for certain
sexual acts, including adultery (Lev 18, 20; Deut 22:20), the right of parents to
execute a "stubborn and rebellious child" (Deut 21:18–21), and the enforced
marriage of a rapist and his victim (Deut 22:28–29)—it is possible to discern
in biblical legislation a tendency toward humanitarianism. Thus, where some
societies consider the slave to be the chattel of his or her master in many respects, the biblical position is somewhat equivocal. In contrast to ancient Near
Eastern collections that lack laws protecting slaves from harsh treatment by
the master (see, for example, MAL A44), the biblical text states that the master who wounds his slave in any way (even losing a tooth) must set him free
(Ex 21:26–27) and a slave who is killed must be avenged (Ex 21:20). Further,
slaves are entitled to the sabbath rest (Ex 20:10, Deut 5:14), and a fugitive slave
cannot be returned to his master (see discussion in Sarna, *Exodus*, 180–182).

You shall not turn over to his master a slave who seeks refuge
with you from his master. He shall live with you in any place he
may choose among the settlements in your midst, wherever he
pleases; you must not ill-treat him. (Deut 23:16–17)

Compare this law from the collection of Hammurapi, which prescribes
death for aiding or sheltering a fugitive slave:

If a man should harbor a fugitive slave or slave woman of either
the palace or of a commoner in his house and not bring him out
at the herald's public proclamation, that householder shall be
killed. (CH 16)

Moreover, the term of service of an Israelite slave is limited to six years in Exodus and Deuteronomy (though the slave may "choose" to make his station permanent). Israelite slavery is prohibited altogether by the priestly code of Leviticus (Lev 25:35–46), although the enslavement of non-Israelites is still permitted.[10]

Other evidence of a tendency toward humanitarianism is the lack of legalized violence in the Bible. The biblical legislation contains no true parallel to the Middle Assyrian laws that legalize wife abuse (a man may pull out his wife's hair, mutilate or twist her ears, A59) and authorize inhumane treatment of a deserting wife (the husband may cut off her ears, A24) and a distrainee living as a debt pledge in an *awīlu*'s house (Sarna, *Exodus*, 176–177).

Greenberg asserts that legal systems express their values by the punishments posited for various transgressions, and undertakes a comparison of the punishments imposed by the ancient Near Eastern and biblical legal materials (24–29). He argues that the Bible's high valuation of human life may be contrasted with the high valuation of property in the extrabiblical codes (see also Sarna, *Exodus*, 178, 180). Hammurapi's collection imposes the death penalty for various *property* crimes: theft and receipt of or trafficking in stolen goods (CH 6–10), housebreaking, theft or robbery following a fire (CH 21–25), defrauding by a female wine seller, and harboring a fugitive slave (CH 108–9). The Middle Assyrian laws impose the death penalty for theft by a wife and for purchasing stolen goods (MAL A3). By contrast, biblical legal writings do not impose the death penalty for violations of ordinary property rights. This punishment is reserved for intentional homicide, certain sexual offenses, and crimes against the deity (sacrilege). Indeed, Num 35 makes it clear that homicide is the one crime for which no monetary punishment can be substituted. The life of the intentional murderer cannot be ransomed—he must pay for the life he took with his own life. The accidental homicide lives out his life in one of six cities of refuge—a kind of social banishment.

> You may not accept a ransom for the life of a murderer who is guilty of a capital crime; he must be put to death. Nor may you accept ransom in lieu of flight to a city of refuge, enabling one to return to live on his land before the death of the priest. You shall not pollute the land in which you live; for blood pollutes the land, and the land can have no expiation for blood that is shed on it,

except by the blood of him who shed it. You shall not defile the
land in which you live, in which I myself abide, for I, Yahweh,
abide among the Israelite people. (Num 35:31–34)

We find no absolute ban on monetary compensation for murder in the extrabiblical collections. According to Greenberg ("Some Postulates," 27) and
Sarna (*Exodus*, 178), these data suggest that for the biblical legislators, the
sanctity of human life is of paramount value, and human life and property
are simply incommensurable. Crimes in the one realm cannot be compensated by punishment in the other realm: There is no death penalty for property crimes and no monetary compensation imposed for homicide. This is
not so in the Middle Assyrian laws and the Hittite laws, for example, where
murder can be compensated monetarily (MAL A10, B2; HL I 1–5), and death
is prescribed for various property crimes, as we have seen. Moreover, in biblical law only the directly guilty party is liable in cases of murder. Deuteronomy 24:16 states explicitly that "parents shall not be put to death for children
nor children be put to death for their parents. A person shall be put to death
only for his own crime." Thus, there is no literal punishment as in the laws of
Hammurapi (if an *awīlu* causes the death of the daughter of an *awīlu*, his
own daughter is put to death [CH 210]; if a builder's negligence causes the
death of another man's son, the builder's son is put to death [CH 230]) or the
Middle Assyrian Laws (if a man rapes, his own wife is raped [MAL A55]).[11]
This may be contrasted with Ex 21:28–32, where the person responsible for
negligent homicide is punished even if the victim is a minor.

It is important to recognize that the biblical legal materials do not
speak with one voice. There are many provisions that contradict one another (see the discussion of the slave laws in Chapter 11), and later versions
of a law, particularly in Deuteronomy, often revise or update earlier versions of a law in, for example, the Covenant Code. Nevertheless, as Greenberg has argued, some common themes and underlying postulates, such as
the sanctity of human life, the value of persons over property, the equality
of free persons in the eyes of the law, the importance of assisting the disadvantaged in society, a tendency toward humanitarianism, and the integration
and interdependence of all aspects of human life, may be discerned despite
some variation.

According to Deut 31:9–13, Yahweh's teaching (Torah) is to be proclaimed publicly, read annually, and studied continually, suggesting that
each person has an obligation to understand and uphold its contents. The
public nature of the study and observance of Yahweh's Torah underscores

the extent to which law and morality are cast in communal terms. It is the community that is in covenant with Yahweh, and it is the community that is the primary moral subject, for individual actions have communal consequences. This communal ethic plays a key role in the cultic symbolism of the priestly writings discussed in the next chapter.

## CHAPTER 10

# The Priestly Legacy

## Cult and Sacrifice, Purity and Holiness

*Readings:* Leviticus 1–20; Numbers 19

Leviticus is the primary exemplar of the Priestly source (P) dealing with matters that were of special concern to, and under the jurisdiction of, priests: the sanctuary, its cultic rituals, the system of sacrifices, and the distinction between the pure and the impure, the holy and the profane. The priestly materials, which are found in a block in Leviticus, in parts of Numbers, and scattered throughout Genesis and Exodus, emerged over a period of centuries. Although they reached their final form in the exilic and postexilic periods, they preserve older cultic and priestly traditions as well.

The book of Leviticus can be broken into the following units. Chapters 1–7 detail the sacrificial system; chapters 8–10 describe the installation of Aaron and his line as priests; chapters 11–15 contain the dietary laws and the laws of ritual purity and impurity; and chapter 16 prescribes the ritual for Yom Kippur (the Day of Atonement). Chapters 17–26 are known as the Holiness Code, a miscellany that includes laws of forbidden sexual relations in chapters 18 and 20 and rules concerning vows and offerings in chapter 27. The special emphasis on holiness in chapters 17–26, as well as variations from the preceding sixteen chapters, has led scholars to the conclusion that chapters 17–26 are from a different priestly school, which they designate as H. The relative dates of P and H are much debated, but increasingly the consensus is that H is later than, and a redactor or editor of, P. (Thus, somewhat confusingly, P can refer to the entirety of the priestly writings that constitute the priestly source, or it can refer to that part of the priestly writings that is not H.)

The priestly materials have long been devalued in academic circles. Biblical scholarship of the nineteenth century and much of the twentieth century is characterized by a deep-seated bias that views impurity rules as primitive and irrational taboos and views sacrifice as a controlled savagery devoid of spiritual meaning. In the latter part of the twentieth century, this situation began to change. As anthropologists and ethnographers began to study the danger avoidance practices, taboos, and rituals of various cultures, including modern western cultures, new avenues for understanding the danger avoidance practices of the Bible emerged. The anthropologist Mary Douglas changed forever the way scholars approach the impurity rules of the Bible by insisting on their interpretation as symbols that conveyed something meaningful to those who constructed and followed them. Biblical scholars attuned to developments in the social sciences, like Jacob Milgrom and more recently Jonathan Klawans, have made very great advances in our understanding of Israelite purity practices. They approach the elaborate and carefully constructed texts of P as part of a system whose meaning derives from the larger cultural matrix or grid in which they are embedded.

To what extent does the system laid out by P represent what ordinary Israelites thought and did? To what extent were these rules actually enacted and followed? To what extent did the priestly authors draw together older random practices, modify them, and impose order on them? To what extent do the priestly texts represent the ideal construction or blueprint of an elite class divorced from lived practice? These are ultimately unanswerable questions. The fact is no one really knows. We do know from living cultures that people do engage in all kinds of ritual and symbolic actions because of genuine beliefs about the importance of those actions and because those rituals and symbols are extraordinarily meaningful to them. Nevertheless, for present purposes, our primary concern is with the program of the texts as they stand before us. Whether the rules were followed or understood by ancient Israelites generally will not concern us here. The main questions we will pursue are: Is there a symbolism operating in P's construction of the cultic realm? What are the key ideas and themes of the priestly material? How does this material align with other aspects of Israelite religion? And what is the ultimate purpose of the priestly writings and the cultic realm they represent?

## Cult and Sacrifice

Like the rest of the ancient world, Israel had a cultic system featuring a sacred sanctuary with holy objects in which priests performed a variety of ritual acts. Israelite-Judean religion shared many cultic forms and rituals with Canaanite and ancient Near Eastern cultures generally. Sanctuaries in the ancient world were understood to be the dwelling place of the deity, and sacrifices were offered to the deity in his or her sanctuary. P texts describe a portable, tentlike sanctuary (*mishkan*) used in the wilderness period (see Figure 7). Woven curtains hung from wooden frames that could be easily assembled and disassembled surrounded the sacred precincts. Within this enclosure a large open courtyard was accessible to all Israelites. The main sacrificial altar stood in this courtyard, as well as a basin used for ablutions. Halfway across this open courtyard was a screen marking the entrance to another enclosure known as "the holy shrine"—the sanctuary proper. Only priests had access to this holy area, which contained an incense altar, a seven-branched lampstand, or *menorah*, and a table for loaves of bread placed be-

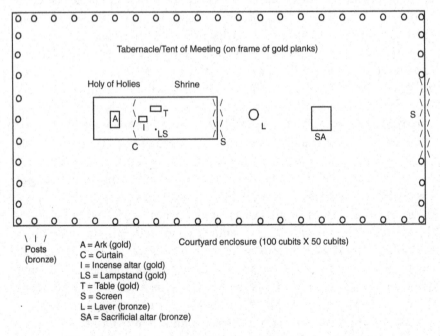

Fig. 7. The structure of the Israelite Tabernacle (sanctuary).
© Ethan Della Rocca.

fore Yahweh each week. The backmost square-shaped chamber was the inner sanctum or Holy of Holies accessible only to the high priest and only on the Day of Atonement following a series of heightened purity observances. Inside the Holy of Holies was the ark, measuring about four feet by two and a half feet. The wooden ark was plated in gold and topped with a *kapporet*, traditionally translated as "mercy seat." Two cherubim (winged lions) flanked the ark and were likely connected to the covering, reminiscent of the thrones of deities highlighted in the iconography and literature of the ancient Near East. In some biblical verses, Yahweh is described as enthroned upon the cherubim, with the ark serving as his footstool. The ark itself contained the tablets of the covenant and was thus a testament to the covenant between Yahweh and Israel. Unlike most ancient sanctuaries, the Israelite tabernacle did not house a statue of the deity—indicative of the aniconic tendency of Israelite religion. Nevertheless, Yahweh was believed to be present in the sanctuary— often in the form of a cloud that descends to fill the tabernacle whenever it is assembled in a new encampment.

## Holiness

It is Yahweh's presence that sanctifies the tabernacle. To understand this requires an understanding of the priestly conception of holiness. The Hebrew word *holy* has a root meaning of "separate." That which is holy is separate, withdrawn from common everyday use. In the priestly view, only Yahweh is intrinsically holy. Yahweh can impart holiness, which is to say he can "sanctify," persons, places, and things when they are brought into a specific kind of relationship to him, best described as a relationship of ownership. What is holy is what is in Yahweh's realm, separated to him. That which is outside Yahweh's realm is common. The Hebrew word for *common* (ḥol) is sometimes translated as "profane," an English word that has a more negative connotation than is evident in the technical Hebrew usage. "Common" is in fact the default status of most objects and things. For a common object to become holy, a special act of dedication or transfer to Yahweh (sanctification) must occur.

So holiness necessarily entails separation in both a positive and a negative sense: separation of an object *to* that which sanctifies it (Yahweh) and separation of that object *from* that which threatens to remove its sanctity. Separation is achieved by means of various restrictions. Holy things are holy because they are separated from the realm of the common by rules of use and safeguards that demarcate them as different and separate. The preservation of holy status depends on these rules and safeguards that protect the holy object from profanation.

It is evident from the schematic representation of the sanctuary in Figure 7 that holiness increases as one moves deeper into the sanctuary. The principle here is that holiness increases as proximity to Yahweh increases. This principle is graphically demonstrated in spatial terms. Outside the Israelite camp is common, profane ground. The Israelite camp bears a certain degree of holiness; the outer courtyard of the sanctuary bears a slightly higher degree of holiness and is accessible to ritually pure Israelites. The sanctuary proper, which is in closer proximity to Yahweh, bears a still higher degree of holiness and is accessible to the priests who are said to be the holy ones within Israel. The inner shrine is the holiest area and is accessed only by the holiest member of the nation—the high priest. Similar concentric circles of holiness characterize the priestly conception of time. There are ordinary profane days. Then there are certain holy days (e.g., the new year, the Passover) separated and demarcated from common time by special rules that mark them as different. Holier that these days is the Sabbath, demarcated by further rules and observances. The holiest day is Yom Kippur, known as the Sabbath of Sabbaths. This day is separated from all other days by additional rules and observances in keeping with its profound holiness. Holiness of persons, objects, space, and time converge on Yom Kippur, for it is only on this most holy day that the most holy high priest enters the most holy of holies and performs a ritual upon the most holy of objects—the ark—itself.

## Ritual Purity

Access to the holy requires purity. Although holiness and purity are often confused in the scholarly literature, the two are not identical. As noted above, to be holy is to belong to or be in the realm of the deity. But things cannot become holy or be in contact with the holy if they are not first pure. Ritual purity—or the absence of impurity—is a *prerequisite* for access to the holy or for holy status. To be in a state of purity simply means that one is qualified to contact the sacred (to enter holy precincts, for example, or handle sacred objects), and to be in a state of impurity simply means that one is not qualified to contact the sacred. The holy is by definition pure. Only that which is free of impurity can access the holy. If an impure object comes into contact with a holy object, the holy object will immediately be rendered impure (defiled) and lose its holy status—it will be profaned.

Normally, to be restored, two things must happen. The object must be purified—in which case it will be pure but still common. The object must then
be rededicated or transferred to the deity. Such an act of transfer will make
it holy again (in addition to being pure). Increased access to the holy requires increased purity. Thus the purity required of a priest, who has access
to the sanctuary proper, is higher than that of an Israelite, who has access to
the outer courtyard only. The purity required of the high priest is even
greater than that of an ordinary priest since the high priest has access to the
innermost shrine, or holy of holies.

   To be pure, one must separate from impurity. But what are the sources
of impurity? Jonathan Klawans has been the most vocal proponent of the
claim that biblical texts speak of two distinct types of impurity: ritual impurity and moral impurity.[1] Ritual impurities are detailed in Lev 12–15,
while moral impurities are discussed in Lev 16 and emphasized by the
Holiness sources (especially Lev 18 and 20). Klawans explains that ritual
impurity arises from physical substances and states that are not in themselves sinful—corpses and carcasses, genital fluxes, skin disease/mold (to be
discussed in greater detail below). Ritual impurity, which is in general permitted, is distinguished by the following characteristic features: (1) It is contagious, transferred, for example, by physical contact or by sharing space
with a source of severe impurity in a covered area; (2) it is impermanent and
can be reduced and removed by some combination of ablutions, time, and/
or ritual observances; and (3) it defiles (which simply means "renders impure") sancta and must be kept separate from it. In severe cases, it defiles
even common objects, and isolation or exclusion of the source of impurity
or the defiled individual may be necessary.

   The concept of ritual impurity was a central and integral feature of
most, if not all, ancient religions. The biblical laws of purity and impurity
strongly resemble those of other ancient Near East cultures—the Egyptians, Mesopotamians, and the ancient Hittites. Certainly there are ancient
Near Eastern and Canaanite roots for many Israelite purity practices. However, the system of ritual purity and impurity as crafted in the priestly writings of the Hebrew Bible represents an attempt to "monotheize" Israelite
purity practices and to create a system that differentiated Israel culturally
from her close neighbors. So for example, impurity was often connected
with a belief in evil spirits and impure demons, and it is quite possible that
Israel's purification rituals originated in, and even long endured as, rituals
of exorcism expelling a demon who was believed to cause the affliction in
question. But in the priestly writings, impurity is, by and large, divorced

from any association with evil spirits. Some scholars theorize that the ritual purity system reflects an original concern with health or hygiene, but this is not very convincing. Only one set of diseases is said to generate ritual impurity, and many substances widely considered unhygienic, such as human and animal excrement, are not sources of ritual impurity in the priestly source. Klawans is among those who insist that any effort to understand the purpose and meaning of Israelite purity practices as systematized by the monotheizing priestly writings in Lev 12–16 would do better to ignore the question of origins and attend to the larger symbolism of impurity and holiness as actually constructed in those writings, in particular the antithetical relationship between impurity and holiness.

Klawans points out that the three main sources of ritual impurity in P are (1) corpses and certain animal carcasses, (2) *zara'at,* skin diseases in humans (a decomposition of the flesh associated with death; see Num 12:12, Job 18:13) and related fungal growths in fabrics and houses, and (3) genital discharges, both normal and diseased. Klawans notes that the physical substances and states labeled impure and thus antithetical to the realm of holiness are associated with death and procreation. Why should this be? The priestly conception of Israel's deity is of an immortal and asexual being (as is clear in the first, or priestly, creation story). To enter the realm of the holy, in which there is neither death nor procreation, requires a separation from death and procreation. Thus, it is an association with death and sexuality that renders one impure and disqualifies one from entering the holy sanctuary. That is not to say that one must not deal with death or sexuality in the ordinary course of life. On the contrary, Yahweh explicitly commands humans to be fruitful and multiply (in the P source no less) and to take proper care of the dead. However, one may not enter the holy sanctuary, Yahweh's realm, when "impure" through contact with death or sexuality. According to Klawans, ritual purification involved separation from those aspects of humanity (death and sex) that are least godlike.[2] To enter Yahweh's realm requires imitation of Yahweh, or *imitatio dei.*

Klawans further argues that the concept of *imitatio dei* also explains the practice of sacrifice—which on the face of it contradicts the idea of avoiding death in connection with the holy, since it entails taking life right in the sanctuary. Klawans argues that "sacrifice involves—in part—the controlled exercise of complete power over an animal's life and death," which is "precisely one of the powers that Israel's god exercises over human beings."[3] Because sacrifice involves a variety of behaviors analogous to behaviors attributed to Yahweh elsewhere in the Bible, the process of sacrifice grants the offerer complete control over life and death and can be understood as an act of *imitatio dei.*

But Klawans asserts that "*imitatio dei* does not exhaustively explain sacrifice in ancient Israel"[4]—indeed, no single theory does. He describes two organizing principles or overriding concerns in the priestly traditions regarding sacrifice. The first is, as we have seen, *imitatio dei.* The second is the desire to attract and maintain the continued presence of Yahweh in the sanctuary.[5] The majority of the sacrifices described in the opening chapters of Leviticus are voluntary sacrifices offered as gifts or in times of celebration. They include (1) the whole or "burnt" offering in which an animal is entirely burned to create a pleasant-smelling smoke (according to P, priests were to offer two such burnt offerings to Yahweh each day); (2) the grain offering, a gift of flour, oil, and incense burned after removal of a portion for the priests; and (3) the well-being offering, which was consumed by the offerer and his family in a feast, after the donation of certain portions to the priests. Well-being offerings are of three main types: a thanksgiving offering, a freewill offering, and a vow offering. These sacrifices are entirely optional and are offered in celebration and thanksgiving or upon the successful completion of a vow. In other words, the sacrificial cult was primarily a vehicle for worshippers' expression of a wide range of emotions—joy over the birth of child, thankfulness for a good harvest, and so on.

Texts from ancient Near Eastern cultures suggest that a central function of the rituals performed in sanctuaries was to secure the perpetual aid of a well-disposed deity. In important ways the Israelite cult was strikingly similar. The Israelites certainly hoped to secure the perpetual aid, blessing, and protection of a well-disposed deity. They believed that blessing and benefaction flowed from Yahweh's presence in the midst of the community and that the rituals performed in the sanctuary were designed to ensure Yahweh's continued residence within and blessing of the community. In particular, the burnt offerings sacrificed by the priests twice daily and emitting a pleasing odor were an effort to attract the deity. Likewise, the gifts, food, and pleasing odors of the sacrifices brought by individual worshippers attracted and maintained the continued presence of Yahweh in the sanctuary.

## Moral Impurity

Just as Yahweh is attracted by some behaviors, he is repelled by others. Grave sins generate an impurity—a moral impurity—that repels the divine presence. Moral impurity is the second kind of impurity described by Klawans.

In contrast to ritual impurity, moral impurity arises from the commission of certain heinous sins, specifically idolatry, homicide, and the sexual transgressions spelled out in Lev 18 and 20. Besides defiling the sinner, moral impurity symbolically defiles various sancta, especially the sanctuary, Yahweh's holy name, and the holy land itself. Moral impurity differs from ritual impurity not only in its origin in sinful behavior but also in the fact that it is not contagious (one does not contract impurity by touching a murderer, for example). Nor is it removed from persons by rituals of bathing and laundering. Moral purity of persons can be achieved only by punishment for heinous sins (such as *karet*, the divine penalty of "cutting-off," or death); atonement for unwitting sins that are later realized, acknowledged, and regretted; or abstention from defiling immoral acts in the first instance. Severe moral impurity defiles the innermost areas of the sanctuary as well as the land. While the sanctuary can be purified of moral impurity (we'll return to this point), land that is repeatedly defiled by sexual transgressions cannot, and eventually it will simply "vomit out" those who dwell upon it (a reference to exile; this is consistent with the priestly representation of the expulsion of the Canaanites from Yahweh's land and repeated warnings to the Israelites not to engage in similar abominable and sinful practices lest they, too, be expelled from the land). The land is also defiled by illicit homicide, whether intentional or unintentional (Num 35:33–34). The manslayer bears "bloodguilt"—a kind of moral impurity—and his life is forfeit. In cases of deliberate murder, bloodguilt and impurity are removed only by the death of the murderer. In cases of accidental homicide, the perpetrator may take refuge in one of five cities designated for this purpose until the death of the high priest, which serves to remove the bloodguilt and impurity of the homicide. Idolatry also defiles the land. Offenders are subject to stoning and the divine penalty of *karet* (cutting off). The Bible repeatedly warns that idols and their cultic appurtenances must be completely destroyed from the holy land (for burning, see Ex 32:20, Deut 7:5, 25, 2 Kgs 10:26; for burying, see Gen 35:4).

In contrast to the land, Yahweh's sanctuary can be purified from moral impurity by means of a special sacrifice: the *ḥattat* sacrifice, often erroneously translated as "sin offering" but more accurately translated as "purification offering." How does the "purification offering" operate? The blood of the sacrifice is the key to the ritual. Just as impurity and sin are associated with death, holiness is associated with life. According to the priestly source, blood represents the life force. This is explicit in the blood prohibition in Gen 9:4, "You must not, however, eat flesh with its life-blood in it," and Lev

17:11, "For the life of the flesh is in the blood, and I have assigned it to you for making expiation for your lives upon the altar; it is the blood as life that effects expiation." The priestly texts couldn't be clearer. Blood represents life, and the blood of sacrificial animals is assigned by Yahweh as a "detergent" to cleanse the sanctuary of the impurities caused by the sinful deeds of the Israelites. All of the sacrifices that purge the sanctuary of ritual and moral impurity—the *hatta't* sacrifices primarily—involve the manipulation of blood. Daubing it on the altar and, on Yom Kippur, sprinkling it on the ark cover itself purifies the defiled object and so symbolizes the victory of the forces of life and holiness over death and impurity. Other purificatory rites involve the use of reddish substitutes as surrogates of blood.

## Atonement

It is widely and mistakenly thought that the purification offering (*hatta't*) purifies the ritual impurity bearer or sinner. But this cannot be true. One can never approach the sanctuary or offer a sacrifice unless one is ritually pure. Purification offerings are brought *after* the genital flux has passed, *after* the scale disease has healed, *after* the appropriate ablutions have been observed. Nor does the *hatta't* rid the sinner of his *moral* impurity because the offering is brought after the sinner has confessed and repented. The offering acts on the sanctuary, purging it of the defilement it symbolically suffered from the offerer's state of ritual impurity or sinfulness. Once the sanctuary is purged, the offerer has settled his debt, repaired the damage he caused, and is fully atoned—"at one" again with Yahweh. Yahweh is no longer repelled by the presence of an impurity that mars his sanctuary.

The defiling effect of lesser transgressions is calibrated to the sinner's intentionality and the presence or absence of repentance. The sanctuary defilement caused by inadvertent sins can be purged by bringing a purification sacrifice. Moreover, deliberate sins that are repented are reduced in severity to the level of unintentional sins—the sanctuary defilement caused by them can then be purged by bringing a purification sacrifice also. By contrast, brazen, unrepented sins and unintentional sins that are never realized stand unremedied. For this reason, the sanctuary must be regularly purged of the accumulated defilements accruing to it as a result of these sins. Leviticus 16 describes the annual ritual carried out on Yom Kippur (the Day of Atonement). A *hatta't* sacrifice is brought on behalf of the entire community to purify the sanctuary of the impurity caused by Israel's sins—particularly brazen, unrepentant sins and unintentional, unrecognized sins. The high priest loads all of the sins and impurities of the Israelites over the head of a goat, which then carries them off into the wilderness away from the sanctuary.

According to Lev 10:10, it is the duty of the priests to teach Israel the distinction between pure and impure on the one hand and holy and common (or profane) on the other so as to avoid impermissible contacts between the holy and the impure. For Yahweh to dwell in Israel's midst requires a ritually pure and holy area in the community (the sanctuary compound).

Purification of the sanctuary is critical to the health and well-being of the community. If the sanctuary is not purged of impurity, it can become polluted to the point that Yahweh is entirely driven out. Jacob Milgrom has argued that there is an Archimedean principle at work here.[6] Every sin creates impurity that displaces or encroaches upon the realm of holiness. Eventually, Yahweh will be displaced and the community left in a godless state—without blessing or protection. Milgrom describes the symbolic function of Israel's purity system in this way: If the sanctuary symbolizes the presence of Yahweh and if impurity represents the wrongdoing of persons, then by saying that impurity is anathema to Yahweh and pollutes his Temple, the priests are able graphically to convey the idea that sin forces Yahweh out of his sanctuary and out of the community. Milgrom describes what he sees as the moral message at the root of this complex symbolic picture: Human actions determine the degree to which Yahweh can dwell on earth among his people. Humans and humans alone are responsible for the reign of wickedness and death or the reign of righteousness and life in their society. The objective of the priestly construction or representation of Israel's impurity laws was to sever impurity from the demonic and reinterpret it as a symbolic system reminding Israel of the divine imperative to reject sin—to behave in ways that attract the presence of Yahweh and do not repel him.

## Priestly Theodicy

Milgrom argues that priestly cultic imagery served as a theodicy, or response to the problem of evil.[7] How can an all-powerful, good deity allow so much evil to exist and even go unpunished? Here is the priestly answer: Every sin pollutes the sanctuary. In other words, while sin may not scar the face of the sinner, it does scar the face of the sanctuary. No wicked deed is therefore without some eventual consequence. The sinner may think he has escaped punishment for his sin, but in fact every act of social exploitation, moral corruption, and cruelty leaves its mark on the sanctuary, polluting it more and more until such time as Yahweh is driven out entirely and human society is consumed by its own viciousness and death dealing. Again, according to Milgrom, the ethical message is that humans are entirely in control of their destiny and the action of every individual influences the fate of society. This is the priestly version of the old doctrine of collective responsibility: Sin affects the entire fabric of society. There is no such thing as an isolated evil—our deeds affect others. And when evildoers are finally punished, they bring others down with them. Yet, those who perish with the wicked are not entirely blameless. After all, they allowed the wicked to flourish and so contributed to the pollution of the sanctuary, that is, the corruption of society. In short, P is informed by the same communal ethic that runs through so much of the Bible until a later period. P simply couches that communal ethic in its own modality—the symbolism of the sanctuary and the cult.

## Dietary Laws

The eleventh chapter of Leviticus contains the dietary laws. Milgrom has argued that the dietary laws of Leviticus are also part of a symbolic system that emphasizes life over death.[8] He points to the major prohibitions of the dietary system as evidence: First, the consumption of animal blood is prohibited in Gen 9:4. In Leviticus, the distinction between permitted and prohibited animals is policed by the double criteria of chewing the cud and possessing split hooves—criteria that seem arbitrary and meaningless in themselves but serve jointly to limit the number of animals that may be eaten to a mere handful out of the many hundreds of living creatures. Milgrom hypothesizes that whatever the origin of various food taboos in Israel may have been, Israel's priests tried to construct a dietary discipline that drives home the point that all life (*nefesh*), even animal life, is inviolable. The one exception, conceded by Yahweh, is the killing of a small number of eligible animals for consumption, provided that the animal is slaughtered properly (i.e., painlessly) and its blood (i.e., its life) is drained and thereby returned to Yahweh.

Milgrom's argument that the system of dietary laws as configured and represented by Israel's priests serves to emphasize reverence for life is a persuasive one. At the same time, these laws serve another important purpose— the formation and maintenance of a differentiated ethnic identity or, in priestly parlance, the formation and maintenance of a holy people separated out from other nations by rules that mark her as Yahweh's people. It is surely significant that the dietary laws are followed by a powerful exhortation to be holy in imitation of Yahweh. Leviticus 11:43–45 reads:

> You shall not draw abomination upon yourselves through any-
> thing that swarms; you shall not make yourselves impure there-
> with and thus become impure. For I Yahweh am your god
> [Elohim]: you shall sanctify yourselves and be holy, for I am
> holy. You shall not make yourselves impure through any swarm-
> ing thing that moves upon the earth. For I Yahweh am he who
> brought you up from the land of Egypt to be your god: you shall
> be holy, for I am holy.[9]

In short, the dietary laws are presented by the priests not as a hygienic regi-
men or as a sensible way to avoid various diseases caused by the lack of re-
frigeration in the desert. Whatever the actual origin of these various dietary
taboos, they are here embedded in a larger ideological framework concerning the need for the people to separate themselves and be holy like their
god, Yahweh. The dietary laws are connected with the theme of *imitatio
dei,* imitation of the deity: As Yahweh is holy (separate and distinct), so you
shall be holy.

## Primary Themes of the Holiness Code

The theme of holiness and especially the exhortation "You shall be holy, for
I, Yahweh your god, am holy" find their fullest expression in Lev 17–26, a
block of text appropriately dubbed the Holiness Code by modern scholars.
There is an important difference between Lev 1–16 and the Holiness Code.
According to Lev 1–16, the priests are a holy class within Israel. They are
singled out by, and dedicated to the service of, Yahweh. Yahweh has assigned them a holy status by separating them to himself and his service and
marking and guarding that separation with various rules and prohibitions
that are incumbent only on them. Israelites may aspire to holiness, but it is
not assumed. However, the Holiness Code that runs from Lev 17 to the end
of the book comes closer to the idea that all of Israel is holy—by virtue of the
fact that Yahweh has set Israel apart from the nations to himself, to belong to
him, just as he set apart the seventh day to himself, to belong to him.

It is only with safeguards that holiness can exist in the created world,
for rules and safeguards keep the holy separate from that which has the
potential to destroy it. These safeguards are naturally addressed to humans

who are charged with the task of preserving the holy in its residence on earth. Thus, although holiness derives from Yahweh, humans play a crucial role in sanctifying the world. This is illustrated well in the case of the Sabbath. The deity sanctified the Sabbath at creation, but Israel must affirm its sanctity by observing those rules and prohibitions that mark it off as holy. Indeed, Israel is doing more than just affirming its holy status. Israel in fact actualizes the holy status of the Sabbath, for if Israel does not observe the prohibitions that distinguish the Sabbath as sacred, the Sabbath is automatically dese-crated (Ex 31:14). "You shall keep the sabbath, for it is holy for you. He who profanes it shall be put to death: whoever does work on it, that person shall be cut off from among his kin." There are therefore two components that are integral and inseparable aspects of the one concept of holiness: (1) initial as-signment of holy status by Yahweh ("selection") and establishment of rules that preserve that holy status in a world that contains threats to it (prohibi-tions) and (2) actualization of a sanctum's holiness by humans (through the observance of positive commandments or negative prohibitions in regard to the sanctum).

Thus, just as the Sabbath is automatically desecrated if the rules that distinguish it as holy are not observed, so Israel's status as a holy people is not actualized or preserved unless Israel observes the rules that distinguish it from the other nations and mark it as the special possession of the deity, as holy. Those rules, many of which are elaborated in H, are the laws and regula-tions of the covenant that mark Israel as distinct from other nations. Indeed, Israel's status as a holy nation, as Yahweh's special possession, is always con-nected with an exhortation to faithfully observe all the details of the Torah or certain key elements thereof, such as the Sabbath or the dietary laws:

> You shall sanctify yourselves and be holy, for I, Yahweh, am your god. You shall faithfully observe my laws: I, Yahweh, make you holy. (Lev 20:7–8)

> Thus you shall be reminded to observe all my commandments and to be holy to your god. (Num 15:40, Lev 22:31–32)

The election of Israel, her holy status, is inseparable from the observance of the teachings and obligations of Yahweh, for they are precisely what sets her apart from other nations.

From the foregoing it is clear that holiness involves a collaboration of divine effort and human effort. This collaboration reaches its most profound expression in the priestly source in the idea that Yahweh and Israel sanctify each other. First, Yahweh sanctifies Israel: Having redeemed Israel, Yahweh made Israel his own special possession from among the nations, sealing the relationship with the giving of a covenant whose instructions would serve as the blueprint for Israel's holy vocation. In turn, Israel sanctifies Yahweh by living out that vocation, by faithfully observing the commandments, and by becoming a holy people. Israel's failure will be a profanation of Yahweh's name, that is, his reputation, which will be sullied in the eyes of all who observe Israel's failure and wickedness. But if Israel succeeds in her sacred calling, Yahweh, too, will be known as holy. In the covenant relationship, Yahweh and Israel meet in a reciprocal sanctification. This is the language, logic, and meaning of Lev 22:31–32.

> You shall faithfully observe my commandments; I am Yahweh.
> You shall not profane my holy name, so that I may be sanctified
> in the midst of the Israelite people—I, Yahweh, who sanctify
> you, I who brought you out of the land of Egypt to be your god,
> I, Yahweh.

What are the moral implications of the holiness model? Holiness in the Holiness Code is a status that is imparted by Yahweh but that is only actualized and preserved by that essential partner in the process—Israel. Holiness in the priestly source must be understood as a divine-human collaboration that awards to humans a huge responsibility. To depict Israel as Yahweh's essential partner in the process of sanctification is to represent humans as full-fledged moral agents, each a powerful force for good (or evil) in the world. Yahweh's battle to sanctify his creation can be Israel's battle. If Israel chooses to turn away, and does not observe the rules, norms, or prohibitions that actualize and preserve sanctity, namely, the laws of Yahweh's Torah, then despite Yahweh's best efforts, desecration occurs: The realm of the holy in the world shrinks. Israel can choose to join with Yahweh in preserving and extending holiness—be it the holiness of objects, time, places, or the community itself—or Israel can drive Yahweh and holiness from the world. This is the moral vision at the heart of the priestly concept of holiness.

## Conclusion

The priestly source of the Pentateuch and particularly the sacrificial and purity systems set forth in Leviticus transformed older Israelite rituals and traditions into symbolic practices that communicated basic convictions about morality and holiness and expounded a communal ethic in addition to an individual morality. Unfortunately, modern critical scholarship often maligned these materials as spiritually impoverished, due to the antipriest, anticult sentiment of European Protestantism. Thus, for Wellhausen, the priestly source with its emphasis on cult and ritual had to represent a late and degenerate stage in the evolution of Israelite religion. According to Wellhausen, the premonarchic period of ancient Israel's history (the patriarchal and early tribal period down to approximately 1000 B.C.E.) was characterized by a free and natural form of religion unsullied by the legalistic and cultic "obsessions" of the priests and their cult. In 586, however, Jerusalem lay in ruins, and the Israelites were sent into exile. It was then in Babylon and in subsequent decades, Wellhausen said, that the priests were able to assume control. Playing on the exiles' overwhelming feelings of guilt and failure, they constructed a new identity and religion that stressed the sinfulness of the people, the need for ritual purity, ritual observance, and legalism as the road back to Yahweh. This, according to Wellhausen, was a degeneration.[10]

Wellhausen's reconstruction of the evolution of Israelite religion is driven more by theological prejudice than by historical evidence and stems from an obvious projection of the Protestant-Catholic tension onto Israelite history and a Christian secessionist account of Judaism as moribund at the time of Jesus. This is not to say that scholars today who date P to the postexilic period are motivated by the same problematic assumptions. Not at all. Scholars of all stripes and allegiances view P as late, and there is some good objective evidence for dating some layers of P (those that serve a redactional and framing purpose) as well as H to the postexilic period.

Most modern scholars would agree that P reached its *final* form in the exilic or postexilic period, as did Deuteronomy and the Pentateuch generally. Nevertheless, there are many data that suggest that the priestly source retains early strata (particularly the ritual and cultic instructions at the core of Leviticus), just as D contains preexilic material. First, postexilic priests turn increasingly to an individual ethic, but P espouses a communal ethic. Second, some sections of P do not assume a central sanctuary, while other sections do. More significant, P contains no universal prohibition of intermarriage, nor does it employ impurity rhetoric to mark an inseparable boundary between classes within Israel or between Israelites and non-Israelite "others." Prohibitions of intermarriage and the use of impurity rhetoric to inscribe boundaries between Israel and other nations emerge in some priestly circles in the postexilic period, and it is difficult to understand P's silence in this regard if it stems entirely from postexilic priestly circles.

Instead of charting an evolution, or rather degeneration, of Israelite religion from JE and D to P as in classical source critical theory, many scholars prefer to see three distinct and roughly contemporaneous strands of ancient Israelite tradition, transmitted and developed over centuries and crystallizing into final form at various times. Thus, we may hypothesize as follows: JE has fragments that are quite old and reached its final form before the centralization of the cult in 622, D contains northern traditions from before 722 that were propounded in late-seventh-century Judah but reached a final redacted form in the exile, and P likewise contains older traditions that reached their full and final redacted form in the exilic or postexilic period. Each of these complex, multilayered sources possesses its own emphases, agenda, and perspectives that at times complement and at times challenge one another but are not best seen as steps in a linear progression. Their diversity has not been flattened or homogenized by a final editor but preserved in a manner that stimulates reflection and debate.

## CHAPTER 11

# On the Steps of Moab

## Deuteronomy and the Figure of Moses

*Readings:* Deuteronomy 1–14, 27–34

### The Figure of Moses

Postbiblical tradition hails Moses as ancient Israel's first and greatest law-giver. Certainly, the biblical narrative depicts Moses as receiving the Torah from Yahweh and conveying it to the Israelites. Yet clearly, Moses is not the compiler of these laws. As noted in Chapter 9, some of the individual laws have roots in older ancient Near Eastern legal tradition, while each of the collections as a whole dates to a later period and is retrojected back to the period in Israel's history in which Moses is said to have lived.

Nevertheless, Moses is the central character in the narrative that extends from Exodus through Deuteronomy, and he serves as a paradigm for Israel's leaders to follow. Yahweh says that none can look upon his face and live (Ex 33:20), yet Moses is described by the biblical narrator as interacting face to face with the deity (Deut 34:10). Clearly, he is an exceptional figure. Why then was he not permitted to see the fulfillment of his labors? Why was he not permitted to enter the Promised Land?

This question must have plagued those who transmitted the traditions of Moses' leadership and life, and the Bible reflects an effort to explain Moses' death on the east side of the Jordan River. When Moses asks to enter the land (Deut 3:25), Yahweh refuses and gives the following reason:

> You shall die on the mountain that you are about to ascend, and
> shall be gathered to your kin, as your brother Aaron died on
> Mount Hor and was gathered to his kin; for you both broke faith
> with me among the Israelite people, at the waters of Meribath-
> kadesh in the wilderness of Zin, by failing to uphold my sanctity
> among the Israelite people. You may view the land from a dis-
> tance, but you shall not enter it—the land that I am giving to the
> Israelite people. (Deut 32:50–52)

What happened at Meribath-kadesh to make Yahweh so angry? The incident is described in Num 20, but the answer is not entirely clear. Perhaps it
is Moses' failure to follow Yahweh's instructions to the letter when producing water for the Israelites that angers him. This answer doesn't satisfy, and
one has the impression that the story in Numbers and Deuteronomy's subsequent claim that it incurred Yahweh's disapproval are an attempt to explain a
long-standing tradition about a great leader who died without entering the
Promised Land. For this to have happened, these writers surmise, he must
have sinned.

After a poignant scene in which Yahweh shows Moses the Promised
Land from a lookout point on the east side of the Jordan, we read of Moses'
death:

> That very day Yahweh spoke to Moses: Ascend these heights of
> Abarim to Mount Nebo, which is in the land of Moab facing
> Jericho, and view the land of Canaan, which I am giving the Is-
> raelites as their holding. (Deut 32:8–9)

> Moses went up from the steppes of Moab to Mount Nebo, to the
> summit of Pisgah, opposite Jericho, and Yahweh showed him the
> whole land: Gilead as far as Dan; all Naphtali; the land of
> Ephraim and Manasseh; the whole land of Judah as far as the
> Western Sea, the Negeb; and the Plain—the Valley of Jericho,
> the city of palm trees—as far as Zoar. And Yahweh said to him,
> "This is the land of which I swore to Abraham, Isaac, and Jacob.
> 'I will assign it to your offspring,' I have let you see it with your
> own eyes, but you shall not cross there." (Deut 34:1–3)

> So Moses the servant of Yahweh died there, in the land of Moab,
> at the command of Yahweh. He buried him in the valley in the

land of Moab, near Beth Peor; and no one knows his burial place to this day. . . . And the Israelites bewailed Moses in the steppes of Moab for thirty days. . . . Never again did there arise in Israel a prophet like Moses—whom Yahweh singled out, face to face, for the various signs and portents that Yahweh sent him to display in the land of Egypt against Pharaoh and all his courtiers and his whole country, and for all the great might and awesome power that Moses displayed before all Israel. (Deut 34:5–6, 8, 10–12)

No other human being in the Bible earns such a tribute.

The force of Moses as a paradigmatic leader of Israel is apparent in the very first leader to succeed him—Joshua. The book of Deuteronomy closes with a transfer of authority from Moses to Joshua.

Now Joshua son of Nun was filled with the spirit of wisdom because Moses had laid his hands upon him; and the Israelites heeded him, doing as Yahweh had commanded Moses. (34:9)

In several ways, Joshua seems to replicate Moses (Coogan, *Old Testament,* 199–201): Moses brings the Israelites across the reed sea, the waters standing in a heap and the people crossing on dry land; Joshua brings the Israelites across the Jordan River into the Promised Land, the waters standing in a heap and the people crossing on dry land (Josh 3:13, 4:7, 5:1). After the crossing, the Israelites observe the Passover, creating a strong link to the Exodus led by Moses at the time of the first Passover (Josh 5:10). Moses beholds the vision of a burning bush and is told to remove his shoes because he is on holy ground; Joshua beholds the vision of a man with a drawn sword who tells him to remove his shoes because he is on holy ground (5:13–15). Moses mediates a covenant between Yahweh and Israel at Sinai; Joshua mediates a renewal of the covenant at Shechem (Josh 24). Moses sends spies to scout out the land, and Joshua sends spies to scout out the land (Josh 2:1). Moses holds out a rod during battle so that Israel will prevail over her enemies, and Joshua holds out his javelin for the same reason (8:18–20).

All of these parallels indicate the narrative importance of Moses as the paradigmatic leader of the Israelites. Indeed, it is said of Joshua after the Israelites cross into the Promised Land: "On that day Yahweh exalted Joshua in the sight of all Israel, so that they revered him all his days as they had revered Moses" (Josh 4:14). No greater praise can be given to a leader than to be compared to Moses.

## Deuteronomy

Israel's wanderings end on the plains of Moab on the east bank of the Jordan River, and it is there that the book of Deuteronomy opens.[1] According to Exodus and Leviticus, Israel received Yahweh's laws at Mt. Sinai, but in Deuteronomy, Moses imparts the full instructions on the plains of Moab, forty years after Sinai and just before the Israelites cross the Jordan. As the Israelites stand poised to enter the Promised Land, Moses delivers three long speeches, which constitute the bulk of the book of Deuteronomy.

Deuteronomy differs stylistically from the other four books of the Pentateuch, which feature an anonymous narrator who describes Yahweh directing his words to Moses, who then speaks on Yahweh's behalf to Israel. But in much of Deuteronomy, Moses speaks directly to the people so that the book is written almost entirely in the first person. Moshe Weinfeld, a leading scholar of Deuteronomy, describes the book as expressing the writer's ideology in a programmatic speech that is placed into the mouth of an ancient great leader[2] (pseudepigraphical writing of this kind is a common practice in Israelite—as in much ancient—historiography).

The basic structure of Deuteronomy is as follows:

1:1–4:43—An introduction to the book including the Israelites' location and Moses' first speech. The speech provides a didactic historical review from Sinai to the present day, underscoring Yahweh's fulfillment of his covenantal promises and urging the Israelites to do their part by obeying his laws.

4:44–28:6—Moses' second speech. This speech also contains a historical review and retells much of the narrative of the earlier books of the Torah (with modifications that reflect a process of inner-biblical interpretation), as well as a central section of laws (Deut 12–26). This central portion of laws is thought to be the earliest core of the book (see below). The Greek title for the book, Deuteronomy, means "repetition of the law" or "second law" and derives from the fact that the bulk of the book consists of a review of the law (again, with modification, revisions, and updates). Chapter 27 describes a covenant renewal ceremony that will take place at Mt. Ebal near Shechem once the Israelites have crossed the Jordan. In ancient Greece, settlers who colonized a new locality at divine instigation would perform ceremonies accompanied by blessings and curses, write sacred laws on stone pillars, build an altar, and offer a sacrifice. These elements all appear in Deut 27's covenant renewal ceremony: The Israelites will erect stones on Mt. Ebal to record the words of the covenant, build an altar for sacrifices, and proclaim blessings and curses. Chapter 28 lists the material rewards that will accrue to Israel if she obeys Yahweh's law and the punishments if she should disobey. The importance of the Deuteronomist's view of history—in which Israel's fate is totally conditioned on her obedience to the covenant—will occupy us in Chapter 14.

29–30—Moses' third speech. This speech emphasizes the degree to which evil fortune is the community's own responsibility. Moses enumerates additional sufferings that will befall Israel if she sins. But, he emphasizes, Israel has a choice. Yahweh has been clear regarding what is required, and it is not beyond Israel's reach to attain life and prosperity:

Surely, this Instruction which I enjoin upon you this day is not too baffling for you, nor is it beyond reach. It is not in the heavens, that you should say, "Who among us can go up to the heavens and get it for us and impart it to us, that we may observe it?" Neither is it beyond the sea, that you should say, "Who among us can cross to the other side of the sea and get it for us and impart it to us, that we may observe it?" No, the thing is very close to you, in your mouth and in your heart, to observe it.

See, I set before you this day life and prosperity, death and adversity. For I command you this day, to love Yahweh your god, to walk in his ways, and to keep his commandments, his laws, and his rules, that you may thrive and increase, and that Yahweh your god may bless you in the land that you are about to enter and possess. But if your heart turns away and you give no heed, and are lured into the worship and service of other gods, I declare to you this day that you shall certainly perish; you shall not long endure on the soil that you are crossing the Jordan to enter and possess. I call heaven and earth to witness against you this day: I have put before you life and death, blessing and curse. Choose life—if you and your offspring would live—by loving Yahweh your god, heeding his commands, and holding fast to him. For thereby you shall have life and shall long endure upon

the soil that Yahweh your god swore to your ancestors, Abraham, Isaac, and Jacob, to give to them. (30:11–20)

All has been given—Israel need only choose to take it.

> 31–34—A series of miscellaneous appendices. Ancient poetry is
> found in the Song of Moses in chapter 32 and the Blessing of
> Moses in chapter 33. Chapter 34 is the story of Moses' death.

Centuries ago, scholars of the Bible noted that Deuteronomy opens with the
verse "These are the words that Moses addressed to all Israel on the other
side of the Jordan," that is, the trans-Jordan. This line is obviously written
from the perspective of someone inside the land of Canaan, looking eastward across the Jordan and describing, in the third person, Moses' speech to
the Israelites before his death in the trans-Jordan. That person could not, of
course, be Moses since Moses never entered the land. Likewise, the last
chapter describing Moses' death and burial could not have been written by
him. Many other textual features point to a period of composition centuries
after the time Moses is supposed to have lived.

Through careful analysis, scholars like Moshe Weinfeld and Bernard
Levinson,[3] have concluded that the original core of Deuteronomy emerged
in the eighth century B.C.E.—probably as a scroll of laws known as the "scroll
of the law [Torah]" (Deut 17:19–20) and roughly equivalent to chapters 12–26
with perhaps a short introduction and conclusion. These laws were put into
the framework of a speech by Moses (chapters 5–11 and 28) in the eighth to
seventh century B.C.E. At some later point, presumably during the exile
(586–538 B.C.E.), framing chapters were added (Deut 1–4 and 31–34), and laws
were updated and passages expanded to reflect the experience of exile (sixth
century B.C.E.). Additionally, Deuteronomy was incorporated into, and
served as the introduction to, the narrative history (referred to as the Deuteronomistic history) that runs from Joshua through 2 Kings. Finally, and
probably in the postexilic period (536 B.C.E. on), Deuteronomy was appended
to the four newly redacted books—Genesis to Numbers—serving as their
conclusion and conferring the title of Torah found in Deut 12 upon them as
well, by implication.

There is much debate over the precise timing of these literary events,
but the postexilic period (post-536 B.C.E.) is the likely time in which this
entire unit—Genesis to Numbers and the lengthy historical appendage
Deuteronomy to 2 Kings—was solidified. The Deuteronomistic history is

an odd conclusion to the Genesis-Numbers material in a way because the expected narrative climax—entry into the land under Moses—does not occur. Levinson suggests that deferring Israel's possession of the land to the future may reflect the historical experience of exile, an experience that challenged the very idea of possession of the land as central to the maintenance of the covenant.[4]

The complex process by which Deuteronomy was formed underscores the fact that modern notions of authorship cannot be applied to biblical texts. Moderns tend to think of an author as an autonomous individual who composes a text at a specific time, but this is not the way important communal texts came into being in the ancient world. As Weinfeld points out, the biblical authors were collectors, compilers, revisers, editors, and interpreters of ancient traditions. Ancient texts were generally the product of many hands over a long stretch of time (perhaps centuries) in which modifications and recontextualizations occurred. We refer to those who transmit and develop a text as a "school"—but this should be understood in a very informal way to refer to authors, compilers, and redactors whose work is connected by common language, themes, and content. Scholars speak of the Deuteronomic school that produced Deuteronomy and the Deuteronomistic school that produced the Deuteronomistic history through 2 Kings (i.e., a history informed by language, themes, and content found in Deuteronomy itself; see Chapters 12 and 13).

## Israel's Legal Collections

The author of Deuteronomy limits the revelation at Sinai to the Decalogue and asserts that the full law as conveyed in Deuteronomy was given to Moses for the Israelites only on the plains of Moab (Deut 5:19, 28:69).[5] The legal core of Deuteronomy (5–26) contains a somewhat expanded version of the Ten Commandments (Deut 5:6–21) and other laws (12–26) that resemble the legal material found in Ex 20–23 and bear some relation to the laws in Leviticus and Numbers. The question is—What is the relationship between these different versions of the same law? Some parallel each other closely; others do not. Are Deuteronomy's legal traditions direct responses to and modifications of the laws in Exodus, Leviticus, or Numbers, or are they best understood as different and independent formulations of a common legal tradition?

Scholars have argued that Deuteronomy revises and reforms previous traditions of the Pentateuch, in accordance with its new notion of centralized cultic worship as well as its humanitarian spirit.[6] The writers employed the literary convention of pseudepigraphy—attributing their work to Moses—as a way of authenticating and authorizing the reforms they advocated.[7] It is thought that Deuteronomy, with its many revisions, would have been seen as an updated replacement of the old book of the Covenant, rather than its complement.

For the most part, Deuteronomy omits much civil law, focusing on Yahweh's moral-religious prescriptions for Israel. The few civil laws that are included are clearly reworked in line with Deuteronomy's humanitarianism. Thus, the rules for the laws of the tithe and the seventh-year release of debts (15:1–11), the rules for the release of slaves (15:12–19), and the rules for the three festivals (16:1–17) are all ancient laws that occur in Exodus but appear in Deuteronomy with modifications reflecting the concerns of the Deuteronomist. A side-by-side comparison of the slave laws in Exodus and Deuteronomy reveals the way in which the Deuteronomist modifies earlier legal tradition.

| *Exodus 21:2–11* | *Deut 15:12–18* |
| --- | --- |
| **I. Six-year limit** | **I. Six-year limit** |
| 2. When you acquire a Hebrew slave, he shall serve six years; in the seventh year he shall go free, without payment. | 12. If a fellow Hebrew, man or woman, is sold to you, he shall serve you six years, and in the seventh year you shall set him free. |
| **II. Parting gifts** | **II. Parting gifts** |
| 3. If he came single, he shall leave single; if he had a wife, his wife shall leave with him. 4. If his master gave him a wife, and she has borne him children, the wife and her children shall belong to the master, and he shall leave alone. | 13. when you set him free, do not let him go empty handed. 14. Furnish him out of the flock, threshing floor, and vat, with which Yahweh your god has blessed you. 15. Bear in mind that you were slaves in the land of Egypt and Yahweh your god redeemed you; therefore I enjoin this commandment upon you today. |
| **III. Option of perpetual servitude** | **III. Option of perpetual servitude** |
| 5. But if the slave declares, "I love my master, and my wife and children: I do not wish to go free," 6. his master shall take | 16. But should he say to you, "I do not want to leave you"—for he loves you and your household and is happy with you—17. you shall take an awl and put |

*(continued)*

| *Exodus 21:2–11* | *Deut 15:12–18* |
|---|---|
| him before Elohim. He shall be brought to the door or the doorpost, and his master shall pierce his ear with an awl; and he shall then remain his slave for life. | it through his ear into the door, and he shall become your slave in perpetuity. |
| **IV. Treatment of the female** | **IV. Treatment of the female** |
| 7. When a man sells his daughter as a slave, she shall not be freed as male slaves are. | 18. Do the same with your female slave. |
| 8. If she proves to be displeasing to her master, who designated her for himself, he must let her be redeemed; he shall not have the right to sell her to outsiders, since he broke faith with her. | |
| 9. And if he designated her for his son, he shall deal with her as is the practice with free maidens. | |
| 10. If he marries another, he must not withhold from this one her food, her clothing, or her conjugal rights. | |
| 11. If he fails her in these three ways she shall go free, without payment. | |
| | **V. Exhortation** |
| | 18. When you do set him free, do not feel aggrieved; for in the six years he has given you double the service of a hired man. Moreover, Yahweh your god will bless you in all you do. |

The two passages deal with essentially the same law, moving from one topic to the next in the same sequence: the limitation of Hebrew slavery to six years, what to give upon the slave's release, the slave's option to remain a perpetual slave, the treatment of the female slave. Deuteronomy then adds an exhortation to follow its rules—if they seem difficult or unfair, know that they are not unfair and will bring Yahweh's blessing.

Despite the similarity in language and sequence, the differences between the two laws are stark. The Deuteronomy law appears to be patterned on the Exodus law in order to revise its terms. First, there is no separate procedure for male and female slaves in Deuteronomy. The Exodus law deals with the male slave first (Sections I–III) and then the female slave (Section IV). The different treatment of the female reveals that the primary function of the female slave is sexual. The Deuteronomy law modifies the Exodus law by noting specifically that the procedure for release or conversion to lifelong enslavement applies to both male and female slaves equally (Section IV), implying that like the male slave, the female slave is a household worker rather than a sexual partner. At precisely the point in the text where Exodus sets out the different terms for the female slave, Deuteronomy reiterates that the female is to be treated exactly as the male (Deut 15:18)—as if to "cancel" Exodus's separate and different provisions for the female altogether.

Second, while the Exodus law protects the rights of the master, the Deuteronomy law shows greater concern for the rights of the slave. In Exodus, if the master gives his slave a wife, she and any offspring of the union belong to the master and do not leave with the slave when his six years of service end. Thus, if the slave wishes to remain with his wife and children, he must renounce his freedom forever. This element of emotional blackmail is absent in Deuteronomy's version of the law. Indeed, the master must give his freed slave gifts to help establish him in his new life. Moreover, the master is exhorted not to consider this a hardship, since he has received inexpensive labor from the slave for six years (Section V). An exhortation of this kind is often a sign that a law is revising an older practice; particularly when the new law imposes greater hardship or sacrifice, its target audience must be urged to accept it. Third, the procedure to be followed in the event that a slave does renounce his freedom is secularized in Deuteronomy—the ear is pierced at the door of the master's home, rather than at the entrance of the sanctuary. This change flows from Deuteronomy's program of cult centralization, which by eliminating the performance of cultic rituals outside Jerusalem necessitated the secularization of many formerly sacral activities. Finally, in Deuteronomy, the law of slave release seems to be incorporated into the seven-year calendrical cycle. Thus, rather than each slave being released on an individual basis when his six years of enslavement is complete (as in Exodus), all slaves are released in the sabbatical year, regardless of when their own term of service actually began. To sum up, an older slave law in Exodus has been updated in a manner that reflects the interests and central themes of Deuteronomy—a greater humanitarianism, the centralization of the cult, and the establishment of a sabbatical cycle.

While the relationship of Deuteronomy to the laws in the Covenant Code is often—not always—one of revision, the relationship between Deuteronomy and the laws in the priestly source is more difficult to characterize. P seems to represent a somewhat contemporaneous and parallel set of legal traditions emanating from different circles and dealing with sacral topics or the sacral implications of general legal topics. Like the D source, P contains legal instructions that contradict legal traditions reflected in the Covenant Code. For example, P abolishes Israelite debt slavery altogether and insists that slaves may be acquired only from foreign nations. Moreover, P proclaims the return of all peoples to their original ancestral land holdings in the Jubilee year (the fiftieth year of the established calendar). This "reset" mechanism restores a fair and equitable distribution of wealth and eliminates the disparities between rich and poor that accrue over time. Leviticus 25:8–10 describes the release of the Jubilee year:

> You shall count off seven weeks of years—seven times seven years—so that the period of seven weeks of years gives you a total of forty-nine years. Then you shall sound the horn loud; in the seventh month, on the tenth day of the month—the Day of Atonement—you shall have the horn sounded throughout your land and you shall hallow the fiftieth year. You shall proclaim release throughout the land for all its inhabitants. It shall be a jubilee for you: each of you shall return to his holding and each of you shall return to his family.

The abolition of Israelite debt slavery is found in Lev 25:39–46, 55:

> If your kinsman under you continues in straits and must give himself over to you, do not subject him to the treatment of a slave. He shall remain with you as a hired or bound laborer; he shall serve with you only until the jubilee year. Then he and his children with him shall be free of your authority; he shall go back to his family and return to his ancestral holding. For they

are my [Yahweh's] servants, whom I freed from the land of Egypt; they may not give themselves over into servitude. You shall not rule over him ruthlessly; you shall fear your god. Such male and female slaves as you may have—it is from the nations round about you that you may acquire male and female slaves. You may also buy them from among the children of aliens resident among you, or from their families that are among you, whom they begot in your land. These shall become your property; you may keep them as a possession for your children after you, for them to inherit as property for all time. Such you may treat as slaves. But as for your Israelite kinsmen, no one shall rule ruthlessly over the other. . . . For it is to me that the Israelites are servants: they are my servants, whom I freed from the land of Egypt, I, Yahweh, your god.

Leviticus's abolition of Israelite debt slavery stems from its covenantal theology. All Israel are the "slaves" of Yahweh and no other. Thus, while an Israelite in extreme financial straits may "give himself over" to his creditor, he is not given over to his creditor as a slave. He works for the creditor, and is to be treated by the creditor, as a hired or bound laborer. Even then, he works only until the jubilee year, at which time he returns to the ancestral land holding he had originally lost.

What is the relationship between Lev 25 and the slave laws in Ex 21 and Deut 15? Certainly, Lev 25 does not exhibit features that would suggest direct literary dependence on Ex 21 in the way that Deut 15 does. D's law closely parallels the law in Exodus in style, structure, and language, suggesting that its composer consciously alluded to and modified, or rewrote, the earlier law. Leviticus 25's law does not echo the style, structure, and language of the Exodus law or the Deuteronomy law. Leviticus 25's instructions on Israelite debt slavery are an integral part of a larger socioeconomic vision ensuring the regular restoration of ancestral land holdings and the cyclical and equitable redistribution of wealth throughout the covenant community. In other words, Lev 25's instructions on Israelite debt slavery appear to be literarily independent of the laws in Exodus and Deuteronomy, expressing a different and competing tradition informed by sacral ideology.

Weinfeld ("Deuteronomy," 177) notes that when Deuteronomy contains laws found also in P, it sometimes presents them in a more rational or desacralized manner—thus D's treatment of sacrifice differs from that of P, as will be shown below. Rather than assuming a direct literary relationship between the two, scholars tend to view large sections of P and D as representing different and roughly contemporaneous streams of ancient Israelite tradition—each containing preexilic and exilic layers.

In short, close textual analysis and comparison leads Weinfeld and many others to conclude that the editors of Deuteronomy updated and revised earlier laws, particularly as reflected in the Covenant Code, in keeping with the circumstances of the eighth through sixth centuries. Deuteronomy thus exemplifies a phenomenon that occurs at several critical junctures in Israel's history—the modification and rewriting of earlier laws and traditions in light of new circumstances and ideas. As such, Deuteronomy is itself an implicit authorization of the process of interpretation. To the extent, then, that we think of the biblical corpus as a canon, it is a canon that allows for the continued unfolding or development of the sacred tradition. The idea of an evolving or flexible canon may seem at odds with modern intuitions about the nature of sacred canons—which are generally thought to be fixed, static, and authoritative precisely because unchanging. But such a view does not capture the reality of the biblical corpus. In Israelite culture, texts representing sacred revelation were modified, revised, updated, and interpreted in the process of transmission and preservation. Indeed, it was precisely because a text or tradition was sacred and authoritative that it was important that it adapt and speak to new circumstances.

## Cultic Centralization

What are the special circumstances and concerns that guide Deuteronomy's revisions? An overriding concern of Deuteronomy is the emphasis on the centralization of all cultic activity at a single shrine. The centralization of the cult represented a radical reform of Israelite religious practice. According to Moses' pronouncements in Deuteronomy, the central sanctuary would be located in a place Yahweh himself would choose—the place where he would cause his name to dwell (12:5, 11, 14). Jerusalem is never explicitly mentioned as the site of the future central sanctuary, though in fact Jerusalem came to fulfill this function.

The striking similarities between Deuteronomy's religious program and the major religious reforms carried out by the eighth-century Judean king Hezekiah and the seventh-century Judean king Josiah (in 622 B.C.E.) has long drawn the attention and speculation of scholars. According to the story in 2 Kgs 22, Temple repairs were undertaken in the time of King Josiah, in the course of which "the scroll of the Torah" was found. When the scroll was read, the king became very distressed because its requirements were not being upheld. The scroll called for the centralization of cultic worship at a central site and the destruction of outlying altars. Josiah took action, assembling the people and publicly reading the scroll. The people agreed to its terms, and Josiah's reforms began. We read that he purged the Temple of vessels made for Baal and Asherah, removed all foreign elements from the cult, and prohibited sacrifice to Yahweh everywhere but in the central sanctuary, destroying the rural shrines or "high places" throughout the countryside where local priests had offered sacrifices.

What was this scroll of the Torah that was "discovered" during Temple repairs. The scholarly consensus is that the scroll described in 2 Kgs 22 was Deuteronomy, or at least its legal core. First, the phrase "scroll of the Torah" appears once in the book of Deuteronomy but does not appear in Genesis through Numbers. Second, rural shrines and pillars in the worship of Yahweh are deemed to be legitimate in J and E; it is only Deuteronomy that contains instructions to destroy worship at local altars. Moreover, the story in 2 Kgs 22 describes the celebration of the Passover after the reforms are instituted. The celebration is not a family observance as depicted in older biblical sources, but a national pilgrimage festival celebrated by all the nation in Jerusalem, precisely as it is described in Deuteronomy. In short, there are several reasons to suppose that the scroll discovered by King Josiah corresponded in many ways to the oldest core of Deuteronomy.

Scholars now think that the core of Deuteronomy (Deut 12–26) was produced in the northern kingdom of Israel in the eighth century, a suggestion supported by affinities with the writings of Hosea, an eighth-century prophet from the northern kingdom, and the E source, also thought to be from the north. In the ninth and eighth centuries, the northern kingdom was the site of a struggle against Baal worship and home to prophets known for their zealotry and exclusive Yahwism. Scholars think northern Yahweh-only traditions brought south by refugees after the fall of the northern kingdom in 722 B.C.E. were placed in the Temple and found about a century later in Josiah's time (622 B.C.E.), but the working of this material into a scroll of the law and the call for centralization were in all likelihood the contribution of Josiah's scribes.

The centralization of the cult must be understood against the political backdrop of the late seventh century B.C.E. The Assyrian threat loomed large. The northern kingdom had already been destroyed, the southern kingdom was paying vassal tribute to Assyria, and a certain amount of religious syncretism had occurred. Second Kings tells of foreign forms of worship being introduced into the Temple. Josiah's reforms were likely an attempt to assert political, religious, and cultural autonomy for Judea. Unregulated worship throughout the land would no longer be tolerated. Josiah hoped to unite the people around a central standardized religious cult purged of foreign influence in order to survive the Assyrian threat to Israel's autonomy and identity. It is in this context that we must consider the strong parallels between Deuteronomy and Assyrian treaties of the late seventh century.

Chapter 8 discussed Hittite treaties as a model for the Israelite covenant, but Deuteronomy is clearly dependent on another model as well—the Assyrian vassal treaty. The best exemplars of these treaties are those of Esarhaddon (681–669 B.C.E.), discovered fifty years ago. Weinfeld has argued at great length that Deuteronomy reworked the second-millennium Hittite model in accordance with the covenantal patterns evident in the first-millennium vassal treaties of Esarhaddon.[8] The Assyrian treaties were loyalty oaths, rather than covenants, imposed upon vassals. Weinfeld argues that Deuteronomy may also be understood as a loyalty oath, although in Israel's case, the people are pledging their loyalty to Yahweh rather than a human king. The exhortations to "love Yahweh your god," "to go after," "to fear," "to listen to the voice of" Yahweh—these are all pledges of loyalty and are paralleled in the Assyrian treaties (where the vassal must love the crown prince, listen to the voice of the crown prince, etc.). And just as the Assyrian treaties warn against prophets, ecstatics, and dream interpreters who will foment sedition, so Deut 13 warns against false prophets urging the people to follow other gods. In short, according to Weinfeld, the Deuteronomic author borrowed a political form but applied it to Israel's relationship with its deity. In a similar vein, Levinson refers to Deuteronomy as a "counter-treaty" shifting the people's loyalty from their Assyrian overlord (Judah was a tribute-paying vassal state of Assyria at this time) and to Yahweh, the true sovereign.[9]

Deuteronomy differs in style, terminology, outlook, and ideological assumptions from the other books of the Torah. As a series of public speeches, it adopts the highly rhetorical and often artificial style of a skilled preacher, employing direct second-person address, a very personal tone, and hortatory phrases such as "with all your heart and soul," "in order that it may go well with you," "a land where milk and honey flow," and "if only you will obey the voice of Yahweh your god." We turn now to some of the major themes of Deuteronomy.

## Themes of Deuteronomy

### *Reform*

The centralization of the cult initiated a series of reforms in Judean religion and socioeconomic conditions. Sacrifices could be offered only at the central sanctuary, necessitating pilgrimage to Jerusalem. By extension, all slaughter of animals for meat in the countryside was no longer sacral, but profane. As a result, many rural Levites who had officiated at small local shrines were put out of business. This explains Deuteronomy's special interest in ensuring that the Levites were well provided for. Many newly unemployed Levites would have gone to Jerusalem seeking employment, and the tension between the Jerusalem priests and these Levite newcomers emerges in other biblical texts.

### *Greater Abstraction of the Deity*

Deuteronomy and related books consistently refer to the sanctuary as the place where Yahweh chose to cause his name to dwell. Yahweh is not said to dwell in the Temple, nor is the Temple described as the house of Yahweh. Rather, the Temple is always the dwelling of his name, and the house is built for his name. Weinfeld ("Deuteronomy," 175) asserts that this formulation is designed to combat the ancient popular belief that Yahweh actually dwells in the sanctuary. Likewise, to eradicate the idea—implicit in earlier sources—that the deity sits enthroned on the cherubim who guard his ark, Deuteronomy emphasizes that the function of the ark is exclusively to house the tablets of the covenant (10:1–5).[10] The ark cover and the cherubim are not mentioned at all. A greater abstraction is also apparent in the shift from visual to aural imagery in describing Yahweh's self-manifestations— one hears but one does not see Yahweh in Deuteronomy.[11]

The sanctuary is understood to be a house of worship as much as a cultic center, in which Israelites and foreigners alike may deliver prayers to Yahweh who dwells in heaven. This is not to say that sacrifice is abolished. Far from it, it is part of Yahweh's service. But Deuteronomy is less interested in cultic matters. The sacrifices that it emphasizes are primarily those that are consumed by the offerer in the sanctuary or are shared with the disenfranchised, the Levite, the alien resident, the orphan, and the widow. By emphasizing the obligation to share the sacrificial meal with the disadvantaged members of society, Deuteronomy gives the impression that the primary purposes of the sacrifice are humanitarian and personal (the fulfillment of a religious obligation or the expression of personal gratitude to Yahweh).[12]

## Ethical Themes

Deuteronomy emphasizes social justice, personal ethics, and neighborly responsibilities. Yahweh's righteous activity on behalf of the weak and oppressed is to be a model for Israel's own. His assistance to the orphan, the widow, and the stranger is the basis of the humanitarianism that runs through the laws of Deuteronomy 12–26.

## Transgenerational Covenant

The covenant concept in Deuteronomy entails the idea that each generation of Israelites understand itself as party to the original covenant: "Yahweh our god made a covenant with us at Horeb. It was not with our fathers that Yahweh made this covenant, but with us, the living, every one of us who is here today" (Deut 5:2–3). That decisive moment at Sinai must be made ever present in each new generation, a goal facilitated by the obligation to study the laws, to recite them daily, and to teach them to one's children (Deut 6:7). Moreover, Deut 31:10–13 proclaims that every seventh year, the Torah is to be read aloud publicly.

## Love

As Weinfeld points out, Assyrian treaties stress the vassal's love (= loyalty) for the crown prince but never a reciprocal love by the crown prince. Deuteronomy (as well as Hittite treaties) differs in this respect, emphasizing Yahweh's gracious and undeserved love for Israel, expressed in his mighty acts on Israel's behalf.[13] The Deuteronomic author makes it clear that Yahweh's great love should awaken Israel's response: love of (i.e., loyalty to) Yahweh. But love and loyalty are mere abstractions without a vehicle for their expression. The vehicle for their expression is Yahweh's Torah—the sum total of his teachings, instructions, laws, and guidelines that are designed to ensure the long life and prosperity of Israel. This idea is found in a passage in Deuteronomy known by its first word, *shema*. The *shema* is the central expression of the love of Yahweh and Israel in the Jewish liturgy to the present day.

> Hear (*shema*), O Israel! Yahweh is our god, Yahweh alone. You
> shall love Yahweh your god with all your heart and with all your
> soul and with all your might. Take to heart these instructions
> with which I charge you this day. Impress them upon your chil-
> dren. Recite them when you stay at home and when you are
> away, when you lie down and when you get up. Bind them as a
> sign on your hand and let them serve as a symbol on your fore-
> head; inscribe them on the doorposts of your house and on your
> gates. (Deut 6:4)

Love of, or loyalty to, Yahweh is the foundation of the Torah; Torah is the
fulfillment of this loyalty.

### The Chosen People

In Deuteronomy, Israel's particular and unique relationship with Yahweh is
expressed in terms of the verb *bahar* = to elect, or choose. Yahweh has chosen
Israel in an act of freely bestowed grace and love to be his special property.

> Mark, the heavens to their uttermost reaches belong to Yahweh
> your god, the earth and all that is on it! Yet it was to your fathers
> that Yahweh was drawn in His love for them, so that He chose
> you, their lineal descendants, from among all peoples—as is
> now the case. (Deut 10:14–15)

This idea of chosenness may be rooted in the ancient Near Eastern political
sphere in which sovereigns singled out vassals for the status of special property. Unlike the priestly materials that portray holiness as a future goal to be
attained through the observance of Yahweh's Torah ("you *shall be* holy to
me" by observing my laws, Lev 11:45; 19:2; emphasis added), Deuteronomy
speaks of Israel as holy through her chosenness and thus bound to observe
Yahweh's Torah ("you *are* a holy people to Yahweh," Deut 7:6; emphasis
added). To put it in the simplest terms, for P, holiness is a goal to be attained
through obedience to Yahweh's Torah; for D, holiness is a status to be lost
through disobedience to Yahweh's Torah.

For Deuteronomy, being a holy people means being separated to Yahweh. That separation entails separation *from* alien peoples and practices
that are inconsistent with the worship of Yahweh. Hence intermarriage
with the Canaanites is prohibited; indeed, they are to be utterly destroyed,

and all alien practices are to be removed from the covenant community. Given that there were probably no Canaanites at the time of Deuteronomy's composition, these texts may be understood as internal polemics against those elements of Israelite society whose practices did not conform to D's Yahweh-only ideals. Separation entails also separation *to* Yahweh's service, which is the observance of his laws, especially the laws of purity and the rejection of pagan practices. The privilege of having been singled out, of being a holy people to Yahweh, entails obligations and responsibility.

At the same time, however, Deuteronomy is aware of the moral danger involved in the notion of election—that it might foster a superiority complex. Thus Deuteronomy warns repeatedly that it is by no special virtue or merit that Israel was chosen, and Moses admonishes the Israelites not to suppose that their inheritance of the land of Canaan is due to their own powers or on account of their righteousness or virtue. Far from it. Israel was chosen by Yahweh in an act of spontaneous love for the patriarchs. This election was entirely Yahweh's initiative and is no cause for Israel to boast.

> For you are a people consecrated to Yahweh your god: of all the peoples on earth Yahweh your god chose you to be his treasured people. It is not because you are the most numerous of peoples that Yahweh set his heart on you and chose you—indeed, you are the smallest of peoples; but it was because Yahweh favored you and kept the oath he made to your fathers that Yahweh freed you with a mighty hand and rescued you from the house of bondage, from the power of Pharaoh king of Egypt. (Deut 7:6–8)

The Israelites must not be tempted, Moses will later warn, to say, "My own power and the might of my own hand have won this wealth for me" (Deut 8:17) or again to say, "Yahweh has enabled us to possess this land because of our virtues" (Deut 9:4). On the contrary, it is only because the wickedness of the Canaanites is so great that Yahweh must drive them from his land. If the Israelites fail to observe Yahweh's covenant, he will drive them out just as he did the Canaanites.

### Divine Providence

Yahweh's providential love and care for Israel is expressed through various metaphors in the Bible. The metaphor of parent and child appears in Deut

8. In Deut 32:10–12, the image that expresses Yahweh's care for Israel is that of an eagle who bears its young on its wings:

> He found him in a desert region,
> In an empty howling waste.
> He engirded him, watched over him,
> Guarded him as the pupil of his eye.
> Like an eagle who rouses his nestlings,
> Gliding down to his young,
> So did he spread his wings and take him,
> Bear him along on his pinions;
> Yahweh alone did guide him,
> No alien god at his side.

Like the eagle who pushes its young from the nest, then repeatedly swoops under them and bears them up until they fly, Yahweh repeatedly tested and corrected the Israelites, until they were ready for the Promised Land.

Deuteronomy's content—the historical review, the farewell speeches, and the death and burial of Moses—make it a fitting capstone to the Pentateuchal narrative. And yet, as mentioned before, it does not bring closure to this narrative. At the end of Deuteronomy, the promises have not yet been fulfilled; the people are still outside the Promised Land. For some scholars this lack of closure points to an exilic date for the work's final composition. Writing for a people living in exile, the Deuteronomic editor wants to emphasize that fidelity to the Torah, and not residence in the land, is of central importance to the covenantal relationship with Yahweh. In any event, Deuteronomy is also the first part of a much longer literary work that runs from Deuteronomy to the end of 2 Kings and has a basic unity of style and outlook. The program and work of this so-called Deuteronomistic School is explored in subsequent chapters.

## CHAPTER 12

# The Deuteronomistic History I

## Joshua

*Readings:* Joshua 1–13, 20, 23–24

### Prophets (Nevi'im)

The second major division of the Tanakh is referred to as Nevi'im (Prophets). The first part, the Former Prophets, encompasses Joshua through 2 Kings and reads as a historical narrative. This theologically oriented account of Israel's history runs from the conquest of Canaan to the destruction of the state by the Babylonians in 586 B.C.E. This material is crucial background for the books of the Latter Prophets, each of which bears the name of the individual to whom the prophecies are attributed.[1] These prophets delivered their messages at critical junctures in the nation's history, and their words are best understood against the backdrop of the particular historical crises they were addressing. The narrative that runs from Joshua through 2 Kings provides this historical background.

Although J, E, and P appear to come to an end here, the Former Prophets (also known as the Historical Prophets), like the books of the Bible reviewed to this point, contain various older sources that have been brought together by a later hand. An editor or group of editors reworked these older sources (oral traditions, records from royal archives, etc.) and wove them into the form we now have—a process referred to as *redaction* (final editing). The anonymous person or group or school responsible for the final composition of these books inserted verses and speeches to frame the older sources and link them together. The redactors' linking and framing passages, as well as their revisions of older sources, exhibit certain features and assumptions characteristic of the book of Deuteronomy, leading the German scholar Martin Noth to surmise that Deuteronomy and the historical books from Joshua through 2 Kings form a literary unit.[2] Joshua to 2 Kings presents and interprets Israel's history in accordance with ideals set out in the book of Deuteronomy, and we refer to the person or persons who redacted this unit as the Deuteronomistic historian or the Deuteronomistic school.[3]

The whole unit was redacted after 622 B.C.E. (because it assumes the centralization of the cult, widely believed to be the achievement of King Josiah). The last dated event mentioned in 2 Kings is the year of the release of King Jehoiachin from prison, 562, so it was probably concluded shortly after that time, during the Babylonian exile (586–536 B.C.E.). Noth assumed one editor, but other scholars have assumed two or even more successive editions of this history because multiple perspectives seem to be represented—the latest being an exilic perspective. Some of the books in this large unit are less influenced by Deuteronomy's main concerns than others, and, as noted above, there are clearly pre-Deuteronomic elements in the material as well.

One of the most salient features of the Deuteronomistic school is the conviction that Israel's residence in the land is a function of its obedience or disobedience to the covenant with Yahweh. That conviction colors the presentation, evaluation, and interpretation of Israel's history in Joshua through 2 Kings. Many scholars would use the term *historiosophy* to describe this material. A historiosophy is more than a narration of events (however selective and partial); it is a *philosophy* of history that seeks to ascertain the *meaning* of events, the larger purpose or design of history, to say not just what happened but why it happened. Many scholars would concur that the Deuteronomistic history is not simply a history of Israel till the destruction of Jerusalem in 586, but a historiosophy that attempts to communicate the meaning and significance of events to that time according to a pattern of reward and punishment (see Chapter 14).

Certain key features of Deuteronomistic thought are evident from Joshua through 2 Kings. These include (1) the centralization of the cult; (2) the belief in the divine election of Jerusalem, of David, and of the royal dynasty that issued from him (indeed, the first four books of the Pentateuch never mention a human king, but Deuteronomy envisages a monarchic regime and contains legislation concerning the king; this feature underscores the connection between Deuteronomy and the books that follow, since the latter focus on the activities of Israel's kings and their degree of fidelity to the major religious reform of the book of Deuteronomy); (3) David as the ideal king; (4) the Yahwist prophets, for example, Elijah and Elisha, as heroes and champions of religious purity; (5) the preference for Judah, the southern kingdom, as compared with the negative presentation of the northern kingdom of Israel (the kings of the northern kingdom will be uniformly denigrated for maintaining cultic centers that rivaled Jerusalem); and (6) the negative presentation of "Canaanites."

## The Land

The books of Joshua and Judges relate the story of the conquest of the land of Canaan by the Israelite tribes and the early years of the settlement. To gain an understanding of the issues involved and the emergence of Israel's tribal structure, it is helpful to know something about the geography of Israel (see Map 2).

It has often been pointed out that in the past 4,000 years, more wars have been fought for possession of the small strip of land known as Canaan than have been fought for almost any other area in the world. In the ancient world, the reason was that this small rectangle—150 miles long and 70 miles wide, about the size of New Hampshire—lies on the way to anywhere worth going in the ancient Near Eastern world. Egypt is to the southeast, Asia Minor is to the northwest, and Mesopotamia is to the northeast. Three main trade routes cross the country. They were used by trading caravans that carried gold, grain, spices, textiles, and other goods between Egypt and the rest of the Fertile Crescent. Control of these international highways brought wealth to the area. But the central location was a double-edged sword that brought prosperity in times of peace but perpetual invasion in times of war. Armies repeatedly crossed the land on their way to greater conquests in Egypt, Asia Minor, or Mesopotamia. This explains the succession of rulers that have held the region: the Egyptians, the Amorites, the Israelites, the Assyrians and Babylonians, the Persians, the Greek Ptolemies and Seleucids, the Romans—and the list continues as we move into the medieval and modern periods.

Despite its small size, the land that would become biblical Israel boasts great geographical diversity. Three main geographical subdivisions run from north to south. First, on the west side of the land, a low coastal

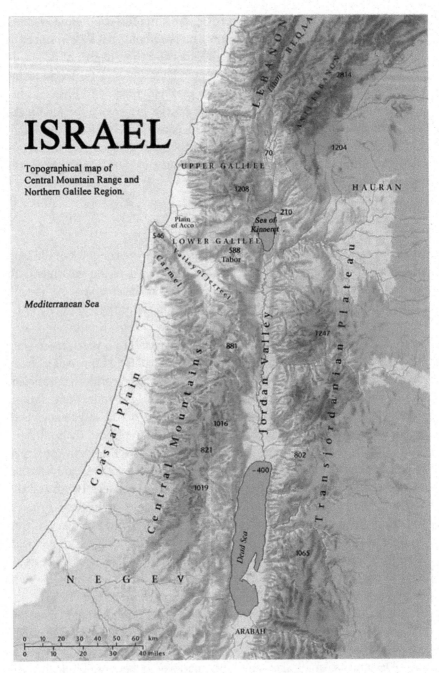

**ISRAEL**

Topographical map of
Central Mountain Range and
Northern Galilee Region.

Map 2. Map of physical features of the land of Canaan. Courtesy of
http://www.science.co.il.

plain about twenty to thirty miles wide provides the chief highway to Egypt. This area was controlled by Egypt at the purported time of the Exodus. Second, running next to the coastal plain, also north to south, is a region of low mountains cut by small valleys—known as the central hill country. Some of the valleys that cut through the mountains are extremely fertile, such as the Plain of Megiddo, which joins with the Valley of Jezreel, an east-west strip that is the most fertile part of the country and the site of many bloody battles in Israel's history. Finally, next to the central hill country, and also running north to south, is the Great Jordan Rift Valley, which extends the full length of the country. The Jordan River runs through this valley, rising in the Kinneret or Sea of Galilee in the north and flowing south sixty-five miles to the Dead Sea. At the northern extreme of the Rift Valley is the snow-covered Mt. Hermon, the highest point in Israel at 10,000 feet. The mountains of the central hill country are between 4,000 and 10,000 feet above sea level (Jerusalem is 2,500 feet above sea level), but the rift valley a few miles to the east is dramatically lower. The Sea of Galilee is 700 feet below sea level, and the Dead Sea is nearly 1,300 feet below sea level, the lowest point on the Earth's land surface. In the north, the river is surrounded on both sides by lush vegetation. However, there is no life in and around the Dead Sea, as the water is 25 percent salts and minerals. It is a desolate area, and tradition identifies this region as the site of Sodom and Gomorrah. The area around the Dead Sea is semidesert. Between Jerusalem and the Dead Sea is the wilderness of Judah.

In short, this relatively tiny area contains radically diverse geographical regions, and this fact held important implications for Israel's history. Unity was difficult. Being somewhat isolated, the inhabitants of each region developed a distinctive economic and cultural character—the small settled farmer, the seminomadic shepherd, the city dweller, merchant, and trader who enjoyed broader cultural contacts.

## The Formation of Israel: Conquest, Immigration, or Revolt?

The book of Joshua divides into two halves. The first twelve chapters form a unit with the following important elements. In chapter 1, Joshua receives his commission from Yahweh to conquer the land. In chapter 2, Joshua sends out spies to reconnoiter the land, and they return with a favorable report. Chapters 3 to 5 recount the crossing of the Jordan and the erection of stones to commemorate the miraculous events, as well as the circumcision of all males born since the Exodus. Chapter 6 contains an account of the defeat of Jericho, involving circumambulations of the people and the ark-bearing priests as blasts are sounded on the horn. Yahweh institutes the *ḥerem*, a form of sacred annihilation of the enemy population and its property practiced in ancient Near Eastern cultures.[4] In chapter 7, the Israelites are routed as they try to capture Ai and learn that the defeat is due to a violation of the *ḥerem*. The guilty party, a man named Achan who retained some of the spoils of war, is finally identified, and his entire household, including the items he appropriated, is destroyed. Ai is taken by the Israelites in chapter 8. In chapter 9, the Israelites are tricked into making a pact with the Gideonites, who become servants of Israel in perpetuity. Further military campaigns are reported in chapters 10 and 11, and the entire conquest is summarized in 10:40, 11:15–20, 23.

> So Joshua defeated the whole land, the hill country and the Negev and the lowland and the slopes and all their kings; he left no one remaining, but utterly destroyed all that breathed. (Josh 10:40)

Chapter 11 stresses that Joshua completed the task begun by Moses.

> Just as Yahweh had commanded His servant Moses, so Moses had charged Joshua, and so Joshua did; he left nothing undone of all that Yahweh had commanded Moses.
>
> Joshua conquered the whole of this region: the hill country [of Judah], the Negev, the whole land of Goshen, the Shephelah, the Arabah, and the hill country and coastal plain of Israel—[everything] from Mount Halak, which ascends to Seir, all the way to Baal-gad in the Valley of the Lebanon at the foot of Mount Hermon; and he captured all the kings there and executed them.
>
> Joshua waged war with all those kings over a long period. Apart from the Hivites who dwelt in Gibeon, not a single city made terms with the Israelites; all were taken in battle. For it was Yahweh's doing to stiffen their hearts to give battle to Israel, in order that they might be proscribed without quarter and wiped out, as Yahweh had commanded Moses. (Josh 11:15–20)

Thus Joshua conquered the whole country, just as Yahweh had promised Moses; and Joshua assigned it to Israel to share ac-

cording to their tribal divisions. And the land had rest from
war. (Josh 11:23)

The division of the land among the twelve tribes[5] is described in the second
half of the book, chapters 13 to 21 (two and a half tribes claim land on the
east side of the Jordan, as explained in chapter 22). Chapter 23 contains
Joshua's farewell address, and chapter 24 describes a covenant renewal ceremony at Shechem.

The narrative in Joshua 2–12 describes the invading Israelites as an
organized confederation of twelve tribes, whose conquest is accomplished
in a few decisive battles under the military leadership of Joshua. The dis-
united Canaanite cities put up little or no resistance, having been paralyzed
by a fear sent by Yahweh. Those who were conquered were put to the ban or
ḥerem—a sacred devotion (i.e., annihilation) of objects or persons to Yahweh. This account expresses the basic idea that Israel's victories would not
have been possible without the wondrous help of Yahweh. Yahweh divided
the Jordan before the Israelites, broke down the walls of Jericho, put fear in
the Canaanites' hearts, and was present at each battle, the ark being the vis-
ible sign of his presence. In this idealized account, the Israelites take the
central hill country in a relatively short time, confining the Philistines to
the coastal plain. Soon after, Israel's tribal structure takes shape, and representatives of all the tribes renew the covenant at Shechem, declaring that
they will be Yahweh's people and worship him alone.

This idealized portrait of the rapid conquest of Canaan is at odds with
statements elsewhere in Joshua and in the book of Judges. For example, Josh
13:1 reads:

Joshua was now old, advanced in years. Yahweh said to him,
"You have grown old, you are advanced in years; and very much
of the land still remains to be taken possession of."

Also, Josh 10:36–39 reports the conquest of several cities in the south, including Hebron and Debir. But in Judges we read that these cities were
captured later, after Joshua's death. Joshua 12:10 reports the defeat of the
king of Jerusalem, but in Judges 1:8, 21, we read that the people of Judah accomplished this, and that despite this victory, they failed to drive out the Jebusites who lived there. Indeed, it is King David, some 200 years later, who,
in a very dramatic story told in 2 Sam 5, will succeed in capturing Jerusalem.

Moreover, the victories in chapters 2–10 are all confined to a small area in what would be the allotment of the tribe of Benjamin, rather than "the whole country" (11:23). Indeed, Jud 1 provides a long list of the places from which the Canaanites were not expelled.

Archaeological evidence contradicts the picture in Joshua also. In the ancient Near East, destroyed cities were leveled and new cities built on top. The slowly rising mounds that resulted from this process are called *tels*. Archaeological excavations reveal the destruction layers under the floor of new cities. Archaeologists familiar with the biblical account have looked for evidence of a large-scale, thirteenth-century B.C.E. destruction of Canaanite cities. But no evidence of *extensive* conquest and destruction has been found in thirteenth- and twelfth-century B.C.E. layers. Indeed, archaeology reveals that some of the sites said to have been destroyed by Joshua and the Israelites were not even occupied in the Late Bronze Age. Excavations of Jericho and Ai indicate that both towns were laid waste 200 years before the probable time of the conquest so that there were no walls in Jericho for Joshua to bring down. Of twenty identifiable sites said to be captured by Joshua and the next generations, only two show destruction layers for this time—Hazor and Bethel—and yet Hazor's capture is contradicted elsewhere in the Bible! In Jud 4 and 5, it is listed among the Canaanite cities that the Israelites failed to take.

It would appear then that Josh 2–12 is a kind of ideological construction. The emergence of Israel in the land of Canaan and the eventual formation of a nation-state were probably much more complicated than the picture painted in Josh 2–12. Scholars have proposed three possible models for understanding the formation of Israel.[6]

The first is the immigration model posed by German scholars. Since the main Canaanite cities were fortified or walled cities on the plains, Israelite immigrants entering the land would have occupied the sparsely populated central highlands, taking control of the plains over time. It is true that the end of the Late Bronze Age (mid-sixteenth century to thirteenth century B.C.E.) and beginning of the Iron Age (1200 B.C.E.) was a time of great upheaval throughout the Mediterranean world following the collapse of the Mycenaean civilization, the Trojan Wars, and the Hittite invasion of Anatolia. These upheavals in Greece and Asia Minor led to migrations of peoples sailing from the mainland and Greek islands to the Near East. Among these "Peoples of the Sea" (probably from the islands and coastal areas of the northeastern Mediterranean) who moved southward in great waves to Phoenicia, the coast of Canaan and Egypt, were the Pelast (which becomes "Philistia" and eventually Palestine). Egypt's hold over Canaan had weakened significantly, which only facilitated the movement of populations into the land. The Pelast took control of a coastal area of Canaan from Jaffa to Gaza and founded the Philistine pentapolis of Gaza, Ashkelon, Gath, Ashdod, and Ekron.

According to the immigration model, Hebrews would have entered the land from the east during the period of population movement that brought the Philistines and other migrants into the western part of the land via the sea—in, approximately, the latter part of the thirteenth century B.C.E. As mentioned in Chapter 7, the Merneptah stele of 1204 (see Figure 2), in which the Egyptian pharaoh boasts that he has wiped out Israel (obviously a hyperbolic boast), indicates that there was an identifiable entity known as Israel in the land of Canaan by the end of the thirteenth century B.C.E.

The problem with the immigration model is, again, the archaeological record. Archaeologists have found hundreds of small sites that were newly established in the thirteenth to eleventh centuries, primarily—but not exclusively—in the central highlands. Many of these new settlements are thought to be Israelite because they appear in places that the Bible identifies as strongholds of Israel. However, these new thirteenth-century settlements are in their material culture (their pots and jars and houses and other material effects) entirely Canaanite, and the inhabitants seem to have been peasant farmers like other Canaanites. (One interesting difference is the absence of pig bones.) This cultural continuity suggests that these new settlements were established peacefully from within and not by foreigners entering the land from some other location.

A second model for understanding the formation of Israel is more consistent with the archaeological evidence for cultural continuity. This is the revolt model. The revolt model proposes that Israel began as a social revolution within Canaanite society. Important support for this model comes from the Amarna letters, an archive of mostly diplomatic correspondence between the Egyptian administration and governors and officials in Canaan and Amurru. The letters date to the fourteenth century B.C.E., a time when Egypt controlled Canaan. The letters contain complaints about groups causing turmoil in Canaan and challenging Egypt's rule—including a group of people called Hab/piru or Ab/piru (whose connection with the biblical "Hebrews," if any, continues to be debated by scholars). These Hapiru were not an ethnic group so much as a marginal social element. They are described in these and other ancient Near Eastern sources as rebels, raiders, outlaws, slaves, and migrant laborers—among other things. Some scholars have suggested that slaves escaping from Egypt may have joined these marginal and disaffected Canaanites in a revolt, establishing their own settlements and worshipping a liberator god named Yahweh. This would account for the continuity in the material culture of these new settlements, as well as the adoption of a new, non-Canaanite deity.

A final, and somewhat similar, model is the model of gradual emergence, which simply holds that Israelites were basically Canaanites who developed a separate identity and settled increasingly in the central highlands. We don't know why they separated. Maybe they were disaffected in some way, maybe they were pushed out of coastal areas by invading Sea Peoples—we do not know, but they withdrew for some reason. How and why they took up the cult of Yahweh is not clear, but it was what marked them as distinct from other Canaanites. The Yahweh cult may have been introduced by people escaping slavery in Egypt. (Most scholars see the Exodus story as evidence for the presence of some escaped slaves among this community.)

Scholars tend toward the view that the Hebrews were probably not at this stage a united people. The various elements that entered into the final mix that would emerge as the nation of Israel may have included local Canaanites who for some reason withdrew and established their own settlements with a continuous material culture and agricultural lifestyle, escaping slaves from Egypt (and there is evidence of *some* destruction suggesting the entry of outsiders), local foreigners (as suggested by biblical narratives recounting affiliations with Midianites, Kenites, and others), and possibly socially or economically marginal groups. Archaeology supports this picture of a merging of peoples rather than a conquest or even large-scale immigration because the new settlements in this period show extensive continuity with the past. The Hebrew tribes themselves were likely still in the process of formation, but the tribal structure of Israelite society that would develop would be strengthened by the natural division of the land into separate geographical areas.[7]

It is entirely possible that some elements within this group brought with them the story of a marvelous escape from Egypt that was believed to be the work of Yahweh, and so the mixed group that would join together to become Israel eventually accepted Yahweh—though probably not exclusively—and adopted the story of the exodus as its own. The union of cultural, religious, and ethnic elements—local Canaanite agriculturalists, the seminomadic Hebrews of the Exodus, escaped slaves, some foreign or migrant elements, perhaps Habiru/Abiru—eventually produced what would be a new political and religious reality called Israel. The ethnic diversity of the community led to various cultural negotiations and contributed to shifting depictions of the deity. Thus, Yahweh was merged with (or usurped but retained characteristics of) the tent-dwelling Canaanite god El, and he was also represented in terms reminiscent of Baal, another god of the settled Canaanite population. In fact, in some biblical narrative texts, Israel's deity is called Baal Berit ("Baal, or master, of the covenant," Jud 8:33, 9:4) or El Berit ("El [or god] of the covenant," Jud 9:46). This assimilation of the features and titles of other gods is an example of convergence, discussed in Chapter 8. Later Yahweh-only prophets will seek to purge these non-Yahweh elements and disassociate the god of Israel from the gods of the Canaanites.

Why does the book of Joshua provide such a different account of the emergence of Israel—one of conquest and war led by the hosts of Yahweh, one in which military skill is less important than ritual preparation and purity? The Israelites march around Jericho for seven days with seven priests carrying seven horns and the Ark of the Covenant, and with a blast and a shout the walls tumble. The conquest is described as a miraculous victory accomplished by Yahweh and "not by your sword or by your bow" (Josh 24:12). And why the claim of an utter destruction (*herem*) of the Canaanites, when, in all likelihood, at least some of those who formed Israel were of Canaanite origin?[8]

Assertions of national identity and independence are often predicated on differentiation from others. If the Israelites were in fact basically Canaanites who had withdrawn from the larger collective for some reason and eventually insisted on the exclusive overlordship of Yahweh, then Canaanites who did not join them were a special threat. The same dynamic of intense sibling rivalry appears again in the first few centuries of the Common Era, when some Jews separated from others and, in differentiating themselves and creating their own identities as Christians, felt it necessary to engage in vituperative and violent rhetoric against their fellow Jews.

There is, however, another voice in the biblical text that adds a level of complexity to this picture. For alongside the idealized portrayal of the Israelite conquest in the first half of the book of Joshua, alongside the call for destruction of the Canaanites, there are tales of alliances with and the incorporation of various Canaanite groups. Indeed, one of the heroes of the battle of Jericho is a Canaanite prostitute named Rahab, who declares her faith in Yahweh and so delivers the city into Joshua's hands. Another Canaanite group—the Gibeonites—tricks the Israelites into making a covenant with them. Michael Coogan (*The Old Testament*, 223) has described such stories as etiological tales, attempting to explain the inclusion of Canaanite groups within Israel (Josh 2:1–21, 6:17, 22–23). At the very least, such stories raise questions about the biblical portrait of invasion, conquest, and utter annihilation; additionally they illustrate the biblical narrator's taste for literary subversion.

## Covenant Renewal: Joshua 23–24

The imperative of preserving a distinct identity based on giving up the worship of older gods and observing all that is written in the law of Moses is reiterated throughout Joshua's farewell address in Josh 23 and the covenant renewal ceremony described in Josh 24. The central idea is that there is one proper response to Yahweh's mighty acts on behalf of Israel: resolute observance of the Book of the Torah of Moses, which entails separation from the practices of other peoples.

In chapters 23 and 24, the Israelites assemble at Shechem to renew the covenant. Joshua recounts Yahweh's mighty deeds on Israel's behalf and exhorts the people to choose whom they will serve—Yahweh who has done everything for them and so undeservedly, or the gods served by their forefathers (the patriarchs)[9] or by the Amorites whom they are presently displacing.

> Do not utter the names of their gods or swear by them; do not serve them or bow down to them. But hold fast to Yahweh your god as you have done to this day. (Josh 23:7b–8)

> Now, therefore, revere Yahweh and serve him with undivided loyalty; put away the gods that your forefathers served beyond the Euphrates and in Egypt, and serve Yahweh. Or, if you are loath to serve Yahweh, choose this day which ones you are going to serve—the gods that your forefathers served beyond the Euphrates, or those of the Amorites in whose land you are settled, but I and my household will serve Yahweh. (Josh 24:14–15)

The people are warned of Yahweh's jealousy—he demands exclusive loyalty and will tolerate no alien gods. Joshua draws a direct connection between intermarriage and the danger of apostasy. Marriage with a Canaanite will lead an Israelite to worship the spouse's gods. Yet, Israel is to show undivided loyalty to Yahweh, or Yahweh will take the gift of land from Israel as he has taken it from the Canaanites.

> For your own sakes therefore, be most mindful to love Yahweh
> your god. For should you turn away and attach yourselves to the
> remnant of these nations—to those that are left among you—and
> intermarry with them, you joining them and they joining you,
> know for certain that Yahweh your god will not continue to drive
> these nations out before you; they shall become a snare and a trap
> for you, a scourge to your sides and thorns in your eyes, until you
> perish from this good land that Yahweh your god has given you.
> (Josh 23:11–13)

Note that the ban on intermarriage articulated in Joshua 23 is not universal but specific to the Canaanites, and for a specific reason—religious purity.

In the sixth century B.C.E., the time of the final editing of the Deuteronomistic history, the Israelites are sitting in exile in Babylon, trying to make sense of the tragedy that had befallen them, the destruction of their god's temple and the loss of the land he had promised them. Interpretations of Israel's history like that presented in Josh 23 and 24 would help to create the conditions for Israel's acceptance of her fate as just punishment for sin and thus bolster faith in Yahweh, as we will see in Chapter 14.

## CHAPTER 13

# The Deuteronomistic History II

## Of Judges, Prophets, and Kings

*Readings:* Judges; 1 Samuel 1–1 Kings 3

## Judges

The book of Judges is set in the transitional period between the death of Joshua and the establishment of the monarchy (1200–1020 B.C.E.) and is an imaginative and embellished reconstruction of that transition (see Map 3). The stories depict local tribal skirmishes rather than confrontations between nations. This depiction probably reflects the reality of the two centuries when the land of Canaan was evolving from the city-states of the Bronze Age to the emerging nations of Israel, Philistia, and Aram. Like Joshua, the book of Judges consists of various sources incorporated into a Deuteronomistic framework. It is in fact a collection of individual stories that center on local heroes, several of whom are socially marginal (the illegitimate son of a prostitute, for example, a bandit, and an irregular Nazirite). These stories have a folkloristic flavor, and they are full of drama and local color: the story of Ehud against the Moabites (Jud 3), Deborah against the Canaanites (Jud 4–5), Gideon against the Midianites (6–9), Jephthah against the Ammonites (Jud 11), and Samson against the Philistines (Jud 13–16). Chapters 17 and 18 tell the story of Micah and his idolatrous shrine, and chapters 19–21 contain the gruesome story of the

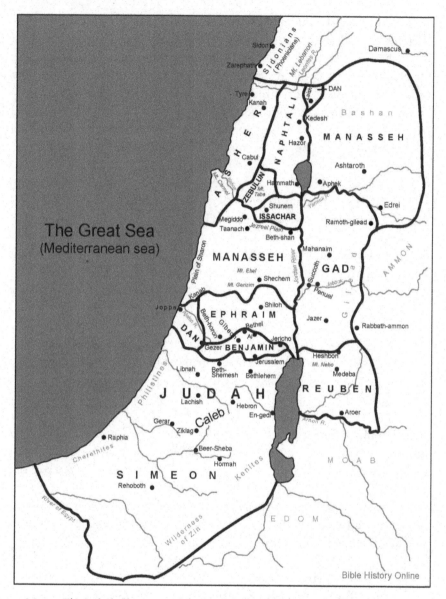

Map 3. The tribal allotment of the land during the transitional period of the
judges. Courtesy of Bible History Online.

Levite's concubine and the civil war of the tribes of Israel against the tribe
of Benjamin.

These stories have been embedded in a Deuteronomistic framework
that provides the editor's view of the period. For the most part, the stories

themselves seem to be largely intact, with only slight interpolations expressing the editor's philosophy of Israel's history. This philosophy of history is best seen in the first chapter, which forms a preface to the book. The chapter provides a detailed summary of the Israelites' situation at the end of Joshua's conquest, listing the extensive area that remained in the hands of Canaanites, starting with Judah and moving northward. In Jud 2:1–5, before Joshua's death, an angel appears. Recounting Yahweh's redemption of the Israelites from Egypt, the angel quotes Yahweh as having said,

> I will never break my covenant with you; And you, for your part, must make no covenant with the inhabitants of the land; you must tear down their altars. (Jud 2:1–2)

Yahweh has pledged to be faithful to his covenant, even as he demands that the Israelites uphold their part—uprooting the inhabitants and their idolatry from the land. The angel then relates that Israel has not, in fact, been obedient, prompting Yahweh to declare,

> But you have not obeyed me—look what you have done! Therefore, I have resolved not to drive them out before you; they shall become your oppressors, and their gods shall be a snare to you. (Jud 2:3)

As punishment for the Israelites' failure to uproot the Canaanites and their idolatry, Yahweh will leave the Canaanites in place as a snare and a trap to test the people's resolve and loyalty. This is a far cry from the idealized portrait of conquest in the first half of the book of Joshua.

The announcement by the angel is followed in 2:10b–3:6 by the editor's own prospective summary of the nation's troubles, expressing the editor's judgment on the nation of this period.

> Another generation arose after them, which had not experienced [the deliverance of] Yahweh or the deeds that he had wrought for Israel. And the Israelites did what was offensive to [evil in the sight of] Yahweh. . . . They followed other gods, from among the gods of the peoples around them, and bowed down to them; they provoked Yahweh. . . . Then Yahweh was incensed at Israel, and he handed them over to foes who plundered them . . . as Yahweh had declared and as Yahweh had sworn to

them; and they were in great distress. Then Yahweh raised up chieftains[1] who delivered them from those who plundered them. But they did not heed their chieftains either; they went astray after other gods and bowed down to them. . . . When Yahweh raised up chieftains for them, Yahweh would be with the chieftain and would save them from their enemies during the chieftain's lifetime; for Yahweh would be moved to pity by their moanings because of those who oppressed and crushed them. But when the chieftain died, they would again act basely, even more than the preceding generation—following other gods, worshiping them, and bowing down to them; they omitted none of their practices and stubborn ways.

In short, it is the view of the Deuteronomistic editor, expressed here in the preface to Judges, that Israel's crises are caused by her infidelity to Yahweh through the worship of Canaanite gods. For this sin Yahweh sells Israel to her enemies. Then, moved to pity he raises leaders (= judges) to deliver her. Sin, punishment, repentance, and deliverance through divinely appointed leaders is the recurring pattern of this book.

However, a Deuteronomistic perspective is not always apparent in the individual stories themselves, which, as mentioned above, appear to be pre-Deuteronomistic folktales about the exploits of local heroes. Thus, Gideon builds an altar despite Deuteronomy's insistence on centralized worship and the prohibition of multiple altars. He is also known by the name Jerubbaal (meaning "Baal will contend"), he erects an idol, and after his death, the people of Shechem continue to worship Baal-berit ("Baal of the covenant"—an interesting merging of Baalism and covenant). The story of Samson also appears to be largely pre-Deuteronomistic. The story was likely a popular and entertaining folktale about a legendary strong man undone by his weakness for foreign women, specifically Philistine women like Delilah, who proves to be his downfall. The behaviors of many of these judges surely scandalized later Deuteronomistic Yahwists. Their stories, when properly framed, were useful in advancing a central Deuteronomistic claim: that foreign gods (often accessed through marriage to foreign women) exercised a fatal attraction for Israel, whose inability to resist the snare of idolatry would lead ultimately to ruin.

The leaders raised by Yahweh are called "judges" (*shofetim*; translated above as "chieftains")—a second-millennium B.C.E. term used to refer to ancient Semitic leaders who exercised many powers, not merely judicial.

The Israelite judge portrayed in the book of Judges was primarily a military leader, commissioned with a specific task only in times of national crisis. The judge had a charismatic quality often expressed by the phrase "the spirit of Yahweh came upon him." Yahweh would raise up the judge to deliver the people. A judge might muster troops from only two or three tribes or even clans, suggesting the lack of a true national entity at this time. The judges differed dramatically from one another in background, class, and even gender (there was one female judge, Deborah). The judges were certainly not chosen for their strength (Gideon is explicitly chosen for his weakness) or for their virtue (Gideon appears as a ruthless fighter and is clearly not a devout Yahwist; Jephthah is an outlaw, and Samson is hardly a moral exemplar). Many judges are representative of the literary type of the crafty trickster so often featured in folklore.

According to the biblical narrative, the phenomenon of judges never led to the formation of a fixed or stable political structure. The idea of a permanent human ruler and the institution of kingship generally is a highly fraught subject in the book of Judges. Several of the individual stories bespeak a deep-seated distrust of kingship. In Jud 8 the people ask the judge, Gideon, to rule permanently as king, but he responds, "I shall not rule over you nor shall my son rule over you; Yahweh shall rule over you" (8:23). Indeed, the short reign of Gideon's ruthless son Abimelech (Jud 9) is a complete disaster. The individual stories depict the position of judge as temporary because Yahweh is viewed as the permanent king in Israel. The temporary authority of the judge is entailed by the eternal kingship of Yahweh; the judge's position could not become absolute as that would be a rejection of Yahweh's leadership.

However, the book of Judges as a redacted whole seems to suggest a progression toward kingship. The final chapters of Judges document Israel's slow slide into disorder and, ultimately, civil war. Chapter 18 opens with the ominous statement that recurs throughout the final four chapters: "In those days there was no king in Israel" (18:1; also 19:1 and 21:25). In addition, it is said that "everyone did as he pleased" or "everyone did what was right in his own eyes" (21:25). By the end of the book, the Israelites find themselves spiraling out of control in an orgy of violence and rape and, in the final chapter, all-out civil war. A Levite's concubine is raped and murdered by the tribe of Benjamin, an atrocity that is to be avenged by all the other tribes, who join together in a holy war—that is, a war of extermination—against Benjamin. Ironically and tragically, the only time all the tribes act in concert is against one of their own. Realizing with regret that the tribe of Benjamin is near extinction, the other tribes then arrange for the kidnapping of women from Shiloh as mates for the few remaining Benjaminites. As a final comment on this horrible symphony of barbarity—rape, murder, civil war, kidnapping, and forced marriage—the Deuteronomist concludes the book of Judges with the refrain: "In those days there was no king in Israel"—no human king *and* no divine king perhaps—"and every man did as he pleased."

The Deuteronomist's explanation for the moral and social bankruptcy of Israel at the end of the period of the judges, on the eve of the monarchy, is Israel's continual infidelity. The prescription for this situation seems to be a king—though this view sits uneasily with the antimonarchic trend of some of the stories that make up the fabric of the book of Judges. But according to the Deuteronomistic historian, the institutional structure of a "kingdom of God" led by inspired judges in times of crisis had failed to establish a stable and continuous government that could provide leadership against Israel's enemies: Ammon and Moab to the east and the Philistines to the west. These enemies soon subjugated the entire land. According to the biblical narrative, the Israelites felt the need for a centralized authority, and the demand for a king was soon heard. In their search for a new political order, the people turn to Samuel, the last in the line of prophet-judges, and ask him to anoint a king for them.

## 1 and 2 Samuel

The books of Samuel deal with the transition from the period of the judges to the period of the monarchy. Chapters 1–4 of 1 Sam recount the birth and career of Israel's last judge, Samuel; chapters 4–7 describe the Philistine crisis and the capture of the ark; chapters 8–15 contain the story of Samuel and Saul and the beginning of the monarchy; chapters 16–31 relate the rise of David and the decline and death of Saul.

First Samuel opens with the story of Samuel's birth to Hannah and her dedication of her son to the service of Yahweh at Shiloh. Shiloh appears to have been the most important shrine prior to the monarchy, and the prophet Jeremiah will refer to it as the place where Yahweh first caused his name to dwell (Jer 7:12). Following the birth of Samuel, a series of crises are revealed. The first is a religious crisis. The priest Eli, also described as a judge but perhaps only in order to fit him into the prevailing pattern of leadership, is said to be aging, and his sons are corrupt. As a result, the word of Yahweh is said to be rare in those days (1 Sam 3:1). The second crisis regards the question of political succession. First Sam 2:12–17 reports that Eli's two sons are clearly unworthy and dissolute: They dishonor the sacrifices and, according to one reading, lie with women at the door of the shrine. Yahweh says he will cut off the power of Eli's house, his two sons will die in one day, and Yahweh will raise up a faithful priest—but in the meantime, no leader is apparent. The third crisis is military. In Jud 4–7, the Israelites suffer a defeat at the hands of the Philistines, Eli's two sons are indeed killed, the ark of Yahweh is captured, and the news of these events causes Eli's sudden demise.

When we first meet Samuel, we wonder whether he is indeed the answer to the crises confronting the people. Chapter 3 says that the word of Yahweh comes to Israel through Samuel (v. 21). In chapter 7, Samuel exhorts the people to stop serving Ashtarot and alien gods and to serve Yahweh, for only then will Yahweh deliver them (v. 3). The people do so, and Samuel leads them—employing prayer, confession, and sacrifice—to a victory over the Philistines at Mitzpah. Yahweh thunders, and the Philistines flee. Thus, Samuel combines many functions in one person: He is a priest offering sacrifices and even building altars, a prophet and seer who receives the word of Yahweh and anoints kings, and a judge who leads the Israelites to a military victory and travels a judicial circuit (mostly within the confines of the tribe of Benjamin) to dispense justice. Yet even Samuel is unable to provide Israel with the leadership required. The Philistine threat reemerges, and the crisis of succession remains because Samuel's own sons are corrupt (1 Sam 8:3). And so the representatives of the twelve tribes come to Samuel to request a king. Samuel is thus a transition figure between Israel, the theocentric confederation of tribes, and Israel, the united monarchy.

## Monarchy

The historical account in 1 Samuel contains many contradictions and duplicates that scholars take as evidence of the existence of various conflicting sources. For example, there are three different accounts of the choice of Saul as king and two accounts of Saul's rejection by Yahweh, of David's entering Saul's service, of David's escape into Philistine territory, of his sparing Saul's life, and of the death of Goliath (only once at the hands of David). More important, however, is the existence of sources that hold opposing views of the institution of kingship. Some passages are clearly antimonarchic; others are promonarchic (or at least report neutrally on the selection and installation of Saul as king).

| Anti-monarchic | 1 Sam 8 | | 1 Sam 10:17–27 | | 1 Sam 12:1–25 |
|---|---|---|---|---|---|
| Pro-monarchic | | 1 Sam 9:1–10:16 | | 1 Sam 11:1–15 | |

First Sam 8 provides a classic example of the antimonarchic perspective. Samuel is initially opposed to the idea of a king, apparently resenting the usurpation of his own powers, until Yahweh tells him:

> Heed the demand of the people in everything they say to you. For it is not you that they have rejected; it is me they have rejected as their king. . . . Heed their demand but warn them solemnly, and tell them about the practices of any king who will rule over them. (1 Sam 8:7, 9)

This Samuel does in verses 11–18. He warns of the rapaciousness and tyranny of kings, the service and sacrifice they will require of the people in order to support their luxurious lifestyle, their bureaucracy, and army. Samuel warns:

> The day will come when you cry out because of the king whom you yourselves have chosen, and Yahweh will not answer you on that day. (1 Sam 8:18)

But the people will not listen and say significantly:

> No we must have a king over us that we may be like all the other nations. Let our king rule over us and go out at our head and fight our battles. (1 Sam 8:19–20)

The people's response is represented as an explicit and ominous rejection of Yahweh and of Israel's distinctiveness from other nations. In Sam 12, Samuel retires, saying, "Henceforth the king will be your leader. As for me, I have grown old and gray" (1 Sam 12:2). He again outlines what is required of a good king and again chastises the people for having asked for a king, warning that Yahweh must be served wholeheartedly.

> Well, Yahweh has set a king over you! Here is the king that you have chosen, that you have asked for. If you will revere Yahweh, worship him, and obey him, and will not flout Yahweh's command, if both you and the king who reigns over you will follow

Yahweh your god, [well and good]. But if you do not obey Yahweh and you flout Yahweh's command, the hand of Yahweh will strike you as it did your fathers. Now stand by and see the marvelous thing that Yahweh will do before your eyes. It is the season of the wheat harvest. I will pray to Yahweh and he will send thunder and rain; then you will take thought and realize what a wicked thing you did in the sight of Yahweh when you asked for a king. (1 Sam 12:13–17)

Some have argued that while the editors who compiled the text preserved the promonarchic perspective of their sources, they chose to frame the promonarchic passages with their own antimonarchic passages, with the result that the antimonarchic passages provide an interpretive framework and are dominant. The implication is that despite positive contemporary evaluations of Israel's kings, from the perspective of a later period, the institution of kingship was considered a disaster for Israel, and that negative assessment is introduced by the Deuteronomistic redactor into the account of the origin of the institution. Others feel that the promonarchic and antimonarchic views were contemporaneous and equally ancient perspectives. Whether one view is older and one later, whether both are ancient or both late—the end result is a complex narrative that includes various views of monarchy in ancient Israel, views that defy easy categorization and that lend the book an air of complexity and sophistication.

Not only is there ambivalence concerning the very institution of monarchy, there is much ambivalence concerning the first occupant of the throne—Saul. Judges contains three accounts of Saul's appointment as king. In 1 Sam 9, it is a private affair between Saul and the prophet Samuel, who installs Saul as king by anointing him with oil. The anointing of kings is also found among the ancient Hittites. In Israel, anointing is a rite of dedication or consecration to Yahweh and is performed at the installation of kings and high priests. In 1 Sam 10, Saul's appointment as king is effected by lottery presided over by Samuel. In 1 Sam 11, Saul is elected by popular choice after his victory over the Ammonites.

Saul is presented in conflicting terms. On the one hand, he is described as tall, handsome, and charismatic, and he is associated with ecstatic prophecy. Saul defended his own tribe of Benjamin from Ammonite raids and was hailed by the tribes as a leader in time of war. As king, he enjoyed some initial victories, driving the Philistines from their garrisons. He was such a popular and natural leader that even Samuel, who at first resented Saul, is said to grieve for him upon his death.

Yet once David enters the story, more negative assessments of Saul appear. It may be that these portrayals stem from circles loyal to the house of David, who will take the throne from Saul and his heirs. Or it may be that Saul's failure and suicide had to be accounted for by identifying some fatal flaw in him. In any event, his ecstatic prophecies are now presented as irrational fits of mad behavior. Where once the spirit of Yahweh had come upon him, Saul is now said to be seized by an evil spirit from Yahweh (1 Sam 16:14) that rushes upon him suddenly and causes him to rave in his house. Elsewhere he commits errors, not obeying Samuel's instructions to the letter, that cost him the support of Samuel and ultimately Yahweh. Two incidents of disobedience are related: In chapter 13 Saul sees the sagging morale of his men and officiates at a sacrifice instead of waiting for Samuel to arrive. This appropriation of a priestly function enrages Samuel, who predicts that Yahweh will not establish Saul's dynasty over Israel (1 Sam 13:13), despite the fact that later kings will offer sacrifice with impunity. In chapter 15, against Samuel's orders, Saul spares the life of an enemy king, Agag, and otherwise violates the command of *ḥerem,* or total destruction of the enemy and the spoils of war. Again, Samuel announces Yahweh's regret over having made Saul king.

> Yahweh has this day torn the kingship over Israel away from you
> and has given it to another who is worthier than you. (15:28)

In any event, with his support eroding, Saul sinks into depression and paranoia. Toward the end of his life, he becomes increasingly obsessed with David and the threat David poses to him and his dynasty. Saul is angry with his own son Jonathan for his deep friendship with David and in jealous rages attempts to kill David or to have him and his supporters killed. In these encounters our sources portray David as something of an innocent victim, protesting his loyalty to and support for Saul, and twice passing up the opportunity to do away with Saul, declaring, "I will not raise my hand against Yahweh's anointed" (1 Sam 24:7; see also 26:10–12). The portrayal of Saul as a raving and paranoid man obsessed with an innocent and loyal David appears to be the work of later apologists for the house of David.

Positive views of Saul's character were not entirely extinguished by the biblical writer. David's own lament for Saul upon learning of his suicide and Jonathan's death (circa 1000 B.C.E.) may reflect Saul's tremendous popularity. David orders the Judahites to learn the Song of the Bow in praise of Saul:

> Your glory, O Israel
> Lies slain on your heights;
> How have the mighty fallen! . . .
> Saul and Jonathan,
> Beloved and cherished,
> Never parted
> In life or in death!
> They were swifter than eagles,
> They were stronger than lions!
> Daughters of Israel,
> Weep over Saul,
> Who clothed you in crimson and finery,
> Who decked your robes with jewels of gold.
> How have the mighty fallen
> In the thick of battle—
> Jonathan, slain on your heights!
> I grieve for you,
> My brother Jonathan,
> You were most dear to me.
> Your love was wonderful to me
> More than the love of women.
> How have the mighty fallen,
> The weapons of war perished! (2 Sam 1:19–27, excerpted)

Of course, representing David as bewailing Saul in these terms serves an apologetic function as well—David is cleared of any part in, or even desire for, the death of Saul (see below).

First Sam 16–2 Sam 5 is the first part of the story of David and has the feel of a historical novel, with a great deal of direct speech and dialogue. Most scholars believe that David was a real person. A recently discovered ninth-century B.C.E. Syrian inscription referring to the "house of David" bolsters this belief, as does the fact that the ruling family in Judah was referred to as the "house of David" for 400 years. Nevertheless, no details of the biblical account can be confirmed.

Surprisingly, David is presented as very human, not a divine or even a particularly virtuous character. This first installment in David's story (1 Sam 16–2 Sam 5) is sympathetic and favorable to David, but it is not entirely obsequious or flattering. In some ways it functions as an apology for David, but on the other hand it is also subtly critical of him. Certainly David is a hero, but reading between the lines, he is also an opportunist, an outlaw, and a mercenary of the Philistines who acts unscrupulously. In short, the biblical account of David's rise to the monarchy is not royal propaganda in the simple sense. The subsequent account of his reign, which takes up the bulk of 2 Samuel, presents him in an even less flattering light.

There are different accounts of David's discovery. In the first, Samuel secretly anoints David king of Judah (i.e., the southern region) in Saul's lifetime. He is the youngest of his father's sons, so this anointment is another reversal of primogeniture and the elevation of the lowly, seen so often in the Bible. In the second account, David is summoned to play music for a disturbed Saul. In the third account, David is introduced as the classic ninety-eight-pound weakling who takes on the legendary Goliath.

After the death of Saul, David will be anointed king in Hebron over his own tribe, Judah. He proceeds to win over or kill those members of Saul's household and retinue that might be a threat to his claim to kingship in the north. Eventually, the northern tribes elect him king, and thus the united kingship of Judah and Israel is finally formed (2 Sam 5:1–4). Once his reign is secure and the nation consolidated behind him, David captures Jerusalem and launches attacks against Israel's neighbors. According to 2 Sam 8:6 and 14, Yahweh gives him victory, and he is depicted as the master of a considerable empire stretching from the desert to the sea, but there is little extrabiblical evidence that Israel actually established lasting control over such a vast region at this time. It is likely that David took advantage of the power vacuum in the area to establish an independent state that was able to dominate its neighbors for a short while—ending the Philistine threat and possibly collecting tribute from Ammon, Moab, and Edom.

## Davidic Covenant

In 2 Sam 7:8–17, the prophet Nathan transmits Yahweh's promise of a covenant to David—a covenant that became the basis for the centuries-long belief in the eternity of the Davidic kingdom:

Thus said Yahweh of Hosts, "I took you from the pasture, from following the flock, to be ruler of my people Israel, and I have been with you wherever you went, and have cut down all your enemies before you. Moreover, I will give you great renown like that of the greatest men on earth. I will establish a home for my people Israel and will plant them firm, so that they shall dwell secure and shall tremble no more. Evil men shall not oppress them any more as in the past, ever since I appointed chieftains over my people Israel. I will give you safety from all your enemies. Yahweh declares to you that he, Yahweh, will establish a house for you. When your days are done and you lie with your fathers, I will raise up your offspring after you, one of your own issue, and I will establish his kingship. He shall build a house for my name, and I will establish his royal throne forever. I will be a father to him, and he shall be a son to me. When he does wrong, I will chastise him with the rod of men and the affliction of mortals; but I will never withdraw my favor from him as I withdrew it from Saul, whom I removed to make room for you. Your house and your kingship shall ever be secure before you; your throne shall be established forever."

So it was that the idea of an eternal and unconditional covenant between Yahweh and the house of David (the fourth biblical covenant) came to be. Yahweh promises in this covenant that he will not take the kingdom away from David and his descendants as he took it from Saul. This does not, however, preclude the possibility of punishment for sin. Indeed, by referring to David as his son, Yahweh asserts the right of the father to discipline his wayward offspring. Michael Coogan points out that the sonship of the king was revolutionary—a deliberate effort to replace an earlier understanding of the entire nation of Israel as the firstborn son of Yahweh.[2] As Yahweh's son, the king now stood between the deity and the people as a whole. Coogan points to two other features of the new royal ideology that represented a shift from previous tradition: (1) a focus on the king's mountain (Mt. Zion, home to the Temple and palace complex from the time of Solomon) rather than the nation's mountain (Mt. Sinai) as the site of revelation and (2) a focus on the king's eternal covenant with Yahweh rather than the people's conditional covenant. This royal ideology, which tends to ignore the main themes of the Pentateuchal narrative such as the Exodus, the covenant at Sinai, and the character of Moses, was resisted in some quarters, as will be discussed in Chapter 14.

Yahweh's oath to preserve the Davidic dynasty and by implication Jerusalem as well led eventually to a popular belief in the invincibility of the holy city. In addition, the belief in Israel's ultimate redemption became bound up with David and his dynasty. David was idealized by later biblical and postbiblical tradition and became the paradigmatic king. The promise of a Davidic dynasty did not die even when Judah fell to the Babylonians in 586 B.C.E. Following the destruction, the community looked to the future for a restoration of the Davidic line, a Davidic king or messiah. The Hebrew word *messiah* means "anointed"—a reference to the fact that kings were initiated into office by means of anointing oil poured on the head. King David was thus a messiah of Yahweh, that is, an anointed king, as was every king and high priest in Israel. And in the exile, Israelites would pray for another messiah—another anointed king of the house of David appointed by Yahweh to rescue them from their enemies and reestablish them as a nation at peace in their land, as David had done. The Jewish hope for a messiah was thus always political and national, involving the restoration of the people in its land under a Davidic king.

The king was subject to Yahweh's will as revealed through his prophets, and thus Israelite monarchy never shifted from its dependence on prophecy. As we will see in Chapter 15, the monarchy's dependence on prophecy is exemplified in dramatic fashion in the remarkable phenomenon of prophetic opposition to and condemnation of kings who violated Yahweh's laws: Samuel against Saul, Nathan against King David, and others.

## David

In the Hebrew Bible, David is second in importance and textual space only to Moses. Three characteristics attributed to David stand out. First, he is depicted as proficient in music and poetry. Later traditions (Amos 6:5, 2 Chr 7:6) attribute to him the invention of instruments and the composition of the book of Psalms. Second, David is credited with great military and tactical skill and confidence, deploying his army on behalf of Israel, but also within Israel against his rivals in a calculating and Machiavellian manner. Third, David is depicted as a shrewd politician who created permanent symbols of Yahweh's election of Israel, David, and David's line to rule over all Israel. David is said to conceive the idea of a royal capital, capturing Jebus, a border town free of any tribal association, and building it up as the city of David (2 Sam 5:6–9) and building a royal palace (2 Sam 5:11–12). This city, renamed Jerusalem, would become the chosen city—the place where Yahweh causes his name to dwell—and a symbol of Israel's kingdom and the dynasty of David. By transferring the ark to Jerusalem (2 Sam 6:1–19), David converted the city into the home of the ancient tablets of the Sinaitic covenant, with the added implication that the Davidic dynasty had inherited the blessing of the covenant and fulfilled the promise to the patriarchs. David is said to have planned a magnificent temple that would become the resting place for the ark and a cultic center for all Israelites, but the building of this temple was left to his son Solomon (1 Chr 22).[3] Still, according to the biblical account, it was David who made the chosen dynasty, city, and (to a lesser extent, the future) Temple into permanent and intertwined symbols of Israel. With David, the history of Jerusalem as the eternal Holy City begins.

Second Sam 9–20 and 1 Kings 1–2 contain an extended historical drama referred to as the Court History or Succession narrative of David. The burning question in this historical narrative is: Who will succeed David? One by one his sons are killed or displaced, until finally Solomon is chosen. This complex drama of intrigue and passion contains a rich array of major and minor characters. It also presents an unusual picture of David. He is weak and indecisive, an antihero who never goes to battle, the primary function of an ancient Near Eastern king. He enters into illicit relations with a married woman, Bathsheba, and then sees to it that her husband is killed in battle in order to cover up the affair. For this double act of murder and adultery, the prophet Nathan upbraids him and Yahweh punishes him with the death of a son and with calamity and rebellion within his own family (2 Sam 12:11, 14). Specifically, David's son Amnon rapes his half-sister (David's daughter) Tamar, earning the undying enmity of his brother Absalom, who has Amnon killed. David's control of those around him declines, and his indecision on the question of succession fuels further resentment, conflicts, and revolts. Absalom stages a revolt against his father, and David is forced to flee from Absalom's forces. He is stripped of his crown and degraded. But when Absalom is killed, David weeps uncontrollably for him, angering his own supporters who fought so earnestly in his defense. By the end of the story, David is impotent and senile. The prophet Nathan and Bathsheba plot to have her son Solomon succeed David. But the hostility of the northern tribes throughout the story (see 2 Sam 20:1–2) is a warning sign of future disunity.

It has been said that the Court History was written by a prose artist of genius. It contains a number of richly drawn characters, who act out scenes of courage, glory, struggle for power, lust, crime, and compassion. The writing is realist. The psychological insight and the uncompromising honesty far surpass the work of any other contemporary writer of historical narrative. David is depicted in very human terms. The flattery and whitewashing found in other ancient Near Eastern dynastic histories and in Chronicles's sanitized retelling of this material is lacking here, and the flaws and weaknesses of David—a national hero—are thinly disguised, complicating the reader's assessment of his character. Indeed, as James Kugel has recently argued, a review of David's rise to power and his dealings with his rivals reveals a ruthless and ambitious guerrilla bent on seizing power but posturing as the pious servant of both Yahweh and his anointed king Saul.[4] The evidence for such a characterization of David is as follows:

David has two opportunities to kill Saul undetected, yet he piously refuses to harm Yahweh's anointed (1 Sam 24:5–8 and 26:10–12) declaring himself Saul's servant. Nevertheless, in 1 Sam 27–28:2, David defects with 600 men to the Philistines—ostensibly so that Saul will stop pursuing him, but he profits greatly from the move. He is given the town of Ziklag by the Philistines and becomes a mercenary for them, engaging in numerous raids and battles (2 Sam 27). David swears loyalty to the Philistines even against Israel (1 Sam 28:1–2), and yet the writer takes pains to point out that David was (forcibly) excluded from the Philistine attack on the Israelites at Mt. Gilboa (1 Sam 29:1–11) in which Saul and his son Jonathan will be killed (1 Sam 31). Thus, despite his defection to the Philistines, David is cleared of any wrongdoing in connection with the death of Yahweh's anointed king. Indeed, while the battle is raging, David's town of Ziklag is attacked by Amalekites. David pursues and routs them and then divides the spoils of war with the elders of several towns throughout Judah (1 Sam 30:26–31), a move calculated to curry favor as David contemplates making a bid for power. His calculation was a good one, as the Judahites will select David as king after the death of Saul (2 Sam 2:4). That David had hoped for the death of the king (despite any protestations to the contrary) was surely no secret, as evidenced by the story of the Amalekite who boasts of having dispatched Saul, on the assumption that David would be pleased and would reward him (2 Sam 1:9–10). Instead, David maintains the facade of pious loyalty to Yahweh's servant Saul and instantly executes the Amalekite for daring to raise his hand against Yahweh's anointed (2 Sam 1:14–15). In a similar vein, David publicly laments the loss of Saul, orders the Israelites to recite "The Song of the Bow" in his honor (2 Sam 1:17), and praises those who buried Saul (2 Sam 2:5–7).

But many in Israel remain loyal to the house of Saul. Saul's army commander Avner, for example, installs Saul's son Ishboshet as king of Benjamin and other areas of Israel (not Judah) in 2 Sam 2:9, and a war between the house of Saul and the house of David ensues (2 Sam 3:1, 6). When Avner and Ishboshet have a falling out (2 Sam 5:7–11), Avner switches his loyalty to David, saying that he will establish the throne of David over Israel and Judah. But David's general Joab suspects Avner of duplicity and kills him (2 Sam 3:22–27), an act justified as personal vengeance for Avner's murder of Joab's brother Asahel. And so another powerful threat to David's ambition is eliminated, with no suspicion cast on David, who emphasizes his personal innocence at great length in 2 Sam 3:28–39.

> Both I and my kingdom are forever innocent before Yahweh of shedding the blood of Avner son of Ner. May the guilt be on the head of Joab and all his father's house. (2 Sam 28b–29a)

David orders everyone to mourn; he makes a great public display of grief, weeping loudly at Avner's graveside and refusing to be comforted so that "all the troops and all Israel knew that is was not by the king's will that Avner son of Ner was killed" (v. 37).

The elimination of potential heirs to Saul's claim to the throne is a dominant theme from 2 Sam 3 on. Prior to Avner's death, David had demanded the return of his former wife Michal, the daughter of Saul, despite her hatred for him and subsequent marriage to another man (2 Sam 3:14–16)—a move likely calculated to prevent the birth of another heir for the house of Saul. In 2 Sam 4, two of Ishboshet's company commanders, Baanah and Rechav, kill Saul's son Ishboshet (vv. 4–6) and bring his head to David, saying they have avenged David on Saul and his offspring. Again, those who commit the foul deed believe they have acted in a way that will please David, and again David's public reaction is one of outrage (vv. 9–12). He promises to avenge Ishboshet's blood, and indeed he orders the two assassins killed.

In 2 Sam 5, the northern tribes plead with David to become their king (vv. 1–3), and he accepts, reigning over them for forty years (2 Sam 5:9). In 2 Sam 9, David shrewdly wins over Mephiboshet, the crippled son of Jonathan, neutralizing any threat that might come from that quarter. Despite David's careful efforts to distance himself from the gradual eradication of Saul's heirs and supporters, some see through his protestations of innocence. When his own son Absalom rebels against him, a member of Saul's clan named Shimei son of Gera hurls stones and dirt at the king and voices a sentiment that was undoubtedly shared by many:

Get out, get out, you criminal, you villain! Yahweh is paying you back for all your crimes against the family of Saul, whose throne you seized. Yahweh is handing over the throne to your son, Absalom; you are in trouble because you are a criminal. (2 Sam 16:7b–8)

It is truly remarkable that the Deuteronomistic historian not only includes the explicit and insulting accusation of Shimei son of Gera but also nowhere denies the content of his charges. Indeed, his narration of events is such that a negative assessment of David's ruthless climb to power requires minimal effort.

Finally, in 2 Sam 21:1–9, all remaining sons of Saul except Mephiboshet are killed. And again, steps are taken to protect David's innocence. The pretext for these murders is the need to end a three-year famine. Upon inquiring of Yahweh, David learns that the famine "is because of the bloodguilt of Saul and [his] house, for he put some Gibeonites to death" (2 Sam 21:1). What can David do then, but hand over to the Gibeonites the remaining seven male heirs of Saul, to be impaled on the mountains before Yahweh (2 Sam 21:7–9)?

With all rivals removed, the question of succession is resolved in Solomon's favor. David's deathbed advice to Solomon reflects his own Machiavellian tactics (1 Kgs 2:1–12). He tells Solomon to kill Joab (presumably because army commanders have a way of trying to seize power) and to kill Shimei the son of Gera.

Implicit in this complex and sophisticated narrative is a critique of kingship, or at least a critique of one of the first and most celebrated occupants of the throne. It is hard to escape the conclusion that the Deuteronomistic historian wishes to stress that David, Solomon, and all the kings of both the northern and southern kingdoms are thoroughly human and in no way divine, subject to sin and error. This will be important in establishing the Deuteronomistic claim that the nation's kings were responsible for bringing down Yahweh's punishment upon the nation.

## CHAPTER 14

# The Kingdoms of Judah and Israel

*Readings:* 2 Samuel 8–1 Kings 3, 10–12, 17–25

## 1 and 2 Kings

First and second Kings contain the history of Israel from the death of King David to the fall of Judah and the Babylonian exile in 586. These books appear to be based on older sources, some of which are explicitly identified, such as the subsequently lost "Book of the Acts of Solomon" (1 Kings 11:41) and the "Book of the Annals of the Kings of Israel" (see, e.g., 1 Kgs 14:19) and the "Book of the Annals of the Kings of Judah" (see, e.g., 1 Kgs 14:29). Annals, or chronicles, were always maintained at royal courts in Egypt and Mesopotamia, and it is highly likely they were maintained in Israel and Judah. These annals are generally lists of events with little narrative, and the first sixteen chapters of 1 Kings contain material of this type. First Kings 17–22 and second Kings 1–9 depart from the annalistic reports on the reigns of kings and contain more developed narratives, generally featuring prophets. Some of the narratives probably circulated independently, particularly those about the prophets Elijah and Elisha. These sources have been embedded in a framework that brings them into line with the religious perspective of the Deuteronomistic historian.

In 1 Kgs 2:12, we read, "And Solomon sat upon the throne of his father David, and his rule was firmly established." With the enthronement of Solomon, the three crises confronting Israel at the opening of 1 Samuel appear to be resolved. The crisis in succession is resolved: David is succeeded by his son Solomon, and according to the biblical narrative, all of the kings of Judah until the destruction in 586 B.C.E. are from the house of David. The military crisis appears to have been resolved by military and diplomatic successes so that Israel is relatively secure. Finally, the religious crisis is resolved. The ark has been retaken from the Philistines and installed in Jerusalem, and a magnificent temple has been planned for the central worship of all Israel.

But the resolution of these crises produced fundamental changes in Israelite society. Out of a loose confederation of tribes united by covenant arises a nation with a strong central administration, headed by a king said to enjoy a special covenant with Yahweh. Rather than charismatic leaders who arise as needed and on a temporary basis, full-fledged kings from a single dynastic line rule in perpetuity. Preserved in the biblical text is a marked tension between the old ideals of the covenant confederation and the new ideology of the monarchy. The new royal ideology combines loyalty to Yahweh and loyalty to the throne so that treason or rebellion against Yahweh's anointed may be perceived as apostasy—rebellion against Yahweh himself.

Jon Levenson points to the deep tension between covenant theology and royal ideology.[1] In covenant theology, Yahweh alone is king. He has a direct suzerain-vassal relationship with the people. The covenant theology implies a negative view of monarchy (as is evidenced on occasion in Judges and Samuel). Monarchy is at best unnecessary and at worst a rejection of Yahweh. Yet despite this critique, kingship was established in Israel, and Levenson sees the royal ideology that developed to support this institution as a major revolution in the structure of the religion of Israel (*Sinai*, 97–101). Where the Sinaitic covenant was contracted between Yahweh and the nation, the Davidic covenant was contracted between Yahweh and a single individual—the king. The covenant with David has been called a covenant of grant by Moshe Weinfeld,[2] a type of ancient Near Eastern covenant granted as a reward for loyal service and deeds. Yahweh rewards David with the gift of an unending dynasty. The contrast with the covenant at Sinai is clear. Where Israel's covenant with Yahweh at Sinai was conditional, premised on the observance of Yahweh's Torah, the covenant with David, his dynastic house, and by implication the Davidic city and its Temple atop Mt. Zion is promissory and will be maintained under all conditions. This royal ideology led some to believe in the inviolability of David's house, city, and sacred mountain, an idea we will return to in subsequent chapters.

Scholars have found various ways to explain the relationship between these two strands of tradition in biblical literature: the covenant theology with its emphasis on the conditional covenant of Moses contracted at Mt. Sinai, on the one hand, and the royal ideology with its emphasis on the unconditional covenant of David focused on Mt. Zion, on the other. One explanation is chronological: Early traditions emphasize Sinai, and later ones emphasize Zion. Another explanation is geographical: The northern kingdom that rejected the Davidide rulers de-emphasized Zion, with its Davidic orientation, and emphasized Sinai. By contrast, the southern kingdom of Judah, where a member of the house of David reigned until the destruction, emphasized Zion and its attendant royal ideology. Levenson rejects the chronological and geographic theories, showing that both the Sinai and Zion traditions can be found in early and in late texts, in northern and in southern sources.[3] The two traditions apparently coexisted, and eventually they would be coordinated. Zion would take on much of the legacy of Sinai—becoming the site of theophany (self-manifestation of Yahweh), the site of covenant renewal, and the site from which Torah goes forth. Nevertheless, later tradition seems to favor the Sinaitic covenant (Levenson, *Sinai*, 211), since the entitlement of the house of David would eventually be made contingent on the observance of Yahweh's Torah. The king is not exempt from the stipulations of the Sinaitic covenant, and though never finally deposed, he could be punished for violations.

David's son Solomon (reigning approximately 961–922 B.C.E.) is given mixed reviews by the Deuteronomistic historian. He ascends to the throne through intrigue and lacks indication of divine choice or approval. Nevertheless, he is described in the biblical text as reigning over something of a golden age (though most scholars view this claim as highly exaggerated). His kingdom is said to extend beyond the borders of Israel, from the Euphrates to the wadi of Egypt (1 Kgs 8:65, 5:4; see Map 4). He made many political and economic alliances throughout the region, sealed through marriages (the daughter of a pharaoh, the daughter of the king of Tyre, and more). According to the biblical text, Solomon built a daunting military establishment, constructed a wall for Jerusalem, and fortified cities like Hazor, Megiddo, and Gezer as bases for his professional army. The army included an expensive chariot force.

According to the biblical narrative, Solomon's accomplishments extended to the realm of industry and trade. He exploited Israel's position to control the major north-south trade routes from Egypt and Arabia to northern Syria, and foreign trade became a source of great wealth to the state. The

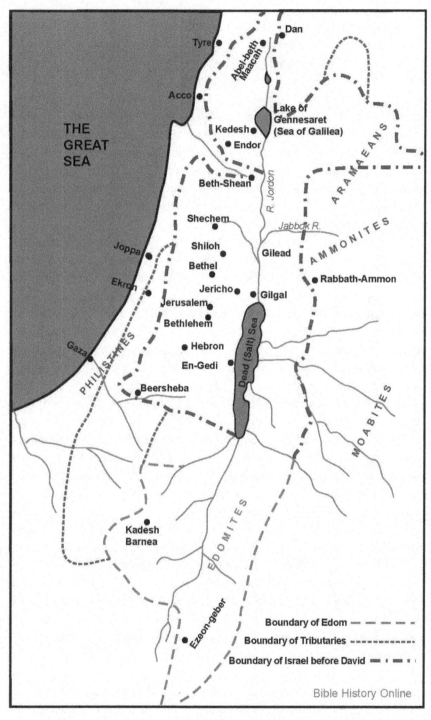

Map 4. Map of the kingdoms of David and Solomon. Courtesy of
Bible History Online.

extensive daily supplies needed to maintain Solomon's lavish court are detailed in 1 Kings 4 and 5. Solomon developed a merchant fleet in the south in conjunction with the Phoenicians under Hiram, king of Tyre. He exploited trade routes through the Red Sea and was able to bring in exotic products from Arabia and possibly the African coast. The famous visit of the Queen of Sheba (the Sabean land in South Arabia) may reflect the movement of peoples and goods along these routes. He engaged in magnificent building operations. Assuming the accuracy of the biblical tradition, earlier scholars hypothesized a flowering of the arts under Solomon. This is the time, some scholars have supposed, that scribes wrote the first imaginative literature—the J source.

But in fact we should be skeptical of this grand picture. To be sure, it is unlikely that the Deuteronomistic historian invented the Solomon material entirely. For some scholars, the many instances in which Solomon openly violates Deuteronomic law (e.g., he sacrifices in high places and worships other gods) suggest that the redactor drew upon older sources.[4] Nevertheless, archaeologists note that Jerusalem was a small town until the end of the eighth century B.C.E., when it suddenly expanded to absorb refugees fleeing the fall of Israel in 722. There are few material remains from the tenth century that attest to a fabulous empire on the scale suggested by the biblical text. Hazor, Megiddo, and Gezer have been excavated, and while some strata do show great gateways, chambers, and even some stables, their dating is uncertain, and some scholars date them to a period after Solomon. Most concur that even if Israel were the most important power in the immediate region at this time, it still would have been relatively insignificant in comparison with the great civilizations of the ancient Near East.

Three features of the biblical representation of Solomon deserve mention. First, Solomon is praised for his wisdom (this is the likely basis for the traditional but incorrect attribution of the books of Proverbs and Ecclesiastes to Solomon). Second, in addition to being praised for his wisdom, Solomon is praised for constructing the Temple. Indeed, the primary focus of the biblical story of Solomon is the building and dedication of the Temple for the Ark of the Covenant in Jerusalem (1 Kgs 6–9:14). Solomon continued the close association between the religious and political leadership by constructing the magnificent new Temple within the palace complex and appointing the high priest himself. In a passage describing the dedication of the Temple (1 Kgs 8), Solomon explains that the Temple is a place where people have access to Yahweh, petition to him, and make atonement for their sins. It is a house of prayer, and it would remain the central focal point of Israelite worship for centuries.

The juxtaposition of the houses of the king and the deity on Mt. Zion was deliberate. This hill, though small, later became a towering and impregnable mountain in the mythic imagination of the nation. According to Levenson, Zion would eventually take on the features of the "cosmic mountain"—a mythic symbol common in the ancient world with potencies that were infinite and universal. Many of the features associated with the cosmic mountain motif are found in Israel in connection with Mt. Zion (Levenson, *Sinai*, 145). The cosmic mountain was viewed as the meeting place of the gods and, more important, the meeting place of heaven and earth, the *axis mundi* or point of junction between the two (Levenson, *Sinai*, 122). In Canaanite religion, the mountain of Baal, known as Mt. Zaphon, was conceived in this manner, and Levenson points to the commonality of language and concept in references to the mountain of Baal, the mountain of El, and the mountain of Yahweh (Levenson, *Sinai*, 124). The Temple on Mt. Zion was sacred space, the Garden of Eden, the place from which the entire world was created, an epitome or microcosm of the world, or the earthly manifestation of the heavenly Temple (Levenson, *Sinai*, 138). The Temple represented an ideal realm and appears as the object of intense longing in some biblical psalms.

His wisdom and his construction of the Temple notwithstanding, Solomon is sharply criticized for a host of sins, including foreign worship (1 Kgs 11:6–13). Solomon's new palace complex had ample room for his harem, which is said to have included 700 wives (many of them foreign princesses and nobility acquired to seal political and business alliances), 300 concubines, and officials and servants (1 Kgs 11:1–5). These numbers are no doubt exaggerated. What's important about these stories is that Solomon's many diplomatic alliances are said to be effected by unions condemned by the Deuteronomistic historian: He is said to have loved many foreign women from the nations that Yahweh had forbidden, and he succumbed to the worship of their gods and goddesses (Levenson, *Sinai*, 138). He built temples for Moabite and Ammonite deities (Levenson, *Sinai*, 138). This may point to a general tolerance of different cults in Jerusalem before the reforms of Josiah in 622, a tolerance of which later editors disapproved. Thus, Solomon's primary flaw in the biblical writer's view is his syncretism, brought on by his marriages to foreign women who introduced their native cults into Jerusalem. Yahweh's punishment for Solomon's infidelity is the division of the kingdom after his death.

In order to support his tremendous court, army, and bureaucracy, Solomon introduced heavy taxation as well as the hated corvée (forced labor on state projects; 1 Kgs 9:14). The urban structure superimposed on agricultural life produced a class distinction between officials, merchants, and large-scale landowners who prospered and the farmers and shepherds who lived at subsistence level. Divisions between town and country, between rich and poor, grew. The tribal democracy was giving way to a schism in society. In addition to the flaws of the kings, the very institution of monarchy itself did not sit well in many quarters because centralized leadership under a human king went against the older traditions of Hebrew tribal society united by covenant with Yahweh and guided by prophets and priests. Before Solomon's death, the northern tribes were completely alienated from the house of David, resenting what they perceived to be Solomon's tyranny.

## Framing Solomon

The Deuteronomistic historian carefully frames his account of the monarchy so as to enable the reader to pass judgment on Solomon and, indeed, on all subsequent kings. Specifically, Solomon is represented as violating explicit prohibitions and warnings issued prior to the establishment of the monarchy. These prohibitions are pseudepigraphically attributed to Moses as a part of the initial covenant, and the warnings are attributed to Samuel at the time of the founding of the monarchy. The prohibitions regarding kings appear in Deut 17:

> If, after you have entered the land that Yahweh your god has assigned to you, and taken possession of it and settled in it, you decide, "I will set a king over me, as do all the nations about me," you shall be free to set a king over yourself, one chosen by Yahweh your god. Be sure to set as king over yourself one of your own people; you must not set a foreigner over you, one who is not your kinsman. Moreover, he shall not keep many horses or send people back to Egypt to add to his horses, since Yahweh has warned you, "You must not go back that way again." And he shall not have many wives, lest his heart go astray; nor shall he amass silver and gold to excess. (Deut 17:14–17)

Kingship is represented here as optional—arising from the Israelites' sense that they would like to be like other nations. But should they decide to install a king, he must be a divinely appointed native Israelite, and he must not multiply horses (particularly from Egypt), wives, silver, or gold. Samuel's warnings appear in 1 Sam 8:

> This will be the practice of the king who will rule over you: He will take your sons and appoint them as his charioteers and horsemen, and they will serve as outrunners for his chariots. He will appoint them as his chiefs of thousands and of fifties; or they will have to plow his fields, reap his harvest, and make his weapons and the equipment for his chariots. He will take your daughters as perfumers, cooks and bakers. He will seize your choice fields, vineyards, and olive groves, and give them to his courtiers. He will take a tenth part of your grain and vintage and give it to his eunuchs and courtiers. He will take your male and female slaves, your choice young men, and your asses, and put them to work for him. He will take a tenth part of your flocks, and you shall become his slaves. The day will come when you cry out because of the king whom you yourselves have chosen; and Yahweh will not answer you on that day. (1 Sam 8:11–18)

In direct violation of Deut 17, Solomon is said to possess 12,000 horses and even to purchase them from Egypt (1 Kgs 10:26–29), to keep many (indeed 1,000!) wives and concubines who turn his heart astray to the worship of foreign gods (1 Kgs 11:1–13), and to amass silver and gold to excess (1 Kgs 9:26–28, 10:1–5, 14–22). Moreover, in fulfillment of Samuel's dire warnings about the abuses of a king, Solomon is said to institute forced labor (1 Kgs 9:15–22) and to establish a lavish court. In short, the list of social and economic ills and abuses prohibited in Deut 17 and enumerated in the warnings of Samuel (1 Sam 8) were realized in the reign of Solomon.

By enumerating Solomon's clear violations of earlier prohibitions and warnings, the Deuteronomistic redactor prepares us to accept the claim that the division of the kingdom after the death of Solomon was just punishment for Solomon's many sins.

> Yahweh was angry with Solomon, because his heart turned away from Yahweh, the god of Israel, who had appeared to him twice and had commanded him about this matter, not to follow other gods; he did not obey what Yahweh had commanded. And Yahweh said to Solomon, "Because you are guilty of this—you

have not kept my covenant and the laws which I enjoined upon you—I will tear the kingdom away from you and give it to one of your servants. But, for the sake of your father David, I will not do it in your lifetime; I will tear it away from your son. However, I will not tear away the whole kingdom; I will give your son one tribe, for the sake of my servant David and for the sake of Jerusalem which I have chosen." (1 Kgs 11:9–13)

## The Divided Monarchy

When Solomon died in 922 B.C.E., the northern tribes, long alienated by the house of David, its tax burden, and forced labor, rebelled against Solomon's son and successor Rehoboam after he refused to relieve their tax burden (1 Kgs 12). The kingdom that had been united under David fell into two rival states of second-rate importance (see Map 5)—Israel, composed of ten tribes in the north, and Judah, composed of the tribes of Judah and Benjamin in the south, each with its own king (see Table 5). In the ensuing centuries, these two states were sometimes at war and sometimes in alliance against a common enemy. Possession of the outlying territories became precarious, and much of the empire, to the extent that it existed, was lost. Toward the end of the eighth century B.C.E., the northern kingdom of Israel fell to the Assyrian empire (722 B.C.E.), and the southern kingdom of Judah, though still viable, was reduced to paying tribute to the new overlord of the Near East. Judah was finally destroyed in 586 B.C.E. by the Babylonians, who had defeated the Assyrians and assumed control over the ancient Near East.

The story of the northern kingdom of Israel presented in Kings is colored by a Judean perspective and is thus highly negative. This kingdom was more divided by tribal rivalries and divergent traditions than Judah, and the first king, Jeroboam (922–901 B.C.E.) did not establish a stable dynasty. First Kings 12 tells of Jeroboam's effort to break the connection with the traditional religious center in Jerusalem by establishing a government at Shechem (a site revered in Hebrew tradition) and royal shrines at Dan in the north and Bethel in the south of the kingdom of Israel. A golden calf was placed in each shrine, an action that is viewed by the biblical writer as a terrible sin. Indeed, the story is written in a manner that deliberately echoes the story of the golden calf made by Aaron in Ex 32—Israel's "primordial" cultic sin. It is entirely possible that the historical Jeroboam—if he did indeed establish alternative cultic centers—was a Yahwist who believed he could establish a site where Yahweh would "cause his name to dwell." But by

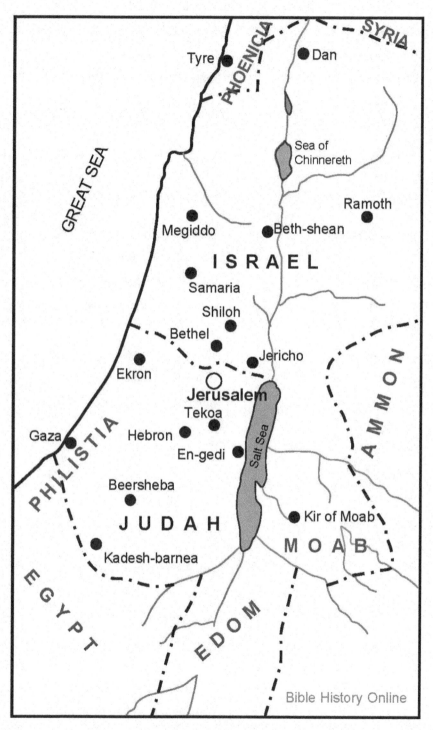

Map 5. Map of the kingdoms of Judah and Israel. Courtesy of
Bible History Online.

## Table 5. Kings of Israel and Judah

| Kings of Israel | Kings of Judah |
|---|---|
| Jeroboam I (928–907) | Rehoboam (928–911) |
| Nadab (907–906) | Abijam (Abijah) (911–908) |
| Baasha (906–883) | Asa (908–867) |
| Elah (883–882) | |
| Zimri (882) | |
| Omri (882–871) | |
| Ahab (871–852) | Jehoshaphat (870–846) |
| Ahaziah (852–851) | Jehoram (Joram) (851–843) |
| Jehoram (Joram) (851–842) | Ahaziah (Jehoahaz) (843–842) |
| Jehu (842–814) | Queen Athaliah (842–836) |
| | Jehoash (Joash) (836–798) |
| Jehoahaz (817–800) | |
| Jehoash (Joash) (800–784) | Amaziah (798–769) |
| Jeroboam II (788–747) | Azariah (Uzziah) (785–733) |
| | Jotham (759–743) |
| Zechariah (747) | |
| Shallum (747) | |
| Menahem (747–737) | |
| Pekahiah (737–735) | Ahaz (745/735–727/715)[1] |
| Pekah (735–732) | |
| Hoshea (732–722) | |
| | Hezekiah (727/715–698/687)[2] |
| | Manasseh (698/687–642)[3] |
| | Amon (641–640) |
| | Josiah (640–609) |
| | Jehoahaz (Shallum) (609) |
| | Jehoiakim (Eliakim) (608–598) |

Data from Michael Coogan, *The Old Testament: A Historical and Literary Introduction to the Hebrew Scriptures*. New York: Oxford University Press, 2006, pp. 290, 308, 328, 351.

[1] The data are inconsistent for the reign of Ahaz.
[2] The data are inconsistent for the reign of Hezekiah.
[3] The data are inconsistent for the beginning of Manasseh's reign.

writing the story as a deliberate echo of the paradigmatic cultic sin of the golden calf, the Deuteronomistic historian parodies Jeroboam's activity and brands his cultic center as illegitimate idolatry. Jeroboam is perceived by the biblical editors as having made unacceptable concessions to Canaanite worship practices and is criticized for this. Despite his best efforts, his kingship remained unstable. Indeed, instability plagued the northern kingdom; in its brief 200-year history, seven different dynasties were to occupy the throne.

Israel enjoyed material prosperity under the rule of Omri and his son Ahab (876–849 B.C.E.). Omri bought and fortified Samaria as the capital of the northern kingdom of Israel (archaeology reveals that it was a magnificent city), but the Deuteronomistic editors judge him as evil for disobeying Yahweh. Omri is the first king of either kingdom to be mentioned in extrabiblical sources. His name appears on the Moabite Stone (see Chapter 12) in which King Mesha of Moab boasts of defeating Omri (see Figure 8).

> As for Omri, king of Israel, he humbled Moab many years (lit. days), for Chemosh was angry at his land. And his son followed him and he also said, "I will humble Moab." In my time he spoke (thus) but I have triumphed over him and over his house, while Israel hath perished for ever! (Now) Omri had occupied the land of Medeba, and (Israel) had dwelt there in his time and half the time of his son (Ahab), forty years; but Chemosh dwelt there in my time.[5]

Omri and his son Ahab were clearly powerful and influential in the region. Ahab is mentioned in an inscription of an Assyrian king, as part of an Aramaean-Israelite coalition that fought the Assyrians. But Ahab and his Phoenician wife Jezebel are said to have established an extravagant court life in the capital of Samaria and are severely condemned by the Deuteronomistic editors. When Jezebel tried to establish the worship of her Phoenician god Baal as an official cult, building a temple for Baal in Samaria, the prophets Elijah and Elisha preached a holy war against the monarchy. We will consider these zealous prophets in the next chapter.

In 842 B.C.E., the army general Jehu led a military coup and was anointed king by the prophet Elisha (2 Kgs 9). His revenge was bloody: Jezebel and the priests of Baal, as well as "all the worshippers of Baal," were slaughtered (2 Kgs 10:21).

Fig. 8. The Mesha Stone commemorating a victory over Israel (mid-ninth century B.C.E.). Radovan/BibleLandPictures.com.

By the eighth century, the new Assyrian Empire was on the rise, and in 722 Sargon II reduced Israel to provincial status. Archaeologists have uncovered inscriptions by Sargon that correspond to the biblical report. They state:

> I besieged and conquered Samaria, led away as booty 27,290 inhabitants of it. . . .

Also:

> [The town I] re[built] better than (it was) before and [settled]
> therein people from countries which [I] myself [had con]quered.
> I placed an officer of mine as governor over them and imposed
> upon them tribute as (is customary) for Assyrian citizens.[6]

There is basic agreement between this and the biblical account, which describes the siege and capture of Samaria and the deportation of Israelites to Assyria (2 Kgs 17:4–6, 18:9–10). These Israelites were eventually lost to history (the famous ten lost tribes of Israel). The few Hebrew farmers and shepherds that remained behind continued in their old ways, and the Assyrians imported new peoples into this territory, which would become the province of Samaria. This ethnically mixed group practiced a form of Israelite religion, but the Deuteronomistic editor does not view it as legitimate. Ultimately these Samaritans came to be despised by the Jews of Judah as foreign corrupters of the faith, always ready to assist Israel's enemies.

We turn our attention now to the southern kingdom, Judah. Composed of the two remaining tribes of Judah and Benjamin, the southern kingdom enjoyed internal stability and remained loyal to the line of David ruling in Jerusalem. Shortly after Israel fell to Assyria in 722, the Judahites under King Hezekiah agreed to terms as subject allies of Assyria. But Hezekiah prepared for rebellion, making alliances with neighbors and prompting the Assyrians to lay siege to Jerusalem in 701 B.C.E. This siege is described in Assyrian sources:

> As to Hezekiah, the Judean,[7] he did not submit to my yoke, I laid
> siege to 46 of his strong cities, walled forts, and to the countless
> small villages in their vicinity . . . I drove out (of them) 200,150
> people. . . . Himself I made a prisoner in Jerusalem, his royal
> residence, like a bird in a cage.[8]

Eventually, the Assyrians withdrew the siege, and Judah was able to preserve its kingship by paying a high tribute. In 612, the Assyrians were defeated (the fall of Ninevah) by the rising Babylonians, and Judah was finally destroyed by Nebuchadrezzar of Babylon in 586 B.C.E. The walls of Jerusalem were dismantled, and many members of the governing class were carried into exile in Babylonia.

That the Hebrews did not fade into oblivion after the loss of their political independence and geographical base is due in large part to the interpretation of events provided by the Deuteronomistic school.

## The Deuteronomistic Historian and Redaction Criticism

As noted before, Deuteronomy may be seen not just as the capstone to the Pentateuch's narrative; it is also the first part of a much longer literary work. It was Martin Noth, a German scholar, who first argued that from the point of view of composition and authorship Deuteronomy has greater stylistic and theological similarity with what follows it (the books of Joshua, Judges, 1 and 2 Samuel, and 1 and 2 Kings) than with what precedes it (Genesis–Numbers). The material from Deuteronomy through 2 Kings constitutes a unit, a history of Israel in its land, from the time of Joshua until the destruction of 586 B.C.E., and has been dubbed the Deuteronomistic history since vocabulary, motifs, and themes characteristic of the book of Deuteronomy continue in the subsequent books. Thus, most scholars now concur that the same group or school that framed and finally edited Deuteronomy also compiled the subsequent historical books through 2 Kings. Since this Deuteronomistic school is looking back at the history of Israel up to and including the defeat and exile of the Israelites in 586, the final form of the work of the Deuteronomistic school must be exilic or, more likely, postexilic, that is, post-536. However, it is very difficult to date the various layers of Deuteronomy with much precision.

The scholarly methodology that led to the positing of the existence of a Deuteronomistic school is redaction criticism. Redaction criticism grew out of a weariness with source criticism and other forms of biblical criticism that fragmented the text into older sources, genres, or tradition units in order to arrive at a history of Israelite religion, with little attention to how the text reached its final form. Redaction criticism rejects the idea that the person or persons who compiled the text from early sources and tradition units did a mechanical scissors-and-paste job. Redaction criticism focuses on identifying the purpose and plan behind the final form of the assembled sources in order to uncover the intention of the person or persons who produced the biblical text in roughly the shape we have it.

Redaction criticism proceeds in the following manner: First, one can usually identify linking passages—passages that join narratives or other units together in an attempt to make the text read smoothly and ease the transition from one source to another. These are assigned to R, the redactor. Also assigned to R are interpretive additions, passages that stand back and comment on or interpret the text—in short, any place where the narrator turns to address the reader directly in order to explain something. For example, statements like "the Canaanites, and Perizzites were then dwelling in the land" (Gen 13:7) or "they tore down the temple of Baal and turned it into latrines, as is still the case" (2 Kgs 10:27) break with the train of the narration in order to comment from the perspective of a later time (the time of the author of the statement). Similarly, etiological comments such as "that is why the children of Israel do X to this day" provide a chronologically later interpretation of the main text. Sometimes a story or book contains a preface that indicates, justifies, or otherwise comments on what is about to be related (Jud 2–3:4), while some passages summarize and offer an interpretation of or justification for what has just been related (2 Kgs 17). By joining together the passages assigned to R, one often sees stylistic similarities and a consistent point of view rarely found in the actual source material that these passages frame. In this way, a clearer understanding of the role of the redactor in the final production of the text and of the redactor's own historical situation, his purposes, and concerns emerges.

## The Historiosophy of the Deuteronomistic Historian

The Deuteronomistic historian responsible for the redaction of Deuteronomy, Joshua, Judges, 1 and 2 Samuel, and 1 and 2 Kings provides not just a history documenting events as they occur but an interpretation of history, a philosophy of history that seeks to ascertain the meaning of events, the larger purpose or design of history—in short, a historiosophy. We find the Deuteronomistic interpretation of Israel's history in the preface to the book of Deuteronomy and in editorial glosses peppered throughout the books of Joshua, Judges, Samuel, and Kings, and we find it especially in the summary of the entire unit contained in 1 Kgs 17. What prompted the Deuteronomist to adopt a particular interpretation of Israel's historical record?

The Deuteronomist was attempting to respond to the first major historical challenge to confront the Israelite people and the Hebrew religion: the collapse of the Israelite nation, the destruction of Yahweh's sanctuary, and the defeat and exile of Yahweh's people. The calamitous events of 722 and particularly 586 raised a critical theological dilemma. Yahweh had promised the patriarchs that their descendants would live in his land. He had promised that the house of David would stand forever. But here the monarchy had collapsed, and the people were defeated and in exile. The challenge presented by this twist of history was twofold: Is Yahweh the god of history, capable of all, imposing and effecting his will? If so, then what about his covenant with the patriarchs and with David? Had he faithlessly abandoned it? That was unthinkable. But if he hadn't abandoned his covenant with his people and with David, then he must not be the god of history, the universal deity over all, since he wasn't able to save his people. Neither idea was acceptable. It was a fundamental tenet of Israelite monotheism that Yahweh is at once the god of history whose will and promise are absolute and at the same time a god of faithfulness who would not abandon his people. How could the disasters of 722 and 586 be reconciled with the convictions that Yahweh controlled history and that he had an eternal covenant with Israel and David?

The historiosophy of Deuteronomy through Kings is the response of one segment of the Israelite community—the Deuteronomistic school (for this use of the term *school,* see Chapter 11). The Deuteronomistic historian's basic idea is that Yahweh's unconditional and eternal covenants with the patriarchs and David do not preclude the possibility of punishment or chastisement for sin, as specified in the conditional Mosaic covenant. This is because although Yahweh is omnipotent, humans have free will and can therefore corrupt the divine plan. So in the Deuteronomistic history, the leaders of Israel are depicted as having the choice of accepting Yahweh's way or rejecting it. Yahweh even tries to help them choose correctly by sending prophets who inform the kings of what Yahweh desires of them. But the wrong choice is made, and it is sin that ultimately brings about the fall of first Israel and then Judah—particularly the idolatrous sins of the kings.

With the deposition and execution of Zedekiah, the last Davidic king, in 586, the Deuteronomistic school reinterpreted the Davidic covenant in conditional terms, on the model of the Mosaic or Sinaitic covenant, according to which Yahweh's favor toward the king depended on loyalty to Yahweh. In this way the fall of the house of David could be seen as justifiable punishment for disobedient rulers like Manasseh. According to the Davidic covenant in 2 Sam 7 formulated in line with Deuteronomistic ideology, Yahweh will punish and chastise his anointed.

According to the Deuteronomistic historian, it is specifically the sin of idolatry and particularly the idolatry of the king for which Israel is punished with exile and destruction. In 2 Kings, a king who permits sacrifice only at the Jerusalem Temple is praised no matter his other faults, and one who does not is condemned no matter his other accomplishments. However, the Deuteronomistic historian is aware of anomalies in the historical record. Some good kings reigned briefly, and some wicked kings (like Manasseh) ruled for long periods of time. Also, disaster sometimes struck after the reign of a faithful king who was religiously devout. The Deuteronomistic historian therefore sounded the theme of delayed punishment. So for example, Solomon's misdeeds in allowing the building of altars for the worship of foreign gods caused the division of the kingdom. But this punishment was mercifully deferred until the time of his sons.

The Deuteronomistic historian sees Israel's defeat in 722 as delayed punishment for Jeroboam's institution of the cultic centers at Dan and Bethel and other idolatrous deeds (2 Kgs 17:16). As for Judah, Hezekiah, who ascended the throne in 727, is judged by the biblical writer to have been a very good king, instituting sweeping reform, destroying the idolatrous altars, and thus retaining semi-independence against the Assyrians. However, his son Manasseh, who reigned from 691 to 638, is remembered as the most wicked king of Judah. Manasseh turned the Jerusalem Temple itself into a pagan pantheon, and for Yahwists this was a disastrous era. Manasseh's eight-year-old grandson, Josiah, came to the throne in 636, and Josiah was considered to be a very good king because he instituted reforms in line with Deuteronomistic ideology. According to 2 Kgs 22, when Josiah was twenty-six, he ordered a refurbishment of the Temple, in the process of which a book of the Torah (believed by most scholars to be something very much like Deut 12–26) was found.[9] Its words alarmed him because its prescriptions regarding sacrifice only at a single central sanctuary were not being fulfilled. Josiah and his priests took this to refer to the Jerusalem Temple, and so all other altars, used in rural areas for centuries, were destroyed.

In the Deuteronomistic historian's view, Josiah was a good king because he purged the country of idolatrous rites and centralized all worship in Jerusalem, but the sin of Manasseh was too great and had to be punished. A prophetess named Huldah told Josiah that though Yahweh planned to bring evil punishment on Judah, it would be after Josiah's lifetime. And indeed in the next generation, Judah fell. In 586, the walls of Jerusalem—the inviolable and eternal city—were breached, the Temple destroyed, and King Zedekiah was blinded and taken into exile in chains with his court. Many of the remaining Judeans fled to Egypt, leaving only the poorest behind.

The result of the Deuteronomistic interpretation was remarkable. In polytheistic societies the defeat of one nation by another was seen as the defeat of that nation's god by the other nation's god, and the conquered peoples would turn from worship of their god to the newly ascendant god. But the Israelites did not renounce Yahweh and take up worship of the Babylonian god Marduk. Their defeat did not lead to despair and apostasy, because it could be explained by the likes of the Deuteronomistic writer(s) as fitting into the monotheistic scheme. Yahweh was punishing Israel for the sin of idolatry, which was in violation of his covenant. To punish Israel, he had raised the Babylonians, who were his tool.

The historiosophy of the Deuteronomistic historian finds its classic expression in 2 Kgs 17:

> In the ninth year of Hoshea, the king of Assyria captured Sa-maria. He deported the Israelites to Assyria and settled them in Halah, at the [river] Habor, at the River Gozan, and in the towns of Media. This happened because the Israelites sinned against Yahweh their god, who had freed them from the land of Egypt, from the hand of Pharaoh king of Egypt. They worshiped other gods and followed the customs . . . which the kings of Israel had practiced. The Israelites committed against the Yahweh their god acts which were not right: They built for themselves shrines in all their settlements, from watchtowers to fortified cities; they set up pillars and sacred posts for themselves on every lofty hill and under every leafy tree; and they offered sacrifices there, at all the shrines, like the nations whom Yahweh had driven into exile before them. They committed wicked acts to vex Yahweh, and they worshiped fetishes concerning which Yahweh had said to them, "You must not do this thing." Yahweh warned Israel and Judah by every prophet and every seer, saying: "Turn back from your wicked ways, and observe my commandments and my laws, according to all the Teaching that I commanded your fathers and that I transmitted to you through my servants the prophets." But they did not obey; they stiffened their necks, like their fathers who did not have faith in Yahweh their god; they spurned his laws and the covenant that he had made with their fathers, and the warnings he had given them. They went after delusion and were deluded; . . . they made molten idols for themselves—two calves— and they made a sacred post and they bowed down to all the host of heaven, and they worshiped Baal. They consigned their sons and daughters to the fire; they practiced augury and divination, and gave themselves over to what was displeasing to Yahweh and vexed Him. Yahweh was incensed at Israel and He banished them from His presence; none was left but the tribe of Judah alone. Nor did Judah keep the commandments of Yahweh their god; they

followed the customs that Israel had practiced. So Yahweh spurned all the offspring of Israel, and he afflicted them and delivered them into the hands of plunderers, and finally he cast them out from his presence. (2 Kgs 17:6–20 excerpted)

According to the Deuteronomistic historian, Israel had been warned from the very beginning that faithlessness and the worship of gods other than Yahweh would be punished with invasion, national collapse, and exile. Deuteronomy 28 contains a long list of curses that will befall the Israelites if they violate the terms of the covenant, and then states:

All these curses shall befall you; they shall pursue you and overtake you, until you are wiped out, because you did not heed Yahweh your god and keep the commandments and laws that he enjoined upon you . . . you shall have to serve—in hunger and thirst, naked and lacking everything—the enemies whom Yahweh will let loose against you. He will put an iron yoke upon your neck until he has wiped you out. Yahweh will bring a nation against you from afar, from the end of the earth, which will swoop down like the eagle—a nation whose language you do not understand, a ruthless nation, that will show the old no regard and the young no mercy. . . . Yahweh will scatter you among all the peoples from one end of the earth to the other, and there you shall serve other gods, wood and stone, whom neither you nor your ancestors have experienced. . . . Yahweh will send you back to Egypt in galleys, by a route which I told you you should not see again. There you shall offer yourselves for sale to your enemies as male and female slaves, but none will buy. (Deut 28:45–46, 48, 64, 68)

If the Deuteronomistic school framed the national history in covenantal terms and laid the blame for the demise of the two kingdoms at the door of the sin of idolatry, particularly the idolatry of the royal house, a different answer was provided by Israel's classical prophets.

# CHAPTER 15

# Israelite Prophecy

*Readings:* 1 Kings 16:29–19:21, 21–22; 2 Kings 1–9, 13

## Nonliterary Prophets

In the historical books of the Former Prophets (i.e., Joshua–Kings, but especially Samuel and Kings), several prophetic characters appear and play an important role in the national drama. The prophets of the tenth and ninth centuries B.C.E. were associated with religious shrines and with the royal court. Beginning in the eighth century, there were prophets whose words were eventually set down in books that would bear their names. These books are found in the section of the Bible known as the Latter Prophets. These prophets are also referred to as the literary or classical prophets in contrast to the prophetic characters whose activities are reported as part of the narrative history in Samuel and Kings. The literary prophets, like the Deuteronomistic historian, struggled to make sense of Israel's suffering and defeat. Their explanation of national events and their message of consolation will concern us in subsequent chapters. This chapter explores the phenomenon of prophecy in ancient Israel generally by examining narratives in Samuel and Kings that feature prophetic characters. This chapter provides important background for chapters that explore the books of the classical or literary prophets in some detail.

Prophecy was widespread in the ancient Near East, though it took different forms in different societies. We know of ecstatic prophets in second-millennium Mesopotamia and in seventh-century Assyria whose primary focus was delivering oracles for the kings, usually favorable. Ecstatic prophecy is also known in the Bible, especially among the earliest prophets. The term *ecstasy* refers to the state of being overcome by such powerful emotions that self-control and reason are suspended. Ecstatics employed music and dance to induce a religious frenzy or emotional seizure that often left the prophet writhing and raving. The Bible attributes this ecstatic state to the spirit of Yahweh, which is said to fall on the prophet and transform him into an instrument of the divine will. Such bizarre behavior is found even among the later literary prophets, who sometimes engaged in outrageous and dramatic acts as a vehicle for the communication of their message.

Not all biblical prophecy has this ecstatic character. The Hebrew word *navi'* means "one who is called" or "one who announces" and refers to one who is called to proclaim Yahweh's message. In biblical religion we find the idea of apostolic prophecy, that is, messenger prophets (apostle = messenger) who are called by Yahweh and charged with a mission (Kaufmann, *Religion of Israel,* 212). The prophet can be elected against his will and must bring the word of Yahweh to the world. The apostolic prophets are represented as the instrument of Yahweh's desire to reveal himself and his will to his people (Kaufmann, *Religion of Israel,* 213). Moses is therefore the first in a long line of apostolic prophets, and Yahweh's call of Moses and Moses' complex response become paradigmatic for the later classical prophetic tradition in Israel. It consists of the following stages found in later prophetic calls: a sudden, unexpected encounter with Yahweh; the summons to deliver a message; the natural reluctance of the individual concerned; and his eventual surrender to Yahweh's overwhelming persuasiveness (cf. Amos 7:14–15, 3:8; Isa 6:5, Jer 1:6, 20:7, 9).[1]

In the Bible, this kind of apostolic prophecy is represented as different from ecstatic prophecy. It is also distinct from divination. Divination is an attempt to uncover the divine will through some technique—perhaps the manipulation of certain substances or the inspection of the entrails of a sacrificed animal. Divination of this type, sorcery, spell casting, and consulting ghosts or spirits are all condemned by Deuteronomy, an almost certain sign that such activities were engaged in by some Israelites. First Samuel 28 contains the famous story of the witch of Endor—who is engaged by Saul to conjure the ghost of Samuel. Moreover, there appears to be a form of divination in the Yahweh cult itself. According to Ex 28:13–30 (see also 1 Sam 14:36–42), the priests were authorized to consult some sort of divinely designated oracular objects—colored stones perhaps—that were manipulated in such as way as to reveal the will of Yahweh. Of course, these "Urim and Thummim" are said to be assigned by Yahweh himself as a means to determine his will, and so they are acceptable, but in general it is the view of the Deuteronomistic historian that divination and sorcery are not only prohibited but also quite distinct from the activity of prophets.

The Hebrew prophet should not be thought of primarily as a prognosticator predicting the future. Rather, the prophet addressed a specific and present historical situation in concrete terms. The prophet revealed Yahweh's immediate intentions but only insofar as he sought to convey Yahweh's response to present circumstances. The goal, however, was to inspire the people to faithful observance of the covenant in the present. Thus any "predictions" made by the classical prophets had reference to the *immediate* future as a response to the *present* situation. The prophet's message was a message about the present, about what was wrong in the prophet's day, and what must be done immediately in order to avert calamity.

There were women prophets in Israel, though none among the literary prophets. Besides Miriam in the Pentateuch, there is Deborah, a tribal leader and a prophet featured in Judges 4–5; Huldah, a prophetess whose advice was sought in the time of King Josiah (2 Kgs 22:13–20; 2 Chr 34:22–28); and Noadiah, who prophesied in the postexilic period (Neh 6:14).

## Prophets and Politics

Biblical narratives depict the king as the anointed one of Yahweh. This anointing is done by prophets, creating a strong bond between the institutions of kingship and prophecy. The first king, Saul, was anointed by the prophet Samuel, but in addition Saul is said to have prophesied himself, in the manner of the ecstatic prophets. After his anointing he is seized by the spirit of Yahweh and joins a band of men playing "harp, tambourine, flute and lyre" (1 Sam 10:5), inducing an ecstasy that transforms him into another man. On another occasion, Saul strips himself naked while prophesying (1 Sam 19:23–24). Likewise David, in addition to being anointed by Yahweh's prophet Samuel, is said to receive Yahweh's spirit or charisma from time to time.

Subsequent monarchs are not said to have been prophets themselves or to be seized by the spirit of Yahweh and to prophesy ecstatically, but the monarchy was always dependent upon and closely connected with the institution of prophecy in Israel. This is exemplified in several ways. First, as noted above, prophets anointed kings. Second, prophets also often announced a king's fall from power. Third, a remarkable motif in biblical narrative is the continued opposition of prophets to kings who violate moral or religious laws: Samuel stands in opposition to Saul, Nathan rebukes King David, Ahijah opposes King Solomon and later King Jeroboam, and the list continues—Elijah and Micaiah against Ahab, Elisha against Jehoram and Ahab's house, Amos against Jeroboam II, Jeremiah against Jehoiakim, and so on. This prophetic opposition to kings is expressed by a standard literary formula: The word of Yahweh came to [prophet] X against [king] Y, "Because you have sinned I will destroy you/wrest the kingship from you, etc."

The complex relationship between the institutions of kingship and prophecy is expressed in the diverse roles assumed by prophets in the narratives in 1 and 2 Samuel and 1 and 2 Kings.

### (1) The "True" Prophet versus the Royal Prophet

Like the kings of Assyria, the kings of Judah and Israel found it politic to employ prophetic guilds. In most instances, the court prophets in the king's employ were little more than endorsers of royal policy. On numerous occasions we see these professional prophets at odds with figures the biblical writer views as true prophets who proclaim the word of Yahweh, regardless of whether it is what the people or the king want to hear. The classic example is Micaiah son of Imlah, who prophesies the truth from Yahweh even though it displeases the king and costs Micaiah his freedom.

First Kings 22 contains the story of the prophet Micaiah and is a pointed critique of the prophetic yes-men who serve as court prophets for, and automatically endorse the royal policy of, the northern kingdom's King Ahab. During the reign of King Ahab in the ninth century, the kingdoms of Judah and Israel form an alliance for the purpose of recapturing territory lost to Aram. But as no military undertaking was launched before obtaining a favorable word from Yahweh, King Ahab's prophets—400 of them—are called, and the king asks:

> "Shall I march upon Ramoth-gilead for battle? Or shall I not?"
> "March," they said, "and Yahweh will deliver it into Your Majesty's hands." (1 Kgs 22:6)

In this instance, the institution of prophecy serves as a source of royal advice. However, the king of Judah, King Jehoshaphat, who had hoped for an oracle against the campaign, asks:

"Isn't there another prophet of Yahweh here through whom we can inquire?" And the king of Israel answered Jehoshaphat, "There is one more man through whom we can inquire of the lord, but I hate him, because he never prophesies anything good for me, but only misfortune—Micaiah son of Imlah." (1 Kgs 22:7–9)

But King Jehoshaphat prevails and Micaiah is summoned. Micaiah is warned by a messenger that he should speak a favorable word like all the other prophets: "Look, the words of the prophets are with one accord favorable to the king. Let your word be like that of the rest of them; speak a favorable word" (v. 13)—an admission that the prophets are little more than yes-men. Micaiah answers the kings' question as to the advisability of the military expedition with the statement: "March and triumph! Yahweh will deliver [it] into your majesty's hands" (v. 15). But Micaiah does not use the prophetic formula "Thus says Yahweh" or give any other indications that he is actually conveying the word of Yahweh. Perhaps sensing Micaiah's deception, the king says, "How many times must I adjure you to tell me nothing but the truth in the name of Yahweh" (v. 16). So Micaiah speaks unrestrained; he tells of the vision he received from Yahweh—a vision of Israel scattered over the hills like sheep without a shepherd, implying that Israel's shepherd, the king, will be killed in battle and the people scattered. The king is irritated by Micaiah's prophecy: "Didn't I tell you . . . that he would not prophesy good fortune for me, but only misfortune?" (v. 18).

Of particular interest is Micaiah's explanation for the fact that he is the lone dissenter. He doesn't accuse the other prophets of being false prophets; instead, he represents them as misled. For the second time, Micaiah delivers the word of Yahweh, and it takes the form of another vision. This time the vision depicts Yahweh himself seated on his throne with the host of heaven gathered around him. Yahweh asks, "Who will entice Ahab so that he will march and fall at Ramoth-gilead?" (v. 20). A certain spirit comes forward to volunteer for the task and reveals his method: "I will go out and be a lying spirit in the mouth of all his prophets" (v. 22a). Yahweh says, "You will entice and you will prevail. Go out and do it" (v. 22b). Micaiah concludes: "So Yahweh has put a lying spirit in the mouth of all these prophets of yours; for Yahweh has decreed disaster upon you" (v. 23). It is all part of Yahweh's plan—Yahweh is setting Ahab up for disaster as punishment for his many sins, just as he set up Pharaoh by hardening his heart against the pleas of Moses to let the Israelites go, and so ensured his demise.

The king doesn't know whom to believe. He doesn't kill Micaiah on the spot but has him imprisoned on rations of bread and water, pending the outcome of the battle. Micaiah agrees to this, saying, "If you ever come home safe, Yahweh has not spoken through me" (v. 28). His prophecy, of course, proves accurate. Despite his effort to disguise himself, the king is killed in battle, and the army scatters.

The story of Micaiah is a critique of what the biblical writer perceived as the nationalization and co-optation of the prophetic guild, at the same time as it offers a portrait of the true prophet. The true prophet is the one who delivers Yahweh's word, even if it is opposed to the view of the king and the majority. He proclaims Yahweh's judgment *against* the king or *against* the nation—a message of doom. While this oppositional stance and characteristic negativity did not always sit well with established interests, in time it would be identified as one mark of a true prophet.

## (2) The Prophet as Yahweh's Zealot

The contrast between true prophets and false prophets is found again in those zealous Yahwists, Elijah and Elisha. The Elijah cycle of stories is found chiefly in 1 Kgs 17–19, 21, while the Elisha cycle appears in 2 Kgs 2–9, 13:14–21. These materials are examples of independent units of tradition that were incorporated into the Deuteronomistic history. The stories are highly folkloristic—lots of drama and color, plenty of miracles, and interesting animal behavior. That this material began as a set of folk stories is also suggested by the fact that there is much overlap in the depiction of the activities of the two prophets. Both multiply food, both predict the death of Ahab's Canaanite wife Queen Jezebel, both part water, and so on. But in their final form here, the stories are interspersed with historical footnotes about these two prophets and set within the framework of the history of the kings of the northern kingdom. They have been appropriated by the Judean-based Deuteronomistic school for the purpose of condemning the northern kingdom and her kings.

Elijah the Tishbite (from the city of Tishbeh in Gilead) is a dramatic character who comes from across the Jordan dressed in a garment of hair and a leather girdle. At the end of the story, he is whisked away by the wind of Yahweh (2 Kgs 2:11). Elijah does battle with the cult of Baal and Asherah, which was introduced by King Ahab in order to please his Baal-worshipping wife, Queen Jezebel (1 Kgs 21:25). As his first act, Elijah announces a drought in the name of Yahweh. This is a direct challenge to Baal, who was believed to control the rain and the general fertility of the land and life itself. Elijah's purpose is to show that it is Yahweh, not Baal, who controls fertility. There is good evidence that Baal was worshipped in the northern kingdom right down to the destruction, and it is quite possible that northerners saw no conflict between the cult of Baal and the cult of Yahweh. But in the Elijah story, the two cults are championed by exclusivists. Jezebel, Ahab's queen, keeps a retinue of 450 Baal prophets and is killing off the prophets of Yahweh. Elijah is equally zealous for Yahweh, refusing to tolerate the worship of any god but Yahweh. He performs miracles—the multiplication of oil and flour, the raising of a dead child—in the name of Yahweh in order to show that it is Yahweh, not Baal, who gives life. As noted in Chapter 8, some scholars argue that biblical religion (Yahwism, as opposed to Israelite-Judean religion) may have originated in the activity of zealous prophets in the northern kingdom of the ninth century who violently opposed attempts to establish the worship of Baal or combine Baal worship and Yahweh worship—prophets like Elijah and Elisha who were exclusive Yahwists tolerating no other deities.

The conflict between the Yahweh cult and the Baal cult reaches a climax in the story in 1 Kgs 18, in which Elijah challenges the prophets of Baal and Asherah to a contest. A severe drought has fallen on the land, which Elihah attributes to Ahab's sin in introducing Baal worship on a broad scale. Elijah has been in hiding from the king, but after three years he returns to Ahab. "Is that you, you troubler of Israel?" Ahab says when he sees Elijah (1 Kgs 18:17). The prophet responds:

> It is not I who have brought trouble on Israel, but you and your
> father's House, by forsaking the commandments of Yahweh and
> going after the Baalim. Now summon all Israel to join me at Mt.
> Carmel together with the four hundred and fifty prophets of
> Baal and the four hundred prophets of Asherah, who eat at Jeze-
> bel's table. (vv. 18–19)

When all are gathered, Elijah challenges the people: "How long will you keep hopping between two opinions? If the Yahweh is god, follow him; and if Baal, follow him!" (v. 20). Met with silence, Elijah prepares for the dramatic contest. Two bulls are slaughtered and laid on altars—one to Baal and one to Yahweh. The 450 prophets of Baal are to invoke their god and Elijah will invoke his to send fire to consume the sacrifice. The god who answers with fire is truly god. The Baal prophets invoke their god morning to noon, shouting, "O Baal, answer us!" What follows is wonderfully satirical:

> But there was no sound, and none who responded; so they performed a hopping dance about the altar that had been set up. When noon came, Elijah mocked them, saying: "Shout louder! After all, he is a god. But he may be in conversation, he may be detained, or he may be on a journey, or perhaps he is asleep and will wake up." So they shouted louder, and gashed themselves with knives and spears, according to their practice, until the blood streamed over them. When noon passed, they kept raving until the hour of presenting the meal offering. Still there was no sound and none who responded or heeded. (1 Kgs 18:26–29)

Then it is Elijah's turn. He sets up twelve stones for the twelve tribes, lays out the bull on the altar, digs a trench around the altar, and orders water to be poured over the whole until it is completely saturated and the trench filled with water. Following these preparations, he calls upon the name of Yahweh: Immediately, a fire descends from Yahweh and consumes offering, wood, stones, earth, and water. The people prostrate themselves and declare, "Yahweh alone is god, Yahweh alone is god." The prophets of Baal are seized and slaughtered.

Elijah expects an end to the drought, and indeed his servant reports that a cloud as small as a man's hand is rising in the west. The sky grows black; there is a strong wind and heavy storm. The drought is over. The language used here is language typically employed for the storm god Baal and drives home the point of the whole satire. Yahweh is the real god of the storm, not Baal. Yahweh controls nature, not Baal. It is Yahweh who is effective; Baal is silent and powerless. Israel's choice should be clear—Yahweh can be the only god for Israel, as for Elijah, whose name (Eli-yah) means "My god is Yahweh."

Jezebel threatens Elijah with execution, and he flees forty days and nights into the desert, to the mountain of Horeb or Sinai, the site of Yahweh's revelation to Moses and the Israelites amid thunder and fire. (Many scholars have pointed out the numerous parallels between Elijah and Moses, suggesting a conscious literary shaping of the Elijah traditions on the model of Moses.) At Sinai, Elijah is in despair; he wishes to die because he feels he has failed in his fight for Yahweh. He hides in a rocky cleft, reminiscent of the cleft in which Moses crouched to catch a glimpse of Yahweh as he passed by. There, hiding in the cleft, Elijah also encounters Yahweh.

Then the word of Yahweh came to him. He said to him, "Why are you here, Elijah?" He replied, "I am moved by zeal for Yahweh, the god of Hosts, for the Israelites have forsaken your covenant, torn down your altars, and put your prophets to the sword. I alone am left, and they are out to take my life." "Come out," he called, "and stand on the mountain before Yahweh."

And lo, Yahweh passed by. There was a great and mighty wind, splitting mountains and shattering rocks by the power of Yahweh; but Yahweh was not in the wind. After the wind—an earthquake; but Yahweh was not in the earthquake. After the earthquake—fire; but Yahweh was not in the fire. And after the fire—a soft murmuring sound. When Elijah heard it, he wrapped his mantle about his face and went out and stood at the entrance of the cave. (1 Kgs 19:9–12)

Elijah is renewed at Sinai—the mountain that was the very source of Israel's covenant with Yahweh. But whereas Yahweh's earlier theophanies there involved earthquake, wind, and fire, the narrative here makes a point of saying that Yahweh is not in the earthquake, wind, and fire, but in the lull after the storm. This story is perhaps a counterpoint or corrective to the immediately preceding story of Elijah on Mt. Carmel. Yahweh may be master of the storm instead of Baal—as Elijah has so dramatically demonstrated—but he is not to be identified with the storm as Baal is. He is not a nature god and can be known in silence—an awesome, vocal silence.

In this theophany, Yahweh instructs Elijah to return to his people and to foment revolution against the royal house. Although this task will be completed by Elijah's disciple and successor Elisha, the importance of this scene is its emphasis on Yahweh as the god of history rather than a nature god. Israel's god acts in history and is made known to humans by his acts in history, and his prophet has no business fleeing to a mountain retreat. He must return and play his part in Yahweh's plans for the nation.

### (3) *The Prophet as Miracle Man and Kingmaker*

The Elijah cycle of stories ends with Elijah's ascent into heaven in a fiery chariot carried on a whirlwind (2 Kgs 2:11), a detail that contributed to the traditional belief that Elijah never died and will return as the harbinger of the Messiah. He left his prophetic cloak to his disciple and successor Elisha (2 Kgs 2:13). Elisha's involvement in the political arena was important also and highlights yet another aspect of the role of the prophet touched on earlier—that of kingmaker and king breaker. Just as Samuel anointed Saul and then David in private meetings, so Elisha sends an associate to secretly anoint Jehu, one of Ahab's ex-captains, as king of Israel. This initiates a bloody civil war in which Jehu massacres all of Ahab's family, supporters, and retinue in Jezreel. Elisha is notable for yet another aspect of the prophetic profile in the books of Samuel and Kings—that of miracle worker. Like Elijah, Elisha performs miracles—he causes an iron ax to float (2 Kgs 6:6), raises a child from the dead (2 Kgs 4:32–35), fills jars of oil (2 Kgs 4:1–7), makes poison soup edible (2 Kgs 4:38–41), causes twenty barley loaves to feed 100 men (2 Kgs 4:42–44), and heals lepers (2 Kgs 5). These legendary stories in which divine intentions are effected by means of the supernatural powers of holy men represent a popular religiosity. People turned to wonder-working holy men when sick or in crisis for help. This kind of popular belief in and fascination with wonder-working charismatics is seen very prominently in the Gospels of the New Testament.

## (4) The Prophet as the Conscience of the King

A final prophetic role is well illustrated by the prophet Nathan. Nathan is the classic example of a prophet who serves as the conscience of the king. Second Samuel 11–12 contains the dramatic story of David and Bathsheba. King David's illicit union with Bathsheba, the wife of Uriah, results in her pregnancy. When David learns that Bathsheba is carrying his child, he first tries to cover up his paternity by granting Uriah a few days' leave from active military duty for the purpose of a conjugal visit. The pious Uriah refuses, and David plans to dispose of him. He orders Uriah's commander to place him in the front lines of battle and then withdraw so that Uriah is exposed and killed—and indeed all transpires as planned. Thus, David has added murder to adultery. But not even the king is above Yahweh's law, and Yahweh sends his prophet Nathan to tell the king a fable:

> "There were two men in the same city, one rich and one poor. And the rich man had very large flocks and herds, but the poor man had only one little ewe lamb that he had bought. He tended it and it grew up together with him and his children: it used to

share his morsel of bread, and drink from his cup, and nestle in his bosom; it was like a daughter to him. One day, a traveler came to the rich man, but he was loathe to take anything from his own flocks or herds to prepare a meal for the guest who had come to him; so he took the poor man's lamb and prepared it for the man who had come to him." David flew into a rage against the man and said to Nathan, "As Yahweh lives, the man who did this deserves to die! He shall pay for the lamb four times over because he did such a thing and showed no pity. And Nathan said to David, "That man is you." (2 Sam 12:1–7)

It is quite remarkable that Nathan escaped with his life after such an accusation. But it is symptomatic of the biblical narrator's view of monarchy, the subjugation of the king to Yahweh and his teachings and prophets, that instead we read that David humbly acknowledged his guilt and repented. He does not escape all punishment for his deed: Yahweh decrees the death of Bathsheba's child, as well as future strife and treachery in David's own household. Indeed, David's son Amnon rapes David's daughter Tamar, and another son, Absalom, will die in an effort to usurp the throne.

Elijah functions as the conscience of King Ahab in 1 Kgs 21. The king covets the vineyard of a man named Naboth. Jezebel falsely accuses Naboth of blasphemy, so that he is stoned to death and his property is transferred to the crown. Shortly after this perversion of justice, Elijah appears and pronounces doom upon Ahab and his descendants for their treatment of Naboth. Ahab admits his sin and repents so that his punishment is delayed, but he is killed later at the Battle of Ramoth-gilead (1 Kgs 22). In these stories we see the prophets functioning as "troublers" whose relationships with the royal house are quite adversarial.

## Literary Prophets

The period of classical prophecy (or literary prophecy) begins with the eighth-century prophets Amos and Hosea. The last of the literary prophets was Malachi (fifth century B.C.E.). The prophets spanned 320 years, from 750 to 430 B.C.E., and responded to urgent crises in the life of the nation. In fact, the prophets can be grouped according to four critical periods: (1) prophets of the Assyrian crisis, (2) prophets of the Babylonian crisis, (3) prophets of the exile, and (4) prophets of the postexilic and restoration community.

In the eighth century, the Assyrian Empire threatened the two king-doms of Israel and Judah. The prophets Amos and Hosea prophesied in the northern kingdom prior to and during the Assyrian crisis and warned of the impending doom that would come as punishment for violations of the Mo-saic Covenant. When Israel fell in 722 and Judah was similarly threatened, two Judean prophets, Micah and Isaiah, carried a similar message to the Judeans. With the fall of Nineveh in 612—an event celebrated in the short book of Nahum—Babylon became the new imperial master of the region. Judah was reduced to the status of vassal state but plotted revolt and sought assistance from Egypt. The prophets Habakkuk and Jeremiah prophesied in Judah prior to and during the Babylonian crisis. Jeremiah urged political submission to Babylon, the agent of Yahweh's just punishment. He wit-nessed the events of the destruction and lived out his final years in Egypt. The sixth-century postexilic prophet Ezekiel spoke to his fellow citizens in exile in Babylonia, asserting the justice of Yahweh's punishment but also offering consolation and encouragement, with visions of a rebuilt temple and glowing future. At the end of the sixth century, when the first of the exiles were permitted to return to their homeland, they faced a harsh life of poverty and toil. To these returnees, the prophets Haggai and Zechariah promised a better future, while the fifth-century prophets Joel and Malachi added eschatological hopes to the mix.

There has long been debate over the degree to which the classical liter-ary prophets were harking back to long-standing Israelite traditions that preceded them or constructing the norms and concepts that would later be viewed as long-standing Israelite tradition.[2] Kaufmann describes the classi-cal prophets as the standard-bearers of the faith of Yahweh.[3] In his view, they were conservatives, and yet the new prophecy conceived of ideas that Israelite thought of an earlier time had not. In this sense, Kaufmann argues, they were also radical. As a result, the prophets had to speak with exaggera-tion and dramatic features. They denounced and chastised the people and were often scoffed at or even persecuted in return. Nevertheless, the nation eventually enshrined their words in its ancient sacred heritage, testimony to the fact that their message served a crucial role in a time of changing politi-cal and religious reality.

## CHAPTER 16

# The Prophetic Response to the Events of History

## Amos as Paradigm

*Readings:* Amos

The individual books of the literary prophets appear to be arranged according to two simultaneous principles: size and chronology. The first three prophetic books are extremely large and appear in chronological order (Isaiah, an eighth-century Judean prophet at the time of the Assyrian crisis; Jeremiah, a seventh- to sixth-century Judean prophet at the time of the Babylonian crisis; and Ezekiel, another Judean prophet at the time of the Babylonian crisis and exile). These three major books are followed by twelve smaller books known as the minor prophets. The minor prophets are arranged in roughly chronological order, though book size also plays a role. In this chapter and in subsequent chapters, the prophetic books will be examined in chronological order rather than canonical order, with close attention to the book's historical context.

As noted in Chapter 14, the Deuteronomistic historian developed an interpretation of the historical catastrophes of 722 and 586 B.C.E. that made it possible to accept the reality of the defeat of Israel without losing faith in Yahweh: The defeat of Israel and the exile of Yahweh's people was not to be taken as evidence that Yahweh was not the one supreme universal god or that Yahweh was a faithless god who had abandoned his people and his covenants. The defeat and exile affirmed precisely the opposite—that Yahweh as the universal god could use other nations to execute judgment upon his people, that Yahweh had brought about the punishment of national collapse and exile—as he had clearly warned he would in the time of Moses—because of the sin of idolatry instigated by sinful kings.

The classical literary prophets (Isaiah, Jeremiah, Ezekiel, and several of the minor prophets) follow the basic thrust of this interpretation of Israel's history. They agree that the defeat and exile are evidence, rather than disproof, of Yahweh's universal sovereignty, that they are Yahweh's just punishment for sin. But they differ from the Deuteronomistic historian in two ways. First, they differ in their identification of the sin that brings national collapse and exile and, second, they differ in their emphasis on a future restoration and glory.

## Amos

The first of the literary prophets, Amos preached in the northern kingdom of Israel during a relatively stable period in the reign of Jeroboam II, around 750 B.C.E., before the Assyrian threat became very apparent. In a brief introduction (Amos 1:1), Amos is described as a sheep breeder from Tekoa (about ten miles from Jerusalem in the southern kingdom). In chapter 7, he adds to this description the datum that he is a tender of sycamore figs (7:14) sent by Yahweh to deliver his prophecies in Bethel, one of the royal sanctuaries of the northern kingdom (7:10–16). It is likely that Amos was not a common shepherd, but a wealthy owner of land or flocks, educated and literate. Judging from the reactions of Amaziah, priest of Bethel, the northerners disliked his message and sought to dispatch him to the southern kingdom. The confrontation between Amos and Amaziah is found in chapter 7.

The book of Amos is structured in four main sections: (1) brief oracles of doom (Amos 1–2); (2) three short oracles (3–6) to the women of Samaria, to the wealthy of Samaria and Jerusalem, and to Israel as a whole; (3) five symbolic visions of judgment: locusts, fire, a plumb line, a basket of fruit, and Yahweh himself by the altar at Bethel (7:1–9:8a); and (4) an epilogue (9:8b–15). Amos contains literary and thematic features that are typical of many of the literary prophets.

## (1) *Editorial Notes*

In Amos, third-person editorial notes occur right at the beginning of the book: "The words of Amos, a sheep breeder from Tekoa, who prophesied concerning Israel in the reigns of Kings Uzziah of Judah and Jeroboam son of Joash of Israel, two years before the earthquake" (Amos 1:1). Almost all prophetic books contain an introduction of this type, identifying the prophet, his place, time, and setting in the third person. Thus we find two types of material in the prophetic books: first-person passages in which the prophet himself speaks and third-person passages about the prophet written by disciples or others when, or after, the prophet's oracles were collected. Amos 7 is another example of the latter type of writing. Here Amos is described in a heated exchange with the priest Amaziah of the shrine at Bethel. This brings us to the second feature of prophetic literature.

## (2) *Diverse Materials*

The prophetic books consist of diverse materials that have been collected, revised, and supplemented. The prophet's oracles, delivered in various situations over a period of time, were apparently saved and then compiled, perhaps by the prophet himself or by his disciples. We know that prophetic oracles were written down and transmitted in other ancient Near Eastern societies as well (in Assyria, for example). The literary nature of the composition accounts for the lack of chronological order, because the prophets or their disciples would combine prophecies according to principles other than chronology. For example, the compiler might employ the principle of a catchword—a word in one oracle corresponds with a word in another oracle, resulting in the juxtaposition of the two oracles. Amos 3:2 reads: "You alone have I known of all the families of the earth." The verb *to know* was probably the catchword for the oracle that follows, which opens with the line "Do two people walk together unless they know each other?" (Amos 3:3). In short, the prophetic books are anthologies of oracles that are often connected for literary rather than chronological or substantive reasons. One cannot assume chronological or narrative sequence, as one might when reading the historical books of Joshua through Kings.

Scholars have long sought to determine the degree to which the prophetic books preserve the actual oracles of historical prophets. There is no question that the prophetic books have undergone revision and supplementation so that not everything in the book of Amos, for example, is from the historical prophet Amos himself. Interpolations and additions have been made to most of the prophetic books. Prompting these changes was the belief that the words of the prophets had enduring significance. Such a belief probably accounts for the oracle prophesying the fall of Judah in Amos 2. This oracle is likely an addition made after Judah's fall in 586 B.C.E. (see below for literary considerations that support this claim). Nevertheless, supplementations and revisions of prophetic writings do not appear to be promiscuous or thoroughgoing. In many instances a prophet's words have not been modified or updated, even though the failure to do so leaves the prophecy out of step with what later proved to be the case. Such inconsistencies between prophecy and later fact suggest a tendency to faithfully preserve the words of the prophet, even as interpolations and revisions attest to a desire to conform the prophet's words to the events of history.

### (3) The Call

Common to many of the books of the literary prophets is a claim to authority as the result of having been called by Yahweh to deliver his word. The irresistibility of the call is illustrated in Amos 3:7–8. After citing a series of proverbs that illustrate inexorable cause and effect, such as "Does a trap spring up from the ground unless it has caught something?" the oracle continues: "A lion has roared, who can but fear? My lord Yahweh has spoken, who can but prophesy?"

### (4) Metaphors

Amos describes his prophecy by means of two primary metaphors: word and vision. Many prophetic oracles are introduced by the phrase "the word of Yahweh came unto prophet X"—conveying the sense that Yahweh speaks to the prophets in language that is then repeated by the prophet. Behind this metaphor is the simple idea that Yahweh communicates with the prophets and the prophets pass on this communication to the people.

In addition to hearing the word of Yahweh, Amos, like many other prophets, is said to *see* visions of various kinds (hence the word *seer* as another designation for the prophet). These visions might be of Yahweh himself speaking or performing some action. Alternatively, they might be visions of extraordinary events or of ordinary objects that carry some symbolic significance. In Amos 7, 8, and 9, the prophet has five visions. One is a vision of Yahweh destroying the worshippers in the Temple (9:1); two are visions of extraordinary things: a locust plague that is about to consume the crop after the king has taken his share for taxes (7:1–3) and a supernatural fire that licks up the subterranean waters that irrigate the earth and threatens the soil itself (7:4–6); two others are visions of ordinary objects that have a special meaning for Israel. For example, a plumb line used by builders symbolizes Yahweh's judgment of Israel (7:7–9), and a basket of summer fruit (in Hebrew, *kayiṣ*) relies on a wordplay to symbolize Israel's end (*keṣ*) (8:1–3).

## (5) Varied Literary Forms

The prophetic corpus employs a variety of literary forms. One commonplace form is "the oracle against the nations." Such oracles occur in Amos but also in the three large prophetic books: Isaiah, Jeremiah, and Ezekiel. Amos 1 and 2 contain seven such oracles that inveigh against the nations. But Amos gives the form a new twist. Six of the seven oracles are directed against surrounding nations who are excoriated for their inhumane treatment of others—Israelite or non-Israelite. As punishment for their war atrocities, a divine fire will break out and destroy their palaces and fortified places. But then comes the twist. After six oracles condemning other nations, Amos turns to address his own people: The same divine power, he declares, will consume the people of Yahweh because of the atrocities and inhumanities they commit not in war but in times of peace! Thus the seventh, climactic oracle announces that Yahweh's wrath will be directed at Israel—surely an unwelcome and shocking proclamation.

The term *Israel* is, of course, ambiguous. Does Amos prophesy against the entire tribal confederation, or does he prophesy against Israel the northern kingdom? Some passages clearly intend the latter, but some statements may be understood as referring to the entire nation. Amos does contain an oracle directed against Judah (Amos 2:4–5), but many scholars view this as a later addition by an editor. There is a central literary consideration that supports this claim. If the oracle against Judah is omitted, we have six oracles plus one (six oracles against foreign nations and one oracle against Israel), and the number 7 is standard in the creation of literary structure. The six plus one pattern is related to another pattern found in Amos: the three plus one pattern (which is simply doubled to create the six plus one pattern): For example, Amos 1:3 reads, "For three transgressions of Damascus, For four I will not revoke it [the decree of punishment]." Also chapter 1, verse 6 regarding

Gaza, verse 9 regarding Tyre, verse 11 regarding Edom, verse 13 regarding the Ammonites, and more, employ the same three plus one pattern.

Other forms employed in the prophetic corpus include hymns, songs or laments (usually mourning for Israel as if her destruction were a fait accompli), and proverbs. Specifically, older proverbs are applied to new situations and so undergo a transformation in meaning. Amos 3–8 contains many such proverbs. Another literary form found in prophetic writing is the covenant lawsuit, or *riv*. Many of the prophetic books feature passages in which Yahweh brings a lawsuit against his people, charging them with breaking the covenant and employing various legal metaphors. In short, the prophetic corpus draws on the entire range of literary forms available in the Israelite tradition, giving these writings a rich and varied texture.

As noted earlier, the book of Amos is a model for the other prophetic books not only in terms of form but also in terms of content, since the book of Amos articulates certain themes that will resound throughout the prophetic literature. These themes, as articulated by Y. Kaufmann (365–368, 386–387, 394–395), are outlined below.

## Denunciation of Social Injustice

First, the literature of the classical prophets is characterized by a vehement denunciation of the moral decay and social injustices of the time.[1] Amos criticizes the sins and attacks the superficial piety of the entire nation—the middle class, the government, the king, and the priesthood. For Amos, as for all the prophets, the idea of covenant prescribes a particular relationship not only with Yahweh but also with one's fellow human beings. Indeed, the two are interlinked so that a sign of closeness with Yahweh is a concern for the poor and needy in Israel's midst. Amos savagely denounces the wealthy and the powerful for their treatment of the poor.

> Hear this word, you cows of Bashan
> On the hill of Samaria—
> Who defraud the poor,
> Who rob the needy;
> Who say to your husbands,
> "Bring and let's carouse!"
> My lord Yahweh swears by his holiness:
> Behold, days are coming upon you

When you will be carried off in baskets,
And, to the last one, in fish baskets,
And taken out [of the city]—
Each one through a breach straight ahead—
And flung on the refuse heap
                                 —declares Yahweh. (Amos 4:1–3)

The pun here is wonderful—the wealthy women of Samaria (the capital of the northern kingdom) are called "cows of Bashan" (an area of rich pastureland in the Transjordan). It was common Canaanite practice to apply terms like *bull, ram,* and *cow* to deities and nobility—thus the term in and of itself does not offend. But the pun here is that these women, praised as healthy bovines, will end up like slabs of meat in the butcher's basket that, when spoiled, are thrown on the refuse heap.

Amos 6:1, 4–7 contains another scathing attack on the idle lives of the carefree rich who ignore the plight of the poor:

Ah, you who are at ease in Zion
And confident on the hill of Samaria,
You notables of the leading nation
On whom the House of Israel pin their hopes. . . .
They lie on ivory beds,
Lolling on their couches,
Feasting on lambs from the flock
And on calves from the stalls.
They hum snatches of song
To the tune of the lute—
They account themselves musicians like David.
They drink [straight] from the wine bowls
And anoint themselves with the choicest oils—
But they are not concerned about the ruin of Joseph.
Assuredly, right soon
They shall head the column of exiles;
They shall loll no more at festive meals.[2]

The moral decay, the greed, and indulgence of the upper classes are directly responsible for the social injustice that outrages Yahweh, as we see in Amos 8:4–6:

Listen to this, you who devour the needy, annihilating the poor of the land, saying "If only the new moon were over, so that we could sell grain; the sabbath, so that we could offer wheat for sale, using an *ephah*[3] that is too small, and a *shekel* that is too big, tilting a dishonest scale, and selling grain refuse as grain! We will buy the poor for silver, the needy for a pair of sandals." Yahweh swears by the Pride of Jacob: "I will never forget any of their doings."

The prophets are prone to extreme formulations and high-flown rhetoric. When one strips away the rhetoric, one sees that the crimes denounced are not murder or rape or physical violence; these would be obvious and grievous violations of social and religious morality. Rather, as Kaufmann and other scholars have long observed, the crimes that are denounced as absolutely unacceptable to Yahweh, the crimes that threaten to bring national collapse and exile, are the crimes prevalent in any society in any era: taking bribes, improper weights and balances, lack of charity to the poor, indifference to the plight of the debtor.

## The Primacy of Morality

A second theme found in classical prophecy is the idea of the primacy of morality—the doctrine that morality is not just an obligation equal in importance to the cult, but that morality is superior to the cult.[4] What Yahweh requires of Israel is morality, not cultic service. The words of the prophets were harsh and shocking. Amos 5:21–24 expresses this idea in first-person direct speech attributed to Yahweh:

I loathe, I spurn your festivals,
I am not appeased by your solemn assemblies.
If you offer me burnt offerings—or your meal offerings—
I will not accept them;
I will pay no heed
To your gifts of fatlings.
Spare me the sound of your hymns,
And let me not hear the music of your lutes.
But let justice well up like water,
Righteousness like an unfailing stream.

The attack on empty piety, on the performance of rituals without proper intention, is stressed repeatedly in the prophetic literature. For Amos, injustice is sacrilege, and the ideals of the covenant are of utmost importance. Without these ideals, the fulfillment of cultic and ritual obligations is a farce.

This prophetic rejection of the cultic activity of the wicked is taken further in some cases. Although the idea is not yet fully formed in Amos, some of the prophets seem to reject the cult of the entire people, not just the wicked: Even if performed properly and by righteous persons, the cult has no inherent or absolute value for Yahweh (see Micah 6:1–8). It may be noted that a forerunner of this view is found even in sources devoted to the cult, since sources like P see the cult as an expression of divine favor and not divine need. In P, the cult has no actual value for Yahweh and does not affect his vitality as in other cultures; the cult was given to humans as a ritual conduit to Yahweh and as a means of procuring atonement for deeds or impurities that temporarily separate one from Yahweh. So the prophetic doctrine of the primacy of morality seems to be reacting to popular assumptions about the automatic efficacy of the cult.

Kaufmann and others have argued that the prophets raised morality to the level of an absolute religious value because they saw morality as essentially divine.[5] For the prophets, moral attributes are the essence of Yahweh himself. He who requires justice, righteousness, and compassion of humans is himself just, righteous, and compassionate. The moral person, then, can be said metaphorically to share in divinity. While pagan religions aspired to apotheosis to deify humans (actual transformation into divine beings after death or even in life), Israelite religion could not embrace such a notion in this life or after death, because of the separation of the divine and human realms. But it did demand that humans become godlike by imitating Yahweh's moral actions.

## The Role of Morality in the National History

A third feature of literary prophecy underscored by Kaufmann concerns the prophets' view of history and their interpretation of the catastrophic events of 722 and 586, an interpretation that centers on their elevation of morality.[6] The prophets insisted that morality—common everyday morality—was a decisive factor in the national history. Israel's acceptance of Yahweh's covenant placed religious and moral obligations upon her, and breaches of the covenant would be punished.

According to the Deuteronomistic view examined in Chapter 14, only one sin is singled out as historically decisive for the nation—the sin of idolatry, particularly as promoted by the nation's monarch. Consequently, the Deuteronomistic historian presents the tragic history of the two kingdoms as a sequence of idolatrous aberrations led by Israel's kings, followed by punishment. In other words, while moral sins and other religious sins in Israel are punished, it is only the worship of other gods that brings the punishment of national collapse and exile. The Deuteronomistic historian's view, exemplified by 2 Kgs 17, makes no mention of strictly moral sins as leading to the collapse of the nation—only idolatry.

By contrast, the view of classical prophecy is that Israel's history is determined by cultic *and* moral factors so that the nation is punished not only for idolatry but also for moral failings. Now while it may not be startling to hear that Yahweh would doom a generation for grave moral sins such as murder and violence (after all, the generation of the flood and the cities of Sodom and Gomorrah were said to be destroyed for such things), the prophets were claiming that the nation was doomed because of commonplace venial sins: bribe taking, false scales in the marketplace. These were the crimes for which destruction and exile would take place.

> Thus said Yahweh:
> For three transgressions of Israel,
> For four, I will not revoke it [the decree of destruction]:
> Because they have sold for silver
> Those whose cause was just,
> And the needy for a pair of sandals.
> [Ah,] you who trample the heads of the poor
> Into the dust of the ground,
> And make the humble walk a twisted course! (Amos 2:6–8)

This, then, is the first difference between the Deuteronomistic interpretation of the catastrophe that befell Israel and the prophetic interpretation: For the prophets, national catastrophes are divine punishment for sin, not just the sin of idolatry, but all sins no matter how petty or venial, since all sins violate the terms of the covenant code given specially to Israel.

Were the prophets harking back to ancient traditions when they emphasized that Israel's election and continued well-being entailed moral obligation? Or were they the originators of this idea, which would later be inserted into the national myth of origins? These questions are hotly debated by scholars and are not likely to be resolved anytime soon. However, it is important to note that the primacy of morality in Israelite religion dates back at least to the time of the earliest prophets of the eighth century B.C.E. and may indeed have antecedents. It is highly unlikely that it arose only in the exile or that it was invented out of whole cloth by the Deuteronomistic historian.

## Consolation and Hope

Another important difference between the Deuteronomistic historian and the prophetic interpretation of Israel's history lies in the fact that the prophets' message of doom is coupled with a message of hope and consolation. The combined themes of doom and consolation find expression in eschatological passages.

Classical prophecy gave a new content to Israelite eschatology (an eschatology is an account of the end or end-time). The prophets warned that without change, the people would suffer the punishment they deserved. In fact, the people's eager expectations for the Day of Yahweh were foolish. The phrase "Day of Yahweh" refers to a popular idea in ancient Israel that on some future occasion Yahweh would dramatically intervene in world affairs on Israel's behalf, lead her in victory over her enemies, and restore her to her former glory. In the popular mind, the Day of Yahweh would be a day of triumph for Israel and vengeance upon her enemies. The people desired the Day of Yahweh, confident that it would be a day of light, of victory and blessing (see Amos 5:18–29 below). But the prophets told a different story. According to them, unless Israel changed course, the Day of Yahweh would not be a day of triumph for Israel or a time of vengeance on Israel's enemies but a dark day of destruction and doom in which Yahweh would finally call his people to account. The classical prophets transformed the popular image of the Day of Yahweh from one of national triumph to one of national judgment.

> Ah, you who wish
> For the day of Yahweh!
> Why should you want
> The day of Yahweh?
> It shall be darkness, not light!—
> As if a man should run from a lion
> And be attacked by a bear;
> Or if he got indoors,

> Should lean his hand on the wall
> And be bitten by a snake!
> Surely the day of Yahweh shall be
> Not light, but darkness,
> Blackest night without a glimmer. (Amos 5:18–20)

A similarly bleak vision is found in Amos 8:9–12:

> And in that day—declares my lord Yahweh—
> I will make the sun set at noon,
> I will darken the earth on a sunny day.
> I will turn your festivals into mourning
> And all your songs into dirges;
> I will put sackcloth on all loins
> And tonsures on every head.
> I will make it mourn as for an only child,
> All of it as on a bitter day.

At the heart of this transformation of the Day of Yahweh into a day of judgment for Israel is an expansion of the idea that Yahweh is the god of history. The claim that Yahweh was the god of history, that Yahweh controlled the destiny and actions of all nations and could summon all nations to judgment, was not a new idea. What the prophets objected to was the assumption held by some that Yahweh's involvement with other nations was always undertaken on behalf of Israel or that Yahweh controlled other nations only by exercising judgment upon them, punishing them, and subjugating them to Israel. The prophets challenged this conventional belief with what would have been perceived as a shocking and extraordinary claim: Yahweh is, of course, the god of history, and he is concerned with all nations, but his involvement with other nations does not extend merely to their subjugation to Israel. If need be, or rather, if Israel so deserves, Yahweh will raise up another nation against her to execute his judgment upon her.

The final chapter of Amos begins by proclaiming the idea of the utter destruction of Israel. "I will slay the last of them with the sword," Yahweh says, "and not one of them shall survive" (Amos 9:1). Wherever they hide—under the earth, in the heavens, at the bottom of the sea—Yahweh will haul them out and slay them. And what of the covenant? The covenant is not a guarantee of privilege or safety—again, for Amos its primary function is to bind Israel to a code of conduct such that violations of that code will be severely punished. And so Amos 9:7–8 contains the startling claim that in Yahweh's eyes, Israel is really no different from the rest of the nations. Just as Yahweh elevated her, so he can lower her:

> To Me, O Israelites, you are
> Just like the Ethiopians—declares Yahweh.
> True I brought Israel up from the land of Egypt.
> But also the Philistines from Caphtor
> And the Arameans from Kir.
> Behold, my lord Yahweh has his eye
> Upon the sinful kingdom [Israel]:
> I will wipe it off
> The face of the earth!

It must be remembered that Amos lived at a time of peace and prosperity (750 B.C.E.), when national confidence was riding high and the people of Israel were convinced that Yahweh was indeed with them. Amos was convinced that despite the outward appearance of health, Israel was diseased. Guilty of social crimes and unfaithfulness to her covenantal obligations, she was headed down a path of destruction. Because of the optimism of his time, Amos emphasized his message of doom. Later prophets speaking in desperate times would provide more of a message of hope. Nevertheless, despite his harsh words, Amos does indicate that his purpose is the reformation and reorientation of the nation. His proclamation of doom is designed to awaken Israel to the urgent need for change.

> Seek good and not evil,
> That you may live,
> And that Yahweh, the god of Hosts,
> May truly be with you,
> As you think.
> Hate evil and love good,
> And establish justice in the gate;
> Perhaps Yahweh, the god of Hosts,
> Will be gracious to the remnant of Joseph. (Amos 5:14–15)

The "perhaps" in the last sentence of this passage is important and indicative of Amos's fatalism. The overriding theme of Amos's message is that punishment is inevitable. This is one reason that most scholars believe the final

verses of Amos (9:8b–15) to be the addition of a later editor. The other reason
is the passage's explicit reference to the fall of Judah and the house of David,
events that occurred more than a century and a half after Amos's time. This
brief epilogue was likely added in order to relieve the gloom and pessimism
of the prophet's message. In it, the prophetic speaker does an immediate
about-face. The oracle of complete and devastating judgment that just concluded in 9:8a, "Behold, my lord Yahweh has His eye upon the sinful kingdom [Israel]. I will wipe it off the face of the earth!" is immediately diluted if
not contradicted in 9:8b:

> But, I will not wholly wipe out
> The House of Jacob—declares Yahweh.
> For I will give the order
> And shake the House of Israel—
> Through all the nations—
> As one shakes [sand] in a sieve,
> And not a pebble falls to the ground.
> All the sinners of my people
> Shall perish by the sword,
> Who boast,
> "Never shall the evil
> Overtake us or come near us."
> In that day,
> I will set up again the fallen booth of David:
> I will mend its breaches and set up its ruins anew.
> I will build it firm as in the days of old . . .
> A time is coming—declares Yahweh . . .
> When the mountains shall drip wine
> And all the hills shall wave [with grain].
> I will restore my people Israel.
> They shall rebuild ruined cities and inhabit them;
> They shall till gardens and eat their fruits.
> And I will plant them upon their soil,
> Nevermore to be uprooted
> From the soil I have given them
>            —said Yahweh your god. (9:8b–11, 13–15)

In other words, Yahweh's punishment of Israel is not the end of the story,
for the affliction serves a purpose. The affliction is designed to chasten

Israel, to purge the dross. Only the sinners will be punished and a remnant—presumably righteous—will be permitted to survive. And in due time that remnant will be restored.

## Conclusion

The book of Amos is a set of oracles by a prophet addressing a concrete situation in the northern kingdom. These oracles were subject to some additions that reflect the perspective of a later editor. Amos's basic message was that all sins and moral failings would be punished by Yahweh on a national level. When the northern kingdom fell, it was understood as the fulfillment of Amos's words—the Assyrians were the instruments of Yahweh's just punishment. Amos's words were preserved in Judah, and after Judah fell, a later editor added a few key passages reflecting knowledge of this later reality: Amos 2:4 containing the oracle against Judah and Amos 9:8b–15 referring to a future day ("on that day") on which the fallen booth of David would be raised. While other literary prophets continue many of the themes apparent in Amos, they also develop new ideas to address changing historical circumstances.

## CHAPTER 17

# Prophets of the Assyrian Crisis

## Hosea and First Isaiah

*Readings:* Hosea 1–14; Isaiah 1–12, 28–33, 36–39

## Hosea

The prophet Hosea is said to be a native of the northern kingdom who prophesied in the time of Jeroboam II (who reigned until 747 B.C.E.) and continued into the reign of Israel's last king, also named Hosea. The prophet appears not to have seen the fall of Israel in 722. Hosea is one of the most difficult prophetic books—the text is quite corrupt, and at times the Hebrew is simply unintelligible. Chapters 1 to 3 tell of the prophet's marriage to a promiscuous woman as a metaphor for Yahweh's relationship with Israel. Chapters 4 to 14 contain an indictment of, or lawsuit against, Israel and comment on the political and religious affairs of Israel. In this chapter, we focus on Hosea 1–4.

The historical background for the book is the Assyrian threat. In the eighth century B.C.E., the Assyrians were wiping out the smaller states of the ancient Near East, and Israel could not be far behind. The line taken by Hosea was to condemn royal attempts to avoid defeat at the hands of Assyria. If Assyria were to conquer Israel, the prophet declared, it would be Yahweh's just punishment. To try to escape and avoid this punishment is simply another kind of rejection of Yahweh and his plans and purpose. To fight against the inevitable showed a lack of trust in the power of Yahweh. Hosea 1:6–7 compares Israel and Judah on this score.

> I will no longer accept the House of Israel or pardon them. But I will accept the House of Judah. And I will give them victory through Yahweh their god; I will not give them victory with bow and sword and battle, by horses and riders.

This attitude is most extraordinary. It must have been seen as nihilistic or treasonous to suggest inaction, but it was a kind of radical faith. Israel was faced with a choice: In whom should she place her trust—her human leaders and their armies or her god? Hosea 10:13 articulates this theme of trusting in humans rather than trusting in Yahweh.

> You have plowed wickedness,
> You have reaped iniquity—
> [And] you shall eat the fruits of treachery—
> Because you relied on your way,
> On your host of warriors.

The book of Hosea is haunted by a sense of impending disaster, as exemplified by Hosea 8:7:

> They sow wind,
> And they shall reap whirlwind—
> Standing stalks devoid of ears
> And yielding no flour.
> If they do yield any,
> Strangers shall devour it.
> Israel is bewildered.

Due to this prevalent theme of unavoidable catastrophe, Hosea has often been described as painting a depressing portrait of unrelieved gloom. Certainly, Hosea's message is grim, and at times he holds out no real hope since the nation must pay the price for its infidelity to Yahweh. But we should look more closely at some other themes in the book before accepting this evaluation entirely.

Hosea follows Amos in his denunciation of the moral decay and social injustice that plagues the land. Hosea 4:1–3 couches this denunciation in the formal style of a *riv* or lawsuit that Yahweh brings against Israel for violating the covenant, the terms of which are abbreviated here.

> Hear the word of Yahweh,
> O people of Israel!
> For Yahweh has a case
> Against the inhabitants of this land,
> Because there is no honesty and no goodness
> And no obedience to Elohim in the land.
> [False] swearing, dishonesty, and murder,
> And theft and adultery are rife;
> Crime follows upon crime!
> For that, the earth is withered:
> Everything that dwells on it languishes—
> Beasts of the field and birds of the sky—
> Even the fish of the sea perish.

Nevertheless, Hosea differs from Amos, who emphasized the theme of social injustice. More prominent in Hosea is a condemnation of Israel's religious faithlessness, or idolatry. He describes in lurid terms Israel's lecherous dealings with and addiction to images and idols. Hosea decries those in positions of leadership—both priests and kings—who have failed to prevent the licentiousness of the people, and he denounces the sacrifices as distracting the people from the real worship of Yahweh.

One of the most striking metaphors employed in Hosea 1–3 to describe the relationship between Yahweh and Israel is the metaphor of marriage, with Israel as an unfaithful, adulterous wife. The adultery of Israel was its Baal worship (biblical narrative sources also depict the north as the scene of much Baal worship). Chapter 1, reported in the third person, contains Yahweh's command that Hosea marry a prostitute as a symbol of Yahweh's own marriage with a faithless wife: "Go, get yourself a wife of whoredom and children of whoredom; for the land will stray from following Yahweh" (Hos 1:2). Hosea marries a prostitute named Gomer, and in due time his wife bears three children with inauspicious names symbolic of Yahweh's anger over Israel's religious infidelity: Jezreel, because Yahweh will punish the house of Jehu for the slaughter of the house of Ahab at Jezreel; Lo-ruhamah, meaning "not loved/forgiven," since Yahweh will no longer love or pardon the house of Israel; and Lo-Ammi, meaning "not my people," a sign that Yahweh had dissolved the covenant bond and rejected his people. There could be no more stark and shocking denial of the covenant than this.

Chapter 3 contains Hosea's first-person account of Yahweh's command to him to marry an adulteress. The adulteress symbolizes Israel, taken from a life of connection with multiple gods, brought into a marriage contract that requires her to remain faithful to one party in contrast to her customary behavior. While chapter 1 focused on the faithlessness of the wife/Israel, chapter 3 focuses on the steadfastness of the husband's/Yahweh's love in the face of his partner's infidelity. Sandwiched between these chapters is a sustained attack on Israel as the unfaithful wife and Yahweh's formal declaration of divorce from Israel: "She is not my wife and I am not her husband" (Hos 2:4).

Hosea also differs from Amos in its stark alternation between prophecies of judgment and prophecies of salvation. Chapters 1–3 do not end without hope of a tender reconciliation and a redemption of the three children apparently cast off from birth. Yahweh's steadfast love (*ḥesed*) will reconcile him to his errant wife and rejected children, just as Hosea is reunited with his faithless wife.

> Assuredly,
> I will speak coaxingly to her
> And lead her through the wilderness
> And speak to her tenderly.
> I will give her her vineyards from there,
> And the Valley of Achor as a plowland of hope.
> There she shall respond as in the days of her youth,
> When she came up from the land of Egypt.
> And in that day—declares Yahweh—
> You will call [me] Ishi,
> And no more will you call me Baali.[1]
> For I will remove the names of the Baalim from her mouth,
> And they shall nevermore be mentioned by name.
> In that day, I will make a covenant for them with the beasts of
>     the field, the birds of the air, and the creeping things of the
>     ground; I will also banish bow, sword, and war from the
>     land. Thus I will let them lie down in safety.
> And I will espouse you forever:
> I will espouse you with righteousness and justice,
> And with goodness and mercy,

> And I will espouse you with faithfulness;
> Then you shall be devoted to Yahweh.
> In that day,
> I will respond—declares Yahweh—
> I will respond to the sky,
> And it shall respond to the earth;
> And the earth shall respond
> With new grain and wine and oil,
> And they shall respond to Jezreel.
> I will sow her in the land as my own;
> And take Lo-ruhamah (not loved) back in favor;
> And I will say to Lo-Ammi, "You are my people,"
> And he will respond "[You are] my god." (Hos 2:16–25)

Thus, Hosea provides a message of consolation to accompany the gloomy portrait of the immediate future, should Israel refuse to repent (though some might argue that the consolation is the addition of a later editor). We have already seen in Amos the idea of a remnant that will survive. This idea and Hosea's idea of reconciliation stem from a conviction that Yahweh cannot and will not desert his people forever.

The prophets' combined message of judgment and doom on the one hand and hope and reconciliation on the other can be connected to the two concepts of covenant in Israelite tradition. The prophets recognized the unconditional and irrevocable covenant that Yahweh established with the patriarchs, which was fulfilled in and henceforth referred to the House of David. This covenant was the basis for a belief in the inviolability of Zion and the assurance that Yahweh would never forsake his people. At the same time, the prophets emphasized the covenant at Sinai, a covenant conditioned on the people's obedience to a set of moral, religious, and civil laws. Violations of this code would be punished. The prophets utilized the themes of both covenant traditions: Israel has violated the covenant, and the curses stipulated by Yahweh—national destruction and exile—will follow. But alienation from Yahweh is not and never will be complete and irreparable, because of the unconditional covenant. Israel will be Yahweh's people forever, despite temporary alienation.

The notion of the election, an act of purely unmerited favor and love on Yahweh's part and not in any way based on any special merit of the people Israel, undergirds the prophetic message of consolation. Hosea paints a poignant and moving portrait of the special and indissoluble love

that Yahweh bears for Israel. Like a parent, Yahweh must discipline his un-
grateful and rebellious child, but he can never entirely forsake that child.

> I fell in love with Israel
> When he was still a child;
> And I have called [him] my son
> Ever since Egypt.
> Thus were they called,
> But they went their own way;
> They sacrifice to Baalim
> And offer to carved images.
> I have pampered Ephraim,
> Taking them in my arms,
> But they have ignored
> My healing care.
> I drew them with human ties,
> With cords of love;
> But I seemed to them as one
> Who imposed a yoke on their jaws,
> Though I was offering them food. . . .
> How can I give you up, O Ephraim?
> How surrender you, O Israel?
> How can I make you like Admah,
> Render you like Zeboiim?
> I have had a change of heart,
> All my tenderness is stirred.
> I will not act on my wrath,
> Will not turn to destroy Ephraim.
> For I am El, not man,
> The Holy One in your midst:
> I will not come in fury. (Hosea 11:1–4, 8–9)

The prophet depicts a passionate struggle within the heart of the deity, a
struggle between his wrath and his love, a struggle that is won ultimately by
his love that will not let Israel (also called Ephraim) go. We will see that
each prophet holds these two covenantal ideas in tension but emphasizes
one or the other, depending on the people's situation. In times of ease and
comfort, a prophet may emphasize the punishment that will befall Israel

for violations of the Sinaitic covenant and downplay Yahweh's eternal commitment to his people. In times of despair and suffering, a prophet may point to violations of the covenant as the cause of distress but emphasize Yahweh's undying love for Israel and so hold out hope for a better future.

## First Isaiah

The book of Isaiah is the longest prophetic book, and the interpretation of many passages as symbolic references to Jesus makes it one of the books of the Bible most quoted by Christians. The historical prophet Isaiah from Jerusalem was a contemporary of Amos and Hosea. However, he was active for a longer period than they—more than fifty years (742–690? B.C.E.). Unlike Amos and Hosea, Isaiah prophesied in the southern kingdom of Judah when the Assyrian Empire threatened and engulfed Israel, then turned to threaten Judah from the reign of Uzziah and into the reign of Hezekiah in Judah.

The claim that prophetic books are anthologies of oracles compiled by the prophet or his disciples may be clearly seen in the book of Isaiah. The book of Isaiah contains some repetitions of material found in other prophetic works. Isaiah 2:2–4 is a verbatim repetition of Micah 4:1–4. Isaiah 15–16 is identical to Jer 48. These repetitions arose as freely circulating prophetic materials were incorporated into more than one prophetic compilation.

The basic structure of the book is as follows:

- 1–11—The memoirs of Isaiah, including a first-person narrative and various oracles about Judah and Jerusalem. In general, these chapters reflect the early period of Isaiah's career from about 742 to 732.
- 12—Hymns.
- 13–23—A set of oracles against foreign nations (as may be found in Amos and Hosea).
- 28–33—Miscellaneous oracles concerning Judah, Ephraim (another name for Israel), and the relationship with Egypt. From a later period (about 715–701), this material also includes counsel to the Judean king Hezekiah during the Assyrian crisis.
- 36–39—A third-person historical narrative about Isaiah and Hezekiah paralleled in 2 Kgs 18–20 (part of the Deuteronomistic history).

Most scholars agree that the remaining material is not the work of the historical Isaiah of Jerusalem and that much of it dates to a period after Isaiah's lifetime. Chapters 24–27 are an apocalypse, a vision of the end of days (the apocalyptic genre will be discussed in Chapter 23). Chapters 40–55 assume a historical setting in which Babylon, not Assyria, dominates the region. These chapters are referred to as Second Isaiah to signal the fact that they do not originate from the historical Isaiah and his circle. Chapters 56–66 contain oracles from the eighth to the early fifth centuries and are referred to as Third Isaiah, again to signal a distinctive provenance. Second and Third Isaiah will be discussed in subsequent chapters. In this chapter we consider the materials associated most closely with the historical Isaiah of Jerusalem (chapters 1–23, 28–39).

## Social Justice

The book of Isaiah is consistent with the book of Amos in identifying moral decay and social injustice as the causes of Yahweh's inevitable punishment.

> Ah,
> Those who add house to house
> And join field to field,
> Till there is room for none but you
> To dwell in the land! . . .
> Ah,
> Those who chase liquor
> From early in the morning,
> And till late in the evening
> Are inflamed by wine! . . .
> Who vindicate him who is in the wrong
> In return for a bribe,
> And withhold vindication
> From him who is in the right. (Isa 5:8, 11, 23)

Isaiah also joins Amos in the assertion that cultic practice without just and moral behavior is anathema to Yahweh.

> Hear the word of Yahweh,
> You chieftains of Sodom;
> Give ear to our god's instruction,

> You folk of Gomorrah!
> "What need have I of all your sacrifices?"
> Says Yahweh.
> "I am sated with burnt offerings of rams,
> And suet of fatlings,
> And blood of bulls;
> And I have no delight in lambs and he-goats. . . .
> Your new moons and fixed seasons
> Fill me with loathing;
> They are become a burden to me,
> I cannot endure them.
> And when you lift up your hands,
> I will turn my eyes away from you;
> Though you pray at length,
> I will not listen.
> Your hands are stained with crime—
> Wash yourselves clean;
> Put your evil doings
> Away from my sight.
> Cease to do evil;
> Learn to do good.
> Devote yourselves to justice;
> Aid the wronged.
> Uphold the rights of the orphan;
> Defend the cause of the widow." (Isa 1:10–11, 14–17)

Like Amos and Hosea, Isaiah asserts that morality is a decisive factor in the fate of the nation.

> Assuredly,
> My people will suffer exile
> For not giving heed,
> Its multitude victims of hunger
> And its masses parched with thirst. (Isa 5:13)

### The Inviolability of Zion

However, Isaiah differs from Amos and Hosea in this: He rarely attributes Yahweh's imminent punishment to the breaking of the Mosaic covenant.

Israel's wilderness tradition and Exodus, so important to the northern prophets Amos and Hosea, have no great influence on the prophecy of the Judean Isaiah, which displays instead an absorbing interest in Davidic theology. Indeed, it is his reliance on Yahweh's special relationship with the Davidic royal line and the sanctity of the Davidic capital, Jerusalem, that undergirds his consistent advice to Judah's kings: Times of great danger are opportunities to demonstrate absolute trust in Yahweh's covenant with the line of David. The king must rely exclusively on Yahweh and Yahweh's promises to David and his city and not on military or diplomatic strategies.

Isaiah's dealings with King Ahaz of Judah during the Syro-Ephraimite war (Ephraim = the northern kingdom of Israel) as depicted in chapter 7 exemplify this idea. As recounted in 2 Kgs 16, the kings of Israel and Syria form an alliance and pressure Judah to join in a coalition against Assyria. Isaiah visits the king to provide counsel. The children of Isaiah bear portentous names—"(only) a remnant will survive," and "Hasten for spoil, hurry for plunder"—names that indicate that deportation and exile lie ahead. Isaiah counsels Ahaz not to fear, for the crisis will pass. Moreover, he tells the king, "If you do not have faith, you will not be made firm" (Isa 7:9), an evocation of Zion theology, according to which one must have faith that Yahweh is in the midst of the city with his people. Isaiah offers Ahaz a sign of the truth of his prophecy, namely, that a young woman who is pregnant will bear a son and call him Immanuel meaning "El is with us" (7:14). Although Christians read this passage out of context as a prophecy of the birth of Jesus,[2] in context the verse most likely refers to the king's wife, who would soon bear Hezekiah. Hezekiah was a celebrated king who kept Judah intact through the Assyrian crisis and about whom it is said "El was with him" (2 Kgs 18:7). The famous verses in Isaiah 9 announcing "for unto us a child is born"—a wonderful counselor, mighty god, everlasting father, prince of peace (again verses utilized in Christian liturgies to this day as a reference to the birth of Jesus)—are understood by most scholars as praise for King Hezekiah. In any event, Ahaz does not heed Isaiah. Indeed, how any king could abstain from seeking political or military solutions is difficult to imagine. Instead, the king appeals to Assyria for help (2 Kgs 16:5–9), a disastrous development in Isaiah's eyes.

Similarly, when Hezekiah forms an alliance with Egypt to stave off the Assyrian threat, Isaiah castigates the king and his men for abandoning Yahweh and relying on the frail reed of Egypt. In support of his counsel, Isaiah parades naked through the streets of Jerusalem to illustrate the exile and slavery that would certainly result from reliance on Egypt—an example of the bizarre and demonstrative behavior engaged in by many of the prophets. Isaiah denounces the "wise men" who serve as political advisors and counsel the king to seek help from Egypt, trusting in horses and chariots. Isaiah scoffingly declares, "The Egyptians are human and not divine; their horses are flesh and not spirit" (31:3). The king should simply trust in Yahweh.

This story can be compared to the narrative accounts of Isaiah's dealings with Hezekiah during the invasion of Sennacherib in chapters 36–38. As the eighth century drew to a close, Sennacherib, the king of Assyria, moved slowly inland through the hill country of Samaria and Judah. He approached Jerusalem from the north and in 701 laid siege to the city. Sennacherib's own annals, discovered by archaeologists, describe Hezekiah shut up in the royal city of Jerusalem like a caged bird (see Chapter 14). During the siege, Isaiah counsels Hezekiah not to capitulate to the Assyrians. This would seem to contradict the prophet's earlier message that Assyria was the rod of Yahweh's anger and that Hezekiah should trust in Yahweh rather than in alliances with mere mortal powers.

But in fact there was a basic consistency to Isaiah's counsel. Just as his earlier counsel to trust in Yahweh rather than Egypt was based on his trust in Yahweh's promises to David and the royal city, so now his counsel not to open the doors of the city to the Assyrians was based on his belief that it was not Yahweh's purpose to destroy his holy city.

> Assuredly, thus said Yahweh concerning the king of Assyria:
> He shall not enter this city;
> He shall not shoot an arrow at it,
> Or advance upon it with a shield,
> Or pile up a siegemound against it.
> He shall go back
> By the way he came,
> He shall not enter this city
> —declares Yahweh;
> I will protect and save this city for my sake
> And for the sake of my servant David. (Isa 37:33–35)

The fact that Jerusalem did indeed escape destruction after the terrifying siege by the Assyrians only fueled the belief in the inviolability of David's city Zion among some ancient Judeans.

## The Call of Isaiah

Isaiah 6 contains a striking account of the call of Isaiah, something that might be expected at the beginning of the book, were chronology the organizing principle. In an extraordinary passage, the call, or commissioning, of Isaiah harks back to the bleakness of Hosea:

> Go, say to that people:
> Hear, indeed, but do not understand;
> See, indeed, but do not grasp.
> Dull that people's mind,
> Stop its ears,
> And seal its eyes—
> Lest, seeing with its eyes
> And hearing with its ears,
> It also grasp with its mind,
> And repent and save itself.[3] (Isa 6:9–10)

It would seem from this passage that destruction is inevitable and that Yahweh's message via his prophet will not be understood. Indeed, Yahweh will see to it that the people do not understand the message, do not heed the call to repent, do not save themselves, and so do not escape Yahweh's just punishment.

This is a fascinating, if theologically difficult, idea. Yahweh tells Isaiah to prevent the people from understanding lest through understanding they turn back to Yahweh and so save themselves. We see Yahweh caught in the balance between his justice and his mercy. As a god of justice, he must punish the sins of Israel with destruction, as he indicated he would do in the Sinaitic covenant. But as a god of mercy, he wishes to bring his people back, send a prophet to warn them of the impending doom, and urge them to repent so that he can forgive them and renounce his plan of destruction. How can Yahweh both punish Israel and fulfill the demands of justice on the one hand, yet save Israel and so fulfill the demands of mercy and love on the other?

## A Remnant Shall Remain

Verses 11–13 of the same chapter provide an answer, employing an idea that appeared in Amos and Hosea also. When Isaiah asks how long the people will fail to hear, to understand, to turn back to Yahweh and save themselves, Yahweh replies:

> Till towns lie waste without inhabitants
> And houses without people,
> And the ground lies waste and desolate—
> For Yahweh will banish the population—
> And deserted sites are many
> In the midst of the land.
> But while a tenth part yet remains in it, it shall return. It shall
>     be ravaged like the terebinth and the oak, of which stumps
>     are left even when they are felled: its stump shall be a holy
>     seed. (Isa 6:11–13)

Yahweh will punish, Yahweh cannot *not* punish Israel, and so the demands of justice will be met and Yahweh will have upheld the terms of the conditional Mosaic covenant. But Yahweh will at the same time effect the salvation of his people in the future. He has sent a prophet with the call to return, and in due time a remnant of the people—a tenth—will understand and heed that call. They will receive Yahweh's mercy, and the covenant will be reestablished. In this way the demands of love and mercy will be met, and Yahweh will have been faithful to his covenantal promise to the patriarchs and the royal house of David. The people's delayed comprehension of the prophet's message will guarantee the operation of Yahweh's just punishment now and his merciful salvation later.

While the notion of a remnant furnishes hope for the future, it was not a consoling message at the time, because prophets such as Isaiah were essentially saying that the current generation would all but cease to exist.

> Only a remnant shall return,
> Only a remnant of Jacob,
> To mighty El.
> Even if your people, O Israel,
> Should be as the sands of the sea,
> Only a remnant of it shall return.
> Destruction is decreed;
> Retribution comes like a flood!
> For my lord Yahweh of Hosts is carrying out
> A decree of destruction upon all the land. (Isa 10:21–23)

The prophetic message of punishment and doom was accompanied by a message of consolation: the promise that a purged and purified remnant would be restored to the Land of Israel. In this, the prophets differ from the Deuteronomistic historian, who is more concerned with the justification of Yahweh's actions against Israel than with painting a vivid portrait of the time of a future restoration. The period of restoration is elaborately envisioned in prophetic writings and takes on an eschatological tenor in some. In Isaiah, for example, the return will be a genuine, wholehearted, and permanent return to Yahweh. It will be the end of sin and idolatry. Yahweh's coming to Jerusalem to save the remnant of Israel and to gather in the dispersed exiles will be a theophany of worldwide scope. All the nations of the earth will recognize the one god, and a new epoch will open in world history in which Yahweh's people will be left in peace. Isaiah is the first to envision the end of the dominion of idolatrous nations.

> In the days to come
> The Mount of Yahweh's House
> Shall stand firm above the mountains
> And tower above the hills;
> And all the nations
> Shall gaze on it with joy.
> And the many peoples shall go and say:
> "Come,
> Let us go up to the Mount of Yahweh,
> To the House of the god of Jacob;
> That he may instruct us in his ways,
> And that we may walk in his paths."
> For instruction shall come forth from Zion,
> The word of Yahweh from Jerusalem.
> Thus he will judge among the nations
> And arbitrate for the many peoples,
> And they shall beat their swords into plowshares
> And their spears into pruning hooks:
> Nation shall not take up
> Sword against nation;
> They shall never again know war. (Isa 2:2–4)

This passage strikes out in a new direction. Genesis (or at least J) represented knowledge of Yahweh as the common heritage of all humans in the very distant past. From their inception, however, the nations turned to the worship of national gods, and several passages in the Torah books suggest that this is simply the way things are. Yahweh is Israel's god, and Israel must be faithful to him, while other nations are expected to be loyal to their gods. But in classical prophecy, universal claims are made on behalf of Yahweh. In the prophetic vision, universal recognition of Yahweh will be established at the end of days; Yahweh will make himself known to all nations as he once did to Israel.

Accompanying the idea of the universal recognition of Yahweh is a transformed understanding of Israel's election. In the Torah books, the election of Israel simply refers to Yahweh's gracious and unmerited choice of Israel as the nation to know him and bind itself to him in covenant. But in the prophetic literature, Israel's election is the election to a mission. Israel was chosen to be the instrument of a universal recognition of Yahweh. When Yahweh comes to rescue the crushed and scattered Israelites, he will be revealed to all of humankind. The nations will abandon their idols, and a messianic period of peace will begin. All humanity will become the object of divine favor.

## Israel's Eschatology

The royal ideology of Judah plays an important role in the eschatological vision of Isaiah. The new peaceful and righteous kingdom will be restored by a king from the branch of Jesse (the father of David; hence, a Davidide). Isaianic passages describing an ideal king succeeding to the throne are likely references to Hezekiah, but Isaiah 11 is different. This passage refers to the *restoration* of the Davidic line, implying its temporary interruption. Because it seems to stem from a time when people hoped for a messiah (anointed king) to arise and *restore* the line of David, many scholars assume an exilic or postexilic provenance for the chapter.

> But a shoot shall grow out of the stump of Jesse,
> A twig shall sprout from his stock.
> The spirit of Yahweh shall alight upon him:
> A spirit of wisdom and insight,
> A spirit of counsel and valor,
> A spirit of devotion and reverence for Yahweh.
> He shall sense the truth by his reverence for Yahweh:
> He shall not judge by what his eyes behold,

Nor decide by what his ears perceive.
Thus he shall judge the poor with equity
And decide with justice for the lowly of the land.
He shall strike down a land with the rod of his mouth
And slay the wicked with the breath of his lips.
Justice shall be the girdle of his loins,
And faithfulness the girdle of his waist.
The wolf shall dwell with the lamb,
The leopard lie down with the kid;
The calf, the beast of prey, and the fatling together,
With a little boy to herd them.
The cow and the bear shall graze,
Their young shall lie down together;
And the lion, like the ox, shall eat straw.
A babe shall play
Over a viper's hole,
And an infant pass his hand
Over an adder's den.
In all of my sacred mount
Nothing evil or vile shall be done;
For the land shall be filled with devotion to Yahweh
As water covers the sea.
In that day,
The stock of Jesse that has remained standing
Shall become a standard to peoples—
Nations shall seek his counsel
And his abode shall be honored.
In that day, Yahweh will apply his hand again to redeeming
   the other part of his people from Assyria—as also from
   Egypt, Pathros, Nubia, Elam, Shinar, Hamath, and the
   coastlands. . . .
Thus there shall be a highway for the other part of his people
   out of Assyria, such as there was for Israel when it left the
   land of Egypt. (Isa 11:1–11, 16)

This new messiah-king will rule by his wisdom and insight. The spirit of
Yahweh will alight on him, a phrase that in the case of the judges, or Saul or
David, was an indication of military might and strength but here refers to a
spirit of counsel and devotion to Yahweh. This king's reign will begin an

ingathering of the exiles of the nation and a transformed world order reminiscent of Eden, when even the beasts shed no blood, and there was no enmity between humans and animals. Isaiah exemplifies the prophetic interpretation of the ancient covenant promises that gave Israel a hope for a better future. Like the other prophets, he declared that the nation was in distress not because Yahweh's promises weren't true but because they weren't believed. But the nation's punishment was a chastisement only, not a revocation of the promises. The prophets pushed the fulfillment of the promises beyond the existing nation. Only after suffering the punishment for present failure would the future redemption be possible. The national hope was thereby retained but thrust ahead.

## CHAPTER 18

# Judean Prophets

## Micah, Zephaniah, Nahum, Habakkuk, Jeremiah

*Readings:* Micah; Zephaniah; Nahum; Habakkuk; Jeremiah 1–8, 18–21, 24, 25–45, 52

### Micah: A Covenant Lawsuit

The second southern prophet to prophesy during the Assyrian crisis was Micah. From the small town of Moreshet twenty-five miles southwest of Jerusalem, Micah was the last of the eighth-century prophets. Unlike the city-bred Isaiah, Micah was a rural prophet who spoke for the poor farmer. Prophesying between 740 and 700 B.C.E., he attacked the Israelites for their idolatries. He follows earlier prophets in also condemning the people for moral failings. Greedy landowners and dishonest merchants (the aristocracy) are the target of his denunciations, as are Judah's priests, judges, royalty, and false prophets.

The starkest contrast between Micah and his contemporary Isaiah lies in his view of the city as inherently corrupt, sinful, and doomed to destruction. Where Isaiah preached the inviolability of David's city Zion, Micah was sharply critical of the Davidic dynasty. He scornfully ridicules the belief that the sanctuary's presence in Jerusalem will protect the city from harm. On the contrary, Yahweh will destroy his city and his own house if need be.

Hear this, you rulers of the House of Jacob,
You chiefs of the House of Israel,
Who detest justice
And make crooked all that is straight,
Who build Zion with crime,
Jerusalem with iniquity!
Her rulers judge for gifts,
Her priests give rulings for a fee,
And her prophets divine for pay;
Yet they rely upon Yahweh, saying,
"Yahweh is in our midst;
No calamity shall overtake us."
Assuredly, because of you
Zion shall be plowed as a field,
And Jerusalem shall become heaps of ruins,
And the Temple Mount
A shrine in the woods. (Micah 3:9–12)

One of the most famous passages in the book, Micah 6:1–8, expresses the prophetic emphasis on the primacy of morality. The passage takes the form of a covenant lawsuit or *riv*, a familiar form in prophetic literature in which the deity sues Israel for breach of the covenant. The structure is as follows:

*Summons, vv. 1–2.* The prophet, acting as Yahweh's attorney, summons the accused and the witnesses. The mountains are the witnesses who will hear Yahweh's case against Israel.

Hear what Yahweh is saying:
Come, present [my] case before the mountains,
And let the hills hear you pleading.
Hear, you mountains, the case of Yahweh—
You firm foundations of the earth!
For Yahweh has a case against his people,
He has a suit against Israel.

*Plaintiff's Charge, vv. 3–5.* Yahweh, through his attorney, states his case and appeals to Israel's memory of the events that manifested Yahweh's love for her, beginning with the Exodus and culminating with the entry into the Promised Land. Israel

seems to have forgotten these deeds performed on her behalf
and the obligations that they entail. Israel's conduct in response to Yahweh's benevolence is appalling.

*Defendant's Plea, vv. 6–7.* Israel speaks but has no case to plead.
Israel knows that she must act to effect reconciliation but does
not know where to begin:

With what shall I approach Yahweh,
Do homage to the god on high?
Shall I approach him with burnt offerings,
With calves a year old?
Would Yahweh be pleased with thousands of rams,
With myriads of streams of oil?
Shall I give my first-born for my transgression,
The fruit of my body for my sins?

*Finding, v. 8.* The prophetic attorney responds to Israel's plea:

He has told you, O humankind, what is good
And what Yahweh requires of you:
Only to do justice,
And to love goodness,
And to walk humbly with your god.[1]

The term translated here as "goodness" is *ḥesed*, a term encountered in Hosea and other prophetic writings, that refers to the steadfast loyal love of
covenantal partners.

The book of Micah alternates three oracles of judgment with three
oracles of restoration that tell of the future glory of Zion. These passages
may seem a little out of keeping with Micah's scathing condemnation of
Judah. Some scholars have suggested that references to Yahweh's unconditional promise to preserve the Davidic kingdom and the optimistic predictions of universal peace (which are almost a verbatim repetition of parts of
Isa 2:2–4; cf. Mic 4:1–4) must be interpolations by a later editor. However,
prophetic writings fluctuate wildly between denunciation and consolation,
so that a shift in theme is not a certain basis for assuming interpolation. A
more reliable guide to interpolation is anachronism. Thus, Micah's explicit
reference to the Babylonian exile is quite likely a later interpolation, as are
passages referring to the rebuilding of Jerusalem's walls, which were not

destroyed until 586 B.C.E. Regardless of whether the book of Micah underwent editorial modification, in its present form it is typical of the common and paradoxical prophetic ambivalence that balances Yahweh's stern judgment and punishment on the one hand with his merciful love for and salvation of his people on the other. (A further paradox lies in the very fact of the preservation of many of the nation's prophetic writings. Presumably, some of these writings were preserved by priests in the Temple, even though both priests and Temple were the target of prophetic denunciation.)

Amos and Hosea in the north and Isaiah and Micah in the south responded to the concrete crisis of the Assyrian threat. Jerusalem's survival of the siege of 701 gave credence to the royal ideology of Isaiah, but Judah emerged considerably weakened, a tribute-paying vassal to Assyria. During the first half of the seventh century, Assyria reached the height of its power, and Assyrian influence penetrated Judah. During this period, King Manasseh reigned in Judah for nearly fifty years. Remarkably, the Deuteronomistic historian devotes a mere eighteen verses to this king, despite the length of his reign. The brief treatment of Manasseh is entirely negative, in contrast to the treatment of King Hezekiah, who preceded him, and his grandson, King Josiah, after him. Manasseh was apparently a loyal Assyrian vassal who reversed the reforms of his father and adopted Assyrian norms. It is in this context that the Deuteronomic reforms of Josiah may be understood.

Toward the end of the seventh century, Assyria—much overextended—began to decline. First Egypt and then Babylon broke away. Josiah came to the throne in 640. Taking advantage of Assyrian weakness, he soon asserted Judean independence, carrying out a series of reforms in 622 that included the centralization of the worship of Yahweh in Jerusalem.

Assyria continued to decline, and in 612, Nineveh, the capital of Assyria, fell to an alliance of Medes and Babylonians. But in 609, Josiah was killed in a battle against the Egyptians in Megiddo, and subsequent kings struggled to resist the advances of Babylon.

## Zephaniah: Future Restoration

Zephaniah was a Judean prophet who prophesied during the reign of King Josiah (640–609). Those of his prophecies that date to the time before Josiah's political and religious reforms in 622 are pessimistic and grim. Judah is condemned for the apostasy and decadence that flourished under the evil king Manasseh, and Yahweh's wrath is said to be imminent. Zephaniah foresees a universal destruction in which all life—human and animal—will be exterminated. As in Amos, the Day of Yahweh is represented in Zephaniah not as a time of triumph and celebration for Israel. Rather, Zephaniah 1:15–18 states:

> That day shall be a day of wrath,
> A day of trouble and distress,
> A day of calamity and desolation,
> A day of darkness and deep gloom,
> A day of densest clouds,
> A day of horn blasts and alarms—
> Against the fortified towns
> And the lofty corner towers.
> I will bring distress on the people,
> And they shall walk like blind men,
> Because they sinned against Yahweh;
> Their blood shall be spilled like dust,
> And their fat like dung.
> Moreover, their silver and gold
> Shall not avail to save them.
> On the day of Yahweh's wrath,
> In the fire of his passion,
> The whole land shall be consumed;
> For he will make a terrible end
> Of all who dwell in the land.

Like the other prophets, however, Zephaniah offers hope. The proud and sinful will be removed, a humble remnant will seek refuge in Yahweh, and the exiles will be gathered and restored, in the sight of all the nations.

> In that day,
> You will no longer be shamed for all the deeds
> By which you have defied me.
> For then I will remove
> The proud and exultant within you,
> And you will be haughty no more
> On my sacred mount.
> But I will leave within you,
> A poor, humble folk,
> And they shall find refuge

In the name of Yahweh.
The remnant of Israel
Shall do no wrong
And speak no falsehood;
A deceitful tongue
Shall not be in their mouths.
Only such as these shall graze and lie down,
With none to trouble them. . . .
At that time I will gather you,
And at [that] time I will bring you [home];
For I will make you renowned and famous
Among all the peoples on earth,
When I restore your fortunes
Before their very eyes. (Zeph 3:11–13, 20)

One particularly joyous passage seems to announce the present deliverance of Judah:

Shout for joy, Fair Zion,
Cry aloud, O Israel!
Rejoice and be glad with all your heart,
Fair Jerusalem!
Yahweh has annulled the judgment against you,
He has swept away your foes.
Israel's sovereign Yahweh is within you;
You need fear misfortune no more. (3:14–15)

Some scholars suggest that these lines register Zephaniah's joyful response to the reforms initiated by Josiah, hailed here as the restoration of Yahweh's presence to the community of Judah.

## Nahum: The Fall of Nineveh

The short book of Nahum differs from most of the other prophetic books of the Hebrew Bible in that it contains no prophecies and does not upbraid the people for their failings. Rather, the book of Nahum is a set of three vivid poems—the first being an acrostic or alphabetic psalm—that rejoice over the fall of Nineveh, the capital of the cruel Assyrian Empire, in 612 B.C.E. The Assyrians, renowned for exceptional brutality and inhumanity in their conquest and empire building, were widely hated in the ancient Near East. They deported populations wholesale and were guilty of atrocities such as the mutilation of captives, the butchering of women and children, and other horrendous deeds attested in both Assyrian and other ancient Near Eastern texts and iconography.

Nahum celebrates the avenging and wrathful Yahweh who has finally turned to destroy his enemies. True, according to Nahum, Yahweh used Assyria as his disciplining rod, to punish Israel and Judah for their sins. But Yahweh is the universal sovereign, and Assyria's savagery was itself to be punished. For Nahum, the fall of Nineveh represents Yahweh's vengeance upon Assyria for her barbaric inhumanity.

Nahum looks forward to a happy era of freedom for Judah and states in 2:15: "for never again shall the wicked come against you." This optimistic declaration was not to be, of course. In a few years, Josiah would be killed, and Judah would fall subject to Egypt and then Babylon, before suffering a final destruction in 586 B.C.E. It is important to note that this glaring error in Nahum was not updated or repaired in order to protect the prophet's reputation. Thus, while some prophetic books contain evidence of editorial manipulation and interpolation, others contain evidence that the basic content of the prophet's oracles were preserved faithfully.

With the fall of Nineveh, national confidence must have been riding high. But things quickly turned sour. The death of Josiah in 609 was a shock. Judah lay trapped, as it were, between two powers: Egypt in the south and Babylon in the north and east. In 605, Babylon defeated Egypt and reduced Judah, under king Jehoiakim, to the status of tributary vassal. But King Jehoiakim rebelled. In response, the Babylonians, under Nebuchadrezzar, laid siege to Jerusalem in 597, killed the king, and took his son into captivity. The puppet king Zedekiah was installed on the throne, but ten years later, Zedekiah also rebelled. The Babylonian king Nebuchadrezzar returned to Jerusalem, and in 586 captured the city, destroyed the sanctuary, and exiled the bulk of the population—ending 400 years of an independent Hebrew nation.

## Habakkuk: How Long?

The book of Habakkuk was apparently written between 600 and 586 B.C.E., a period in which the Babylonians twice attacked Jerusalem—once in 597 and finally in 586. Habakkuk is another unusual prophetic book, containing not so much prophecies as philosophical musings on the conduct of

Yahweh. Habakkuk 1–2 is a kind of poetic dialogue between Habakkuk and Yahweh. The prophet complains bitterly of Yahweh's inaction:

> How long, O Yahweh, shall I cry out
> And you not listen,
> Shall I shout to you, "Violence!"
> And you not save?
> Why do you make me see iniquity,
> [Why] do you look upon wrong?—
> Raiding and violence are before me,
> Strife continues and contention goes on. . . .
> You whose eyes are too pure to look upon evil,
> Who cannot countenance wrongdoing,
> Why do you countenance treachery,
> And stand by idle
> While the one in the wrong devours
> The one in the right?
> You have made mankind like the fish of the sea,
> Like creeping things that have no ruler. (Hab 1:2–3, 13–14)

Yahweh responds to the charge by asserting that the Babylonians are the instruments of his justice, though they ascribe their might and success to their own gods rather than Yahweh. The idea that conquering nations serve as the instruments of Yahweh's punishment is familiar from the Deuteronomistic history and from other prophetic writings. However, Habakkuk is unusual in that he does not couch this idea in the larger argument that Judah deserves so catastrophic a punishment. Unlike the Deuteronomistic historian, Habakkuk does not assert that the people are suffering for their sins. Habakkuk thus struggles with what appears to be a basic lack of justice: "Decision fails and justice never emerges; for the villain hedges in the just man—therefore judgment emerges deformed" (1:4). It is not merely that the wicked and the just suffer the same fate; rather, the wicked seem to fare better than the just, reducing humankind to the level of fish and creeping things for whom sheer power and not morality is the principal consideration.

Having made this charge, Habakkuk awaits Yahweh's answer:

> I will stand on my watch,
> Take up my station at the post,
> And wait to see what he will say to me,

What he will reply to my complaint.
Yahweh answered me and said:
Write the prophecy down,
Inscribe it clearly on tablets,
So that it can be read easily. . . .
But the righteous man is rewarded with life
For his fidelity.
How much less then shall the defiant go unpunished. (2:1–2,
  4b–5a)

In short, the righteous must simply have faith that justice will prevail, and this faith must sustain them through vicissitudes and trials.

The third chapter shifts gears, so much so that some scholars see it as an interpolation—but again, dramatic shifts in theme and tone are not uncommon in the prophetic books. Here Yahweh is described as a warrior god who thunders from the east, hurling his spear and seeking vengeance on Israel's oppressors. It may be that this passage is an editor's effort to respond to Habakkuk's skepticism that Yahweh will bring justice—and bring it soon. This image of Yahweh as the avenging warrior answers Habakkuk's opening question, which was in all likelihood rhetorical: How long will Yahweh stand by and be silent while the Babylonians rape and pillage? On the other hand, it is possible that Habakkuk exhibits the paradoxical tension that we have seen in other prophetic books. Specifically, he holds the paradoxical view that Yahweh's justice is slow in coming, yet the righteous man must have complete faith in its ultimate execution.

The book of Habakkuk has raised the problem of theodicy and locates the problem's resolution in a vision of the future. In this respect, Habakkuk anticipates the interest in theodicy that characterizes later Israelite literature, particularly apocalyptic literature, which defers hope to a future event.

## Jeremiah: Prophet of the Destruction

The prophet who lived at the time of the final destruction of Judah and the fall of Jerusalem at the hands of the Babylonians in 586 B.C.E. was Jeremiah. Born of a priestly family in Anathoth, a village near Jerusalem, he began prophesying while still a boy. He was a contemporary of King Josiah and so witnessed the brief renaissance that occurred under his leadership—the sweeping cultic reform, the eradication of the Assyrian influences that had been welcomed by Manasseh, and the renewal of the covenant. When Josiah died, Jeremiah added his lament to the grief of the nation. Jeremiah also witnessed the final destruction and the exile.

The book of Jeremiah is a collection of very different types of material, with no clear organization or chronological order: prophecies, anecdotes, diatribes against pagan nations, poems, biographical narratives, and a brief historical appendix resembling 2 Kgs 24–25. The literary history of Jeremiah is complex, and there is great variation among ancient witnesses to that text. The Septuagint version (a third- to second-century B.C.E. Greek translation) is much shorter than the Hebrew version and has a different arrangement. There are also significant differences in fragments found among the Dead Sea Scrolls, all attesting to the open-ended nature of written compositions in antiquity.

The book of Jeremiah contains three types of material: poetic oracles attributed to Jeremiah, biographical narratives about the prophet attributed to his amanuensis and assistant, Baruch son of Neriah, and editorial notes about him contributed by a Deuteronomistic editor. The influence of the Deuteronomistic historian on Jeremiah—in both substance and style—is clear.

A basic outline of the book follows:

1–25—An introduction and account of Jeremiah's call, as well as poetic oracles and an occasional biographical narrative.

26–29—Narratives of Jeremiah's conflicts with other prophets and authority figures.

30–33—Messages of hope and consolation.

34–45—Prose stories centering around and after the time of the final destruction.

46–51—Oracles against the nations (some from other writers).

52—A historical appendix about the fall of Jerusalem extracted from 2 Kgs 24:18–25:30.

### The Temple Sermon

Jeremiah preached that the nation's doom was inevitable because of its violation of the covenant, the very charter for Israel's existence. His descriptions are vivid and terrifying. He denounces Israel's leaders. The professional prophets with whom he has numerous encounters are accused of lying when they prophesy peace. There are a few negative references to priests, but King Jehoiakim, the son of Josiah, is especially criticized.

Jeremiah can be compared to Micah in attacking the popular ideology of the inviolability of Zion. As long as injustice and oppression are practiced in Judah, the presence of the Temple is no guarantee of anything. Judah will suffer the fate she deserves for failure to fulfill her covenantal obligations. Yahweh tells Jeremiah to stand at the gate of the Temple and speak these words, in a passage that is often referred to as the Temple Sermon:

> Thus said Yahweh of Hosts, the god of Israel: Mend your ways and your actions, and I will let you dwell in this place. Don't put your trust in illusions and say, "The Temple of Yahweh, the Temple of Yahweh, the Temple of Yahweh are these [buildings]." No, if you really mend your ways and your actions, if you execute justice between one man and another; if you do not oppress the stranger, the orphan, and the widow; if you do not shed the blood of the innocent in this place; if you do not follow other gods to your own hurt—then only will I let you dwell in this place, in the land that I gave to your fathers for all time. See you are relying on illusions that are of no avail. Will you steal and murder and commit adultery and swear falsely, and sacrifice to Baal, and follow other gods whom you have not experienced, and then come and stand before me in this House which bears my name and say, "We are safe?" Safe to do all these abhorrent things! Do you consider this House which bears my name to be a den of thieves? As for me, I have been watching—declares Yahweh. (7:3–11)

To attack the doctrine of the inviolability of Zion and the eternity of the House of David was iconoclastic in the extreme. As support for this radical idea, Jeremiah needed only to point to history. He cites the example of Shiloh as an object lesson (7:12–15): In the time of the judges, the presence of the ark at Shiloh proved to be no guarantee against the Philistine aggressor, who not only destroyed the sanctuary but captured the ark itself. The belief that Yahweh would not allow his Temple, his city, and his anointed ruler to be destroyed is, in Jeremiah's view, a deception and an illusion.

### Resistance Is Futile

Jeremiah resembles his predecessors in his political message. The nation's pathetic attempts to resist the great powers and to enter into alliances against them were completely futile. To dramatically illustrate the destruction and slavery that would inevitably follow resistance, Jeremiah paraded about Jerusalem, first in a wooden yoke and then an iron one (chapters 27–28), as a symbol of the slavery to come. In 27:6, he announces Yahweh's declaration that "I herewith deliver all these lands to my servant, King Nebuchadrezzar of Babylon."

To refer to the man responsible for the destruction of the nation as Yahweh's servant would have been shocking, not to say dangerous. Yet in several passages, Jeremiah exhorts the king to submit to the Babylonian forces surrounding Jerusalem in acceptance of Yahweh's will, passages thought by some scholars to be added during the exile, when it would be in the interest of the community to appear accepting of Babylonian rule.

## Baruch Son of Neriah

To ensure the preservation of his words, Jeremiah had his amanuensis Baruch (see Figure 9) write down everything conveyed to him by Yahweh. Chapter 36 records the process by which Jeremiah's words were transcribed. Yahweh commands Jeremiah:

Fig. 9. Bullae believed to belong to Baruch ben Neriah, scribe of the prophet Jeremiah in sixth-century B.C.E. Jerusalem.
Photo: Z. Radovan/BibleLandPictures.com. Illustration:
Kyle Pope, Ancient Road Publications, http://ancientroadpublications.com.

> Get a scroll and write upon it all the words that I have spoken to
> you—concerning Israel and Judah and all the nations—from
> the time I first spoke to you in the days of Josiah to this day. . . .
> So Jeremiah called Baruch son of Neriah and Baruch wrote
> down in the scroll, at Jeremiah's dictation, all the words which
> Yahweh had spoken to him. (Jer 36:2, 4)

Because Jeremiah is in hiding, he instructs Baruch to take the scroll to the
Temple and read it to the people. The king's officials report to the king
about the subversive message delivered by Baruch. Baruch goes into hiding,
and the scroll is torn into strips and burned. Yahweh orders Jeremiah to get
another scroll and repeat the process and so he does:

> So Jeremiah got another scroll and gave it to the scribe Baruch
> son of Neriah. And at Jeremiah's dictation, he wrote in it the
> whole text of the scroll that King Jehoiakim of Judah had burned;
> and more of the like was added. (v. 32)

Some believe that the written oracles referred to are the oracles in chapters
1–25, though prior perhaps to some Deuteronomistic editing. In any event,
this story gives us some insight into the practice of prophecy: It was not off
the cuff. The compositions of the prophets were committed to memory and
could be dictated again.[2]

### The Confessions of Jeremiah

Jeremiah was rejected, despised, and persecuted by his fellow Judeans,
many of whom regarded him as a traitor. During his lifetime he was flogged,
imprisoned, and frequently in hiding. He was a troubled man living in
troubled times, who felt intensely all the suffering that would come upon his
people and who wept over the fate of Jerusalem (8:18–9:3). Jeremiah provides
insight into the inner turmoil he suffered—as other prophets do not—in a
group of passages referred to as the Confessions of Jeremiah (11:18–12:6;
15:10–21; 17:14–18; 18:18–23; 20:7–13; 20:15–18). While the authenticity of these
passages is in question, they do paint a fascinating portrait of the prophet.
He curses the day he was born. He accuses Yahweh of deceiving him, of en-
ticing him to act as Yahweh's messenger only in order to be met with humiliation and shame. Yet he cannot hold it in—Yahweh's word rages within

him, and he must prophesy. It would be better had he not been born at all, than to be born to such ceaseless suffering.

> You enticed me, O Yahweh, and I was enticed;
> You overpowered me and you prevailed.
> I have become a constant laughingstock,
> Everyone jeers at me.
> For every time I speak, I must cry out,
> Must shout, "Lawlessness and rapine!"
> For the word of Yahweh causes me
> Constant disgrace and contempt.
> I thought, "I will not mention him,
> No more will I speak in his name"—
> But [his word] was like a raging fire in my heart,
> Shut up in my bones;
> I could not hold it in, I was helpless.
> I heard the whispers of the crowd—
> Terror all around:
> "Inform! Let us inform against him!" . . .
> Accursed be the day that I was born! . . .
> Accursed be the man
> Who brought my father the news
> And said, "A boy
> Is born to you,"
> And gave him such joy!
> Let that man become like the cities
> Which Yahweh overthrew without relenting! . . .
> Because he did not kill me before birth
> So that my mother might be my grave,
> And her womb big [with me] for all time.
> Why did I ever issue from the womb,
> To see misery and woe,
> To spend all my days in shame! (20:7–10, 14–15, 17–18)

Shortly after the fall of Jerusalem, Jeremiah was taken forcibly to Egypt. There he lived out his final years, violently denouncing fellow refugees for worshipping the Queen of Heaven (Jer 43–45). As before, it seems that few heeded him, preferring other explanations of the nation's woes.

Thereupon they answered Jeremiah—all the men who knew that
their wives made offerings to other gods; all the women present,
a large gathering; and all the people who lived in Pathros in the
land of Egypt: "We will not listen to you in the matter about
which you spoke to us in the name of Yahweh. On the contrary,
we will do everything that we have vowed—to make offerings to
the Queen of Heaven and to pour libations to her, as we used to
do, we and our fathers, our kings and our officials, in the towns
of Judah and the streets of Jerusalem. For then we had plenty to
eat, we were well-off, and suffered no misfortune. But ever since
we stopped making offerings to the Queen of Heaven and pour-
ing libations to her, we have lacked everything, and we have been
consumed by the sword and by famine. And when we make offerings to the Queen of Heaven and pour libations to her, is it
without our husbands' approval that we have made cakes in her
likeness and poured libations to her?" (Jer 44:15–19)

This fascinating passage reveals the diversity of practice and belief in ancient
Israel. The same historical events were interpreted differently by different
people. Some were convinced that Jeremiah had contributed to the nation's
misery by dissuading his fellow Judeans from the worship of the Queen of
Heaven. Jeremiah countered that it was the people's failure entirely to desist
from their idolatry that forced Yahweh to punish them, and to do so severely.

Despite the hostility of his audience, and despite Jeremiah's harsh criticism of established authorities and even scribes, the prophet's words were
preserved by scribes and Deuteronomistic editors.

### Consolation

Like the earlier prophets, Jeremiah balanced his message of doom with a
message of consolation, especially in the so-called Book of Consolation
(chapters 30–33). Jeremiah envisages an end to the exile and a restoration of
the community. Indeed, Jeremiah was the first to set a time limit to the "dominion of the idolaters"—a time limit of seventy years. Jeremiah's letter to
the first group of deportees taken to Babylon in 597 before the final destruction in 586, in chapter 29, is remarkable for its counsel to the exiles to settle
down in their adopted home to wait out the appointed time. Jeremiah warns
the people not to listen to prophets who say they will return shortly. They are
lying; the Israelites must "serve the king of Babylon and live" (Jer 27:16–17).

> Thus said Yahweh of Hosts, the god of Israel, to the whole com-
> munity which I exiled from Jerusalem to Babylon: Build houses
> and live in them, plant gardens and eat their fruit. Take wives
> and beget sons and daughters; and take wives for your sons, and
> give your daughters to husbands, that they may bear sons and
> daughters. Multiply there, do not decrease. And seek the welfare
> of the city to which I have exiled you and pray to Yahweh in its
> behalf; for in its prosperity you shall prosper. (Jer 29:4–7)

In other words, the people must not be deceived by the idle dreams of false
prophets who tell them return is imminent (vv. 8–9). Yahweh has other
plans—plans for welfare and not for evil—to give the people a future and a
hope (29:11). At the end of seventy years (29:10), Jeremiah said, Yahweh will
make an end of the nations among whom the Israelites are dispersed (30:11),
and the exiles will return to their land (31:7–14). Zion, he declared, will be
acknowledged as the holy city, and a new Davidic king will reign (33:20–21,
25–26). At that time, a new covenant will be made with Israel—this time a
covenant etched on the heart, encoded as it were into human nature.

> See, a time is coming—declares Yahweh—when I will make a
> new covenant with the House of Israel and the House of Judah.
> It will not be like the covenant I made with their fathers, when I
> took them by the hand to lead them out of the land of Egypt, a
> covenant which they broke, though I espoused them—declares
> Yahweh. But such is the covenant I will make with the House of
> Israel after these days—declares Yahweh: I will put my Teaching
> into their inmost being and inscribe it upon their hearts. Then I
> will be their god, and they shall be my people. No longer will they
> need to teach one another and say to one another, "Heed Yah-
> weh"; for all of them, from the least of them to the greatest, shall
> heed me—declares Yahweh. (Jer 31:31–34)

The new covenant described by Jeremiah does not appear to be new in its
content. Yahweh will continue to impart his teachings in this covenant.
What is different is that the covenant will be inscribed directly upon the
heart, built into human nature so that there will be no need to study and
learn what Yahweh requires. Thus, it is human nature that will change, not
the teachings of Yahweh; humans will be hardwired to obey these teachings. In this remarkable passage, Jeremiah registers his dissatisfaction with

the element of free will so crucial to the biblical notion of covenant. The biblical story of the Garden of Eden establishes the moral freedom of human beings, accepting that such freedom will occasionally be exercised in disobedience resulting in evil. But in Jeremiah's vision of an ideal future, humans will simply know and obey the teachings of Yahweh. To a defeated people, yearning for reconciliation with their god, Jeremiah's "robo-righteousness" was a comforting and inspiring vision, even if it did run counter to the biblical conception of humans as free moral agents. This tension will be seen in later texts as well.

In one very beautiful passage, Jeremiah describes a future restoration of the Temple, the bringing of offerings and the singing of psalms of praise. In contrast to chapter 25, where he warned that Yahweh would banish "the sound of mirth and gladness, the voice of bridegroom and bride," leaving the land a desolate ruin, Jeremiah now says:

> Again there shall be heard in this place . . . in the towns of Judah and the streets of Jerusalem that are desolate, without man, without inhabitants, without beast—the sound of mirth and gladness, the voice of bridegroom and bride, the voice of those who cry, "Give thanks to Yahweh of Hosts, for Yahweh is good, for his kindness is everlasting!" as they bring thanksgiving offerings to the house of Yahweh. For I will restore the fortunes of the land as of old—said Yahweh. (33:10–11)

## Summary of Preexilic Prophets

The fall of Jerusalem shattered the national and territorial bases of Israel's culture and religion. The Babylonians burned the Temple to the ground and carried away most of the people to live in exile in Babylon, leaving only the poorest members of society to till the earth. It was the completion of a tragedy that had begun centuries earlier and was seen as the fulfillment of the covenant curses. It was the end of the Davidic monarchy, the end of the Temple and its priesthood, the end of Israel as a nation. The Israelites were now confronted by a great test. One option would have been to see in these events a sign that Yahweh had abandoned his people to, and had been defeated by, the god of the Babylonians; Marduk would replace Yahweh as the Israelites assimilated themselves to their new home. Certainly, there were Israelites who went this route. But others, firmly rooted in an exclusive Yahwism, did not.

How could their faith survive outside the framework of Israelite national culture, away from Temple and land? Uprooted and scattered, could Israelite group identity live on without its national foundations and institutions and on foreign soil, or would Israel go the way of other national groups? The pain and despair are expressed in the words of the psalmist:

> By the rivers of Babylon, there we sat, sat and wept, as we thought of Zion. There on the poplars we hung up our lyres, for our captors asked us there for songs, our tormentors, for amusement, "sing us one of the songs of Zion." How can we sing a song of Yahweh on alien soil? If I forget you, O Jerusalem, let my right hand wither; let my tongue stick to my palate if I cease to think of you, if I do not keep Jerusalem in memory even at my happiest hour. (Ps 137)

It was the message of the prophets that helped some Israelites make sense of their situation and remain distinct and invulnerable to identity loss. This was one reason for the preservation of the writings of prophets who had often been despised and unheeded in their own lifetimes. Yahweh had not been defeated, these prophets claimed. The nation's calamities were not disproof of his power and covenant but proof of it. Later generations decided that the prophets had spoken truly when they said that destruction would follow if the people did not turn from their moral and religious violations of Yahweh's law. Rather than undermine faith in Yahweh, the defeat and exile when interpreted in the prophetic manner had the potential to convince Jews of the need to show absolute and undivided devotion to Yahweh and his commandments. Paradoxically, the moment of greatest national despair was transformed by the prophets into an occasion for the renewal of religious faith.

The great contribution of the prophets was their emphasis on Yahweh's desire for morality as expressed in the ancient covenant. The great contribution of Jeremiah was his insistence on Yahweh's everlasting connection with his people even outside its land and despite the loss of central national religious symbols—Temple, holy city, and Davidic king. This insistence that the faithful person's relationship with Yahweh was not broken even in an idolatrous land, when added to Jeremiah's hope for a new covenant and future restoration, provided the exiles with the ideas that would transform the nation of Israel into the religion of Judaism.

CHAPTER 19

# Responses to the Destruction

## Ezekiel and 2–3 Isaiah

*Readings:* Ezekiel 1–5:4, 8–11, 16–18, 23, 25, 33, 36–37, 40, 47; Isaiah 40–42, 49–55

### Ezekiel

Sixth-century prophetic literature confronts the issues raised by the final destruction. What was the meaning of this event? How could it be reconciled with the concept of Israel as Yahweh's elect? How could such tremendous evil and suffering be reconciled with the nature of Yahweh himself? In classical terms, if Yahweh is god, he is not good, and if Yahweh is good, then he is not an all-powerful god, since he failed to prevent this evil.

Ezekiel was a priest and a prophet deported in the first deportation of 597 B.C.E. with King Jehoiachin. He was in Babylon during the final destruction of Jerusalem in 586. His priestly background and interests are reflected in his prophecies, which accuse the Israelites of failing to observe the cultic and ritual laws, and in his promises for a future centered around a renewed Temple. There is a striking correspondence of language and theme between Ezekiel and the priestly sources of the Bible, particularly H.

The prophecies of Ezekiel follow a chronological order and date from the late 590s to the 560s B.C.E.

The structure of the book is as follows:

1–24—Prophecies delivered in Babylon and dating to the predestruction period (pre-586 B.C.E.).

1–3 contain an account of Ezekiel's call and commission as
prophet. Ezekiel receives an inaugural vision; other visions
and symbols are related.

4–24 contain colorful oracles of condemnation for Judah and
Israel. Includes the departure of Yahweh's glory in chapters 8–11 and an emphasis on individual responsibility for
sin in chapter 18.

25–32—Oracles against foreign nations (as in Jeremiah and Isaiah) designated in Ezekiel as "the uncircumcised." The tone is
vengeful and gloating; these oracles have exerted a strong influence on the New Testament book of Revelation.

33–48—Prophecies delivered after the destruction (post-586
B.C.E.).

33–39—The fall of Jerusalem is related in chapter 33, followed
by oracles of promise and hope for the future.

40–48—Visions of restoration, the new Temple, and a new
Jerusalem.

## Call and Early Visions

The book opens with a narrative account of Ezekiel's call, in 593 in a Jewish
community on the River Chebar, a large irrigation canal near the Euphrates, in Babylon. This is the first instance of a call to a prophet occurring outside the land of Israel. Chapter 1's remarkable vision, like many of the visions
in this book, has a surrealistic, almost hallucinatory, quality and is reminiscent of descriptions of the storm god Baal. The text describes a stormy wind,
a huge cloud, and flashing fire. Yahweh rides upon a throne-chariot supported by four magnificent creatures, each with a human body and four faces
(that of a human, a lion, an ox, and an eagle). Four huge wheels gleam like
beryl beneath a vast and awe-inspiring expanse or dome that gleams like
crystal, and above this expanse is the semblance of a throne like sapphire. On
the throne was the semblance of a human form gleaming like amber, fire en-
cased in a frame with radiance all about. This *kavod*, or cloud that contained
and hid the fire of Yahweh's presence, is the term used in the Torah (in the
priestly source) to describe the presence of Yahweh among the people. It set-
tles on Mt. Sinai in Ex 24, and in Ex 40 the cloud covers the tent of meeting
and fills the tabernacle. Seeing it now, Ezekiel says, that it

was the appearance of the semblance of the Presence of Yahweh. When I beheld it I flung myself down on my face. And I heard the voice of someone speaking. (Ezek 1:28)

The language of "semblance," "appearance," and "presence" emphasizes the transcendent nature of the deity who cannot be directly perceived. By contrast, the prophet's humanity is emphasized by the phrase "son of man," the Hebrew term for a mortal human that appears throughout the book.

The call of Ezekiel in chapter 2 is reminiscent of the call of Jeremiah and Isaiah. He is sent to a nation of rebels who will not listen to him (2:3–5). His commission is symbolized by a scroll on which are inscribed lamentations, dirges, and woes. Ezekiel is handed the scroll and commanded to eat it, after which he must go and speak to the House of Israel (2:8–3:1). He swallows the scroll with its dismal contents and it tastes as sweet as honey. His task is spelled out in chapter 3—he is to be a watchman, one who gives warning of danger. People will either heed him or not—but each is ultimately responsible for his own fate (3:11, 16–21).

In a vision in chapter 8, an angel transports Ezekiel to Jerusalem and into the Temple courts. The vivid description of the shocking abominations occurring there is an attempt to justify the destruction of the city and is characterized by the customary prophetic hyperbole. After witnessing the slaughter and destruction wreaked by Yahweh, Ezekiel then sees the *kavod*, the light-filled cloud that is the presence of Yahweh, arise from the Temple and travel east.

> The Presence of Yahweh left the platform of the House and stopped above the cherubs. And I saw the cherubs lift their wings and rise from the earth, with the wheels beside them as they departed; and they stopped at the entrance of the eastern gate of the House of Yahweh, with the Presence of the god of Israel above them. (10:18–19)

> The Presence of Yahweh ascended from the midst of the city and stood on the hill east of the city. A spirit carried me away and brought me in a vision by the spirit of Elohim to the exiled community in Chaldea. Then the vision that I had seen left me, and I told the exiles all the things that Yahweh had shown me. (11:23–25)

This vision draws on ancient Near Eastern traditions in which gods abandon their cities in anger, leaving them to their destruction by another god.[1] The primary difference here is that Yahweh, rather than another god, brings the destruction himself. Moreover, Yahweh does not retire to the heavens or remain with those left behind in Judah. In Ezekiel, those left behind are guilty. Instead, Yahweh moves east with the exiles who have been spared.

The end of the book relates a further vision of the restored Temple (Ezek 43). In this vision, Ezekiel sees the *kavod*, returning from the east.

> And there, coming from the east with a roar like the roar of mighty waters, was the Presence of the god of Israel, and the earth was lit up by his Presence. . . . The Presence of Yahweh entered the Temple by the gate that faced eastward. A spirit carried me into the inner court, and lo, the presence of Yahweh filled the Temple. (43:2, 4–5)

Just as the divine presence went eastward with the exiles in chapter 8, so it will return with the exiles at the time of the reestablishment of Israel in her home. What is significant here is the idea that Yahweh is not linked to a particular place, but to a particular people. Yahweh is with his people even in exile.

### Predestruction Prophecies and the Principle of Individual Responsibility

Like his prophetic predecessors and contemporaries, Ezekiel preaches a message of doom and judgment, and his condemnations emphasize the people's idolatry and moral impurity. Ezekiel's denunciations of Jerusalem are the most violent, graphic, and lurid in the biblical corpus. These prophecies were likely delivered after the first deportation in 597 in the hope of staving off a final destruction, which nevertheless occurred in 586. Ezekiel warns that Jerusalem will fall, deservedly, and that rebellion against Babylon is treason against Yahweh. He employs a wide range of vivid metaphors to describe Israel's situation: Jerusalem is Sodom's sister, only more vile (Ezek 16); Jerusalem is a vine, but a wild or burned one, producing nothing of use (Ezek 15). Purity language is employed metaphorically in images intended to inspire extreme revulsion: Ezekiel asserts that Jerusalem has been utterly defiled so that destruction is the only possible remedy. Metaphors of sexual promiscuity abound: Yahweh's destruction of Israel is figured as the horrific abuse doled out by an insanely jealous and violent husband (16:38–42; 23:45–49). The images are disturbingly pornographic, shocking, nightmarish (Ezek 16 and 23).

Ezekiel engages in various dramatic prophetic signs to convey his message, some so bizarre and extreme that he was accused of insanity.[2] He cooks his food on a fire of human excrement to symbolize the fact that those besieged by Nebuchadrezzar will be forced to eat unclean food (4:9–17). He does not mourn his wife when she dies to illustrate that Yahweh will not mourn the loss of his temple (24:15–27). He binds himself in ropes and lies on his left side 390 days to symbolize the 390 years of the exile of Israel and then forty days on the right side to symbolize the length of Judah's captivity (4:1–8)—of course, neither of these turns out to be correct. Finally, he shaves his beard and hair, burning a third, striking a third with a sword, and scattering a third to the winds, retaining only a few hairs bound up in his robe (5:1–17). This symbolizes the destruction of a third of the people by pestilence and famine, a third by violence, and the exile of a third to Babylon (note the correspondence to the covenant curse in Lev 26:23–33 assigned to H). Yahweh will allow only a few to escape.

Ezekiel makes it clear that only those who ignore the warning are doomed; those who heed it will be spared, and in this he sounds the theme of *individual responsibility* that is characteristic of him. The following verses emphasizing individual responsibility for sin may be contrasted with Torah passages that emphasize collective and transgenerational responsibility for sin.

> The word of Yahweh came to me: What do you mean by quoting this proverb upon the soil of Israel, "Parents eat sour grapes and their children's teeth are blunted?" As I live—declares my lord Yahweh—this proverb shall no longer be current among you in Israel. Consider, all lives are mine; the life of the parent and the life of the child are both mine. The person who sins, only he shall die.
>
> . . . A child shall not share the burden of a parent's guilt, nor shall a parent share the burden of a child's guilt; the righteousness of the righteous shall be accounted to him alone, and the wickedness of the wicked shall be accounted to him alone. Moreover if the wicked one repents of all the sins that he committed and keeps all my laws and does what is just and right, he shall live; he shall not die.

. . . Is it my desire that a wicked person shall die?—says my lord Yahweh. It is rather that he shall turn back from his ways and live. So too, if a righteous persons turns away from his righteousness and does wrong, practicing the very abominations that the wicked person practiced, shall he live? None of the righteous deeds that he did shall be remembered; because of the treachery he has practiced and the sins he has committed—because of these he shall die.

. . . Be assured, O House of Israel, I will judge each one of you according to his ways—declares my lord Yahweh. Repent and turn back from all your transgressions; let them not be a stumbling block of guilt for you. Cast away all the transgressions by which you have offended, and get yourselves a new heart and a new spirit that you may not die, O House of Israel. For it is not my desire that anyone shall die—declares my lord Yahweh. Repent, therefore, and live! (18:1–4, 20–21, 23–24, 30–32)

The Torah principles of collective and transgenerational punishment, found most famously in the second commandment's declaration that Yahweh punishes children for the sins of their fathers unto the fourth generation, is rejected in this passage. To be sure, the passage deals with divine justice, not human justice. In the human sphere, only the guilty are to be punished by those in authority, but many Pentateuchal texts indicate that Yahweh operates according to a different principle—the principle of collective responsibility. In the Torah books, this principle is understood positively: that the sins of the father should be visited upon the children is an expression of Yahweh's *mercy*. Exodus 34:6–7 describes Yahweh as merciful and gracious, slow to anger, abounding in steadfast love and faithfulness, and forgiving the wicked, but he does not excuse the wicked entirely. Instead, he spreads their punishment over three or four generations rather than exacting full punishment on a single individual all at once. Likewise, the Deuteronomistic historian used the idea of delayed punishment to explain disasters that befell virtuous kings—these disasters were merciful postponements of the punishment of a previous generation. However, what was once perceived as a mercy came increasingly to be seen as the unjust punishment of the innocent. Several biblical passages try to bring greater justice to this picture. Exodus 20:5–6 emphasizes that those punished in the third and fourth generations are *themselves* wicked, and those rewarded in the thousandth generation are themselves virtuous.[3] The Deuteronomistic notion of delayed punishment is rejected by the Chronicler. Thus, 1 and 2 Chronicles present the same historical narrative as 1 and 2 Kings but rewritten so that no catastrophe is ever explained as punishment for the guilt of anyone other than the one experiencing the catastrophe.

After 586, some accepted the idea that the nation was suffering because of the accumulated guilt of previous generations (notably the Deuteronomistic historian), but for others the idea of accumulated guilt and transgenerational punishment lost much of its explanatory power.[4] The destruction and exile were devastatingly severe punishments that were difficult to justify as delayed punishment for an earlier generation's violations.

Ezekiel is among those who reject the doctrine of collective responsibility in the execution of divine justice. In chapter 18, he responds to the idea of suffering for one's ancestors' sins by declaring that times have changed. Yahweh will no longer punish the people collectively—each person will be judged individually, and only the sinner will be punished. This was a major departure from Ex 34 and even from the roughly contemporaneous view of the Deuteronomistic school.

It should be noted that this kind of departure, this kind of polyphony, did not impinge upon the authority of the Hebrew Bible for the nation of Israel. The Bible's authority did not derive from some supposed consistency or univocality. The philosophical tradition so influential in western culture that defines truth in monistic terms—that is, only that which contains no contradiction is true, and only that which is true is authoritative—is alien to the ancient non-Hellenized world. The Hebrew Bible is not a work of philosophy and does not strive to present philosophical truth. The various books of the Hebrew Bible present the best efforts of sages, prophets, scribes, and visionaries to respond to and explain the experiences and crises of the nation over a period of centuries. The Bible's authority derives from the explanatory power of its insights into and understanding of Yahweh's governance of the world and his plans for Israel. Those insights and understandings may shift and even stand in contradiction with one another, but they are not mutually exclusive, and their contradictions do not affect their authoritative status within the community, their ability to explain and to console, and their ability to nourish the faith of a people convinced that Yahweh would never desert them, no matter how difficult it may be to understand his interactions with them.

*Postdestruction Prophecies and Metaphors of Restoration*

Ezekiel 33 states that in the year 586, a fugitive brought the news of the fall of Jerusalem, and Ezekiel exchanged his message of doom for a message of hope. Before the fall of the city, his task had been to shatter the people's illusions, shake them out of their complacency. Now that they were reduced to despair and remorse, his task was to offer reassurance and hope. Yahweh would initiate a new beginning.

Though Israel's punishment was deserved, it did not, according to Ezekiel, betoken the end of the relationship between Yahweh and his people. A new Israel would rise from the remnant of Judah and Israel. He expresses this restoration by means of various metaphors and visions. Chapter 34 condemns the shepherds (a common ancient Near Eastern metaphor for leaders) of the people and promises to set up in the future one shepherd of the house of David to be prince among the people. Chapter 36 describes the restoration using metaphors of purity and cleansing. Israel will be cleansed from the impurities of her past and given a new covenant of the heart.

> I will take you from among the nations and gather you from all the countries, and I will bring you back to your own land. I will sprinkle clean water upon you, and you shall be clean: I will cleanse you from all your uncleanness and from all your fetishes. And I will give you a new heart and put a new spirit into you: I will remove the heart of stone from your body and give you a heart of flesh; and I will put my spirit into you. Thus I will cause you to follow my laws and faithfully to observe my rules. Then you shall dwell in the land which I gave to your fathers, and you shall be my people and I will be your god. (36:24–25)

Here, as in Jeremiah, a utopian redesign of human nature is envisaged, one in which the problems associated with the exercise of human free will will be obviated. Yahweh's law, teachings, and commandments will not change; human nature will be transformed. Yahweh will cause humans to obey his instructions, implying the elimination of free will: Yahweh's Torah will be observed in a kind of robo-righteousness.

Another metaphor used for the restoration of a new Israel out of the remnant of the old is the metaphor of revival from death, found in chapter 37.

The hand of Yahweh came upon me. He took me out by the spirit of Yahweh and set me down in the valley. It was full of bones. He led me all around them; there were very many of them spread over the valley and they were very dry. He said to me, "O mortal can these bones live again?" I replied, "my lord Yahweh, only you know." And He said to me, "Prophesy over these bones and say to them: O dry bones, hear the word of Yahweh! Thus said my lord Yahweh to these bones: I will cause breath to enter you and you shall live again. I will lay sinews upon you, and cover you with flesh, and form skin over you. And I will put breath into you, and you shall live again. And you shall know that I am Yahweh!" I prophesied as I had been commanded. And while I was prophesying, suddenly there was a sound of rattling, and the bones came together, bone to matching bone. I looked and there were sinews on them, and flesh had grown, and skin had formed over them. . . . The breath entered them, and they came to life and stood up on their feet, a vast multitude. And He said to me, "O mortal, these bones are the whole House of Israel. They say, 'Our bones are dried up, our house is gone; we are doomed.' Prophesy therefore and say to them: Thus said my lord Yahweh: I am going to open your graves and lift you out of the graves, O my people, and bring you to the land of Israel. You shall know, O my people, that I am Yahweh, when I have opened your graves and lifted you out of your graves. I will put my breath into you and you shall live again, and I will set you upon your own soil. Then you shall know that I Yahweh have spoken and have acted"—declares Yahweh. (37:1–8, 10–14)

In the interpretation that follows this vision, the bones are said to be "the whole House of Israel" who say, "Our bones are dried up and our hope is lost" (37:11). Yahweh promises to raise Israel from the "grave," a metaphor for exile, and restore her to her homeland—as one people, north and south with one prince to rule over her. This famous "Valley of Dry Bones" passage has often been decontextualized and cited as a source for the doctrine of a literal resurrection after death. But in its context it is clearly one of many metaphors employed by the prophet Ezekiel to describe Israel's redemption from exile and restoration in its land.

Chapter 47 describes the restored land and city: At the center of the restored community is a new Jerusalem, and at its center a rebuilt Temple described in detail in the last nine chapters of the book. In Ezekiel's utopian vision, the land is equally allotted among all twelve tribes. Jerusalem lies in the center with twelve great gates (one for each tribe), its Temple the source of a never-ending river that will make the Dead Sea flow with fresh water. Zadokite priests preside, assisted by Levite menials, and no foreigners are permitted entry (a view not shared by others in the post-destruction era).

While Ezekiel believed that Yahweh would restore a purified Israel to the land under a Davidic monarch and prophesied to this effect, he (like Jeremiah) also maintained that a relationship with Yahweh was possible in the meantime, a relationship outside of the chosen land. Thus, Ezekiel's response to the national disaster and exile may be summarized as follows: although Israel's punishment was fully deserved, Yahweh is with his people in exile. Even following the destruction, a relationship with Yahweh remains possible in the diaspora.

The Jewish Diaspora was a religious-national body the like of which had never before been seen. A people remained loyal to its god while in exile from its own land, and without worshipping that god cultically or by means of sacrifice (since Jerusalem was the only legitimate altar site). In time, a new worship would be fashioned—one without sacrifice, consisting of prayer, confession, fasts, and ritual observance. Three times a day Jews would pray in the direction of Jerusalem. Worship in synagogues would come into being. The importance of the Sabbath would grow as a memorial of the covenant and symbol of Jewish faith. And as a new development, non-Jews would join themselves to Yahweh, adopting the *religious worship* of Israel out of religious conviction. It has been said with only some exaggeration that as the history of Israel as a nation comes to an end, the history of Judaism begins.

## Second Isaiah (Isaiah 40–55)

A second response to the destruction and exile can be found in the anonymous writings appended to the book of Isaiah. There are two discrete units of material appended to Isaiah—chapters 40–55, known as Second Isaiah, and chapters 56–66, known as Third Isaiah. These chapters differ from Isaiah proper in several ways. First, it is clear that Second Isaiah and parts of Third Isaiah were written after the exile, whereas the historical Isaiah was active in the late eighth and early seventh centuries B.C.E. Assyria was Israel's oppressor in the time of the historical Isaiah, but in Second and Third

Isaiah Babylon is referred to as the oppressor, Jerusalem is referred to as destroyed, and the audience addressed is living in exile. Indeed, the appended materials even know of the overthrow of Babylon by Cyrus of Persia around 539 B.C.E. and express some of the euphoria that attended Cyrus's authorization of the Jews to return from Babylon to Jerusalem and rebuild their Temple (Isa 44:28). Moreover, there are stylistic differences between First Isaiah and Second and Third Isaiah. The latter units contain no biographical data, for example.[5] Finally, these materials evidence a new theology of history, a new attitude to foreign nations, and a renewed emphasis on monotheism.

### Comfort Ye

Second Isaiah appears to be an entirely postdestruction work. The inaugural oracle in chapter 40 is an oracle of consolation and comfort. The prophet envisions a straight and level highway prepared in the wilderness for a dramatic procession of Yahweh, the shepherd, leading his people back to Jerusalem.

> Comfort, oh comfort my people,
> Says your god.
> Speak tenderly to Jerusalem,
> And declare to her
> That her term of service is over,
> That iniquity is expiated;
> For she has received at the hand of Yahweh
> Double for all her sins.
> A voice rings out:
> "Clear in the desert
> A road for Yahweh!
> Level in the wilderness
> A highway for our god!
> Let every valley be raised,
> Every hill and mount made low.
> Let the rugged ground become level
> And the ridges become a plain.
> The Presence of Yahweh shall appear,
> And all flesh, as one, shall behold—
> For Yahweh himself has spoken."

> A voice rings out: "Proclaim!"
> Another asks, "What shall I proclaim?"
> "All flesh is grass,
> All its goodness like flowers of the field:
> Grass withers, flowers fade
> . . . But the word of our god is always fulfilled!"
>
> . . . Behold, my lord Yahweh comes in might,
>
> . . . Like a shepherd he pastures his flock:
> He gathers the lambs in his arms
> And carries them in his bosom;
> Gently he drives the mother sheep. (40:1–8, 10, 11)

A voice cries out to proclaim a literal return from exile. Yahweh is opening a highway and leading his flock home like a shepherd at the head of a new exodus, an idea so important that it recurs at the end of the unit in chapter 55. A second key theme of Second Isaiah is sounded at both the beginning and end of the unit: The word of our god is always fulfilled or, in some translations, the word of our god stands forever. This idea is the essence of the Israelites' hope during the period of captivity and exile. It appears in the first oracle of Second Isaiah and is beautifully restated in the last oracle in chapter 55.

> For as the rain or snow drops from heaven
> And returns not there,
> But soaks the earth
> And makes it bring forth vegetation,
> Yielding seed for sowing and bread for eating,
> So is the word that issues from my mouth:
> It does not come back to me unfulfilled,
> But performs what I purpose,
> Achieves what I sent it to do.
> Yea, you shall leave in joy and be led home
>     secure.
> Before you, mount and hill shall shout aloud,
> And all the trees of the field shall clap their hands. (55:10–12)

The everlasting word of Yahweh, its guaranteed fulfillment, specifically to bring his people home in a new exodus—these are the ideas that form an envelope or inclusio around the entire unit of Second Isaiah.

*Monotheism*

The monotheism implicit in First Isaiah becomes explicit in Second Isaiah. For Second Isaiah, coming to terms with the destruction of 586 B.C.E. means accepting that Israel's punishment was deserved and asserting that Yahweh controls the history of not just Israel but also the nations. There is no power other than Yahweh. Referring to the rise and fall of nations, 41:4 states:

> Who has wrought and achieved this?
> He who announced the generations from the start—
> I, Yahweh, who was first
> And will be with the last as well.

Yahweh is the first and the last, which is to say—everything. There is no deity but Yahweh. Isaiah 44 satirizes those nations who make and worship idols and ridicules the folly of ascribing divinity to that which one has created with one's own hands! In Isa 41 Yahweh states his case against these vain and useless idols, summoning them to answer for themselves and to show that they are gods by announcing what will occur.

> Let them approach and tell us what will happen.
> Tell us what has occurred,
> And we will take note of it;
> Or announce to us what will occur,
> That we may know the outcome.
> Foretell what is yet to happen,
> That we may know that you are gods!
> Do anything, good or bad,
> That we may be awed and see.
> Why, you are less than nothing,
> Your effect is less than nullity;
> One who chooses you is an abomination. (41:22–24)

But this is only half the picture. Not only are the gods of the nations no-gods, but Yahweh is the true god of all nations. Who raised Cyrus of Persia from the north to sweep through the ancient Near East? No one but Yahweh.

> I have roused him from the north, and he has come . . .
> And he has trampled rulers like mud,
> Like a potter treading clay
> . . . The things once predicted to Zion—
> Behold here they are! (41:25, 27)

In these passages Second Isaiah articulates the last in a series of transformations. Yahweh, once a southern deity imported into Canaan, then the national god of Israel, has become here the lord of universal history. The only god is the god of Israel.

## The Suffering Servant

Second Isaiah also contains the famous Servant Songs (42:1–4, 49:1–6, 50:4–9, 52:13–53:12). The identity of the servant in these passages has been a puzzle to biblical interpreters for centuries, especially because the servant is at times a collective figure and at times an individual figure. In chapter 49 the servant is described as a prophet but with a universal message, rather than a message for the Israelites alone. The servant or prophet is first identified as Israel herself.

> Yahweh appointed me before I was born,
> He named me while I was in my mother's womb.
> He made my mouth like a sharpened blade,
> He hid me in the shadow of his hand,
> And he made me like a polished arrow;
> He concealed me in his quiver.
> And he said to me, "You are my servant,
> Israel in whom I glory." (49:1–3)

Yet in verse 5 it would appear that the prophet/servant has a mission to Israel, to bring her back to Yahweh, and therefore is not to be identified with Israel.

> And now Yahweh has resolved—
> He who formed me in the womb to be his servant—

> To bring back Jacob to himself,
> That Israel may be restored to him. (49:5)

This mission is then expanded in verse 6:

> For he has said: it is too little that you should be my servant
> In that I raise up the tribes of Jacob
> And restore the survivors of Israel:
> I will also make you a light of nations,
> That My salvation may reach the ends of the earth.

Chapter 50 speaks of the servant as rebellious and persecuted.

> I offered my back to the floggers,
> And my cheeks to those who tore out my hair.
> I did not hide my face
> From insult and spittle. (Isa 50:6)

But it is the famous and difficult passage in Isa 53 that most movingly describes the suffering and sorrow of Yahweh's servant.

> He was despised, we held him of no account.
> Yet it was our sickness that he was bearing,
> Our suffering that he endured.
> We accounted him plagued,
> Smitten and afflicted by Elohim
> But he was wounded because of our sins,
> Crushed because of our iniquities.
> He bore the chastisement that made us whole,
> And by his bruises we were healed.
> We all went astray like sheep,
> Each going his own way;
> And Yahweh visited upon him
> The guilt of all of us.
> He was maltreated, yet he was submissive,
> He did not open his mouth;
> Like a sheep being led to slaughter,
> Like a ewe, dumb before those who shear her,
> He did not open his mouth.

> . . . And his grave was set among the wicked,
> And with the rich, in his death—
> Though he had done no injustice
> And had spoken no falsehood.
> But Yahweh chose to crush him by disease,
> That, if he made himself an offering for guilt,
> He might see offspring and have long life,
> And that through him Yahweh's purpose might prosper. (53:3–11)

There have been many attempts to equate this man of sorrows with all kinds of figures. Early on, Jesus' followers saw Jesus as the suffering servant of Yahweh in Isaiah. The New Testament writers borrowed passages from Isaiah, particularly chapter 53, when constructing their narratives of Jesus' life and death.[6] He is depicted as the innocent and righteous servant who suffered for the sins of others. In the teachings of Paul, however, Christians are identified as the servant who suffers with and for Jesus. Despite these later theological interpretations, the anonymous writer of Second Isaiah was not writing about a remote Nazarene teacher and charismatic healer who would live more than five centuries later. Examined in its original context, it appears most likely that the servant is Israel herself, described metaphorically as an individual whose present suffering and humiliation is due to the sins of other nations, but whose future restoration and exaltation will cause astonishment among those nations, who will then be humbled to Yahweh. There are problems with even this interpretation. The main objection to interpreting the servant as Israel is Isa 49:5, which describes the servant as having a mission to Israel. It seems a little odd to say that Israel bears a mission to Israel. However, this problem can be solved if we remember that Israel is often a divided entity in prophetic thought, so that perhaps the writer envisions a mission of one part—the righteous part—to the other—the part that has gone astray. Leaving aside this difficulty, the more prominent motif in the Servant Song of Isaiah is that the servant has a mission to the world—a role that would suit Israel quite well. Furthermore, the phrase "Israel, my servant" appears in Second Isaiah eight times so that the idea of Israel as Yahweh's servant to the nations is clearly a part of Isaiah's conceptual world. And since we are dealing with poetry rather than a rigorously consistent metaphysical treatise, it should not be too surprising that sometimes the servant is spoken of as a collectivity and sometimes as an individual (the same holds true of Israel, in fact). Thus, in its original context it is likely that the servant is Israel herself.

*Israel's Mission*

If the servant is Israel, then we can see how Second Isaiah offers yet another interpretation of the events of 586—an ultimately positive interpretation. The punishment Israel suffered, even if excessive (and Isa 40 claims that Israel has received double for all her sins), is not meaningless. It will lead to national redemption. Israel will be healed by her wounds. In addition, suffering leads to a new role for Israel among the nations. Second Isaiah expresses a new self-awareness that was beginning to take hold in the exile. Some Israelites saw themselves as the faithful Servant of Yahweh, a servant whose loyalty to Yahweh in dark times would broadcast the knowledge of Yahweh throughout the nations. Israel was chosen from the womb to serve Yahweh's universal purpose. Israel's suffering, observed by others, would lead to the recognition of Yahweh by those others. Where once Yahweh had covenanted with David to lead his people Israel, he now covenants with all Israel to lead the nations of the world in Yahweh's way, as may be seen in the following passage:

> Incline your ear and come to me;
> Harken, and you shall be revived.
> And I will make with you an everlasting covenant,
> The enduring loyalty promised to David.[7]
> As I made him a leader of peoples,
> A prince and commander of peoples,
> So you shall summon a nation who you did not know,
> And a nation that did not know you,
> Shall come running to you—
> For the sake of Yahweh your god,
> The Holy One of Israel who has glorified you. (55:3–5)

Yahweh makes an eternal covenant with Israel like the covenant he once concluded with David. The functions of the institutions of the old order are transferred to the nation as a whole. What kings, priests, and prophets did for Israel, Israel will now do for the whole world. As the mediator between the only god and the nations of the world, Israel is a light unto them. All will ascend to her, because from her comes Torah, or instruction in the divine will.

## CHAPTER 20

# Responses to the Destruction

## Lamentations and Wisdom

*Readings:* Lamentations; Proverbs 1–13, 32; Job 1–11, 21–31, 38–42

## Lamentations

When Nebuchadrezzar burned the Temple and destroyed Jerusalem, the initial reaction of the nation was one of overpowering grief and sadness, reflected in the book of Lamentations. This short book of dirges lamenting the loss of Jerusalem as the death of a beloved person is traditionally attributed to Jeremiah, but the biblical text does not itself make this claim. The attribution may have arisen because, of all the prophets, Jeremiah reveals the most about his personal suffering and grief and because he was present at the destruction as an eyewitness. Likewise, the traditional attribution of the book of Psalms to David probably arose because the biblical narrative describes him as a musician.

There is no logical development of ideas in Lamentations, primarily because of the artificial device guiding its construction. Four of the five chapters are acrostic poems, with each verse, or series of verses, beginning with a letter of the alphabet in sequence (in chapter 3, there are three verses per letter). This gives the poem formal unity but no logical flow. It has been pointed out that this form is particularly appropriate for an expression of grief that is too profound and all-encompassing to be logical.

There are ancient Near Eastern prototypes of laments for destroyed cities, understood as the result of a deity's decision to abandon the city.[1] The biblical book of Lamentations belongs to the same genre. The lamentations over Jerusalem resemble David's lamentation over Saul—the former beauty and wealth of the beloved are contrasted with his or her present state. At the same time we are given a picture of the great suffering that accompanied the final collapse.

> Alas!
> Lonely sits the city
> Once great with people!
> She that was great among nations
> Is become like a widow:
> The princess among states
> Is become a thrall. (1:1)

> Alas!
> The gold is dulled,
> Debased the finest gold!
> The sacred gems are spilled
> At every street corner.
> The precious children of Zion;
> Once valued as gold—
> Alas, they are accounted as earthen pots,
> Work of a potter's hands!
> Even jackals offer the breast
> And suckle their young;
> But my poor people has turned cruel,
> Like ostriches of the desert.
> The tongue of the suckling cleaves
> To its palate for thirst.
> Little children beg for bread;
> None gives them a morsel.
> Those who feasted on dainties
> Lie famished in the streets;
> Those who were reared in purple
> Have embraced refuse heaps.
> The guilt of my poor people
> Exceeded the iniquity of Sodom,

Which was overthrown in a moment,
Without a hand striking it.
Her elect were purer than snow,
Whiter than milk.
Their limbs were ruddier than coral,
Their bodies were like sapphire.
Now their faces are blacker than soot,
They are not recognized in the streets;
Their skin has shriveled on their bones,
It has become dry as wood.
Better off were the slain of the sword
Than those slain by famine,
Who pined away, [as though] wounded,
For lack of the fruits of the field.
With their own hands, tenderhearted women
Have cooked their children;
Such became their fare,
In the disaster of my poor people. (4:1–10)

The poet adopts the standard Deuteronomistic interpretation of events—an interpretation that infers sin from suffering and therefore harps on the sin and impurity of Jerusalem that brought on the calamity. The poet singles out the corrupt prophets and priests for blame and attacks the popular ideology of the inviolability of Zion. In this way Yahweh is justified: Israel's many sins caused Yahweh to pour out his wrath and destroy Jerusalem utterly. Yet the descriptions of Yahweh's consuming rage are some of the most powerful and disturbingly violent poetry in the Hebrew Bible (see, for example, 2:3–7, 9–12, 17–18, 20–22) and divert attention from the people's guilt to their suffering—children crying for bread and starving to death, women raped and men abused. Implicitly, then, Yahweh's justice is challenged—a challenge that will reach full and explicit expression in other biblical books.

In chapter 3, the poet switches to the first person, and Jerusalem speaks like one pursued and beaten by an angry and violent master.

I am the man who has known affliction
Under the rod of his wrath;
Me he drove on and on
In unrelieved darkness;
On none but me he brings down his hand

Again and again, without cease.
He has worn away my flesh and skin;
He has shattered my bones.
All around me he has built
Misery and hardship;
He has made me dwell in darkness,
Like those long dead.
He has walled me in and I cannot break out;
He has weighed me down with chains.
And when I cry and plead,
He shuts out my prayer;
He has walled in my ways with hewn blocks,
He has made my paths a maze.
He is a lurking bear to me,
A lion in hiding.
He has forced me off my way and mangled me,
He has left me numb. (3:1–11)

In a remarkable passage, the poet describes Yahweh as refusing to hear the
prayers of Israel.

We have transgressed and rebelled
But you have not forgiven.
You have clothed yourself in anger and pursued us,
You have slain without pity.
You have screened yourself off with a cloud,
That no prayer may pass through.
You have made us filth and refuse
In the midst of the peoples. (3:42–45)

The poem ends with a plea for reconciliation.

But you, O Yahweh, are enthroned forever,
Your throne endures through the ages.
Why have you forgotten us utterly,
Forsaken us for all time?
Take us back, O Yahweh to yourself,
And let us come back;
Renew our days as of old!

> For truly, you have rejected us,
> Bitterly raged against us.
> Take us back, O Yahweh, to yourself,
> And let us come back;
> Renew our days as of old! (5:19–22)

Lamentations represents one response to the fall of Jerusalem—an over-whelming sense of loss, grief, misery, and a longing to return. The two centuries following the destruction would prove to be a crucial period of transition, and Israelite literature in this period reflects the nation's con-tinuing struggle with the philosophical and religious challenges posed by the destruction. How could this disastrous event be explained? The re-sponse of the Deuteronomistic school was outlined in Chapter 14: Israel was collectively punished for the sinful idolatry of her kings; history simply reflects divine justice on a national and international level. The prophetic response was outlined in Chapter 16: Israel was punished for violations of the covenant, but a purified and righteous remnant will be restored. Jere-miah and Ezekiel promoted the idea of a continuing relationship with Yah-weh in exile while awaiting a fantastic restoration and redesign of human nature, while Second Isaiah emphasized a universal significance for the suffering of Yahweh's servant Israel: Israel's suffering served a larger divine plan by preparing her for a new role in world history.

Still other responses are to be found in the books collected in the third section of the Hebrew Bible known as the Writings (Heb: Ketuvim). While some of the books in the third section of the Bible may have origi-nated in the predestruction era, it is widely believed that they became au-thoritative for the community in the postexilic period. As such, they served the postexilic community as a prism through which to view and come to grips with Israel's tragic history.

## Wisdom Literature

The so-called wisdom books of the Hebrew Bible are Proverbs, Job, and Ecclesiastes.[2] Israelite wisdom literature belongs to a larger scribal tradition of wisdom literature in the ancient Near East. Very little in biblical wisdom texts, apart from their monotheism, lacks a parallel in the wisdom litera-ture of Egypt and Mesopotamia. Ancient Near Eastern wisdom literature is characterized by its praise of human intelligence applied to understanding the ways of the world. Often presenting traditional advice that has been found to be tried and true, ancient Near Eastern wisdom literature is universal and humanistic in its orientation. Likewise, Israelite wisdom literature does not speak to the particular and historical condition of Israel but to the general human condition.[3] Biblical wisdom texts make no special claim to having been divinely revealed—these texts contain observational wisdom that can be weighed, confirmed, or disputed by experience.

The Hebrew word for wisdom, *hokhmah,* means literally "skill" and refers to the skill of living properly, morally, or well. The biblical corpus contains various types of wisdom material.

- (1) Clan/family wisdom—commonsense observations and aphorisms typical of many cultures. Many sound like advice passed on from parent to child. Although these aphorisms are scattered throughout the Hebrew Bible, many are contained in the book of Proverbs:

  Better a meal of vegetables where there is love than a fattened ox where there is hate. (15:17)
  "Bad, bad," says the buyer, but having moved off he congratulates himself. (20:14)
  The door turns on its hinge, and the lazy man on his bed. (26:14)
  Like cold water to a parched throat is good news from a distant land. (25:25)

  (2) Court wisdom—produced to serve the needs of the court, a genre well attested in ancient Egypt. Court wisdom consists of bureaucratic or administrative advice and practical instruction on manners, diplomacy, and how to live well and prosper.

  Put your external affairs in order, get ready what you have in the field, then build yourself a home. (24:27)
  He who guards his mouth and tongue guards himself from trouble. (21:23)
  For want of strategy an army falls, but victory comes with much planning. (11:14)
  He who loves discipline loves knowledge, he who spurns reproof is a brutish man. (12:1)

  (3) Reflective probing into the critical problems of human existence. The biblical books that exemplify this type of wisdom literature, the books of Job and Ecclesiastes, will be discussed below.

According to Jewish tradition, King Solomon is to be credited with the composition of Proverbs and Ecclesiastes, as well as several noncanonical wisdom works. This tradition presumably arises from 1 Kgs 5:9–14, which describes Solomon as the wisest of all men, composing 3,000 proverbs and 1,005 poems. Like the attribution of the entire Pentateuch to Moses, the entire book of Psalms to David, and the book of Lamentations to Jeremiah, the attribution of Proverbs and Ecclesiastes to Solomon does not withstand scrutiny.

As noted above, the wisdom literature of the Hebrew Bible tends to be universalistic, ahistorical, and humanistic. There is nothing particularly Israelite about these works—no mention of the Exodus, of Sinai, of Moses, or any of the narrative traditions of the nation—and they are paralleled in great abundance in the writings of other peoples of the ancient Near East. In the book of Proverbs, wisdom is connected with Yahweh and adherence to his ways. However, biblical wisdom, like ancient Near Eastern wisdom generally, grounds morality on somewhat nonparticularistic notions of prudence and "god/Yahweh-fearing" rather than on Israel's historical covenant with Yahweh.

## Proverbs

A classic book of Israelite wisdom, Proverbs may contain some material of considerable antiquity, even if it reached its final form only in postexilic times. The many affinities between Proverbs and Egyptian, Canaanite, and Babylonian literature suggest that Israel assimilated wisdom material from her wider environment.[4] Like wisdom literature in general, the book of Proverbs ignores the historical odyssey of the Israelites, issues of sacrifice, idolatry, and even social injustice and is cosmopolitan and universal in flavor. The chief aim of Proverbs seems to be the inculcation of wisdom as the means to social tranquility and a happy life. Young people should master their impulses and lead productive and sensible lives. Many maxims are intended to educate sons (there is no mention of daughters), and much of chapters 1–9 is formally pedagogical. These chapters warn against the seductions of foreign women and urge young men to pursue wisdom—figured here as a virtuous woman—created before all other created things and assisting Yahweh in ordering the universe. Proverbs values hard work and diligence and warns against excessive sleep, sex, and wine. The book recommends honesty in business affairs, kindness, loyalty, impartiality, sobriety, humility, restraint, and sincerity. Wealth is not to be desired at the cost of calmness and peace.

The wisdom sayings of Proverbs are usually short, two-line sentences in which the second line runs parallel to the first. Parallelism establishes various connections between the two parts of a verse. An example of *synonymous parallelism,* in which the two parallel units are essentially synonymous, is found in Prov 22:1 and is a classic feature of biblical poetry in general:

> A good name is to be chosen rather than great riches, and favor
> is better than silver and gold.

In *antithetic parallelism,* the two lines form a balanced pair of opposites, as in Prov 10:1:

> A wise son makes a glad father, but a foolish son is a sorrow to
> his mother.

When the second line completes or intensifies the thought of the first, it is termed *ascending parallelism,* as may be seen in Prov 11:22:

> Like a gold ring in the snout of a pig is a beautiful woman bereft
> of sense.

In the book of Proverbs, wisdom itself is established as a religious concept. In some passages, wisdom is personified as a woman who promises insight and counsel (1:20–33, 8:1–36, 9:1–6). In other passages, wisdom is described as being present when the world was created (3:19, 8:22–30). Already in the first chapter of Proverbs, wisdom is ascribed a religious value and is linked with reverence for and obedience to Yahweh.

> The fear of Yahweh is the beginning of wisdom; fools despise
> wisdom and discipline. (1:7)

Similarly,

> Trust in Yahweh with all your heart, and do not rely on your
> own understanding. (3:5–8)

Wisdom guards one from evil. The wise person accepts the sufferings with which Yahweh disciplines him. If a righteous man suffers, then he is being chastised by Yahweh as a son is disciplined by his father, and he should not reject this reproof.

> For Yahweh reproves him whom he loves, as a father the son in
> whom he delights. (3:12)

Most striking is the book of Proverbs' optimism and even complacency. There is an almost smug certainty in the book that the righteous and the wicked of the world receive what they deserve in this life. Yahweh's just providence and the existence of a moral world order are presuppositions that the book does not question. The wise person's deeds are good and will bring him happiness and success. The foolish person's deeds are evil and lead to failure and ruin. The truly wise person knows that the world is essentially coherent and ethically ordered, that clear laws of reward and punishment exist in the world:

> He who digs a pit will fall into it, and a stone will come back
> upon him who starts it rolling. (26:27)
> Righteousness protects him whose way is blameless; wickedness
> subverts the sinner. (13:6)

This insistence on the basic justice of the world and the power of wisdom or fear of Yahweh to guarantee success and security was one strand of ancient Israelite thought that reached crystallization in the book of Proverbs and was available as a response to, an explanation of, the catastrophes that had befallen the nation. The same insistence may be seen in the work of the Deuteronomistic school, unwilling to relinquish the idea of a moral deity in control of history and preferring to infer the nation's sinfulness from its suffering and calamity. Better to blame the sufferer—Israel—and so keep Yahweh and the system of divine retributive justice intact. But it is precisely this formulaic and conventional piety that is challenged in two other wisdom books of the Bible—Job and Ecclesiastes. In Job we find the idea that suffering is not always punitive; it is not always a sign of wickedness; it is not always explicable. This is the first of several subversions of fundamental biblical principles that the reader encounters in the book of Job.

## Job

The book of Job, which is probably no earlier than the sixth century B.C.E. (though scholars disagree), can be one of the hardest books of the Bible for many moderns to read because its conclusions seem to fly in the face of basic religious convictions. But Job's charges against the deity must be taken seriously. After all, the narrator makes it clear that Yahweh takes them seriously. Yahweh nowhere denies Job's charges, and in fact at the end of the story, Yahweh states that Job has spoken truly (Job 42:7).

Job attacks the optimistic conventional piety typified in the book of Proverbs and challenges the assumption that there is a moral world order. The issues raised in the book of Job are (1) why the deity permits blatant injustice and undeserved suffering and evil to exist in the world and (2) whether people will be virtuous when they are afflicted and suffering; that is, are people righteous only because the deity will reward them for it, or are they righteous because of the intrinsic or inherent value of righteousness?

In literary terms, the book contains two primary units.[5] First is a simple prose story that provides a framework for the book, chapters 1, 2, and 42. This narrative framework, which tells of a scrupulously righteous man named Job afflicted by horrendous calamity, was probably a standard ancient Near Eastern folktale of great antiquity. The story is set not in Israel but in Edom, and Job is not an Israelite but an eastern magnate dwelling in the country of Uz.

However, the Israelite author of the book of Job inserts a lengthy poetic dialogue (some thirty-nine chapters long) into the middle of this simple folktale. The addition of this second literary unit transforms the legend dramatically. While the Job of the narrative frame seems to accept his fate, the Job of the poetic dialogue rails against the injustice of the universe and the deity. These two characterizations of Job are already hinted at in his name, which is bivalent in meaning. The name Job (pronounced Iyyov) can mean "enemy" (in Hebrew) or "the repentant one" (in Aramaic). And indeed, as the story progresses, both senses of the name will be appropriate.

The book's structure is outlined in Table 6. Chapters 1 and 2 contain the prose prologue about the pious and prosperous Job and his devastation as the result of a challenge put to Yahweh. At the end of the prologue, three friends come to comfort him and to sit with him in silence for seven days (2:13). After this week of mourning, Job and his friends are not silent. Their discourse is represented in the large poetic section that extends from chapter 3 to 42:7.

Table 6. Structure of the Book of Job

**Narrative Prologue—Chapters 1-2**
  Poetic Dialogue 3:1–42:6

  *1st Cycle, 3–11*
  Job speaks, 3
    Eliphaz replies, 4–5
  Job speaks, 6–7
    Bildad replies, 8
  Job speaks, 9–10
    Zophar replies, 11

  *2nd Cycle, 12–20*
  Job speaks, 12:1–14:22
    Eliphaz replies, 15:1–35
  Job speaks, 16:1–17:16
    Bildad replies, 18:1–21
  Job speaks, 19:1–29
    Zophar replies, 20:1–29

  3rd *Cycle, 21–31*
  Job speaks, 21
    Eliphaz replies, 22
  Job speaks, 23–24
    Bildad replies, 25
  Job speaks, 26–31

  Elihu's Speech, 32–37
      1. 32–33
      2. 34
      3. 35
      4. 36–37

  Yahweh's Speech, 38:1–42:6
    Yahweh, 38:1–40:2
    Job, 40:3–5
    Yahweh, 40:6–41:34
    Job, 42:1–6
**Narrative Epilogue 42:7–17**

First, there is a dialogue between Job and his three friends (3:1–31:40) that can be divided into three cycles of speeches. Job opens each cycle, and then his friends speak in a regular pattern, first Eliphaz (with Job responding), then Bildad (with Job responding), then Zophar. This pattern of six speeches occurs three times, but the third set omits a speech by Zophar. This deviation ensures that Job has the first and the last word (a summation speech in chapters 29–31). At first, the friends seek to comfort Job and to explain his suffering, but their comfort turns increasingly cold and dissolves ultimately in a callous contempt for Job's condition. This section closes with a long speech by Job (29–31) lamenting the loss of his past pleasant life, protesting his innocence, and calling on his god to answer (31:35). Then Elihu, a previously unannounced fourth friend appears and gives four speeches (32–37) admonishing Job and defending divine justice. This is followed by a poetic discourse between Yahweh—who poses a series of rhetorical questions—and Job—who appears contrite. This section also falls into four parts: two long speeches by Yahweh and two short ones by Job. A concluding prose epilogue vindicates Job. Yahweh criticizes the friends, and a rather unexpected happy ending sees Job restored to his fortunes before experiencing a peaceful death.

A closer examination of the book reveals a fascinating narrative progression. The story opens by introducing Job, a *blameless and upright* man, who fears Yahweh and shuns evil (1:1). The moral virtue and innocence of Job is thus established in the opening line as a nonnegotiable narrative fact. Yet this Job is to become the victim of a challenge issued by the satan (= the accuser) in the Heavenly Council. The satan is not to be confused with the character Satan. Satan, or the Devil, does not appear in the Hebrew Bible, where Yahweh has no evil adversary. He is the creation of later literature. The satan, however, occurs four times in the Hebrew Bible (Job, Num 22:32, Zech 3:1–4, and 1 Chr 21:1).[6] The satan is simply a member of the divine council (one of Yahweh's minions), whose function it is to investigate affairs on earth and act as a kind of prosecuting attorney, bringing evildoers to justice. Only in later Jewish and especially Christian thought does the term lose the definite article and become a proper name—Satan—for an enemy or opponent of Yahweh (the Devil). This later concept of Satan develops as a useful means of explaining the existence of evil in the world without attributing it directly to Yahweh. But that is not the function of the satan (the prosecutor) here. He works for Yahweh, and when Yahweh boasts of his pious servant Job, the prosecuting angel wonders, as his portfolio requires him to do, whether Job's piety is sincere. Perhaps it is motivated by self-interest. Since he has been blessed with such good fortune and prosperity,

Job is, naturally enough, pious and righteous. But would his piety survive suffering and affliction? Deprived of his wealth, would he not curse Yahweh?[7] Yahweh is confident that Job's piety is not superficial or driven by the desire for reward, and he permits the satan to put Job to the test. Job's children are killed, and all his cattle and property are destroyed. But Job's response in 1:21 is:

> Naked came I forth from the belly of my mother
>   and naked shall I return thither:
> Yahweh gave, and Yahweh took away;
>   blessed be the name of Yahweh. (Gr)[8]

The narrator adds, "In all this, Job did not sin or accuse Elohim of anything unworthy" (1:22; Gr). Yahweh again praises Job to the satan, saying, "and still he holds on to his integrity, so you incited me to destroy him for nothing" (2:3; Gr). In response, the satan proposes increasing the suffering, and Yahweh agrees, with the condition that Job's life be preserved. The satan then strikes Job's body with terrible, painful sores in an effort to crush his spirit. Job's wife rages, "Do you still hold on to your integrity? Bless Elohim [i.e., curse him] and die!" (2:9; Gr). But still Job will not sin, will not curse his deity. He insists on remaining virtuous and responds, "Shall we then accept the good from Elohim and not accept the bad?" (2:10; Gr).

At first glance, it would appear that Job accepts his bitter fate. But note that after the first round of suffering, the narrator observed that in all this Job did not sin with his lips or impute anything unsavory to Elohim. But now he merely observes, "In all this Job did not sin with his lips" (2:10; Gr)—not with his lips perhaps, but is the reader to suppose that in his heart he did impute unsavory things to the deity (Greenberg, "Job," 285)?

Moving directly to the conclusion of the folktale in 42:7, the reader discovers that Job is fully rewarded for his patience and steadfast loyalty, and his household and belongings are restored twice over. Thus, the folktale standing alone could be read as the story of an innocent man tested by horrific suffering, who accepts his fate, retains his faith, and is rewarded. Standing alone, the tale appears to reflect the values and conventional piety of wisdom literature and the Deuteronomistic school. Suffering must be borne by the righteous as the disciplining chastisement of a father.

However, the folktale does not stand alone. The anonymous author of Job uses the legend concerning the righteous man Job as a frame for his own purposes. The hint at the end of the prologue (2:10) that implies Job's imputation of unsavory things to Elohim points forward to the extensive dialogue of the poetic section. In these chapters are Job's unsavory accusations against the deity. Here, a most *im*patient, furious Job will charge his god with gross mismanagement of the world and eventually deny the existence of a moral order altogether. The two literary units that compose the book—the prose frame and the poetic dialogue—appear to be in tension. Yet interwoven as they now are, they work together, the one shaping our reading of the other. Specifically, our rejection of the accusations of Job's friends in the poetic dialogue is necessitated by the prose framework's assertion of Job's innocence. Because of the nonnegotiable narrative fact of Job's righteousness, we know that Job's friends lie when they say Job is suffering for some hidden sin and that Job's assertion that he has not deserved this suffering is correct.

Let us rehearse the arguments advanced in the central core of the book following the excellent analysis of Edwin M. Good.[9] Though Job doesn't exactly curse the deity in his first speech, he does curse the day of his birth, and in a passage that alludes repeatedly to creation, Job essentially curses all that the deity has accomplished as creator of the cosmos. He wishes he were dead. At this point he doesn't ask why so much suffering has come upon him, but only why he should be alive when he prefers death.

Eliphaz's reply (chapters 4–5) is long and elaborate. He seems to offer comfort until he injects a new element into the discussion—the issue of justice (Good, *Turns of Tempest*, 212–213). Job has not mentioned the issue of justice, but Eliphaz says:

> Think now, what innocent man ever perished?
> Where have the upright been destroyed?
> As I have seen, those who plow evil
> And sow mischief reap them. (4:7–8)

Eliphaz hands Job the standard line of biblical wisdom literature as exemplified by the book of Proverbs, which reflects a belief in a system of divine retributive justice. By definition, there can be no undeserved suffering. The implication is that Job has deserved his suffering—a thought that apparently had not occurred to him—and the question of undeserved suffering dominates the rest of the book.

Job's second speech (chapters 6–7) is disorderly, full of wild contradictory images (Good, *Turns of Tempest*, 213–214) reflecting the shock, pain, and rage that now overwhelm him. Haunted by Eliphaz's connection of his suffering with some sin, he turns to address the deity directly. He admits he is not perfect, but surely, he objects, he does not deserve such affliction.

Bildad's speech in chapter 8 is tactless and unkind (Good, *Turns of Tempest*, 217–218). He says:

> Will El pervert the right?
> Will the Almighty pervert justice?
> If your sons sinned against Him,
> He dispatched them for their transgressions. (8:3–4)

In other words, El is perfectly just, and ultimately all get what they deserve. Indeed, Job's children died because they sinned, and Job would be well advised to simply search for the deity and ask for mercy.

The friends' speeches lead Job to conclude that the deity must be indifferent to moral status. He doesn't follow the rules that he demands of humans but "finishes off both perfect and wicked" (9:22; G). When Job complains that "he wounds me much for nothing" (9:17; Gr) he echoes Yahweh's own words of complaint to the satan in the prologue ("you have incited me to destroy him *for nothing*"—emphasis added). The reader suspects that the verbal coincidence between Yahweh's words and Job's words ("for nothing") attests to the truth of Job's complaint: He is suffering for nothing!

Legal terms dominate as Job calls for the charges against him to be published. Job hurls countercharges in a suit against the deity—charges of unworthy conduct, of spurning his creatures while smiling on the wicked, of scrutinizing Job though he knows Job to be innocent. This countersuit is a subversion of the common prophetic genre of the *riv*, or covenant lawsuit, in which Yahweh through his prophets charges Israel with flagrant violation of the terms of his covenant and warns of inevitable punishment. In Job, it is the human who arraigns the deity. And yet, Job asserts, since his adversary is divine and not human, there is no fair way for the lawsuit between them to be tried or arbitrated: "man cannot win a suit against El" (9:2; Gr). Job is powerless in the face of this injustice.

These ideas find expression in Job 10:1–7:

> I am disgusted with life;
> I will give rein to my complaint,
> Speak in the bitterness of my soul.
> I say to Eloah, "Do not condemn me;

Let me know what you charge me with.
Does it benefit you to defraud,
To despise the toil of your hands,
While smiling on the counsel of the wicked?
Do you have the eyes of flesh?
Is your vision that of mere men?
Are your days the days of a mortal?
Are your years the years of a man,
That you seek my iniquity
And search out my sin?
You know that I am not guilty,
And that there is none to deliver from your hand.

Job repeats his wish to die, but this time less because of his suffering and more because his worldview has collapsed (Good, *Turns of Tempest*, 229). Divine power, he now sees, is utterly divorced from justice—a second fundamental biblical assumption subverted.

Job's words seem to egg on his interlocutors. Eliphaz had only implied Job was a sinner, Bildad baldly asserted that his children died for their sins, and now Zophar claims that Job is suffering *less* than he actually deserves. But Job will not be persuaded that he has sinned or, more precisely, that he has sinned in proportion to his punishment. The deity is simply unjust. The Job of the poetic dialogue portion of this book is hardly patient or pious. He is angry and violent; he argues, complains, and vehemently insists upon his innocence.

In his fourth speech (which opens the second cycle of speeches), Job appeals to creation. The deity's controlling power is arbitrary and unprincipled as he interferes with both nature and the human order—a subversion of the Genesis portrait of creation as a process whose goal and crown is man. Again, Job demands a trial in a widely quoted and mistranslated verse:

He may well slay me; I may have no hope;
But I must argue my case before him. (13:15)

In other words, Job knows he can't win, but he still wants his day in court, to make his accusation of the deity's mismanagement, to voice his protest though it will gain him nothing. In a pun on his name Iyyov, Job asks, "Why do you hide your face and treat me like an enemy [oyev]?" (13:24).

In his second speech, Job fully expects to be murdered—not justly executed, but murdered—by the deity and hopes only that the evidence of his murder will not be concealed. "Earth, do not cover my blood" (16:18). Job's third speech reiterates his desire that the wrong against him not be forgotten:

> Would that my words were written,
> Would that they were engraved in an inscription,
> With an iron stylus and lead,
> Forever in rock they were incised. (19:23–24; G)

Job's three speeches in the second cycle become increasingly emotional. For their part, Job's friends in this cycle become increasingly cruel (Good, *Turns of Tempest*, 260–261). Their insistence that suffering is always a sure sign of sin seems to justify hostility toward and contempt for Job, who is now depicted as universally mocked, humiliated, and abused. One cannot help but see in this characterization of Job's so-called friends an incisive commentary on the callous human propensity to blame the victim, and to do so lest our tidy and comfortable picture of a moral universe in which the righteous do not suffer should fall apart, as Job's has.

Job opens the third cycle of speeches urging his friends to look—really see—his situation, for then they must be appalled. Job's situation, looked at honestly, requires the admission that the deity has done this for no reason (Good, *Turns of Tempest*, 266) and that the friends' understanding of the world is a lie. Job asserts baldly that there is no retributive justice, no coherent and orderly system of morality in this life or any other, since there is no immortality and no afterlife.

> Why do the wicked live on,
> Prosper and grow wealthy?
> Their children are with them always,
> And they see their children's children.
> Their homes are secure, without fear;
> They do not feel the rod of Eloah.
> . . . their children skip about.
> They sing to the music of timbrel and lute,
> And revel to the tune of the pipe;
> They spend their days in happiness,
> And go down to Sheol in peace.

> . . . How seldom does the lamp of the wicked fail,
> Does the calamity they deserve befall them?
> . . . [You say,] "Eloah is reserving his punishment for his sons";
> Let it be paid back to him that he may feel it,
> . . . One man dies in robust health,
> All tranquil and untroubled;
> His pails are full of milk;
> The marrow of his bones is juicy.
> Another dies embittered,
> Never having tasted happiness.
> They both lie in the dust
> And are covered with worms. (21:7–9, 11b–13, 17, 19, 23–26)

But despite Job's words, his friends cannot look honestly at him, cannot allow that indeed a righteous man would suffer horribly (Good, *Turns of Tempest*, 273).

By the end of the third cycle, Job is ready and eager for his trial, but he can't find his god. Job's final speech in the third cycle focuses on divine absence (Good, *Turns of Tempest*, 278). The deity is irresponsibly absent from his world, and the result is human wickedness. From the idea that the deity is morally neutral, Job has moved to the implicit charge that he is *responsible* for wickedness, he *rewards* wickedness, he *causes* wickedness (Good, *Turns of Tempest*, 279). By his absence, his failure to govern properly, the deity is both corrupt and a corrupter of others (Good, *Turns of Tempest*, 281). "If it is not so, who will prove me a liar and bring my words to nought?" (24:25; Gr).

Yet even in the depths of his anguish, and even though he is now convinced that the deity does not enforce a moral law in the universe, Job clings to one value. Righteousness is a virtue in and of itself, and even if it goes unrewarded, Job will not give up his righteousness (Good, *Turns of Tempest*, 287). Face to face with the shocking insight that good and evil are met with indifference by the deity, that righteousness brings no reward and wickedness no punishment, Job—though bitter—refuses to succumb to moral nihilism.

> By El who has deprived me of justice!
> By Shaddai who has embittered my life!
> As long as there is life in me,
> And Eloah's breath is in my nostrils,

My lips will speak no wrong,
Nor my tongue utter deceit.
Far be it from me to say you are right;
Until I die I will maintain my integrity.
I persist in my righteousness and will not yield;
I shall be free of reproach as long as I live. (27:2–6)

These last lines recall the words of Yahweh and the satan in the prelude.
There the satan said that a man would not hold on to virtue or righteousness
in the face of suffering but would give everything away for his life. That narrative setup determines our interpretation of Job's statement here. Though
he is losing his life, Job will not give away anything but holds on to his integrity. As Yahweh said to the satan in 2:3: "Still he holds on to his integrity—
you have incited me to destroy him *for nothing*" (Gr).

In his darkest, most bitter hour, with all hope of reward gone, Job
clings to the one thing he has—his own righteousness. In fact, when all hope
of a just reward is gone, righteousness becomes an intrinsic value. As Y.
Kaufmann writes: "The poet raises Job to the bleak summit of righteousness
bereft of hope, bereft of faith in divine justice."[10] Or in the words of Moshe
Greenberg, Job displays

> the sheer heroism of a naked man, forsaken by his God and his
> friends and bereft of a clue to understand his suffering, still
> maintaining faith in the value of his virtue and in the absolute
> duty of man to be virtuous. The universe has turned its back on
> him yet Job persists in the affirmation of his own worth and the
> transcendent worth of unrewarded good.[11]

In a way then, for all their differences in style and manner, the patient Job
of the legend and the raging Job of the poetic dialogue are basically the
same man—each ultimately remains firm in his moral character—clinging
to righteousness because of its intrinsic value and not because it will be rewarded: Indeed, Job appears to know bitterly that it will not. And this is,
after all, precisely the question that was at issue between Yahweh and the
satan: "Still he holds on to his integrity," Yahweh declared in 2:3—and so he
does even in the poetic dialogue, not quietly or patiently, but in the furious
rage of disillusionment and complete alienation from all that he has believed
to be true about his god. Again, punning on his name and in a reversal of his
earlier assertion that his god views him as an enemy, Job now declares that it

is the deity who is the enemy (27:7; Good, *Turns of Tempest*, 287–288). And yet despite this sobering realization, Job would be righteous.

At the end of his outburst, Job sues his god. He issues him a summons and demands that the deity reveal to him the reason for his suffering. Job pronounces a series of curses to clear himself from the accusations against him, specifying the sins he has not committed and ending as he began in chapter 3 with a curse on his birthday. We expect to hear from the deity; instead, we hear from an unannounced stranger named Elihu.

Elihu is the only one of the four interlocutors to refer to and address Job by name. Elihu repeats the trite assertions of Job's friends. However, he also affirms, as the three friends did not, that not all suffering is punitive and that contemplation of nature's elements can open the mind to a new awareness of the deity. In these two respects (Greenberg, "Job," 297), Elihu's speech moves us toward Yahweh's answer from the storm.

Job 38:1 introduces the climactic moment in which Yahweh addresses Job in an extraordinary theophany, or self-manifestation, speaking out of a tempest or whirlwind. "Who is this who darkens counsel, speaking without knowledge?" (38:2). Is this a reference to Job? To Elihu? To the three friends? To all of them? Yahweh has heard enough—it is his turn to ask questions, the answers to which are clearly implied.

> Where were you when I laid the earth's foundations?
> Speak if you have understanding.
> Do you know who fixed its dimensions
> Or who measured it with a line?
> ... Have you ever commanded the day to break,
> Assigned the dawn its place,
> ... Have you penetrated to the sources of the sea,
> Or walked in the recesses of the deep? (38:4–5, 12, 16)

Yahweh continues with rhetorical questions regarding nature and animals. But what, the reader wonders, is the purpose of all these questions? Isn't all of this in some sense irrelevant (Good, *Turns of Tempest*, 339)? Job has posed some specific challenges: Why am I suffering? Is there a pattern to existence? Is Yahweh's refusal to answer these challenges a way of saying that there is no answer? Is this Yahweh's way of saying that his justice is beyond human understanding? Or is this theophany of Yahweh in the forces and order of nature an implicit assault on the fundamental tenet of Israelite religion that Yahweh is known and made manifest through his interactions with humans? That Yahweh is a god of history rather than a nature god?

The rise of monotheism in Israel is generally understood to have effected a break from mythological conceptions of the gods as manifested in various natural forces and limited by metadivine powers and forces in the cosmos. The biblical god[12] was not identical to ancient Near Eastern or Canaanite nature gods, because he was understood to transcend nature. In the most monotheizing sources of the Bible, Yahweh is encountered not through the involuntary and recurring cycles of nature but through his freely willed and nonrepeating actions in historical time. It is this view of Yahweh that underwrites the whole notion of retributive justice. Only an essentially good god transcending and unconstrained by mechanistic natural forces can establish and administer a system of retributive justice, doling out punishment and reward in response to the actions of humans in time. Is the author of Job suggesting that history and the events that befall the just and unjust are not the medium of revelation? Is Yahweh a god of nature after all, encountered in the repeating cycles of the natural world and not in the unpredictable and incoherent arena of human history and action? If so, then this is a third radical subversion of a fundamental biblical assumption.

Yahweh's second major speech to Job is found in chapter 40: "Would you impugn my justice? Would you condemn me that you may be right?" (40:8). Now Yahweh gets at the heart of the matter. Job's friends were wrong—they condemned Job, attributed sin to Job, so that they might be right. But Job, too, has been wrong, condemning *Yahweh*, attributing wickedness to *Yahweh* so that he might be right. Yahweh invites Job to try *his* hand at righting wrongs (Greenberg, "Job," 298):

> Scatter wide your raging anger,
> See every proud man and bring him low. . . .
> Then even I would praise you
> For the triumph your right hand won you. (40:11, 14)

After that, Yahweh continues, Job can go on to deal with Behemoth and Leviathan, two mythical monsters. The implication is that dispensing justice, like wrestling with monsters, isn't so easy.

Yahweh seems to say that the world doesn't work as Job supposes at all (Good, *Turns of Tempest,* 355–356). Job's friends erred because they assumed that there is a system of retributive justice at work in the world.

That assumption led them to infer that all who suffer are sinful, a blatant falsehood. But Job also errs if he assumes that although there isn't a system of distributive justice, there *ought* to be one. That assumption leads him to infer that suffering is the sign of an indifferent or wicked god, equally a falsehood. In a nutshell, Yahweh refuses to be seen as a moral accountant (Greenberg, "Job," 300). The idea of Yahweh as moral accountant is responsible for two major errors: the interpretation of suffering as an indicator of sin on the one hand (the error of Job's friends) and the ascription of injustice to Yahweh on the other (the error of Job).

In his final speech, Job confesses to a new firsthand knowledge of Yahweh that he lacked before. As a result of his knowledge, Job repents. "Therefore I recant and relent, being but dust and ashes" (42:6; Good, *Turns of Tempest*, 375). Here the other meaning of Job's name—one who repents—suddenly leaps to mind. But for what does Job repent? He surely does not repent for sin—Yahweh has not upheld the friends' accusations against Job (indeed, he will state explicitly in a moment that they were wrong). Yahweh *has* indicated that guilt and innocence, reward and punishment are not what the game is all about. And while Job has long been disabused of the notion that the wicked and righteous actually get what they deserve, he nevertheless clung to the idea that they should. And it is that mistaken idea, an idea that led him to ascribe wickedness to Yahweh, that Job now recants. With his new understanding of Yahweh ("I had heard You with my ears/But now I see You with my eyes," 42:5), Job is liberated from what he would now understand to be the false expectations raised by the Deuteronomistic notion of a system of divine retributive justice (Good, *Turns of Tempest*, 373–377).

Following this dialogue with Yahweh, Job is restored to his fortunes. Yahweh asserts that Job did not suffer for any evil or sin that he had done. The conventional, impeccably Deuteronomistic views of the three friends—that suffering is always punishment for sin, that only the wicked suffer, and no suffering is undeserved—is denounced by Yahweh when he says that they "have not spoken of me what is right as my servant Job has" (42:7). For some, the ending seems anticlimactic, a capitulation to the demand for a happy ending of just deserts that runs counter to the thrust of the whole book. And yet, in a way the ending is superbly fitting—the last in a series of reversals subverting our expectations (Greenberg, "Job," 300). Suffering comes inexplicably, but so does restoration. Blessed be the name of Yahweh.

Yahweh nowhere attempts to justify or explain Job's suffering to him, and yet by the end of the dialogue, our grumbling, embittered, raging Job is satisfied. Perhaps Job has realized that an automatic principle of reward and punishment would make it impossible for humans to do the good for purely disinterested motives. It is precisely when righteousness is seen to be absurd and meaningless that the choice to be righteous paradoxically becomes meaningful. However we are to interpret Yahweh's speech and Job's response, one thing is certain: Yahweh and Job are reconciled.

The suffering and injustice that characterize the world have baffled humankind for millennia. The book of Job provides no answer in the sense of an explanation or a justification of suffering and injustice. What it does offer is a stern warning to avoid the Scylla of blaspheming against the victims by assuming their wickedness and the Charybdis of blaspheming against Yahweh by assuming his (Greenberg, "Job," 301). Nor is moral nihilism an option as Job, yearning for but ultimately renouncing divine order and justice, clings to his integrity and chooses virtue—for nothing.

## CHAPTER 21

# Canonical Criticism

## Ecclesiastes, Psalms, and the Song of Songs

*Readings:* Ecclesiastes 1–12; Psalms 1, 2, 8, 19, 21, 32, 37, 44, 46, 49, 52, 72–74, 78–80, 90, 93, 96–99, 103–106, 109, 110, 112, 114, 115, 118, 119, 128, 131, 136, 137, 139, 150; Song of Songs

Chapter 5 introduced source criticism (or historical criticism), form criticism, and tradition criticism as modern methods of analyzing the biblical text. These are not the only methods employed by contemporary biblical scholars. One method that can be useful when considering works of uncertain provenance is the *canonical approach.* The canonical approach is a method that grew out of a dissatisfaction with the scholarly focus on original, historical meanings to the exclusion of the function and meaning of biblical texts for believing communities in various times and places. The historical-critical method was always primarily interested in what was *really* said and done by the original biblical contributors. The canonical approach assumes that biblical texts were generated, transmitted, reworked, and preserved in communities for which they were authoritative and that biblical study should examine how these texts functioned in the believing communities that received and cherished them. Emphasis is on the final, received form of the text, rather than stages in its development, on the function of the fixed text in the first communities to receive it, and on the process of adaptation by which the community resignified earlier traditions to function authoritatively in a new situation. The canonical approach might ask: What meaning, authority, or value did a biblical writer seek in a tradition or story when he employed it? What meaning, authority, or value would his community have found in it and what meanings or values would later communities find in it? Why did the religious communities accept what they did as canonical?

The third section of the Hebrew Bible, known as *Kethuvim* or "Writings," contains works of diverse and at times uncertain provenance. One thing is certain: These works were revered in the postexilic period. They became important to and authoritative for the community of Israel after the fifth century B.C.E., and thus there is virtue in considering these works through the eyes of the postexilic community for whom they were canonical and authoritative. The canonical approach would ask: Why were these books important in the postdestruction, postexilic era? Is it possible to understand the community's embrace of these works as a response to the historical odyssey of the nation? Even if some of these works originated in the preexilic period, what can be learned from the fact that they were adopted and cherished by the postexilic community? Whatever the circumstances and time of their composition and final redaction, how did these works serve the postexilic community as a prism through which to view Israel's tragic history?

It is surely no accident that many of the books in this third section of the Bible explore the very questions raised by the events of Israel's history after the fifth century B.C.E.: questions of suffering and evil, the possibility of sustaining faith in Yahweh in the midst of suffering and disappointed national aspirations, and the place of non-Jews in the divine economy. These are the themes that will occupy us in these final chapters.

## Ecclesiastes

The conventional religious piety of Proverbs and the firm belief in a just system of divine reward and punishment that is so important to the Deuteronomist is challenged not only in the book of Job but also in the book of Ecclesiastes. Ecclesiastes is couched in the first person except for a third-person introduction and epilogue. The introduction reads: "The words of Koheleth, son of David, king in Jerusalem" (Eccl 1:1). The Hebrew term *kohelet* may mean preacher, hence the Greek name for the book is Ecclesiastes (meaning "preacher"). Tradition attributes the work to David's son King Solomon, reputed to have been wise, but the attribution is fictive. Linguistic and literary features suggest a later, perhaps fourth-century B.C.E., date, and the book's themes evoke Hellenistic models. While Ecclesiastes is presented as the musings and ruminations of an individual, its inclusion in the "national library" made new conceptual tools available to a nation struggling to make sense of its history and its god, even though no reference is made to that history at all.

The deity is referred to by the general term Elohim and not by his personal Israelite name Yahweh. The prominent tone of the book is one of alienated cynicism and a weary melancholy. The theme repeated throughout the book is the emptiness of human effort. All is vanity (in the sense of futility), all is for nought.

> Utter futility!—said Koheleth—
> Utter futility! All is futile!
> What real value is there for a man
> In all the gains he makes beneath the sun?
> One generation goes, another comes,
> But the earth remains the same forever. . . .
> Only that shall happen
> Which has happened,
> Only that occur
> Which has occurred;
> There is nothing new
> Beneath the sun! (1:1–4, 9)

Contemplation of the endless repeated cycles of the natural world—the rising and setting of the sun and the moon, the ebb and flow of the tide—leads to the conclusion that nothing is permanent, all is fleeting. We do not find in Kohelet the linear view of time or the sense of progress in history that scholars, rightly or wrongly, associate with the Bible, but rather the cyclic view of time associated with mythology. There are also the endless repeated cycles of the human world—birth and death, breaking down and building up, weeping and laughter, love and hate, killing and healing. In one of the most famous (and misunderstood) passages from this book, Kohelet expresses the idea that everything has its season or time, with the consequence that the effort of humans to alter or effect anything is meaningless.

> For everything there is a season, and a time for every matter
>     under heaven: A time to be born, and a time to die;

A time to plant and a time to pluck up what is planted;
A time to kill and a time to heal;
A time to break down and a time to build up;
A time to weep, and a time to laugh;
A time to mourn, and a time to dance;
A time to cast away stones and a time to gather stones together;
A time to embrace and a time to refrain from embracing;
A time to seek and a time to lose;
A time to keep and a time to cast away,
A time to rend and a time to sew,
A time to keep silence and a time to speak,
A time to love and a time to hate, a time for war and a time for
  peace. (3:1–8, RSV translation)
What value, then, can the man of affairs get from what he earns? I
have observed the business that Elohim gave man to be concerned
with: He brings everything to pass precisely at its time. (3:9–11a)

The burden of this passage is that all things come to pass and return in end-less cycles, and we add nothing by our efforts!

Kohelet reports that he has tried everything in his search for some-thing permanent, not evanescent. Physical pleasure is unsatisfying and transient. Wealth brings anxiety. Wisdom is better than power, but even knowledge brings great pain.

And so I set my mind to appraise wisdom and to appraise
  madness and folly. And I learned—that this too was pursuit
  of wind.
For as wisdom grows, vexation grows;
To increase learning is to increase heartache. (1:17–18)

Even if we concede that wisdom is superior to ignorance, we must still face the fact that ultimately death obliterates everything—death is the great equalizer:

I found that
wisdom is superior to folly
As light is superior to darkness;
A wise man has his eyes in his head,
Whereas a fool walks in darkness.

> But I also realized that the same fate awaits them both. So I
> reflected: "The fate of the fool is also destined for me; to
> what advantage, then have I been wise?" And I came to the
> conclusion that that too was futile, because the wise man,
> just like the fool, is not remembered forever, for as the
> succeeding days roll by, both are forgotten. Alas, the wise
> man dies, just like the fool! And so I loathed life. For I
> was distressed by all that goes on under the sun, because
> everything is futile and pursuit of wind. (2:13–17)

Even more explicitly than Job, Ecclesiastes attacks the principle of divine
providence and retributive justice. There is no principle of reward or punishment; indeed, the wicked prosper while the innocent suffer. Even the
principle of delayed punishment, so important to the Deuteronomic historians, is openly attacked as unjust.

> And here is another frustration: the fact that the sentence im-
> posed for evil deeds is not executed swiftly, which is why men are
> emboldened to do evil—the fact that a sinner may do evil a hun-
> dred times and his [punishment] still be delayed . . . sometimes
> an upright man is requited according to the conduct of the scoun-
> drel; and sometimes the scoundrel is requited according to the
> conduct of the upright. I say all that is frustration. (8:10b–12, 14)

In a more famous passage,

> I have further observed under the sun that the race is not won
> by the swift, nor the battle by the valiant, nor is bread won by
> the wise, nor wealth by the intelligent, nor favor by the learned.
> For the time of mischance comes to all, and a man cannot even
> know his time. (9:11–12)

Ultimately, for Kohelet it is the inexorable fact of death that makes life entirely meaningless—the starting point of modern schools of existentialist
philosophy. Death is the bottom line, and he rejects the idea of any life after
death.

> For the same fate is in store for all: for the righteous, and for the
> wicked; for the good and pure, and for the impure; for him who

sacrifices, and for him who does not; for him who is pleasing and for him who is displeasing; and for him who swears, and for him who shuns oaths. That is the sad thing about all that goes on under the sun: that the same fate is in store for all. . . . For he who is reckoned among the living has something to look forward to . . . since the living know they will die. But the dead know nothing; they have no more recompense, for even the memory of them has died. Their loves, their hates, their jealousies have long since perished; and they have no more share till the end of time in all that goes on under the sun. (9:2–6)

Nevertheless, for all the despair and cynicism, there is a positive note in Ecclesiastes. The writer does not, after all, recommend nihilism or suicide, despite the lack of purpose or meaning in life. In fact, he does quite the opposite. He states that every life does have its moments of happiness, and these one should seize while one can.

Go, eat your bread in gladness, and drink your wine in joy; for your action was long ago approved by Elohim. Let your clothes always be freshly washed, and your head never lack ointment. Enjoy happiness with a woman you love all the fleeting days of life that have been granted to you under the sun—all your fleeting days. For that alone is what you can get out of life and out of the means you acquire under the sun. Whatever it is in your power to do, do with all your might. For there is no action, no reasoning, no learning, no wisdom in Sheol,[1] where you are going. (9:7–10)

Similarly,

Only this, I have found, is a real good: that one should eat and drink and get pleasure with all the gains he makes under the sun, during the numbered days of life that Elohim has given him; for that is his portion. (5:17)

Or

Thus I realized that the only worthwhile thing there is for them is to enjoy themselves and do what is good in their lifetime; also,

> that whenever a man does eat and drink and get enjoyment out
> of all his wealth, it is a gift of Elohim. (3:12–13)[2]

We must not delude ourselves. There is no grand plan, no absolute value or meaning to our labors, and no life in the hereafter that we are working toward. (Here Kohelet may be polemicizing against the belief in an afterlife of reward or punishment that was taking root in Jewish writings of the Hellenistic period under the influence of Greek thought.) But one can still find happiness and love, and with these, one should be content. Striving after anything more is a striving after wind that leaves one weary and bitter. One must accept the reality of death and enjoy what one can in the short time one has. Indeed, it is precisely the reality of death that makes life precious— whatever it is in one's power to do must be done with all one's might, because there is only this single, brief chance. Eternal unlimited life with endless opportunities to act would make any single act meaningless. Given the fact of death and the limitations it imposes, taking pleasure in the ordinary activities and labors of life becomes not meaningless, but precisely meaningful.

Kohelet is an unusual, if not subversive, book, and its inclusion in the national library was apparently a matter of some controversy. Its controversial character is reflected in the pious editorial postscript that appears at the end of the book:

> The sayings of the wise are like goads, like nails fixed in
>     prodding sticks. They were given by one Shepherd.
> A further word: Against them, my son, be warned!
> The making of many books is without limit
> And much study is a wearying of the flesh.
>     The sum of the matter, when all is said and done: Revere
>     Elohim and observe his commandments! For this applies to
>     all mankind: that Elohim will call every creature to account
>     for everything unknown, be it good or bad. (12:11–13)

To fear Elohim and obey his commands because he will reward the good and punish the evil is simply not the message of Kohelet, and it is very likely that these lines come from a later editor who was disturbed by the thrust of Kohelet's preaching. Juxtaposed in this one book, then, are two responses to the suffering, pain, and injustice in the world, providing two ways of interpreting the tragedy that had befallen the nation Israel. One asserts the deity's providence and justice and urges obedience and faithfulness to his commandments. The other asserts the lack of justice and providence in the world and preaches simple existential pleasures as the source of life's meaning. The richness of the Hebrew Bible derives precisely from its juxtaposition of radically diverse points of view.

## Psalms

The book of Psalms contains the principal collection of religious lyric poetry in the Bible, consisting of 150 poems or ritual recitations addressed directly to the deity, to the worshipping community, or to a cultic or ceremonial actor. The title "Psalms," the Septuagint's title for the Hebrew book "Tehillim" (= "praises"), derives from Greek *psalmoi,* which denotes religious songs performed to the musical accompaniment of the psalterion (a stringed instrument). The psalms were likely collected into a book in the postexilic period—but many, particularly those attributed to professional Temple musical guilds, are thought to have been used in the Temple service and date from early preexilic times. It is believed that the Temple staff provided the psalms with musical and liturgical notes preserved in the text, but these markings are largely a mystery to modern scholars. It seems that some superscriptions and notes indicate the tune or kind of musical accompaniment—stringed instruments or flutes—that is intended.

Most psalms tell us very little about the time and circumstance of their composition. Several were apparently composed for use at royal coronations, which would mean they were written when Davidic kings still ruled Jerusalem. For example, Psalm 45 is a love song written in celebration of the king's marriage with a foreign bride, addressed to the bride herself.

> Take heed, lass, and note,
>     incline your ear:
> forget your people and your father's house,
> and let the king be aroused by your beauty;
> since he is your lord, bow to him.
> O Tyrian lass,
>     the wealthiest people will court your favor with gifts,
> goods of all sorts.
> The royal princess,

> her dress embroidered with golden mountings,
> is led inside to the king;
> maidens in her train, her companions,
> are presented to you.
> They are led in with joy and gladness;
> they enter the palace of the king.
> Your sons will succeed your ancestors;
> you will appoint them princes throughout the land.
> I commemorate your fame for all generations,
> so peoples will praise you forever and ever. (45:11–18)

Scholars divide the psalter into five collections or books, each concluding with a doxology: Book 1 = 1–41; Book 2 = 42–72; Book 3 = 73–89; Book 4 = 90–106; Book 5 = 107–150. Book 5 is probably the last to reach fixed form because the manuscripts of this section found among the Dead Sea Scrolls show great variation suggestive of textual fluidity. Book 2 concludes with the postscript "The prayers of David, the son of Jesse are ended" (72:20)—so at one time the Davidic psalms were thought to end with Ps 72. Almost all of the psalms of Book 1 are prefaced with the phrase "to/of David."[3] To this old First Temple nucleus, other collections gravitated. For example, each of psalms 120 to 134 bears the title "A Song of Ascents," suggesting that these psalms were sung by pilgrims ascending to Jerusalem during pilgrimage festivals. Nevertheless, tradition attributes the entire book of Psalms to King David. This attribution stems from the fact that seventy-three of the 150 psalms are explicitly said to be psalms to/for/of David (see note 4) and that David is said to be a man of musical talent, according to the Deuteronomistic narrative. However, the superscriptions are all late additions, so perhaps the psalms are Davidic in that they were the result of royal patronage of poetry by the house of David in general. The biblical text itself lists other authors for some psalms: Ps 72 is ascribed to Solomon, Ps 90 to Moses, and others to Asaph and the sons of Korah, the ancestor of a priestly family. Some are clearly postexilic, such as Ps 74, which laments the destruction of the Temple, and Ps 137: "By the rivers of Babylon, there we sat, sat and wept as we thought of Zion." Thus the book as a whole is an anthology of religious expressions deriving from many centuries of Israel's history. Despite the claim of religious tradition, the psalms were not all penned by David.

Some of the psalms seem to be oriented to community worship and some to individual worship, but in ancient Israel there wasn't always a sharp distinction between the two. The ancient Israelite in the Temple prayed to the deity as a member of a larger community bound by a covenant and not as a lone individual. In the words of Ps 34:3, "Exalt Yahweh with me; let us extol His name together."

The book of Psalms has been studied using the techniques of form criticism. The pioneer in this area was Hermann Gunkel, and his work was further advanced by Sigmund Mowinckel.[4] Form critics classify psalms according to their form, or literary genre, and then attempt to place these literary types within their cultic setting, or *Sitz im Leben*. Gunkel and Mowinckel identified numerous genres to which psalms can be assigned on the basis of formal and thematic features. Several of these genres are listed below, but combined into broader groupings for ease of presentation. (It should be noted that many psalms are of mixed genre.)

(1) Hymns of praise, thanksgiving or trust (see, for example, Pss 8, 19, 23, 24, 46,103, 104, 114, 115, 118, 131, 136, 139 150).

This is the largest category of psalms. Many celebrate Yahweh's majesty, wisdom, and power, such as this creation hymn:

O Yahweh, our lord,
   How majestic is your name throughout the earth,
You who have covered the heavens with your splendor. . . .
When I behold your heavens, the work of your fingers,
   the moon and stars that you set in place,
   what is man that you have been mindful of him,
   mortal man that you have taken note of him,
   and adorned him with glory and majesty;
   You have made him master over your handiwork,
   laying the world at his feet,
   sheep and oxen, all of them,
   and wild beasts, too;
   the birds of the heavens, the fish of the sea,
   whatever travels the paths of the seas.
O Yahweh, our lord, how majestic is your name throughout the
   earth. (8:2, 4–10)

The tiny Ps 117 contains in just two verses all of the classic formal elements of a song of praise or thanksgiving: an opening invocation to worship (A), followed by a motive clause giving the reason for worship (B), and then a recapitulation or renewed call to praise (A').

(A) Praise Yahweh, all you nations;
   extol him, all you peoples
(B) For great is his steadfast love toward us;
   the faithfulness of Yahweh endures forever
(A') Hallelujah (117:1–2)

Psalm 136 punctuates a recitation of Yahweh's great deeds (the creation, the Exodus, the conquest of the Promised Land) with the phrase "His steadfast love is eternal" and is an excellent illustration of how Israel's praise is inspired by remembering what Yahweh has done. Still other psalms extol Yahweh in his role as creator (Ps 104) or as lawgiver. A striking characteristic of this category of psalms is the variety of metaphors used to describe the deity: King, Shield, Stronghold, Refuge, Rock, Shelter, and many more.

The paradigmatic psalm of trust is Ps 23, which employs the metaphor of a shepherd to describe Yahweh guiding the individual in straight paths through a frightening valley. The speaker's trust contributes to a sense of deep tranquility that is sustained even in the presence of enemies.

> Yahweh is my shepherd,
> I shall not want;
> He makes me lie down in green pastures.
> He leads me beside still waters;
> He restores my soul.
> He leads me in paths of righteousness
> For his name's sake.
> Even though I walk through the valley of the shadow of death,
> I fear no evil;
> For thou art with me;
> Thy rod and thy staff, they comfort me.
> Thou preparest a table before me in the presence of my
>    enemies;
> Thou anointest my head with oil,
> My cup overflows.
> Surely goodness and mercy shall follow me all the days of my
>    life;
> And I shall dwell in the house of Yahweh forever. (23:1–6, based
>    on RSV translation)

The short Psalm 131 invokes the image of a mother and child to express an even greater tranquility:

> O Yahweh, my heart is not lifted up,
> My eyes are not raised too high;
> I do not occupy myself with things too great
> and too marvelous for me.
> But I have calmed and quieted my soul
> like a child quieted at its mother's breast;
> like a child that is quieted is my soul.
> O Israel, hope in Yahweh,
> from this time forth and for evermore. (131:1–3; RSV translation)

These and similar psalms contain some of the most personal descriptions of biblical faith, of confidence or simple trust in Yahweh.

(2) Enthronement (see for example Pss 93, 96, 97, 98, 99), Royal or Messianic Psalms (see for example Pss 2, 21, 45, 72, 110).

Enthronement or kingship psalms celebrate Yahweh as the sovereign ruler of the heavens or as the sovereign over foreign nations. Their descriptions of Yahweh employ the language and themes associated with the deities of ancient Near Eastern mythology, particularly Baal the storm god. Some psalms allude to the defeat of a sea monster as key to Yahweh's role as creator and king (Ps 74). Others contain demythologized allusions to the old ancient Near Eastern combat creation stories. In Ps 29, the assembly of the gods praises Yahweh, who thunders over the mighty waters and is enthroned at the flood. Similarly, Ps 93 depicts the sea as a natural entity rather than a divine antagonist:

> Yahweh is king,
>     He is robed in grandeur;
>     Yahweh is robed,
>     He is girded with strength.
> The world stands firm;
>     it cannot be shaken.
> Your throne stands firm from of old;
>     from eternity you have existed.

The ocean sounds, O Yahweh,
   the ocean sounds its thunder,
   the ocean sounds its pounding.
Above the thunder of the mighty waters,
   more majestic than the breakers of the sea
   is Yahweh, majestic on high.
Your decrees are indeed enduring;
   holiness befits Your house,
   O Yahweh, for all times. (93:1–5)

Royal psalms praise Yahweh's anointed king. Some scholars believe that these psalms were recited at coronations.

Yahweh said to my lord,
   "Sit at my right hand
while I make your enemies your footstool."
Yahweh will stretch forth from Zion your mighty scepter;
hold sway over your enemies!
Your people come forward willingly on your day of battle.
In majestic holiness, from the womb,
   from the dawn, yours was the dew of youth.
Yahweh has sworn and will not relent,
"You are a priest forever, a rightful king by my decree."
Yahweh is at your right hand.
He crushes kings in the day of his anger. (110:1–5)

Not all royal psalms are concerned primarily with military success. Some seek to ensure that the king is bestowed with other qualities necessary for good stewardship.

O Elohim, endow the king with your judgments,
   the king's son with your righteousness;
   that he may judge your people rightly,
   Your lowly ones, justly. . . .
Let him champion the lowly among the people,
   deliver the needy folk,
   and crush those who wrong them. . . .
Let him be like rain that falls on a mown field,
   like a downpour of rain on the ground,

that the righteous may flourish in his time,
and well-being abound, till the moon is no more. (72:1–2, 4, 6)

(3) Psalms of Lament, Petition, and Indebtedness (see, for example, Pss 13, 22, 44, 55, 74, 78, 79, 80, 105, 106).

Songs of lament can be voiced in the plural as a communal supplication or in the voice of the individual. Although individual laments may open with an invocation to or praise of the deity, some launch immediately into a desperate plea for deliverance from some suffering or crisis—often expressed metaphorically—and for vengeance upon one's enemies. After presenting his complaint, the psalmist usually confesses his trust in Yahweh, asks for help or forgiveness, and then concludes with a vow that he will praise Yahweh again. We sometimes see an acknowledgment of a divine response. Psalm 13 has many of these features.

How long, O Yahweh; will You ignore me forever?
How long will you hide your face from me?
How long will I have cares on my mind,
    grief in my heart all day?
How long will my enemy have the upper hand?
Look at me, answer me, O Yahweh, my god!
Restore the luster to my eyes,
    lest I sleep the sleep of death;
lest my enemy say, "I have overcome him,"
my foes exult when I totter.
But I trust in your faithfulness.
    My heart will exult in your deliverance.
I will sing to Yahweh,
    for he has been good to me. (13:2–6)

Psalm 55 asks for deliverance from the treachery of a deceitful friend:

It is not an enemy who reviles me
    —I could bear that;
    it is not my foe who vaunts himself against me
    —I could hide from him;
    but it is you, my equal,
    my companion, my friend;

    sweet was our fellowship;
      we walked together in Elohim's house.
  Let him [Yahweh] incite death against them;
    may they go down alive into Sheol!
  For where they dwell
    there evil is. . . .
  He harmed his ally,
    he broke his pact;
    his talk was smoother than butter,
    yet his mind was on war;
    his words were more soothing than oil,
    yet they were drawn swords.
  Cast your burden upon Yahweh and he shall sustain
    you;
    He will never let the righteous man collapse. (55:13–16, 21–23)

Some laments are pleas for the forgiveness of personal sins. Psalm 51, attributed to David after the prophet Nathan rebukes him for his illicit relationship with Bathsheba, contains a striking example of the parallelism that typifies biblical poetry.

  Have mercy on me, O Elohim,
    according to thy steadfast love;
    according to thy abundant mercy
    blot out my transgressions.
  Wash me thoroughly from my iniquity,
    and cleanse me from my sin!
    For I know my transgressions,
    and my sin is ever before me.
  Against thee, thee only, have I sinned,
    and done that which is evil in thy sight,
    so that thou art justified in thy sentence
    and blameless in thy judgment. . . .
  Create in me a clean heart, O Elohim,
    and put a new and right spirit within me.
  Cast me not away from thy presence
    and take not thy holy Spirit from me.
  Restore to me the joy of thy salvation,

and uphold me with a willing spirit. (51:3–6,12–14, based on
RSV translation)

Communal laments bewail Israel's misfortunes and urge Yahweh's vengeance upon Israel's oppressors, sometimes reminding the deity of his historic relationship with Israel and his covenantal obligation. Psalm 74 is a
case in point. Its explicit reference to the destruction of the sanctuary reveals its postexilic date. As a response to the catastrophe, it gives expression
to despair, bewilderment, and even anger that the deity has forgotten his
obligation to Israel.

Why, O Elohim, do you forever reject us,
    do you fume in anger at the flock that you tend?
Remember the community you made yours long ago,
    Your very own tribe that you redeemed,
    Mount Zion, where you dwell.
Bestir yourself because of the perpetual tumult,
    all the outrages of the enemy in the sanctuary.
Your foes roar inside your meeting-place;
    they take their signs for true signs.
It is like men wielding axes
    against a gnarled tree;
    with hatchet and pike
    they hacked away at its carved work.
They made your sanctuary go up in flames;
    they brought low in dishonor the dwelling place of your
    presence.
They resolved, "Let us destroy them altogether!"
    They burned all El's tabernacles in the land.
No signs appear for us;
    there is no longer any prophet;
    no one among us knows for how long.
Till when, O Elohim, will the foe blaspheme,
    will the enemy forever revile your name?
Why do you hold back your hand, your right hand?
Draw it out of your bosom! . . .
Do not deliver your dove to the wild beast,
    do not ignore forever the band of Your lowly ones.

> Look to the covenant! . . .
> Rise, O Elohim, champion your cause. (74:1–11, 19–20a, 22b)

The psalmist is bewildered. Why has this happened? Why doesn't the deity act? There is no mention of Israel's sin and no indication that the destruction was just punishment for sin. Psalm 44 goes even further and explicitly rejects the traditional Deuteronomistic view. Psalm 44 states flatly that the people had not sinned, had not been faithless. Yahweh's desertion is thus incomprehensible, and he is rebuked for his inaction on behalf of faithful Israel.

> In Elohim we glory at all times,
>     and praise your name unceasingly.
> Yet you have rejected and disgraced us;
>     you do not go with our armies. . . .
> You let them devour us like sheep;
>     You disperse us among the nations.
> You sell your people for no fortune,
>     You set no high price on them. . . .
> All this has come upon us,
>     yet we have not forgotten you,
>     or been false to your covenant.
> Our hearts have not gone astray,
>     nor have our feet swerved from your path,
>     though you cast us, crushed, to where the sea monster is,
>     and covered us over with deepest darkness.
> If we forgot the name of our god
>     and spread forth our hands to a foreign god,
>     Elohim would surely search it out,
>     for He knows the secrets of the heart.
> It is for your sake that we are slain all day long,
>     that we are regarded as sheep to be slaughtered.
> Rouse yourself, why do you sleep, my lord!
> Awaken, do not reject us forever!
> Why do you hide your face,
>     ignoring our affliction and distress?
> We lie prostrate in the dust;
>     our body clings to the ground.
> Arise and help us,
>     redeem us, as befits your faithfulness. (44:9–10, 12–13, 18–27)

This psalm contains an explicit denial of the rhetorically inflamed charges against Israel found in the books of the prophets. We have not gone astray, the psalmist protests, we have not swerved from your path. This astonishing protestation of innocence that accuses the deity of sleeping on the job is reminiscent of Job and represents a different perspective on the destruction and exile—one that asserts the deity's inaction rather than Israel's guilt.

But Pss 74 and 44 can be contrasted with Psalms 78 and 106. These psalms belong to the category of hymns in celebration of divine action in Israel's history. Both of these psalms toe the Deuteronomistic line in their recapitulation of Israel's history—from the creation, through the Exodus, and on to the conquest of the Promised Land. These psalms stress Israel's utter indebtedness to her god and the latter's patience with Israel's constant faithlessness.

> He performed marvels in the sight of their fathers,
>     in the land of Egypt, the plain of Zoan.
> He split the sea and took them through it;
>     He made the waters stand like a wall.
> He led them with a cloud by day,
>     and throughout the night by the light of fire.
> He split rocks in the wilderness
>     and gave them drink as if from the great deep.
> He brought forth streams from a rock
>     and made them flow down like a river.
> But they went on sinning against him,
>     defying the most high in the parched land.
> To test El was in their mind
>     when they demanded food for themselves.
> They spoke against Elohim, saying,
>     "Can El spread a feast in the wilderness?
>     True, he struck the rock and waters flowed,
>     streams gushed forth;
>     but can he provide bread?
> Can he supply his people with meat?" (78:12–20)

Yahweh's faithful actions and Israel's faithless responses are similarly featured in Ps 106's historical review. In these two psalms, as in the Deuteronomistic literature, we see a clear attempt to explain Israel's tragic end, and in this instance the psalmist chooses to blame Israel and justify the deity at all costs.

> (4) Psalms of Blessing and Cursing (see, for example, Pss 1, 109, 137).

These psalms invoke the deity to bless the righteous—either the nation Israel or the righteous within the nation—and punish and afflict the wicked—either enemy nations or the wicked within Israel and other nations. These psalms can be shocking in their violent fury. For example, Ps 137 calls for vengeance on the Babylonians who destroyed Fair Jerusalem:

> Fair Babylon, you predator,
> > a blessing on him who repays you in kind
> > what you have inflicted on us;
> > a blessing on him who seizes your babies
> > and dashes them against the rocks! (137:8–9)

Psalm 109 contains a lengthy list of afflictions with which the psalmist would have Yahweh smite his wicked and deceitful foes:

> May his days be few;
> > may another take over his position.
> May his children be orphans,
> > his wife a widow.
> May his children wander from their hovels,
> > begging in search of [bread]. . . .
> May he be clothed in a curse like a garment,
> > may it enter his body like water,
> > his bones like oil.
> Let it be like the cloak he wraps around him,
> > like the belt he always wears.
> May Yahweh thus repay my accusers,
> > all those who speak evil against me. (109:8–10, 18–20)

> (5) Psalms of Wisdom, Meditation, and Instruction (see, for example, Pss 32, 37, 49, 52, 73, 90, 112, 119, 128).

Wisdom psalms are almost proverbial in nature, possess a reflective, medi-
tative tone, and often open with the stock phrase "Happy is the man who/
Happy are all who X." For example, Ps 128 begins

> Happy are all who fear Yahweh,
>    who follow his ways.
> You shall enjoy the fruit of your labors;
>    you shall be happy and you shall prosper.
> Your wife shall be like a fruitful vine within your
>       house;
>    your sons, like olive saplings around your table.
> So shall the man who fears Yahweh be blessed. (128:1–4)

Many psalms presuppose worship in the Temple and even have an
antiphonal—echo and response—character suggestive of liturgical recitation. However, others seem to envisage individual meditation upon and delight in the Torah (for example, Pss 1, 19, and 119). One of these, Ps 119, is the
longest psalm, with stanzas of eight lines beginning with the same Hebrew
letter, and each successive stanza beginning with the next letter of the alphabet. This Psalm represents the Torah as an object of study and devotion. The
study of Torah makes one wise and happy:

> The teaching of Yahweh is perfect,
>    renewing life;
>    the decrees of Yahweh are enduring,
>    making the simple wise;
> The precepts of Yahweh are just,
>    rejoicing the heart;
>    the instruction of Yahweh is lucid,
>    making the eyes light up.
> The fear of Yahweh is pure,
>    abiding forever;
>    the judgments of Yahweh are true,
>    righteous altogether,
>    more desirable than gold,
>    than much fine gold;
>    sweeter than honey,
>    than drippings of the comb. (19:8–11)

The elevation of Torah reflects a shift occurring in the late Second Temple period in which the Torah takes on increased importance and its study is almost a form of worship.

There are many ways to categorize and classify the psalms, and many individual psalms combine units that belong to different genres, for example, Ps 22, which opens as a lament, "My God, my God, why have you forsaken me?" (in the well-known RSV translation), then changes to a hymn of praise and confident triumph. At least one psalm, Ps 68, defies categorization altogether.

From this brief sampling, it should be apparent that the psalms are a microcosm of the religious insights and convictions of ancient Israel. Perhaps because so many lack historical specificity, the psalms have become a great source for personal spirituality in western civilization. Although some of the psalms may have been composed as much as 3,000 years ago, they are inspiring and relevant for many contemporary readers, providing opportunities to confess one's failings; proclaim good intentions; complain about misfortunes; cry out against injustice; request assistance; affirm trust in divine providence; express emotions of praise, joy, and wonder at creation; and reflect on human finitude in the face of divine infinitude.

## Song of Songs

For many readers, the most surprising book to be included in the Hebrew Bible is a poem known as the Song of Songs, a beautiful and erotic love song that celebrates physical passion and human sexuality. The opening verse is a late superscription that attributes the song to Solomon. In fact, these sensuous love lyrics are probably postexilic, and the attribution to Solomon was likely fueled by the statement in 1 Kgs 4:32 that Solomon uttered 3,000 proverbs and 1,005 songs. The speaker of the poem alternates, but most often it is a woman, sometimes addressing her beloved, sometimes addressing the daughters of Jerusalem. At times the speaker is a man. Although Solomon is mentioned six times in the poem, he is not said to be one of the speakers.

The setting of the book is pastoral; the two young lovers express their passion through and amid the beauties of nature with frequent references to gardens, vineyards, fruit, flowers, perfumes, doves, flocks of goats, and shorn ewes. There are vivid descriptions of the physical beauty of the lovers and some highly erotic passages. The poem is unique in giving expression to the erotic feelings of a woman.

I slept, but my heart was awake.
Listen, my lover is knocking.
"Open to me my sister, my love,
my dove, my perfect one,
for my head is wet with dew. . . ."
My lover thrusts his hand into the hole,
and my insides yearned for him,
I arose to open to my lover,
and my hands dripped with myrrh,
my fingers with liquid myrrh,
upon the handles of the lock.
I opened to my lover,
but he was gone.[5]

Adopting a canonical approach, we may ask why this secular poem was incorporated into the national library of the postexilic community. What was the intention of those who included it? Did they feel that its representation of the lover's frustrated and yet unflagging search for the beloved somehow captured the experience of the postexilic community? How was the poem received and read by the earliest communities for whom it was a part of Scripture? Did they draw inspiration from the portrait of a passionate love that is never extinguished, even when the beloved is ceaselessly sought but not found?

We do know that for some religious authorities over the centuries, the candid descriptions of passionate love proved to be too much, and the explicit content of the book—which contains no reference to the deity and was certainly a secular poem originally—was interpreted away. Christians allegorized the song as an expression of Christ's love for his "bride"—the spiritual church. Jewish tradition read the book as an expression of Yahweh's love for his chosen people Israel.

It is said that the ancient rabbis debated whether the Song of Songs should be included in the canon. It was R. Akiva, arguing for its inclusion, who prevailed, declaring: "The whole world was only created, so to speak, for the day on which the Song of Songs would be given to it. Why? Because all the writings are holy but the song of songs is the Holy of Holies."[6]

CHAPTER 22

# The Restoration

## Ezra-Nehemiah and Ruth

*Readings:* Ezra 1–10; Nehemiah 10, 13

### The Persian Period

In 539 B.C.E., the Babylonian Empire was defeated by the Persians under the leadership of Cyrus. Cyrus established the largest empire yet seen in the ancient Near East, stretching from Egypt to Asia Minor and eastern Iran. Unlike other ancient masters, the Persians held to a policy of cultural and religious independence for their conquered subjects.

The famous Cyrus Cylinder (see Figure 10) discovered by archaeologists is a nine-inch fired clay cylinder covered in cuneiform writing that tells of Cyrus's conquest of Babylon at the command of Babylon's god Marduk and his policy of allowing captives to return to their homelands and rebuild their temples. The cylinder's inscription is consistent with the picture presented in the biblical books of Ezra, Nehemiah, and Chronicles, according to which Cyrus, in 538, gave the Judean exiles permission to return to Jerusalem and reconstruct the Temple—an event that kindled hope in the hearts of many Judeans. The book of 2 Chronicles concludes with the decree of Cyrus permitting the Jewish captives to return to their homeland and build their temple:

And in the first year of King Cyrus of Persia, when the word of Yahweh spoken by Jeremiah was fulfilled, Yahweh roused the

Fig. 10. Cyrus Cylinder describing the Persian king Cyrus's decree allowing departed peoples to return to their places of origin (fifth century B.C.E.). Z. Radovan/BibleLandPictures.com.

spirit of King Cyrus of Persia to issue a proclamation throughout his realm by word of mouth and in writing, as follows: Thus said King Cyrus of Persia: Yahweh, the god of Heaven has given me all the kingdoms of the earth, and has charged me with building him a House in Jerusalem, which is in Judah. Any one of you of all his people, may Yahweh his god be with him and let him go up. (2 Chr 36:22–23)[1]

The king's decree is described as fulfilling the word of the prophet Jeremiah, who prophesied that the Babylonian exile would last seventy years. From the time of the departure of the first group of exiles in 597 to the return in 538 is sixty years; from the destruction of the first Temple in 586 to the building of the second between 521 and 515 is approximately seventy years. Either way, in the eyes of the Chronicler, it was close enough to be deemed a fulfillment of Jeremiah's prophecy.

A fuller version of the decree, which is consistent with the Persian ruler's policy of tolerating and even encouraging local religious cults, is in Ezra, which adds:

Let him go up to Jerusalem that is in Judah and build the House of Yahweh, the god of Israel, the god that is in Jerusalem; and all

who stay behind, wherever he may be living, let the people of his
place assist him with silver, gold, goods, and livestock, besides
the freewill offering to the House of Elohim that is in Jerusalem.
(Ezra 1:3b–4)

The exiles returned to what was now a Persian province—Yehud—where
they held a certain degree of self-determination.

The periodization of Jewish history centers on these events. The period from 586 to the 530s B.C.E. is known as the exilic period, a time in
which—most scholars would maintain—the traditions of P and D reached
their final form; the period following the return of the exiles is known as
the Restoration, the Persian period, or the beginning of the Second Temple
period, since the Second Temple is completed somewhere between 521 and
515 (in contrast to the First Temple period from the time of Solomon, about
950 to 586).

## Ezra-Nehemiah

The books of Ezra and Nehemiah (often combined as Ezra-Nehemiah) give
an account of the return of the Babylonian exiles in the late sixth and fifth
centuries B.C.E. Ezra and Nehemiah were regarded as a unit in Hebrew Bibles until the Middle Ages.[2] For many years, scholars believed that Ezra-
Nehemiah was the second part of a larger historical work that included
1 and 2 Chronicles, with which they have much in common. But recently the
suggestion that these works derive from the same author has come under
attack due to their differing theological assumptions and language use. In
any event, Ezra and Nehemiah draw on a number of different documents
and sources (including, it seems, the first-person memoirs of Nehemiah for
the book of Nehemiah). Events recorded in Ezra-Nehemiah include the
initial return of the exiles, the rebuilding of the Temple, the career of Ezra,
and the career of Nehemiah. All four books were probably edited in the late
fourth century B.C.E., when Judah was a small province within the massive
Persian Empire (though some scholars propose a later date) (see Map 6).

The books of Ezra and Nehemiah contain conflicting information
about the return and restoration, and as a result, our knowledge of the timing of various events is rather poor. It is not clear who first returned to help
rebuild Jerusalem—Ezra, a priest and scribe, or Nehemiah, the Persian-
appointed governor of Judah. Even though the Chronicler dates events according to the year of the reign of the Persian king Artaxerxes, there were

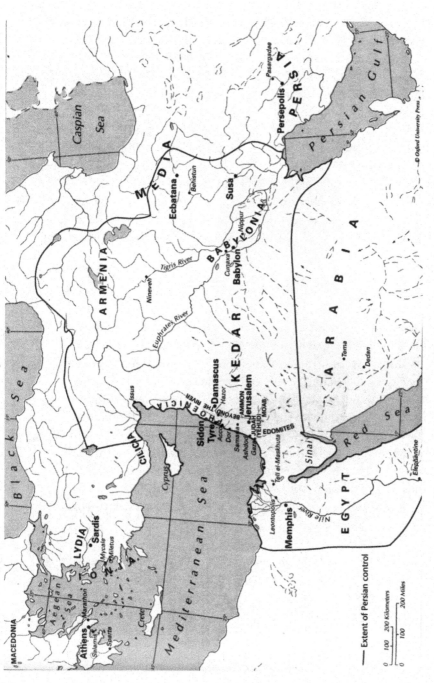

Map 6. Map of the Persian Empire with the province of Yehud.

From Michael Coogan, *The Old Testament: A Historical and Literary Introduction to the Hebrew Scriptures*. New York: Oxford University Press, Inc., 2006, p. 403.

two kings named Artaxerxes in the fifth century and one in the fourth century. Thus, scholars are not agreed on the sequence of events in this period. Somewhat arbitrarily perhaps, the following discussion presents the career of Nehemiah and then the career of Ezra. Moreover, information is drawn from both the book of Ezra and the book of Nehemiah in a nonlinear fashion, since events do not appear in chronological sequence.

The book of Ezra opens with Cyrus's decree and then provides a long list of the exiles who returned to Judah after 538. The exiles were led by Sheshbazzar, and among them were the priest Yeshua and Zerubbabel, a grandson of King Jehoiachin of the House of David. Jehoiachin had been among the exiles in 597—he was kept under house arrest in Babylon but eventually released. Now his grandson—a Davidide—was returning to Jerusalem. Chapter 3 of Ezra describes the sacrifices offered on the rebuilt altar and the beginning of the process of rebuilding the Temple in approximately 521 B.C.E.

> When the builders had laid the foundation of the Temple of Yahweh, priests in their vestments with trumpets, and Levites, sons of Asaph, with cymbals were stationed to give praise to Yahweh, as King David of Israel had ordained. They sang songs extolling and praising Yahweh, "For he is good, his steadfast love for Israel is eternal." All the people raised a great shout extolling Yahweh because the foundation of the House of Yahweh had been laid. Many of the priests and Levites and the chiefs of the clans, the old men who had seen the first house, wept loudly at the sight of the founding of this house. Many others shouted joyously at the top of their voices. The people could not distinguish the shouts of joy from the people's weeping, for the people raised a great shout, the sound of which could be heard from afar. (Ezra 3:10–13)

Evidently, the older generations who remember the magnificence of the Temple of Solomon shed tears while the young people shouted for joy at the establishment of a new Temple.

The building does not proceed peacefully due to hostilities with peoples of the surrounding communities referred to as "adversaries of Judah and Benjamin." In Ezra 4–6, these Samaritans offer to assist in the project of reconstruction, but their offer is rejected. As a result, the Samaritans persuade the Persians that rebuilding a potentially rebellious city is a bad idea, and the Persians order the rebuilding to stop. Two prophets—Haggai and Zechariah—urge the continuation of the building. A Persian official objects, and the Jews appeal to the new Persian emperor Darius. They ask him to search the court records for the original authorization by Cyrus. Cyrus's edict is found, and Darius agrees not only to enforce it but to honor his obligation to supply the money for the rebuilding and the procurement of sacrifices. The Temple is dedicated about 515 B.C.E., and a Passover celebration is celebrated in the sanctuary.

There are other social tensions, specifically, friction between those who had remained in Judea and the returning exiles who, while few in number, enjoyed imperial support. These self-styled "children of the exile" referred to the local Judeans as "peoples of the land"—a derogatory term that cast aspersions on the latter's very status as Jews. As we will soon see, radically different views of Jewish identity were to emerge during this period.

The following events referred to in the books of Ezra and Nehemiah are generally ascribed to the mid-fifth century: Nehemiah, a Jewish subject of Persia, was the official cupbearer to the Persian emperor Artaxerxes I in the court at Susa, a position that likely entailed his being a eunuch. The book of Nehemiah opens with a description of Nehemiah's grief upon hearing the report of the terrible conditions of his people in Jerusalem in the mid-fifth century. Weeping, he asks for the consent of the emperor to go to Jerusalem and rebuild the city. Nehemiah travels to Jerusalem (some date his arrival to 445 B.C.E.) and undertakes the refortification of the city. He meets with opposition—some internal opposition led by Noadiah, a female prophetess (Neh 6:14), and some external opposition from Israel's neighbors, the Samaritans, the Ammonites, and some Arabs, who represent this reconstruction of the city's defensive walls as an affront to Persian rule. But Nehemiah continues, providing his workmen with weapons against enemy attack, and the walls are quickly completed. These fortifications help to reestablish Jerusalem as an urban center. In time, Nehemiah is appointed governor of Judah under Persian dominion. He institutes economic and social reforms to improve the situation of the poor and works to establish public order. The governorship of Nehemiah may have overlapped to some degree with the mission of Ezra, whose activities are also reported in the books of Ezra and Nehemiah, but scholars differ on this point.

Chapter 7 of the book of Ezra introduces Ezra, a Babylonian Jew of a priestly family who is described in verse 6 as a scribe expert in the Teaching of Moses. In verse 10 it is said that Ezra had dedicated himself to study the Teaching of Yahweh so as to observe it and to teach laws and rules to Israel. Ezra is commissioned by Emperor Artaxerxes, in a letter the text of which is in 7:12–26, to travel to Jerusalem to supervise the Temple and to assess the implementation of Mosaic standards in the Judean province. He is also charged with the appointment of scribes and judges to administer civil and moral order. This was evidently the imperial policy of the Persians—to commission loyal subjects to regulate their own local cults—and Ezra's work must be understood in this light.[3]

> For you are commissioned by the king and his seven advisers to regulate Judah and Jerusalem according to the law of your god, which is in your care.... And you, Ezra, by the divine wisdom you possess, appoint magistrates and judges to judge all the people in the province of Beyond the River [Cis-Jordan] who know the laws of your god, and to teach those who do not know them. Let anyone who does not obey the law of your god and the law of the king be punished with dispatch, whether by death, corporal punishment, confiscation of possessions or imprisonment. (Ezra 7:14, 25–26)

In addition, Ezra is appointed to bring treasures of silver and gold to the Temple. Ezra brings with him a copy of the Mosaic Torah (precisely what that might have been will be considered below) in order to regulate and unify Jewish life in the restored community, and together Ezra and Nehemiah bring about a revival. Ezra's reforms were aimed at strengthening the religious identity of the Judahites, revitalizing their morale, and preventing the decline of Yahweh worship. His two most important acts are his dissolution of foreign marriages and his renewal of the covenant.

### Dissolution of Foreign Marriages/Separatism

Ezra was distressed to discover that many of the returned exiles had married with non-Israelite women who followed pagan practices. Chapters 9 and 10 describe his efforts to reverse this trend. He begs Yahweh to forgive the people for this violation of his law, and then, at a great assembly, he calls upon the people to divorce their foreign spouses.

This is not in fact Pentateuchal law. The prohibition of marriage with any and all foreigners is a great innovation on Ezra's part, one that we shall see was not universally accepted. The high incidence and acceptance of intermarriage is indicated by the fact that it took several months to identify all those who had intermarried and to send away their spouses and children. Even priests were among those who did not view intermarriage as a violation of the covenant (Ezra 10:18–19), an additional sign that Ezra was deviating from long-accepted tradition.

The text of Ezra's prayer before Yahweh is a fascinating presentation of Ezra's interpretation of Israel's tragic history and constitutes yet another response to the calamity that had befallen the nation:

> From the time of your fathers to this very day we have been deep in guilt. Because of our iniquities, we, our kings, and our priests have been handed over to foreign kings, to the sword, to captivity, to pillage, and to humiliation, as is now the case. But now, for a short while, there has been a reprieve from Yahweh our god, who has granted us a surviving remnant and given us a stake in his holy place; our Elohim has restored the luster to our eyes and furnished us with a little sustenance in our bondage.... Now what can we say in the face of this, O our Elohim, for we have forsaken your commandments, which you gave us through your servants the prophets, when you said "The land that you are about to possess is a land unclean through the uncleanness of the peoples of the land, through their abhorrent practices with which they, in their impurity, have filled it from one end to the other. Now then, do not give your daughters in marriage to their sons or let their daughters marry your sons; do nothing for their well-being or advantage, then you will be strong and enjoy the bounty of the land and bequeath it to your children forever." After all that has happened to us because of our evil deeds and our deep guilt— though you, our Elohim, have been forbearing, [punishing us] less than our iniquity [deserves] in that you have granted us such a remnant as this—shall we once again violate your commandments by intermarrying with these peoples who follow such abhorrent practices? Will you not rage against us till we are destroyed without remnant or survivor? (Ezra 9:7–8, 10–14)

Ezra's argument toes the Deuteronomistic line that states that Israel's tragic fate has befallen her because of her sins. Indeed, she has not been punished as fully as she deserves. In addition, like the prophets, Ezra asserts that the covenant was not abrogated and a remnant has been saved and restored. What is different in Ezra is the identification of the sin for which Israel was punished: Israel has mixed its "holy seed" with "common seed" through unions with "the peoples of the land"—a reference to foreigners certainly, but possibly also to Judeans who had remained in the land during the exile and who had adopted the language and customs of their neighbors (see further below). And if history is any guide, Ezra argues, the community is placing itself at great risk again by intermarrying with persons who will lead them into the worship of other gods and the performance of abhorrent practices. Surely this time Yahweh will not be so merciful as to spare even a remnant!

Ezra's interpretation of the Mosaic prohibitions against intermarriage is expansive.[4] The Torah prohibits intermarriage with the native Canaanite peoples (Ex 23:27–33, Deut 7:1–5), a prohibition rationalized by the claim that the Canaanites would lead the Israelites into abhorrent pagan practices, child sacrifice, and so on (a moral-religious rationale). Deuteronomy 23:4–8 also prohibits marriage with certain foreigners for historical reasons, specifically, Moabites and Ammonites because of their cruel treatment of the Israelites during their trek to the Promised Land. Egyptians are not prohibited after the third generation, and there is no prohibition against marriage with other foreign groups (for example, Phoenicians, Midianites, and Ishmaelites), so long as the foreign partner enters into the covenant community of Yahweh and does not lead the Israelite partner into the worship of other gods. Indeed, there is good evidence that the assimilation of foreigners was generally accepted in both the preexilic and postexilic eras (even when the ideal of not leading the Israelite astray was *not* met): Non-Israelites married Israelites and assimilated into the larger community (Moses himself married a Midianite woman and a Cushite woman). Israel's kings regularly married foreign women without compromising the Israelite identity of their royal offspring, who ascended to the throne unchallenged, an indication that Israelite identity originally passed through the male line. But Ezra seeks to limit foreign influence because he fears a dilution of Israelite identity will erode commitment to the covenant. Zealous for Yahweh and wary of his wrath, Ezra interprets and expands these prohibitions as a general ban on intermarriage with any and every non-Israelite.

However, the old moral-religious rationale could not sustain a universal ban on intermarriage. The moral-religious rationale established a permeable boundary between Israelites and non-Israelites because any non-Israelite who renounced immorality and idolatry could marry into the covenantal community and acquire Israelite identity. Sustaining a new *universal* ban on intermarriage required a *new* rationale capable of establishing an impermeable boundary between Israelite and non-Israelite. Ezra provided just such a rationale—the "holy seed" rationale.

Ezra rationalized his innovative universal ban on intermarriage by asserting that all Israelites are "holy seed" and that intermarriage with non-Israelites created a forbidden mixture of holy seed with profane seed—a sacrilege (*ma'al*) that would require expiation by means of a sacrificial offering (Ezra 9:4, 10:2, 6, 10). Substituting a "holy seed" rationale for the old moral-religious rationale enabled Ezra not only to construct a universal prohibition of intermarriage (even a morally righteous and Yahweh-revering non-Israelite would be prohibited because he was of profane seed) but also to make Israelite identity contingent on the status of both mother and father. Both parents must be of the "holy seed" in order to establish a claim of Israelite identity.

Ezra's new rationale may have been suggested by the juxtaposition of the themes of intermarriage and holiness in Deuteronomy (assuming Ezra possessed something like the Deuteronomy we currently have). Deuteronomy 7:2b–5 prohibits intermarriage with Canaanites and is followed immediately by the statement:

> For you are a people consecrated [holy] to Yahweh your god: of
> all the peoples on earth Yahweh your god chose you to be his
> treasured people. (Deut 7:6)

If verse 6 is understood to be the rationale for the immediately preceding prohibition in verses 2b–5, one might conclude that intermarriage with Canaanites is forbidden *because* the Israelites are a holy people (consecrated to Yahweh) and non-Israelites are not, and that intermarriage must be a profanation of the holy seed of the Israel.

Deuteronomy 23:2–5's prohibitions on admission into the congregation of Yahweh were also interpreted as banning the physical entry of foreigners into the sanctuary, as attested in Neh 13:1, 3–5, 7–9.

> At that time they read to the people from the Book of Moses,
> and it was found written that no Ammonite or Moabite might
> ever enter the congregation of Elohim. . . . When they heard the
> Teaching, they separated all the alien admixture from Israel.
> Earlier, the priest Eliashib, a relative of Tobiah, who had been
> appointed over the rooms in the House of our Elohim, had

assigned to him [Tobiah, the Ammonite] a large room where they used to store the meal offering, the frankincense, the equipment, the tithes of grain, wine, and oil, the dues of the Levites, singers and gatekeepers, and the gifts for the priests. . . .

When I [Nehemiah] arrived in Jerusalem, I learned of the outrage perpetrated by Eliashib on behalf of Tobiah in assigning him a room in the courts of the House of Elohim. I was greatly displeased, and had all the household gear of Tobiah thrown out of the room; I gave orders to purify the rooms, and had the equipment of the House of Elohim and the meal offering and the frankincense put back.

According to this passage, the influential Tobiad family, originally Ammonite but joined in marriage with prominent Judeans, had gained access to a storeroom in the sanctuary. Nehemiah is incensed when he learns of this violation. He throws them out and has the rooms purified.

Likewise, Nehemiah interprets the similar wording in Deut 23:2 as banning eunuchs like himself from entering the sanctuary. Some scholars believe that this interpretation accounts for his refusal to flee to the sanctuary in order to escape his enemies (Neh 6:11–13).

### Renewal of the Mosaic Covenant

Ezra's most important public act—an extended public reading of the Torah of Moses, followed by a renewal of the Mosaic covenant—is reported in Nehemiah 8.

When the seventh month arrived—the Israelites being [settled] in their towns—the entire people assembled as one man in the square before the Water Gate, and they asked Ezra the scribe to bring the scroll of the Teaching of Moses with which Yahweh had charged Israel. On the first day of the seventh month, Ezra the priest brought the Teaching before the congregation, men and women and all who could listen with understanding. He read from it, facing the square before the Water Gate, from the first light until midday, to the men and the women and those who could understand; the ears of all the people were given to the scroll of the Teaching. Ezra the scribe stood upon a wooden tower made for the purpose. . . . Ezra opened the scroll in the sight of all

the people, for he was above all the people; as he opened it, all the
people stood up. Ezra blessed Yahweh, the great Elohim, and all
the people answered, "Amen, Amen," with hands upraised. . . .
[The leaders and] the Levites explained the Teaching to the people
while the people stood in their places. They read from the scroll of
the Teaching of Elohim, translating it and giving the sense; so
they understood the reading. (Neh 8:1–3, 4a, 5–8)

From this passage, it appears that the assembled people no longer understood the classical Hebrew of the Bible. Ezra and his assistants had to trans-
late it into Aramaic, the lingua franca of the Persian Empire, and give the
sense of the text as it was read. It is impossible to determine precisely what
it was that Ezra presented to the people. It may have been the Pentateuch
basically in the form we now have it, since both D and P are strongly reflected
in Ezra. In any event this "torah" was to become the basis and standard for
the Jewish community from that time forward.

At a festival celebration, a few weeks later, there was an additional public teaching of the law and a recital of Israel's history that laid special emphasis on Israel's covenantal obligations to Yahweh. This recital of Israel's
history is found in Neh 9, and as an interpretation of the calamities faced by
the nation, it is consistent with the prayer in Ezra 9: Yahweh has withheld
nothing from Israel, yet Israel has defied Yahweh, rebelled against him, and
killed the prophets who urged them to turn back to the covenant. Yahweh
tolerated Israel's sin as long as he could, but finally he had to punish her.
Even so, in his great compassion Yahweh did not abandon Israel completely. The Levites and leaders address Yahweh directly: "Surely you are in
the right with respect to all that has come upon us, for you have acted faithfully, and we have been wicked" (Neh 9:33). Like the Deuteronomistic historian, Nehemiah completely justifies Yahweh and blames the Israelites for
all that has befallen them.

All this is but a prelude to the people's reaffirmation and recommit-
ment to the covenant—a reaffirmation spelled out in great detail in Neh
10–13. Chapter 10 opens: "In view of all this, we make this pledge and put it
in writing." There follows a list of all the officials, Levites, priests, and the
heads of the people, who in conjunction with all the rest of the people declare that they will

join with their noble brothers, and take an oath with sanctions to
follow the Teaching of Elohim, given through Moses the servant

of Elohim, and to observe carefully all the commandments of Yahweh our god, his rules and laws, Namely: we will not give our daughters in marriage to the peoples of the land, or take their daughters for our sons. (Neh 10:30–31)

There follows a list of obligations to which the people commit themselves, including observance of the Sabbath day and the Sabbath year and the supply and upkeep of the Temple. It is surely significant that the ban on intermarriage and the observance of the Sabbath top the list of covenantal obligations. These two provisions are the centerpiece of the renewed covenant zealously promoted and enforced by Ezra and Nehemiah. Chapter 13 describes Nehemiah's efforts to see that the people lived up to this pledge. He scurries about Jerusalem enforcing cessation of work on the Sabbath and persuading certain individuals to give up their foreign wives. Indeed, a reputation for (if not a reality of) endogamy, Sabbath observance, and circumcision will emerge as primary characteristics of a male Jew in the ancient world.

Ezra and Nehemiah's reforms may be seen as a direct response to the events of Israel's history: What had happened before cannot, they believed, be allowed to happen again. Israel's tragic history must be read as a cautionary tale that calls upon the people to make the changes needed to avoid a repeat disaster. There is only one way to guarantee that Israel will never again be destroyed. She must live up to the covenant she failed to honor in the past. She must rededicate herself to the covenant, and this time she must be single-minded in her devotion to Yahweh, for history has shown that Yahweh does not fail to punish faithlessness and betrayal. Israel cannot be led astray by the beliefs and practices of her neighbors, and a strict policy of separation must be enforced if she is to be cured of the desire for idols.

## Other Voices: Isaiah 56

Ezra and Nehemiah, represented in the biblical sources as possessing the backing of Persian imperial authority, sought to create and preserve a national and religious identity for the Judean community at a precarious time in its existence. Under Ezra, the Torah became the official and authoritative norm for Israel, but this did not in itself result in a single, uniform set of practices and beliefs. Adopting the Torah as a communal norm simply meant that practices and beliefs were deemed authentic to the degree that they accorded with the sense of Scripture. But interpretation of Scripture varied dramatically, so that widely divergent Judean groups in the Persian and Hellenistic periods would claim biblical warrant for their specific practices and beliefs. Thus, while Ezra and Nehemiah may have unified the Restoration community around a common text, they did not unify them around a common interpretation of that text.

This lack of unity may be seen in other postexilic biblical texts that express opposition to the separatism envisaged in Ezra-Nehemiah. For example, although Nehemiah understands Deut 23 as banning all foreigners and eunuchs from entering the sanctuary (a view endorsed in Ezek 44:6–14), the following passage from Third Isaiah holds out a different vision:

> Let not the foreigner say,
> Who has attached himself to Yahweh,
> "Yahweh will keep me apart from his people";
> And let not the eunuch say,
> "I am a withered tree."
> For thus said Yahweh:
> "As for the eunuchs who keep my Sabbaths,
> Who have chosen what I desire
> And hold fast to my covenant—
> I will give them, in my House
> And within my walls,
> A monument and a name
> Better than sons or daughters.
> I will give them an everlasting name
> Which shall not perish.
> As for the foreigners
> Who attach themselves to Yahweh,
> To minister to him,
> And to love the name of Yahweh,
> To be his servants—
> All who keep the sabbath and do not profane it,
> And who hold fast to my covenant—
> I will bring them to my sacred mount
> And let them rejoice in my house of prayer.
> Their burnt offerings and sacrifices
> Shall be welcome on my altar;
> For my House shall be called
> A house of prayer for all peoples." (Isa 56:3–7)

This passage, dated by most scholars to the postexilic period, sounds a theme of openness and inclusion and reassures foreigners and eunuchs who have joined themselves to Yahweh that they will be welcome in the holy Temple and may even minister to Yahweh. As regards Judean identity, the insistence on unmixed genealogy did not become the norm for the transmission of Judean and later Jewish identity; similarly, access to Israelite identity remained open to foreigners who accepted the norms of the community. The strongest repudiation of Ezra's genealogical definition of Judean identity and rejection of intermarriage and assimilation may be found in the little book of Ruth.

## Ruth

The book of Ruth is set in the days of the Judges but it was certainly written later—whether in the preexilic or postexilic period is not certain. Rather than focusing on the book's provenance, the canonical critic would ask: How did this book function for Second Temple Judeans when it entered the library of canonical texts? How would it have resonated for those familiar with the legacy of Ezra and Nehemiah? This short tale of a foreign woman (Ruth's foreign status is continually emphasized throughout the book) who acts nobly and enters the community of Israel by choice, stood in pointed opposition to the negative view of foreigners, the ban on intermarriage, and the purely genealogical definition of Israelite identity promulgated by Ezra and Nehemiah in the postexilic period.

The story's plot is as follows: A famine in Judah causes a Bethlehemite named Elimelech, his wife Naomi, and their two sons to leave Judah to reside in the country of Moab. The two sons marry Moabite women, one named Orpah and the other named Ruth. Consider the effect that the opening verses of the story would have had on a late fifth- or fourth-century Judean audience. While the nation of Moab had long ceased to exist, biblical tradition prohibited intermarriage with Moabites (Deut 23), who were hated for their ill treatment of the Israelites en route to Canaan. Biblical tradition also contained a degrading story of the Moabites' descent from the incestuous union of Lot and his daughter after the fall of Sodom (Gen 19:30–38). And yet this story begins with the matter-of-fact report of a Bethlehemite family traveling to Moab and securing Moabite wives for its sons! Surely, a Judean audience would have been surprised, if not shocked.

In short order, Elimelech and his two sons—appropriately named "Sickness" (Machlon) and "Death" (Chilion)—die. The Israelite widow Naomi is left with no blood relation, only her two Moabite daughters-in-law. Naomi tearfully tells them that they should return to their fathers' homes since she will never be able to support them as a poor widow, and she has no further sons to give them. It is clear they have no legal obligation or tie to Naomi.

> But Naomi replied, "Turn back, my daughters! Why should you go with me? Have I any more sons in my body who might be husbands for you? Turn back, my daughters, for I am too old to be married. Even if I thought there was hope for me, even if I were married tonight and I also bore sons, should you wait for them to grow up? Should you on their account debar yourselves from marriage? Oh no, my daughters! My lot is far more bitter than yours, for the hand of Yahweh has struck out against me." They broke into weeping again, and Orpah kissed her mother-in-law farewell. But Ruth clung to her. So she said, "See, your sister-in-law has returned to her people and her gods. Go follow your sister-in-law." But Ruth replied, "Do not urge me to leave you, to turn back and not follow you. For wherever you go, I will go; wherever you lodge, I will lodge; your people shall be my people and your god my god. Where you die, I will die, and there I will be buried. Thus and more may Yahweh do to me if even death parts me from you." When [Naomi] saw how determined she was to go with her, she ceased to argue with her; and the two went on until they reached Bethlehem. (1:11–19a)

By the force of sheer conviction, Ruth joins herself to the people of her mother-in-law. Returning to Judah, Ruth supports her mother-in-law and herself by gleaning the fallen sheaves behind the reapers in the field. According to Pentateuchal law, the sheaves that fall from the workers' hands must be left for the poor to collect. Ruth gleans in the field of a kinsman of Naomi, named Boaz, a man of substance. She is diligent and soon comes to his attention. Boaz is kind to her, securing her safety among the rough field-workers and providing her with water, for he has heard of all that Ruth has done for Naomi, how she left her home and family to come to a people she did not know. He blesses her,

May Yahweh reward your deeds. May you have a full recompense from Yahweh, the god of Israel, under whose wings you
have sought refuge. (2:12)

Boaz increases his generosity, sharing his meal with Ruth and giving to her
from the harvested grain in addition to her gleanings.

Naomi is delighted with Ruth's gleanings, which more than suffice for
their needs, but she is even more pleased to learn that Ruth met with the
kindness and generosity of Boaz, since, as she points out, he is among their
redeeming kinsmen. A redeemer, or *go'el,* is a person who, as a close relative,
has certain legal obligations to that relative. These obligations include redeeming the relative or his property if sold to a stranger due to poverty,
marrying the childless widow of a deceased relative and producing offspring
for the deceased (a duty that fell first to the deceased's brother), and, in the
case of a blood-redeemer avenging the blood of a slain kinsman. Though
Boaz is a somewhat distant relative, Naomi believes he is the answer to their
dual problem of poverty on the one hand and Ruth's widowhood on the
other. In chapter 3, she urges Ruth to visit Boaz as he winnows barley on
the threshing floor. Ruth is to bathe, anoint herself, dress, and go at night
to the threshing floor. Naomi seems to be planning Ruth's seduction of
Boaz. She instructs Ruth not to reveal herself until Boaz has finished eating
and drinking. When he lies down, Ruth is to approach him, uncover his
"feet"—which may well be a sexual euphemism—and lie down.[5] He will tell
her what she is to do. Ruth did as instructed by her mother-in-law.

Boaz ate and drank, and in a cheerful mood went to lie down beside the grainpile. Then she went over stealthily and uncovered
his feet and lay down. In the middle of the night, the man gave a
start and pulled back—there was a woman lying at his feet! "Who
are you?" he asked. And she replied, "I am your handmaid Ruth.
Spread your robe over your handmaid for you are a redeeming
kinsman." He exclaimed, "Be blessed of Yahweh, daughter! Your
latest deed of loyalty is greater than the first, in that you have not
turned to younger men, whether poor or rich. And now daughter,
have no fear, I will do in your behalf whatever you ask, for all the
elders of my town know what a fine woman you are." (Ruth 3:7–11)

Ruth's request is that Boaz act as her redeemer and spread his robe over her,
a formal act of protection and espousal. Boaz assures her that he will redeem

her, but he points out that there is another kinsman who is actually a closer relation and thus has first right of refusal (3:12). Boaz will settle the matter legally in the morning—we are left wondering what transpired in the night—and indeed in chapter 4 we read of the legal proceeding by which the other kinsman is freed of his obligation and claim to Ruth, enabling Boaz to marry her. But the punchline to the whole story is yet to come:

> So Boaz married Ruth; she became his wife, and he cohabited with her. Yahweh let her conceive, and she bore a son. And the women said to Naomi, "Blessed be Yahweh, who has not withheld a redeemer from you today! May his name be perpetuated in Israel! He will renew your life and sustain your old age; for he is born of your daughter-in-law who loves you and is better to you than seven sons." Naomi took the child and held it to her bosom. She became its foster mother, and the women neighbors gave him a name, saying "A son is born to Naomi!" They named him Obed; he was the father of Jesse, father of David. (4:13–17)

David, Yahweh's anointed king over Israel; David with whom Yahweh covenanted that his house should reign forever; David from whose line would come the Messianic king to rule in the final age—David is said to be the direct descendant (the great-grandson) of a foreign woman from a country of idol worshippers, a Moabite woman no less! This short and moving story represents a strand of thought that stood in opposition to the line of thinking found, for example, in Ezra's call for a ban on intermarriage as the only sure means of ensuring faithfulness to Israel's god. Not only is Ruth the Moabite not guilty of abominable practices, she is the ancestor of Yahweh's chosen monarch, and she is praised by all who know her as a paragon of ḥesed—the steadfast love and loyalty that binds the members of the covenant community to one another and to Yahweh. Ruth the Moabite stood by an elderly widow to whom she had no legal or moral obligation and was accepted into the covenant community.

## Conclusion

Despite Ezra's polemical efforts to exclude foreigners from the community, Ezra's reforms never became normative for the entire community. Postexilic and later rabbinic Judaism never adopted Ezra's holy seed ideology or his purely genealogical definition of Jewish identity and continued to allow the assimilation (eventually conversion) and marriage into the covenant community by persons of foreign birth who accepted the god of Israel. Ezra's extreme views were popular among sectarian groups (Ezran exclusivism is championed in writings found at Qumran) and exerted some influence on early Christian bans on marriage between believers and unbelievers,[6] but it is the book of Ruth that features prominently in the Jewish conversion ceremony to this day.

# CHAPTER 23

# Postexilic Prophets and the Rise
# of Apocalyptic

Israel's literary prophets had spoken of a remnant of Israel that would be restored gloriously in its land. But the returned exiles faced a life of great hardship. The reality of poverty, the difficulties in rebuilding the Temple, the hostility of the Judeans who had remained behind as well as that of the surrounding peoples, and the absence of any real political independence under a Davidic king—all this fell far short of the earlier prophets' glorious descriptions of the restored kingdom. In the postexilic period, new prophets arose to address the community's disappointment.

## Haggai and Zechariah

The short book of Haggai contains the words of the prophet Haggai to Zerubbabel, the governor of Judea. Prophesying in 520, Haggai declared that the nation's difficulties, the repeated agricultural setbacks, and famine were signs of Yahweh's displeasure that his Temple had not been completed (1:2–11). Zerubbabel was convinced, and the people returned to the task enthusiastically (1:14–15). Haggai promised that the rebuilt but humble structure would soon be filled with treasures flowing in from all nations (2:6–9). The promises of restoration made by the prophets of old were just around the corner.

Haggai longed not only for a rebuilt Temple, but for the reestablishment of Judah's independence under a Davidic king—and he held out hope for Zerubbabel, who was a descendant of David, to serve as Yahweh's messiah or appointed king (2:20–23). This hope burns even more strongly in the work of Haggai's contemporary, the prophet Zechariah. Chapters 1–8 of Zechariah contain prophecies attributed to the historical Zechariah from around 520 B.C.E. (Chapters 9–14, referred to by scholars as Second Zechariah, contain obscure writings from a later hand or school in the apocalyptic vein. These chapters will be discussed below.)

Zechariah prophesied for about two years around the year 520 B.C.E. In Chapters 1–8, he, too, urges the rebuilding of the Temple. The first six chapters contain a series of eight elaborate and symbolic visions revealed by an angel or divine messenger (a mode of revelation that is even more highly developed in apocalyptic literature). These visions focus hope on Zerubbabel, the governor, and Yeshua, the high priest, who will rule in a kind of diarchy as monarch and priest. At some point, however, the Persians ousted Zerubbabel (perhaps because he gave rise to messianic hope), and Zechariah's prophecies were adjusted to refer solely to Yeshua. Specifically, textual irregularities lead some scholars to hypothesize that Zech 6:9–15 originally referred to Zerubbabel and/or Yeshua, but now depict Yeshua as a shoot or branch from Jesse's stock (i.e., a Davidide since Jesse was the father of David) who will rebuild the sanctuary and wear the royal insignia (Zech 6:13). In general, the elevation of the high priest is a feature of Judean society in the Restoration period.

Chapters 7 and 8 declare Yahweh's promise to turn and do good things for Jerusalem and the House of Judah, so long as the people turn from their unjust and evil ways. Zechariah points forward to a glorious day when all the nations of the world will eagerly come to seek Yahweh in Jerusalem and to entreat his favor (8:22). For Zechariah, there is a place for all nations in the divine economy of the fully restored future.

> Thus said Yahweh of Hosts: In those days, ten men from nations of every tongue will take hold—they will take hold of every Judean by a corner of his cloak and say, "Let us go with you, for we have heard that Elohim is with you." (8:23)

## The Eschatological Turn—Third Isaiah

The last wave of Israelite prophetic writings addresses the disappointment and disillusionment of postexilic Judeans with a consistent message: The earlier prophets' promises of future glory for the restored remnant are all

true—but the future they promised is not now. It is only in the eschaton—
the final day—that the glory of Jerusalem and a Messianic ruler will be restored. The hope that must sustain the community through the bleak present
is an eschatological hope—for in the end of days, all will be set right.

Parts of the book of Third Isaiah depict the bitter reality of life in
postexilic Judah. The anonymous prophetic author of these chapters (Isa
56–66) denounces the failings of the exiles, but in addition he advances an
eschatology (an account of the end of days). This eschatology differs from
the depiction of Zion's future glory found in earlier prophets. Earlier prophetic pronouncements generally referred to a reestablishment of Judah's
fortunes in historical time. But eschatological works like Third Isaiah look
beyond historical time to a time of a "new heaven and a new earth" when
Judah's sins will be forgotten and the land will become an earthly paradise
blessed with peace, prosperity, and length of days.

> For behold! I am creating
> A new heaven and a new earth;
> The former things shall not be remembered,
> They shall never come to mind.
> Be glad, then, and rejoice forever
> In what I am creating.
> For I shall create Jerusalem as a joy,
> And her people as a delight. . . .
> Never again shall be heard there
> The sounds of weeping and wailing.
> No more shall there be an infant or graybeard
> Who does not live out his days.
> He who dies at a hundred years
> Shall be reckoned a youth,
> And he who fails to reach a hundred
> Shall be reckoned accursed. . . .
> For the days of my people shall be
> As long as the days of a tree,
> My chosen ones shall outlive
> The work of their hands.
> They shall not toil to no purpose;
> They shall not bear children for terror,
> But they shall be a people blessed by Yahweh,
> And their offspring shall remain with them.

Before they pray, I will answer;
While they are still speaking, I will respond.
The wolf and the lamb shall graze together,
And the lion shall eat straw like the ox,
And the serpent's food shall be earth.
In all my sacred mount
Nothing evil or vile shall be done—said Yahweh. (65:17–20,
    22–25)

Third Isaiah envisions something new on earth—Jerusalem re-created as a
joy and delight, without suffering or sadness. The curses of Eden will be
reversed. Instead of shortened lives of toil and hardship, people will enjoy
extended lifespans and the blessings of productive labor and happy families. The enmity between predator and prey will be eliminated as the wolf
and the lion return to their original vegetarian state, and the serpent ceases
to bite at the heels of humans. The misery of the years between the original
Eden and this future Eden "shall never come to mind."

. But not all postexilic eschatologies are suffused with the tranquility of
this Edenic vision. Eschatologies of an apocalyptic tenor spoke of a terrifying, cataclysmic end-time.

## The Apocalyptic Genre: Zechariah and Joel

Only one biblical book—the book of Daniel—belongs to the genre of literature
known as apocalyptic. The term derives from the Greek *apocalypsis,* which
means "a revealing." An apocalypse is a revelation of things to come, and as
apocalypses generally predict the end of historical time and the beginning of
a new world order, they are concerned with eschatology. However, while
apocalyptic literature is concerned with eschatology, not all eschatological
literature is apocalyptic. Apocalyptic literature—within the Bible and outside
it—is characterized by the following distinguishing characteristics:

1. *Pseudonymy*—Most apocalyptic works are attributed to important figures of the past.
2. *Mediated revelation*—Revelation is mediated through a heavenly messenger or angel in visions or dreams.
3. *Symbolism*—Apocalyptic works are highly symbolic and employ bizarre and surreal images of beasts and monsters, usually

to depict foreign nations. These visions are organized in a systematic chronology that represents the march of history—past, present, and future—in a coded form that requires interpretation, often by the divine messenger.

4. *Catastrophes*—Apocalypses predict a series of catastrophes that signal the coming of the end. Motifs from ancient myths, such as ancient stories of battles with sea monsters, are often used to describe these future catastrophes.

5. *Dualism*—Apocalypses divide humankind into two mutually exclusive groups: the righteous, who are a tiny minority, and the wicked, who are the vast majority. In a final public judgment, the former will be saved and the latter destroyed. In this respect, later apocalypses may show the influence of Persian thought, which is dualist in nature, opposing light and darkness, good and evil, life and death.

6. *Divine king*—The deity generally appears in an apocalypse as an enthroned king who brings all history to a crashing end, thereby demonstrating his sovereignty and confounding the wicked all at once.

7. *Mythological elements*—Apocalyptic literature often incorporates mythological motifs and imagery, especially the motif of a battle between the deity and primordial chaotic forces, in its depiction of the final battle.

8. *Judgment and life after death*—Apocalypses generally depict a judgment of the individual dead, followed by everlasting life or punishment. This idea of a life after death is not found in the Hebrew Bible until the very late apocalyptic book of Daniel. The idea is very influential in the Dead Sea Scrolls and in the writings of the New Testament. A belief in personal immortality or a general resurrection of the dead arises from a negative view of this world as a place where justice cannot be obtained. Apocalyptic writers examined the world they lived in and drew the conclusion that reward and punishment would be made in an afterlife, as they were certainly not doled out in this life. This is a marked break from the general conviction of the Hebrew Bible that human life is limited to this world and that the fundamental concern of humans is morality in this life and not immortality in another.

9. *Despair and hope*—Apocalyptic literature can be described as
a literature of despair and hope. It is a literature of despair or
pessimism because its basic premise is that this world holds out
no promise for the righteous. It is a literature of hope or optimism because it affirms that the deity will intervene in human
history and set everything right, interrupting the natural order
and destroying the world as we know it in order to rescue the
righteous and humiliate the wicked. The hope for supreme and
ultimate vindication is thrust off into the future. Thus, the apocalyptic genre constitutes yet one more response to the traumatic
events, crises, and disappointments of Israelite history.

Apocalyptic passages of varying length appear in several postexilic books
of the Hebrew Bible. Second Zechariah (9–14) is a collection of diverse oracles, probably fifth century or later, that contain strange visions and predictions. While their meaning cannot always be fathomed, they focus on the
Day of Yahweh, the restoration of Jerusalem, and the rise of a new and
humble king who will rule in peace. Chapter 14 is a vision of the global battle
that will bring an end to history. Yahweh will bring the nations to Jerusalem,
where they will plunder the city and kill almost all its inhabitants. But at the
last moment Yahweh will intervene and fight for Israel, exacting revenge on
her enemies. Following the battle, Yahweh will transform the earth into a
paradise. Israel's enemies will rage against one another, while the surviving
nations will pilgrimage to Jerusalem, elevated above all other cities, to worship at the Temple. Yahweh will be sovereign over the world.

The short book of Joel, probably the latest prophetic book, also contains apocalyptic material. It can be divided into two parts. Joel 1:2–2:27
describes a military invasion, symbolized by an army of locusts and interpreted as the divine punishment that will precede the Day of Yahweh. The
third and fourth chapters contain an apocalyptic description of the final
day of terror.

> Before the great and terrible day of Yahweh comes,
> I will set portents in the sky and on earth:
> Blood and fire and pillars of smoke;
> The sun will be turned to darkness
> And the moon to blood. (Joel 3:3–4)

But the righteous will survive:

> But everyone who invokes the name of Yahweh shall escape; for
> there shall be a remnant on Mount Zion and in Jerusalem, as
> Yahweh promised. Anyone who invokes Yahweh will be among
> the survivors. (Joel 3:5)

In chapter 4, the Day of Yahweh is envisaged as a Judgment Day for all
peoples, issuing in a new age (an idea that will be elaborated upon in the
book of Daniel and in nonbiblical apocalyptic writings). On this Judgment
day, Yahweh will summon all the godless nations to the Valley of Judgment
(the Valley of Jehoshaphat). Here the final battle between good and evil will
take place, after which Yahweh's people will be blessed and Yahweh's holy
city will never again suffer shame.

> For lo! in those days
> And in that time,
> When I restore the fortunes
> Of Judah and Jerusalem,
> I will gather all the nations
> And bring them down to the Valley of Jehoshaphat.
> There I will contend with them
> Over my very own people, Israel,
> Which they scattered among the nations. (4:1–3)

> Let the nations rouse themselves and march up
> To the Valley of Jehoshaphat,
> For there I will sit in judgment
> Over all the nations roundabout.
> Swing the sickle,
> For the crop is ripe;
> Come and tread,
> For the winepress is full,
> The vats are overflowing!
> For great is their wickedness. . . .
> But Yahweh will be a shelter to his people,
> A refuge to the children of Israel. . . .
> And Jerusalem shall be holy;
> Nevermore shall strangers pass through it.
> And in that day,
> The mountains shall drip with wine,

The hills shall flow with milk,
And all the water courses of Judah shall flow with water.
A spring shall issue from the House of Yahweh
And shall water the Wadi of Acacias. . . .
Judah shall be inhabited forever,
And Jerusalem throughout the ages. (4:12–13, 16b–18, 20)

The eschatological features of Joel are (1) a series of disasters that signal the impending wrath of Yahweh; (2) a cosmic battle in which Yahweh triumphs over Israel's enemies; (3) a final judgment of all nations; (4) an outpouring of blessings on Yahweh's people, city, and land; and (5) a new reality that including Yahweh's continued protection and presence.

There are important differences between classical prophecy and eschatologies of a more apocalyptic bent, as are found in Joel. Both speak about final things or an end-time, but the classical prophets did not in general expect that the course of human affairs would come to an end—only that Israel's rebellion would end and Israel would live under a perfect king anointed by Yahweh. In the apocalyptic imagination, history as it was known would end and a new age, a new world order, would begin. The present age and the age to come are qualitatively distinct. The present age is under the dominion of evil powers (in postbiblical apocalyptic writings and the New Testament, that power will be Satan, who becomes the archenemy of the deity). The age to come will be free of all evil, moral corruption, and death. But Yahweh himself must intervene to bring the present age to a crashing halt and initiate the new world order.

## Daniel

The second half of the book of Daniel contains the only fully apocalyptic material in the Hebrew Bible. The first six chapters of the work are what may be called "heroic fiction"—like the book of Esther to be discussed in Chapter 24, they feature a Jew in a Gentile court saved from disaster. They recount Daniel's adventures under King Nebuchadrezzar, Belshazzar (the latter is mistakenly said to be a king), King Darius, and the Persian King Cyrus. Historical inaccuracies abound. The chronology of more than a century is telescoped, Belshazzar was not a king but a Babylonian prince, and he was defeated by Cyrus, not Darius. The historical inaccuracy of the work is a sign that it was written at a later time (perhaps the end of the third century B.C.E.) when there was no clear historical knowledge of the Babylonian and early Persian period. Chapters 7–12 are fully apocalyptic in genre and were probably composed between 167 and 164 B.C.E., when Jews were suffering intense persecution at the hands of the Syrian king Antiochus IV Epiphanes. (Daniel is thus the latest book of the Hebrew Bible.) However, the author writes covertly, disguising his references to contemporary historical events and personalities in narratives and visions attributed to a remote era of the past.

In chapters 1–6, Daniel is represented as a loyal Jew living in the Babylonian exile among idol worshippers. He refuses to bow down to any other god, observes the dietary laws, and prays facing Jerusalem. He occupies a position of some honor, has the power to interpret dreams and predict the future, and though severely tested, remains true to Yahweh, who aids him in more than one miraculous escape from danger.

The two primary themes of this first section of the book are Daniel's interpretation of the dreams of Nebuchadrezzar and Daniel's allegiance to his god. In chapter 2, Nebuchadrezzar dreams of a huge statue with a head of gold, torso and arms of silver, belly and thighs of bronze, legs of iron, and feet of mixed iron and clay. A great stone uncut by human hands flies from heaven and smashes the clay feet of the statue. The statue crumbles, and the stone becomes a mountain that fills all the earth. Daniel decodes the dream's historical symbolism. Each metal represents a kingdom that ruled the ancient Near East: Daniel explicitly decodes only gold—it is Babylon. One may suppose, then, that silver is Media, bronze is Persia, and iron is Macedonian Greece, which conquered the ancient Near East under Alexander in 332, initiating the Hellenistic period of ancient Near Eastern history. After Alexander's death, his empire was divided into smaller Hellenistic kingdoms—Egypt, ruled by the Ptolemies, and Syria, ruled by the Seleucids—that wrangled for control of the land between them, including Judea. Thus, the iron and clay feet of the statue in Daniel's dream represent the lesser Hellenistic kingdoms of Egypt and Syria that succeeded Alexander's empire. The stone from heaven represents the future kingdom of the god of heaven that will destroy these godless kingdoms and fill all the earth forever.

Chapter 3 tells the story of Daniel's three companions who refuse to worship a giant gold statue and are thrown into a fiery furnace. When they emerge unscathed, the king is duly impressed and acknowledges the god of Israel. In chapter 4, a second dream is interpreted by Daniel as a sign that Nebuchadrezzar will be struck down seven times, losing his reason and his throne, until he realizes that the god of heaven is the source of all human and divine power. When these events come to pass—when Nebuchadrezzar suffers a fit of insanity that drives him from society—he praises the heavenly deity proclaimed by Daniel as the universal king. In chapter 6, Daniel's enemies at court trick the Median king Darius into issuing an edict against those who pray to anyone but the king. Daniel violates the edict and is arrested and thrown into a den of lions but emerges unharmed. The result is that Darius recognizes the supremacy of "the living god" and orders all in his kingdom to revere the god of Daniel.

There is, of course, no historical merit to these stories of Babylonian, Median, and Persian kings acknowledging or adopting the god of the Judeans who lived in exile among them. These stories gave voice to the hope—or fantasy—that a cruel and impious monarch who had humbled Yahweh's people might be taught humility by Yahweh and come to recognize and praise the god of Israel as the universal creator-god. They also provide a model for life in the diaspora—Jews can live in the Gentile world (indeed, Daniel attains a high position in the royal court) but must never forget their god and his laws.

The second half of Daniel—chapters 7–12—switches from third-person to first-person narration and is fully apocalyptic. Daniel has a series of visions and dreams that are interpreted for him by an angel—a classic feature of the apocalyptic genre. These visions survey Near Eastern history from the sixth to the second centuries B.C.E. Chapter 7 again represents the succession of kingdoms—the Babylonian, Median, Persian, and Macedonian empires—this time as beasts: a lion, a bear, a winged leopard, and an ogre. The horns of the ogre represent the Ptolemies of Egypt and the Seleucids of Syria. The arrogant little horn is the Syrian king Antiochus Epiphanes himself. In a second vision, the "Ancient of Days" (the deity in a white robe and beard seated on a fiery chariot throne) confers glory and kingship on one who is said to be "like a son of man." This figure establishes an everlasting kingdom to replace the bestial kingdoms that have preceded it. He overwhelms the little horn (Antiochus) who is making war on saints (= loyal Jews) by trying to change their law and abolish their religion (a reference to the second-century persecution of Jews under Antiochus Epiphanes).

In chapter 8, the manlike figure is identified as the angel Gabriel, who explains another vision. Later, Gabriel appears again to make known to Daniel the details of the final age and refers to the angel Michael, who joins him in leading forces against Persia and Greece (10:20–21).

In another vision in chapter 8, the horn that represents Antiochus is said to move toward the Land of Splendor (= Israel), to challenge the very chief of the army of heaven, and to remove the perpetual sacrifice (a reference to the fact that Antiochus halted the sacrificial service in the Jerusalem Temple). Chapter 9 also describes the installation of an "abomination of desolation" (the pagan altar set up on the Temple's sacrificial altar and the statue of Zeus erected in the sanctuary). The various persecutions under Antiochus are thus presented by the author in veiled form, for reasons of safety.

Chapter 9 also contains a moving prayer for deliverance. The angel Gabriel assures Daniel that the end is near and that it was even predicted by Jeremiah, who said that Jerusalem would lie desolate for seventy years. Jeremiah prophesied in the early sixth century, of course, and these chapters of the book of Daniel were written many centuries later, in the 160s B.C.E. Daniel 9 "rescues" Jeremiah's prophecy by interpreting his "seventy years" as "seventy weeks of years," that is, 490 years, that would pass before the consummation of all things. The last week, namely, the last seven years, was the reign of Antiochus Epiphanes.[1] Thus the writer maintained that he was living in the "last days," in the final moments of the last week of years—very typical of apocalyptic literature. The time is at hand; Israel's god will soon win victory through a mighty act and introduce the messianic age, ending the nation's long years of desolation.

Apocalyptic literature sees history as determined—a closed drama that must be played out and requiring no action on the part of humans except faithful waiting. The divine kingdom will come solely by the deity's power, but it must be preceded by a time of great trouble—which is nothing but the birth pangs of the messianic age. The faithful, whose names are recorded in the deity's book, will be rescued. Chapter 12 imagines a resurrection of the dead as a compensation to those who died under the Syrian persecution—a clear attempt to deal with the injustice that mars this world. This is the only passage of the Bible to explicitly espouse the idea of individual life after death, breaking with a longer Israelite tradition that is vague or silent on the issue. Not all Jews accepted the idea, but it would be essential to the rise of Christianity, which is deeply indebted to apocalyptic thinking, and through Christianity, it came to have a far-reaching impact on western civilization.

The Book of Daniel is a response to specific historical circumstances. It is a response to the crisis of persecution and martyrdom in the second century B.C.E.—a new kind of crisis that led to a new kind of response. The earlier crises of 722 and 586 could be explained as punishment for sin and faithlessness. But now in the second century, Jews were dying not because they were faithless but precisely because they were faithful, because they refused to obey the decrees of Antiochus and to violate their law and covenant! This new phenomenon of martyrdom required a new response, and the book of Daniel provides a fully apocalyptic one: remain faithful, wait, Daniel urges, and know that all will be set right by the god of heaven, not in historical time but at the end of history in an ultimate and cataclysmic triumph of life and faith over death and evil—and it will be soon. Daniel emphasizes the deity's firm control of history and in this way bolsters loyal Jews suffering indignities, torture, and even death because of their faith.

We have seen the zealous fifth-century response of Ezra and Nehemiah to the fateful events in Israel's history. They believed that Israel's rededication to her god and the covenant involved as a first step the cessation of intimate relations with foreigners and separation from their abominable practices. We have seen the very different view of Third Isaiah and Ruth that would integrate foreigners in the community and sanctuary of Yahweh. We have also seen the later emergence of apocalyptic as an expression of present despair and future hope that entailed the divinely orchestrated and cataclysmic defeat of the wicked enemies who persecute Israel. In the next and final chapter, we will examine two books of the Hebrew Bible that take different approaches to the question of Israel and the nations.

## CHAPTER 24

# Israel and the Nations

## Esther and Jonah

*Readings:* Esther, Jonah

### Esther

The book of Esther is an interesting counterpoint to the apocalyptic reliance on Yahweh's cataclysmic consummation of history in order to dole out justice to righteous Israel and the wicked nations. This short novella is set in fifth-century B.C.E. Persia during the reign of Ahashverosh (Xerxes, 486–465), although it was probably written in the fourth century B.C.E. Like Daniel, Esther is another work of heroic fiction featuring a Jew in the court of a Gentile king. The Jews of Persia are threatened with genocide and are saved not by divine intervention, but through their own efforts. Indeed, the book of Esther does not mention the deity even once.

The story revolves around Mordechai, a pious Jew who sits at the gate of the Persian King Ahasverosh (Xerxes), and his beautiful niece, Esther, whom he has adopted as his own. There is much comic irony in this story. When the Persian king divorces his wife Vashti because she refuses to appear in the royal diadem before his male courtiers—presumably in nothing but the royal diadem—Esther's great beauty commends her to the king, and she becomes queen. Mordechai advises her to be discreet about her Jewish identity, for safety's sake.

Esther did not reveal her people or her kindred, for Mordechai had told her not to reveal it. Every single day Mordechai would walk about in front of the court of the harem, to learn how Esther was faring and what was happening to her. (2:10–11)

Some time later, the king promotes Haman the Agagite to the post of chief administrator, and all in the palace gate kneel down to Haman as the king had ordered—all except Mordechai. Day after day he refuses, and finally the matter is reported to Haman.

When they spoke to him day after day and he would not listen to them, they told Haman, in order to see whether Mordechai's resolve would prevail; for he had explained to them that he was a Jew. When Haman saw that Mordechai would not kneel or bow low to him, Haman was filled with rage. But he disdained to lay hands on Mordechai alone; having been told who Mordechai's people were, Haman plotted to do away with all the Jews, Mordechai's people, throughout the kingdom of Ahasverosh. (3:4–6)

Haman casts lots (*purim*) to determine the date of the massacre and then offers the king a handsome bribe in return for permission to kill the Jews of the kingdom:

"There is a certain people, scattered and dispersed among the other peoples in all the provinces of your realm, whose laws are different from those of any other people and who do not obey the king's laws; and it is not in Your Majesty's interest to tolerate them. If it please Your Majesty, let an edict be drawn for their destruction, and I will pay ten thousand talents of silver to the stewards for deposit in the royal treasury." Thereupon the king removed his signet ring from his hand and gave it to Haman son of Hammedatha the Agagite, the foe of the Jews. And the king said, "The money and the people are yours to do with as you see fit." (3:8–11)

An edict goes out to every province to destroy, massacre, and exterminate all the Jews, young and old, children and women, on a single day—the thirteenth day of the month of Adar. Jews everywhere fast, weep, and mourn in sackcloth and ashes. Esther sends to Mordechai for an explanation of the commotion. He sends a message informing her of the decree and urging her to appeal to the king and plead for her people. Esther hesitates—to appear unbidden before the king carries a penalty of death. Mordechai responds with the following message:

> "Do not imagine that you, of all the Jews, will escape with your life by being in the king's palace. On the contrary, if you keep silent in this crisis, relief and deliverance will come to the Jews from another quarter, while you and your father's house will perish. And who knows, perhaps you have attained to royal position for just such a crisis." Then Esther sent back this answer to Mordechai: "Go assemble all the Jews who live in Shushan, and fast in my behalf; do not eat or drink for three days, night or day. I and my maidens will observe the same fast. Then I shall go to the king, though it is contrary to the law; and if I am to perish, I shall perish!" So Mordechai went about [the city] and did just as Esther had commanded him. (4:13b–16)

In a tense scene, Esther approaches the king. She is permitted entry by the king, who offers to grant her every request. She asks that the king and Haman attend a banquet she is preparing. At Esther's banquet, the king offers to grant Esther any request she might wish to make. Her request shows her loyalty to her people:

> "If Your Majesty will do me the favor, and if it pleases Your Majesty, let my life be granted me as my wish, and my people as my request. For we have been sold, my people and I, to be destroyed, massacred and exterminated. Had we only been sold as bondmen and bondwomen, I would have kept silent; for the adversary is not worthy of the king's trouble." Thereupon King Ahasverosh demanded of Queen Esther, "Who is he and where is he who dared to do this?" "The adversary and enemy" replied Esther, "is this evil Haman!" And Haman cringed in terror before the king and queen. (7:3b–6)

Esther boldly reveals her Jewish identity to the king, expressing her solidarity in phrases like "we" and "my people and I." In the comedy of errors that follows, the king leaves the room in a rage, and Haman falls prostrate on

Queen Esther's couch to plead for his life. When the king reenters to find Haman in so compromising a position, he declares, "Does he mean to ravish the queen in my own palace?" In an ironic reversal, the king orders Haman impaled on the stake that Haman had originally set up for Mordechai, and Mordechai is elevated in Haman's stead. But the Jews are still in danger because an edict of the king's cannot be revoked. The solution is a second edict, in which Ahasverosh charges the Jews to arm and defend themselves. In yet another of the many reversals that fill this story, what was to be a day of defeat becomes a day of triumph, as the Jews slay those who were bent on murdering them.

The victory celebration, the feast of Purim, is commemorated by Jews to this day. The melodramatic story of the luxurious court life of the Persians and its attendant political intrigue is re-created annually in raucous carnival-like dramatizations. According to the Talmud, on Purim it is a mitzvah—a commandment or good deed—to get so drunk that you cannot distinguish Haman from Mordechai. But beyond the theatrics, there are important and striking themes in this story. First, the ethnic element of Jewish identity, rather than the religious, comes to the fore in the book of Esther. The presentation is entirely secular: The Jews are described as a people, an ethnos. Esther is fully assimilated to her Gentile environment, unlike Daniel who prays toward Jerusalem daily and observes dietary laws. Second, there is a very human and antiapocalyptic message to this story. It gives expression to the conviction that solidarity and heroic resistance are necessary in the face of overwhelming anti-Jewish aggression, to ensure Jewish survival. According to the book of Esther—so different from the book of Daniel—the lesson to be learned from Israel's history is this: resistance, not martyrdom; action and self-help, not passive hope in divine intervention.

## Jonah

If the book of Esther presents one alternative to the postexilic eschatologies in which Yahweh intervenes to consume Israel's enemies, the book of Jonah offers yet another. The book of Jonah is found among the prophetic books of the Bible because in 2 Kgs 14:25, Jonah, son of Amittai is identified as a prophet. Yet the book of Jonah differs in certain significant ways from the other prophetic books. First, it is not a collection of oracles but a comic tall tale about a reluctant prophet named Jonah. Second, Jonah is commissioned by Yahweh to carry a message to the people of Nineveh, the capital of Assyria—not to the people of Israel.

The Israelite concept of divine mercy receives its full expression in the book of Jonah. In the first chapter Jonah receives his call from Yahweh. Yahweh instructs him to go to Nineveh, whose wickedness is great, and to proclaim Yahweh's judgment.

> The word of Yahweh came to Jonah son of Amittai: Go at once to Nineveh, that great city, and proclaim judgment upon it; for their wickedness has come before me. Jonah, however, started out to flee to Tarshish from Yahweh's service. He went down to Joppa and found a ship going to Tarshish. He paid the fare and went aboard to sail with the others to Tarshish, away from the service of Yahweh. (1:1–3)

In a humorous touch, of which there are many in this short book, Jonah does an immediate about face and sets sail for Spain, at the other end of the Mediterranean, the farthest extent of the known world at that time. But of course Jonah cannot escape from Yahweh, and Yahweh sends a storm that threatens to destroy the ship. The non-Israelite sailors pray to their gods and then finally cast lots in order to discover who has brought this danger to the ship. The lot falls to Jonah. Jonah confesses that he is a Hebrew who worships a god named Yahweh who (as he now realizes) made both land *and* sea—a fact that strikes terror in the hearts of the sailors. Jonah further adds that he is fleeing from Yahweh's service, implying that his flight is the cause of the terrible storm. Jonah proposes that he be thrown overboard to save the ship, but the sailors (rather nobly) consider this step an option of last resort and strive mightily to row to shore. This proves impossible, and finally in despair they pray to Yahweh by name, asking him to forgive them for killing an innocent man. They heave Jonah overboard, and the sea is calm. The narrator reports that the men revere Yahweh, offer a sacrifice to him, and make vows.

In the meantime Yahweh has appointed a huge fish to swallow Jonah, thus preserving his life.

From the belly of the fish, Jonah prays to Yahweh. This prayer or psalm is not entirely appropriate to the context. The deity did not drive Jonah away, nor is there any evidence that Jonah longs for the Temple, as stated in verse 5. The psalm is probably an insertion by a later writer, triggered by references to drowning and crying out to Yahweh from the "belly" of Sheol, just as Jonah is said to be in the "belly" of the fish (a catchword connection). In response to Jonah's prayer, Yahweh orders the fish to spew Jonah out onto dry land.

Chapter 3 represents Jonah's second chance. Yahweh calls him again, and in contrast to his response to the first call, Jonah sets out for Nineveh at once. He proclaims Yahweh's message: In forty days Nineveh will be overthrown. Then comes the shocker:

> The people of Nineveh believed Elohim. They proclaimed a fast, and great and small alike put on sackcloth. When the news reached the king of Nineveh, he rose from his throne, took off his robe, put on sackcloth, and sat in ashes. And he had the word cried through Nineveh: "By decree of the king and his nobles: No man or beast—of flock or herd—shall taste anything! They shall not graze, and they shall not drink water! They shall be covered with sackcloth—man and beast—and shall cry mightily to Elohim. Let everyone turn back from his evil ways and from the injustice of which he is guilty. Who knows but that the deity may turn and relent? He may turn back from His wrath, so that we do not perish." The deity saw what they did, how they were turning back from their evil ways. And the deity renounced the punishment he had planned to bring upon them, and did not carry it out. (Jonah 3:5–10)

Idolatrous Nineveh is said to believe Elohim. Here, the writer employs the generic term "Elohim" rather than the more specifically Israelite name "Yahweh." Evidently what is desired of the Ninevites is a general god-fearing moral reform rather than a recognition and worship of Yahweh. The Ninevites humble themselves before the deity, hoping to arouse his mercy. In yet another humorous touch, the narrator reports that even the animals wear sackcloth, fast, and cry out to the deity! From the greatest to the least, the inhabitants of Nineveh turn back from their evil ways, and Yahweh's mercy is aroused.

There is a wonderful irony in the fact that this reluctant prophet produces maximal results with minimal effort. In chapter 1 he made no effort to convince the sailors of anything except the desirability of throwing him overboard, and yet after their encounter with Jonah, the sailors revere Yahweh, offer him sacrifices, and make vows. Similarly, once in Nineveh, Jonah utters a mere five words (literally, "forty days more, Nineveh overthrown"), and in response even the cattle are crying out to heaven. Jonah does not fulminate against the people, speak of Yahweh or any divine power at all, or call upon the people to repent and save themselves. Unlike the classical Israelite prophets who railed against the people, enumerating the causes of Yahweh's anger and charting a clear path to forgiveness through repentance, Jonah offers no instruction, no counsel, no comfort, and no insight, in fact, into the situation in which the Ninevites find themselves. It is the Ninevite king who simply surmises that turning back from sin might prompt the deity to turn back from his wrath! And so every last Ninevite—and all their livestock—repents. Jonah, it seems, is incapable of failure. Unintentionally, indeed against his will, he succeeds in bringing a group of non-Israelite sailors to the worship of Yahweh and precipitates the moral reform of wicked Ninevites! Isaiah, Jeremiah, and Ezekiel would have given their eyeteeth to have had so powerful an effect with so few words.

The Assyrians are spared. And Jonah is furious:

> This displeased Jonah greatly and he was grieved. He prayed to Yahweh, saying, "O Yahweh! Isn't this just what I said when I was still in my own country? That is why I fled beforehand to Tarshish. For I know that you are a compassionate and gracious god, slow to anger, abounding in kindness, renouncing punishment. Please, Yahweh, take my life, for I would rather die than live." Yahweh replied, "Are you that deeply grieved?" (4:1–4)

There is no response from Jonah, who leaves the city to sulk. His complaint seems to be twofold: If you are going to punish the wicked, then just punish them, and if you are planning to spare them, then just spare them, and don't waste my time with messages and oracles. But the stronger problem for Jonah seems to be the lack of punishment for the wicked. Jonah is indignant that the Assyrians did not get what they deserved. What happened was just what he knew would happen, right from the outset, and that is why he refused what would ultimately be a fool's errand.

The words of Jonah's complaint are carefully chosen. Comparing his description of Yahweh with the similar description of Yahweh given by Moses in Ex 34:6–7, we see what Jonah omits. Moses proclaimed:

> Yahweh! Yahweh! A god [El] compassionate and gracious, slow to anger, abounding in kindness and truth [emet], extending kindness to the thousandth generation, forgiving iniquity, transgression and sin; yet he does not remit all punishment, but visits the iniquity of parents upon children and children's children, upon the third and fourth generations.

Jonah's catalog of divine attributes differs from Moses' in two ways. First, he omits the word "truth" (*emet*).[1] Second, where Moses describes the deity's mercy as temporarily but not entirely canceling punishment of the wicked, Jonah describes the deity as forgiving iniquity and remitting all punishment entirely. These two changes are interrelated. As far as Jonah is concerned, Yahweh's complete forgiveness of iniquity is a kind of falsehood, a lack of concern for truth. If Yahweh were true to the demands of justice and the explicit terms of his covenant, he would *not* forgive all iniquity; he would reward and punish as true justice dictates. This then is Jonah's complaint: Yahweh's mercy perverts his truth and justice, because some things ought not to be forgiven. People must be held to account for their evil actions. How can Yahweh *not* do justice?

As Jonah sits in a small booth he has constructed, Yahweh causes a leafy plant to grow up over him, providing shade and saving him from much discomfort. The plant is to be the source of a final lesson for Jonah.

> Jonah was very happy about the plant. But the next day at dawn the deity provided a worm, which attacked the plant so that it withered. And when the sun rose, Elohim provided a sultry east wind; the sun beat down on Jonah's head, and he became faint. He begged for death, saying, "I would rather die than live." Then Elohim said to Jonah, "Are you deeply grieved about the plant?" "Yes" he replied, "so deeply that I want to die." Then Yahweh said: "You cared about the plant, which you did not work for and which you did not grow, which appeared overnight and perished overnight. And should not I care about Nineveh, that great city, in which there are more than a hundred and twenty thousand persons who do not yet know their right hand from their left, and many beasts as well!" (4:6b–11)

How can Yahweh *not* be compassionate? For even the most evil of peoples are no less his creation than precious Israel, and if they will only turn to him in humility, he will wipe the slate clean, show compassion, and forgive. It is only human to long for the punishment of the wicked, but Yahweh longs for their reformation and return. This short book addresses the problem of Yahweh's justice versus his mercy. Jonah is a champion of divine justice and believes that sin should be punished. He is outraged at Yahweh's forgiveness. But Jonah learns that a change of heart is enough to obtain mercy and that the true role of the prophet is to move people to reform, to repent, to return.

The date of the book of Jonah cannot be ascertained. Most scholars date it to the Persian period, partly on the (unreliable) assumption that books that are more universal in scope are influenced by the teachings of later classical prophecy, but some argue that the story is at least at base an old one. First, the Nineveh of this book is not the capital of a huge empire. Its ruler is not the ruler of world-conquering Assyria but merely the king of the town of Nineveh, and its sin is not the oppression and enslavement of Israel but the violence of its citizens, which might suggest a date before 722 B.C.E. Nineveh is another Sodom, and this story is therefore in keeping with Torah traditions in which it is assumed that Yahweh punishes non-Israelites or the nations for immorality but not for idolatry. Other nations are not obligated to accept monotheism, but they are bound by the basic moral law of the Noahide covenant.

Although a Persian provenance is likely but not entirely certain, a canonical approach can consider what the book's reception in the postexilic period might have been. The very idea of a prophet being sent to Nineveh—the capital of the hated Assyrian Empire, the home of the people who destroyed the northern kingdom of Israel in 722 and dispersed the ten tribes forever, then laid siege to Jerusalem and exacted tribute from Judah—must have been startling. Ultimately, then, this book would represent a strand of thought in postexilic Judah very different from the eschatological fervor that delighted in fantasies of the destruction of Israel's enemies, such as is found in Joel and as would be featured later in Daniel and in postbiblical apocalyptic literature, most notably the Christian book of Revelation. The book of Jonah reminded Israel that the universal god is desirous of the reform and return of all his creation and proposes that the Israelite prophet is called upon to carry the message of divine forgiveness to other nations, even those that have humiliated and despised Yahweh's chosen. Wittingly or unwittingly—we will never know—the author of this short and comic tale fostered a postexilic sense of Israel as a light unto the nations.

# Epilogue

The literature of the Hebrew Bible relates the odyssey of Israel from its earliest beginnings in the stories of individual patriarchs worshipping a local deity to its maturity as a nation forced by history to look beyond its own horizons and concerns. The Israelites were lifted up to become something greater than they could ever have planned. They came to see themselves as Yahweh's servants to the world at the same time that they struggled and argued with their god and criticized themselves for their very human weaknesses and failings.

From another vantage point, the Bible can also be seen as an anthology of works written by authors who struggled against great odds to sustain a people's covenantal relationship with its god, Yahweh. The contrast between reality and the religious-moral ideal that good prospers and evil is defeated was a distressing and perplexing problem that occupied the biblical writers (Kaufmann, *Religion of Israel,* 332). The existence of evil, the suffering of the righteous, the defeat of Yahweh's chosen—all this seemed basically incompatible with certain fundamental monotheistic intuitions, that Yahweh holds supreme power in the universe, Yahweh is essentially good and just, and his providential care extends throughout creation. How can faith in such a god be upheld in the face of evil and suffering?

Although all ancient cultures struggled with the problem of evil, it had particular poignancy for Israel. In other ancient Near Eastern literatures, we find doubts about the existence of a moral order, but only in Israel does the absence of a moral order and the question of evil touch on the very essence of the deity and the very foundation of religious faith (Kaufmann,

400

*Religion of Israel,* 332). Paganism posits the existence of primordial evil demons or gods, and thus the existence of evil and suffering does not impugn the good gods themselves. Later religious systems that grow out of the Bible increasingly posit demons or a devil to account for evil in the world. Undeserved suffering, outrageous and frustrating as it might be, can be explained at least by the jealousy or caprice of the evil gods or demons who are indifferent to human fate. But in biblical religion, there is no independent evil principle. Thus, undeserved suffering and rampant evil impugn the goodness and the justice of the deity himself. Biblical persons have no refuge from evil and suffering other than their faith in Yahweh's justice. And if that justice is slow in coming, despair and doubt threaten. For this reason, Israelite theodicy is charged with great pathos because the stakes are so high—if one loses faith in an essentially moral universe, one loses one's god or at least, as we saw in the book of Job, one loses a god who governs the world according to a clear moral standard.

The biblical writers do not approach the problem as philosophers or theologians might. For the philosopher, theodicy is primarily a logical problem, a contradiction (how can a just and good god allow evil and suffering to exist?), and like any other logical problem, it is best solved through the careful construction of a systematic argument. This is not the method or the approach of the biblical writers. For them, the problem is not philosophical—it is personal, psychological, and spiritual. The burning question is really this: How can one sustain a commitment to Israel's god in the face of national catastrophe and personal suffering? How can one have the strength to embrace, to trust, to love this god knowing that unpredictable suffering and chaos have struck and may again strike at any moment?

Various writers from various periods add their voices to Israel's struggle to come to terms with the problem of sustaining faith in the midst of evil and suffering. The aim of these writers is not to solve the philosophical problem of theodicy so much as to enable the relationship with Yahweh to survive all shocks, to make life in covenant with Yahweh a viable option, despite the evil and suffering experienced by the faithful. The Bible does not offer one single model of how to cope with this problem. A dynamic relationship with a living, personal god (rather than the static god of the philosophers) is too complex to be captured in a single one-dimensional theology. Systematic theology could not do justice to the variegated experiences of the nation and of an individual life. And so, various models are presented—not all consistent with one another, but each serving a particular segment of the community, coping with a particular challenge at a particular time. Each is an attempt to sustain Israel's relationship with Yahweh in the face of challenges to that continued relationship. Biblical writers tell stories and interpret history in order to illustrate the many ways in which various individuals and the nation as a whole have managed to make sense of their covenantal relationship with Yahweh. There is room for multiple models, multiple images of Yahweh and his relationship to Israel, and as modern readers of the Bible, we can only marvel at the unresolved polyphony of this ancient anthology.

It is as if the rabbis who were later to canonize this collection saw the truth of the words of Kohelet—to everything there is a season and a time for every purpose under heaven—and so included books with very different approaches to the fundamental problems that faced the ancient Israelites as Israelites and as human beings. After 586 B.C.E., the Deuteronomistic historian salvaged Yahwism from going the way of other defeated national religions by arguing that Israel had suffered not because Yahweh's promises weren't true but because they weren't believed. This enabled the Israelites to continue to be faithful to their god, despite the destruction of his sanctuary, chosen city, and ruler. The prophets emphasized the moral and communal aspects of the covenant, without which all sacrificial worship was anathema, and thereby unwittingly prepared the way for a worship without sacrifice in the Diaspora and in later Judaism. The Psalms give expression to the deepest emotions of the worshipper struggling with personal despair or brimming over with faith and joy. Job gives vent to the outrage we feel over unjust suffering, while Ecclesiastes preaches existential pleasures and labor as a solace for the vanity of all human endeavor. Ezra and Nehemiah confront the very real problem of assimilation with a call to Israel to close ranks, while Jonah and Ruth remind Jews of the universal providence of their god. Esther and Daniel provide encouragement of radically different kinds for Jews under threat of persecution and massacre—one a plea for self-reliance and solidarity, the other a promise of divine intervention in an apocalypse.

Do these books contradict each other? No more than a man contradicts himself when he says that today he feels happy but yesterday he felt anxious. These books capture different realities, moments, and experiences in the ever-shifting historical odyssey of the nation. Israel's relationship with her god has always been dynamic and complex. To each of these books there was a time and a purpose in the past, and as countless readers of the Bible have discovered over the centuries, these books offer continued teaching and inspiration in the shifting moments of any age.

# Notes

## Preface

1. Genesis, Exodus, Leviticus, Numbers, Deuteronomy, Joshua, Judges, 1–2 Samuel, 1–2 Kings, Isaiah, Jeremiah, Ezekiel, The Book of the Twelve (Hosea, Joel, Amos, Obadiah, Jonah, Micah, Nahum, Habakkuk, Zephaniah, Haggai, Zechariah, Malachi), Psalms, Job, Proverbs, Ruth, Song of Songs, Ecclesiastes, Lamentations, Esther, Daniel, Ezra-Nehemiah, 1–2 Chronicles.

2. As will be explained in Chapter 1, the term Old Testament is an imperfect title for both the course and the present volume. Hence I have adopted the neutral term "Bible" for the title of the present volume, because the subject of our study is the collection of books common to all Jewish and Christian Bibles. Despite the difference in titles, this volume (*Introduction to the Bible*) with its twenty-four chapters closely corresponds to the online course (*Introduction to the Old Testament*) and its twenty-four lectures. Throughout this work I refer to the object of our study variously as the Hebrew Bible or the Tanakh (see further, Chapter 1). Not all books are covered in equal depth, and a few of the smaller prophetic writings and 1–2 Chronicles receive only summary attention. Introducing students to the entire Bible in twenty-four lectures of fifty minutes each necessitated hard choices. Another teacher might have made other, equally reasonable choices of what to include and what to omit.

3. This translation now appears in *The Jewish Study Bible* (henceforth *JSB*), edited by Adele Berlin, Mark Zvi Brettler, and Michael Fishbane (Oxford: Oxford University Press, 2004).

4. Likewise, I do not capitalize pronouns that refer to the Israelite deity.

5. This does not apply when context indicates that the word Elohim is being used in the sense of "deity" or "god." Thus on occasion ha-Elohim (lit. "the god") will be rendered as "the deity" or "the god." Likewise, the phrase Yahweh Eloheykha (and similar forms) will be translated "Yahweh your god," while phrases like Yahweh Elohey Israel will be translated "Yahweh, the god of Israel."

6. For example, the year 586 B.C.E. is equivalent to the year 586 B.C.

## CHAPTER 1
## The Legacy of Ancient Israel

1. As noted in the Preface, *Israel* and *Israelite* are more general terms for a member of the Israelite ethnos, whereas *Judean* refers to a person who hails from the southern kingdom of Judah or, later, the Persian province of Yehud (536–332 B.C.E.) and subsequently the Greek and Roman province of Judea. With the destruction of the northern kingdom of Israel in 722, the only Israelites remaining were the Judeans, and thus the terms *Israelite* and *Judean* become somewhat interchangeable (except

in contexts that refer clearly to the former inhabitants of the destroyed kingdom of Israel). In the late biblical period, the term *Yehudi* (often translated "Jew" but more properly "Judean") referred to an inhabitant of Yehud/Judea. It would be some centuries before the term *Yehudi* or *Jew* was understood to designate an adherent of the tradition of Judaism, rather than an inhabitant of the province of Yehud/Judea.

2. How fair this statement is as a description of ancient religious conceptions is a matter of considerable debate. For our purposes, however, it is a useful starting position because it is the position that—fairly or not—is polemicized against by certain biblical writers. It is also the position that—right or wrong—has informed much modern biblical scholarship.

3. The name *The Bible* is from the Greek *ta biblia,* a plural form that translates literally as "the books."

4. Exodus 31:18 does describe the stone tablets of the covenant as being divinely inscribed. See also Ex 34:1 and Deut 10:12.

5. It is only in the fifth century B.C.E. that the term *Torah* clearly refers to something like the Pentateuch (or Five Books of Moses). In the Pentateuch itself, the term *torah* means a specific rule or teaching and not the complete literary work of Genesis through Deuteronomy.

6. Canonization, from the Greek *kanon,* meaning a measuring rod or ruler, refers to the process by which a work came to be included in a list of authoritative writings, or Scripture. Different communities possess different canons of the Bible.

7. The number 24 is reached by counting 1 and 2 Samuel as one book, 1 and 2 Kings as one book, 1 and 2 Chronicles as one book, the twelve minor prophets as one book, and Ezra and Nehemiah as one book—as was the practice in antiquity.

8. A challenge to the long-standing hypothesis that the settlement at Qumran near the Dead Sea was home to a monastic sect was issued by archaeologists Yitzhak Magen and Yuval Peleg. In "Back to Qumran: Ten Years of Excavations and Research, 1993–2004," in *The Site of the Dead Sea Scrolls: Archaeological Interpretation and Debate,* edited by Katharina Galor, Jean-Baptiste Humbert, and Jurgen Zangenberg (Leiden: Brill, 2006), Magen and Peleg argue that Qumran was the site of a pottery factory and that there is no essential connection between the activity of the site and the library of scrolls found in nearby caves. The view has raised interest but has not replaced the prevailing consensus that the scrolls were the library of a sect that lived at Qumran.

## CHAPTER 2
### Understanding Biblical Monotheism

1. Yehezkel Kaufmann, *The Religion of Israel,* trans. Moshe Greenberg (New York: Schocken Books, 1972), p. 22. The following presentation of Kaufmann's views draws extensively on pp. 21–121 of *The Religion of Israel.*

2. Yehezkel Kaufmann, "The Genesis of Israel," in *Great Ages and Ideas of the Jewish People,* edited by Leo W. Schwarz (New York: Modern Library, 1956), pp. 3–29, pp. 12–13.

3. Stephen A. Geller, "The Religion of the Bible," in *The Jewish Study Bible,* edited by Adele Berlin and Marc Zvi Brettler (New York: Oxford University Press, 2004), pp. 2021–2040.

4.  I cite here the more user-friendly translation/paraphrase found in Victor H. Matthews and Don C. Benjamin, *Old Testament Parallels: Laws and Stories from the Ancient Near East*, 2nd ed. (New York: Paulist Press, 1997), pp. 7–8. Readers interested in a full translation may consult James B. Pritchard's *Ancient Near Eastern Texts Relating to the Old Testament* (henceforth *ANET*), 2nd ed. (Princeton, NJ: Princeton University Press, 1955), p. 6.

5.  Citing again the more user-friendly translation/paraphrase found in *Old Testament Parallels*, pp. 4–5. Readers interested in a full translation may consult Pritchard, *ANET*, pp. 4–5.

## CHAPTER 3
## Genesis 1–3

1.  Nahum Sarna, *Understanding Genesis* (New York: Schocken Books, 1966). The various works of Michael Coogan have also been consulted for this chapter, especially *The Old Testament: A Historical and Literary Introduction to the Hebrew Scriptures* (New York: Oxford University Press, 2006).

2.  "The Creation Epic," trans. E. A. Speiser, in Pritchard, *ANET*, pp. 60–71. All subsequent citations of *Enuma Elish* are from the same translation.

3.  We focus here on the first creation story. The second creation story, in Gen 2:4b–3, contains many features that are at odds with a thoroughgoing monotheism.

4.  Hayes's translation following Jacob Milgrom, "Leviticus 1–16: A New Translation with Introduction and Commentary," in vol. 1 of *The Anchor Bible Dictionary* (henceforth *ABD*), edited by David Noel Freedman (New York: Doubleday, 1992) p. 705.

5.  Hayes's translation.

6.  Many readers mistakenly refer to this tree as "the tree of knowledge" and assume that it confers wisdom in a general sense. In fact, it is "the tree of the knowledge of *good and evil*," and, as will be argued here, this tree is the occasion for the first human pair to learn that they possess moral freedom (the ability to know and to choose good or evil actions).

## CHAPTER 4
## Doublets and Contradictions

1.  For example, in Gen 1, Elohim creates whole species, including earthlings—both male and female—at once, while in Gen 2, Yahweh creates a single male individual and only later a female. In the first story humans are the final creation, but in the second story humans are created *before* the animals.

2.  All translations of the *Epic of Gilgamesh* are taken from the translation in Pritchard, *ANET*, pp. 72–99.

3.  Unlike the first creation story, the second creation story refers to the deity as Yahweh. See the Preface for an explanation of the appellations of Israel's deity and the principle for rendering those names that is employed in this volume.

4.  The "satan" will be discussed further in Chapter 20.

5.  Later biblical and religious traditions understand *adam* to be a proper name.

6.  The woman is finally given a personal name, Eve, after the expulsion.

7. Sarna (*Understanding Genesis*, 28), however, disputes this interpretation, arguing that there is no evidence for the denigration of the farming life in biblical literature generally.

8. This is not to say that Yahweh does not change his mind and adjust his plans. He does, but in response to human actions that are sometimes unpredictable to him. Indeed, the very decision to destroy humans in the first place arose in response to the unexpected evil that they performed, leading Yahweh to regret having made them at all. Again, Yahweh is not depicted in these early stories as possessing the attributes of the "God" constructed by later western theology: foreknowledge and immutability.

9. The universal worship of Yahweh is an idea that appears in other biblical texts, as we shall see.

10. Hayes's translation following Milgrom, *Leviticus 1–16*, p. 705.

## CHAPTER 5
## The Modern Critical Study of the Bible

1. Later published as *Prolegomena to the History of Israel*.

2. As noted earlier, to avoid confusion with the "God" constructed by later western theology, I avoid this translation in this volume and employ the untranslated term "Elohim" or simply "the deity" or "Israel's god."

3. For a readable introduction to and illustration of literary criticism, see Norman C. Habel's *Literary Criticism of the Old Testament* (Philadelphia: Fortress Press, 1971). A popular but excellent introduction that critiques Wellhausen and the Christian-centric biases of many source critics is Richard Friedman's *Who Wrote the Bible* (New York: Summit, 1987).

4. A distinction must be made between P materials of a redactional nature (genealogical tables that effect a transition between Pentateuchal narratives, framing materials such as Gen 1 and Deut 34 that open and close the entire Pentateuch) that likely originate in the sixth century or a little later and the cultic and ritual materials in Leviticus and Numbers that likely derive from priestly circles in the First Temple period.

5. Marc Zvi Brettler, *How to Read the Bible* (Philadelphia: Jewish Publication Society, 2005), p. 21.

## CHAPTER 6
## Biblical Narrative

1. See Chapter 7 for a brief discussion of this name.

2. The same verb is used in Gen 17:17 to describe Abraham's reaction to the same news. He, too, mocks as absurd the very idea of Sarah having a child. The Hebrew root *ṣ.ḥ.q.* is often translated as "laugh," but this is a poor translation since the unqualified English term *laugh* bears a positive connotation. By contrast, the unqualified Hebrew term has a contemptuous and derisive connotation and, depending on context, will refer to (1) a mocking or scoffing laughter (Ezra 23:32), (2) jesting (Gen 19:14), (3) "toying with" someone (Gen 39:17), (4) lewd or sexual conduct (Gen 26:8), (5) making sport of someone (Jud 16:25), or (6) aggressive and even violent interac-

tion (2 Sam 2:14). The root *s.h.q.* has a positive connotation (laughter in the positive sense) only when it is qualified by an explicit marker of joy or in a context clearly indicating joy (as in Ps 126:2, where the speaker imagines a dreamlike state of great happiness; Eccl 2:2, where the term is parallel to *simḥah,* or joy; and arguably Job 8:21, though there the term may mean triumphant and thus slightly mocking laughter).

3. Sarah's fear of usurpation finds some footing in the narrator's artful description of Ishmael as *meṣaḥeq*—which can be taken as a pun on Isaac's name, meaning "Isaac-ing"—playing or taking the part of Isaac!

4. New York: Basic Books, 1985, 2011.

5. Erich Auerbach's study of Gen 22 in *Mimesis: The Representation of Reality in Western Literature,* trans. Willard R. Trask (Princeton, NJ: Princeton University Press, 1968), contrasts the expansive and fully foregrounded style of Homer with the terse and laconic style of the biblical writer.

6. The deity who issues the order to sacrifice Isaac is referred to as "[the] Elohim" (vv. 1, 8-9), but the name Yahweh is used in the second half of the story when Abraham is told to desist and is praised for his readiness to obey (vv. 11, 14, and following).

7. See James Kugel, *How to Read the Bible* (New York: Free Press, 2008), 131, and Jon D. Levenson, *The Death and Resurrection of the Beloved Son* (New Haven, CT: Yale University Press, 1993), p. 5.

8. The older is Esau from whom the Edomites descend, and the younger is Jacob, or Israel. Historically, the nations of Israel and Edom were enemies, and Edom was subjugated for a time by Israel in the reign of David.

9. Although, as we have seen, the characterization of Abraham as faithfully fulfilling the divine plan may not withstand close scrutiny.

10. Coogan, *The Old Testament,* p. 72.

## CHAPTER 7
## Israel in Egypt

1. Nahum Sarna, *Exploring Exodus: The Heritage of Biblical Israel* (New York: Schocken Books, 1986), p. 8. The discussion of Exodus in this chapter and the next draws heavily from Sarna.

2. Citing the translation/paraphrase found in Matthews and Benjamin, *Old Testament Parallels,* pp. 91–93. Readers interested in a full translation may consult Pritchard, *ANET,* p. 376.

3. The Sargon Legend, third millennium B.C.E. (twenty-third century B.C.E.), in Pritchard, *ANET,* p. 119.

4. Or possibly, the statement is causative: "I will cause to be what I will cause to be."

5. The story is likely an ex post facto etiological account of the name Yahweh, whose origins were lost.

6. Coogan, *The Old Testament,* p. 82.

7. The following information on divine nomenclature and the Canaanite pantheon may be found in Coogan, *The Old Testament,* pp. 81–82.

8. Mark S. Smith, *The Early History of God: Yahweh and the Other Deities in Ancient Israel,* 2nd ed. (Grand Rapids, MI: William B. Eerdmans, 2002), p. 7.

CHAPTER 8
## From Egypt to Sinai

1. John Collins, *Introduction to the Hebrew Bible with CD-Rom* (Minneapolis, MN: Augsburg Fortress, 2004), pp. 115–119.
2. Because of Israel's monotheism, Yahweh is not said to be a new god who overthrows an older god; rather, he is said to be the same god but with a new name. Henceforth El is to be known as Yahweh.
3. Jon Levenson, *Sinai and Zion: An Entry into the Jewish Bible* (San Francisco, CA: Harper, 1985), Introduction.
4. See also Sarna, *Exploring Exodus,* pp. 136–137, and Coogan, *The Old Testament,* p. 110, all drawing on the scholarship of G. E. Mendenhall.

CHAPTER 9
## Biblical Law

1. This point is not uncontested in the biblical text. According to Ex 20:1-18, the people hear all ten utterances and are filled with fear. They ask Moses to serve as intermediary, conveying Yahweh's words to them, because they fear for their lives. That Yahweh's revelation to the entire community encompassed no more and no less than the Ten Commandments is reiterated in Deut 5:19. However, Deut 5:5 suggests that Moses served as intermediary even for the Ten Commandments because of the people's great fear.
2. The commandments are differently enumerated by Jews and Christians and among different Christian denominations. See Table 4.
3. Brettler, *How to Read the Bible,* p. 66.
4. All translations of these collections are taken from Martha T. Roth, *Law Collections from Mesopotamia and Asia Minor,* 2nd ed. (Atlanta, GA: Society of Biblical Literature, 1997).
5. Moshe Greenberg, "Some Postulates of Biblical Criminal Law," in *Yehezkel Kaufmann Jubilee Volume* (Jerusalem: Magnes Press, 1960). Reprinted in *The Jewish Expression,* edited by Judah Goldin (New Haven, CT: Yale University Press, 1976). Greenberg's article was critiqued by Bernard Jackson in "Reflections of Biblical Criminal Law," in *Essays on Jewish and Comparative Legal History* (Leiden: Brill, 1975), pp. 25–63, who questions the very enterprise of identifying the postulates that underlie a collection of laws. Greenberg answers these criticisms in "More Reflections on Biblical Criminal Law," in *Studies in Bible,* Scripta Hierosolymitana 31, edited by S. Japhet (Jerusalem: Magnes, 1986), pp. 1–48.
6. Much information is also drawn from Nahum Sarna, *Exploring Exodus,* pp. 158–189.
7. The ancient Near Eastern collections use three terms to refer to persons: *awilum, mushkenum,* and *wardum. Wardum* is clearly a slave and is so translated. *Awilum* is used in two ways. It is the term for a general, nonspecific person as the subject of the provision of law in question and is thus translated by Roth as "man" (as in the text just cited). However, when it stands in opposition to *mushkenum* or *wardum,* it refers to a member of the highest privileged class, and *mushkenum* refers to a person of lower social prestige (perhaps a serf?) than the *awilum* (perhaps a free citizen?). Roth translates *mushkenum* as commoner and, in these contexts, leaves *awilum*

untranslated. See discussion in Roth, p. 8, and glossary entries, pp. 268 and 271. See also Sarna, *Exploring Exodus*, p. 166.

8. While social distinctions among *free* persons are eliminated in biblical criminal and bodily injury law, slavery is still an accepted institution. Slaves are not entitled to the same protections and rights as free persons. Slavery will be discussed more fully in Chapter 11.

9. Keeping in mind that *citizen* refers to free male householders and excludes slaves. On the other hand, the personal injury laws include the resident alien within their purview. There are indications that women may also have been deemed as persons rather than property for the purposes of personal injury and homicide law (see Ex 21:28-32, which equates male and female in the laws of the goring ox, and Lev 24:17-22, which refers to death or injury to any "human being"—presumably without regard for gender).

10. A comparison of the slave laws is taken up in Chapter 11.

11. Such punishments are often described in the secondary literature as "vicarious punishment" (Greenberg, "Some Postulates," p. 29; Sarna, *Exploring Exodus,* p. 176), but this is inaccurate as the principle at work is not a principle of substitution. Rather, these cases assume the male head of household is the legal actor or subject. Any loss he causes another legal actor (another male head of household) of equal status must be punished in a literal equivalence (the principle of talion). Thus, since the legal actor caused another legal actor to lose his daughter or son, he must suffer the same loss as punishment, and therefore his daughter or son is put to death. The minor in these cases is not deemed an independent legal actor but the "property" of the father. In the Middle Assyrian Laws, the raped wife is likewise not deemed a legal actor, and therefore the offense is against her husband. The rapist must suffer the same harm he inflicted: Since he has harmed *a man* by raping his wife, the literally equivalent punishment is that he should be punished by having his wife raped. The biblical legislation rejects all such punishments in the administration of human justice. However, divine justice works differently. Yahweh does punish collectively and transgenerationally in the Torah books; see Greenberg, pp. 29–30.

## CHAPTER 10
## The Priestly Legacy

1. Jonathan Klawans, *Impurity and Sin in Ancient Israel* (New York: Oxford University Press, 2000). See also Klawans's excellent and very readable summary, "Concepts of Purity in the Bible," in *JSB*, pp. 2041–2047.

2. Klawans, "Concepts," pp. 2044, 2046.

3. Jonathan Klawans, *Purity, Sacrifice and the Temple: Symbolism and Supersessionism in the Study of Ancient Judaism* (New York: Oxford University Press, 2006), p. 58.

4. Klawans, *Purity,* p. 68.

5. Klawans, *Purity,* pp. 72–73.

6. Jacob Milgrom, "Israel's Sanctuary: The Priestly 'Picture of Dorian Gray,' " in *Studies in Cultic Theology and Terminology* (Leiden: Brill, 1983), pp. 75–84.

7. Milgrom, "Israel's Sanctuary," p. 82.

8. Jacob Milgrom, "Leviticus 1–16," pp. 704–741.

9. JPS translation, but substituting the more accurate "impure" for "unclean" as a translation of Hebrew *tame'*.
10. For Wellhausen's views on religion, see Patrick D. Miller Jr., "Wellhausen and the History of Israelite Religion," in *Semeia* 25 (1982): 61–73.

CHAPTER 11
## On the Steps of Moab

1. The name Deuteronomy means "second law" and reflects the fact that the book repeats many of the instructions and laws found in Ex 19–23. The relationship between the various legal collections in the Pentateuch will be discussed below.
2. Moshe Weinfeld, "Deuteronomy, Book of," in *ABD*, pp. 168–183, p. 169.
3. Bernard Levinson, "Introduction to Deuteronomy," in *JSB*, pp. 356–362, p. 359.
4. See Levinson, "Introduction to Deuteronomy," p. 359: "Had possession of the land remained central to the covenant, Israelite religion would have collapsed. The fulfillment of the Torah is thus redactionally redefined as obedience to the requirements of covenantal law rather than the acquisition of a finite possession."
5. Weinfeld, "Deuteronomy, Book of," p. 168.
6. Weinfeld, "Deuteronomy, Book of," p. 169. For an excellent discussion of Deuteronomy as a radical reform document, transforming multiple aspects of Israelite culture, see Levinson, *Deuteronomy and the Hermeneutics of Legal Innovation* (Oxford: Oxford University Press, 1997).
7. See Levinson, "Introduction to Deuteronomy," p. 350, and further, Levinson, *Deuteronomy*, esp. chapter 1.
8. Weinfeld, *ABD*, p. 170.
9. Levinson, "Introduction to Deuteronomy," p. 358, and Coogan, *Old Testament*, p. 181.
10. Coogan, *Old Testament*, p. 176.
11. Coogan, *Old Testament*, p. 176.
12. Coogan, *Old Testament*, p. 177.
13. Coogan, *Old Testament*, p. 170.

CHAPTER 12
## The Deuteronomistic History I

1. An exception is the book of Jonah, which is a short story about a prophet named Jonah.
2. For an example of parallel language, compare Deut 11:24 with Josh 1:3 and Deut 4:39 with Josh 2:11.
3. Noth lays out his ideas in *The Deuteronomistic History* (*JSOT* supplement), trans. J. Doull (Sheffield, England: Sheffield Academic Press, 1981).
4. An excellent example of the institution of *herem* outside biblical Israel may be found in the Moabite stone discovered by archaeologists in 1868. In the inscription on the stone, the ninth-century B.C.E. King Mesha of Moab boasts of devoting (i.e., slaying) thousands of Israelites to his god Astar-Chemosh. For the hyperbolic nature of these texts, see note 8 below.

5. The twelve tribes among whom the land is divided do not correspond exactly to the twelve sons of Jacob as listed in the birth narratives of Gen 29–30 and the deathbed blessings delivered by Jacob in Gen 49: six sons by Leah, four sons by the concubines, Bilhah and Zilpah, and two sons by Rachel (Joseph and Benjamin). According to Numbers 26 and Josh 13–20, two tribes stem from Joseph through his two sons—Ephraim and Manasseh. The number of land allotments remains at twelve, however, because the Levites are not assigned land. As the priestly class, they are to be supported by the perquisites of the cult (sacrifices), tithes, and other gifts.

6. For a full discussion of the three models for the emergence of Israel (the immigration, conquest, and revolt models), see Norman Gottwald, *The Tribes of Yahweh: A Sociology of the Religion of Liberated Israel, 1250–1050 BCE* (Sheffield, England: Sheffield Academic Press, 1999), pp. 191–236.

7. See the discussion of the emergence of Israel in Coogan, *Old Testament,* pp. 220–224.

8. The claims of utter destruction are hyperbolic. Compare the inscription of King Mesha of Moab from the ninth century B.C.E. that boasts: "And [the god] Chemosh said to me, 'Go take Nebo from Israel.' So I went by night and fought against it from the break of dawn until noon, taking it and slaying all seven thousand men, boys, women, girls, and maid-servants, for I had devoted them to destruction for (the god) Ashtar-Chemosh." King Mesha's declarations of absolute victory and utter destruction of Israel are hyperbolic, and in all likelihood the author of the book of Joshua engages in the same braggadocio. Nevertheless, this doesn't lessen the shock value for a modern reader, even though war atrocities in modern times have been no less savage and brutal. For the full text of this inscription, see Pritchard, *ANET,* pp. 320–321.

9. This explicit reference to the fact that the patriarchs were not strict Yahwists is noteworthy.

## CHAPTER 13
## The Deuteronomistic History II

1. The Hebrew term translated here as "chieftains" is the word *shofetim,* more commonly translated "judges." The translation "chieftain" reflects the fact that the primary activity of the *shofetim* was military rather than judicial.

2. Coogan, *Old Testament,* p. 278.

3. Second Samuel contains no such tradition. In 2 Sam 7:1-7, David expresses a wish to build a temple to house the ark, but Yahweh dismisses the idea as unnecessary, promising instead to make a house (i.e., a dynasty) for David.

4. Kugel, *How to Read the Bible* (New York: Free Press, 2007), pp. 482–484.

## CHAPTER 14
## The Kingdoms of Judah and Israel

1. This claim is argued throughout Jon D. Levenson, *Sinai and Zion: An Entry into the Jewish Bible* (San Francisco, CA: Harper, 1985).

2. Moshe Weinfeld, "The Covenant of Grant in the Old Testament and in the Ancient Near East," *Journal of the American Oriental Society* 90 (1970): 184–203.

3. Levenson, *Sinai and Zion,* pp. 187–206.

4. On the other hand, insofar as the Deuteronomistic historian seeks to blame Israel's kings for the nation's demise, Solomon's violations are key to its characterization of him, so the existence of material damaging to Solomon's reputation is not necessarily a sign of older sources.

5. Pritchard, *ANET,* p. 320. Mesha is mentioned in 2 Kgs 3:1–8, 24–27, where he is said to battle with Omri's grandson Jehoram.

6. Both translations are from Pritchard, *ANET,* p. 284.

7. "Judean" is a more accurate translation than "Jew," which appears in Pritchard, *ANET,* pp. 287–288.

8. Pritchard, *ANET,* pp. 287–288.

9. Levinson, "Deuteronomy," *JSB,* pp. 357–358. It is thought that the legal core of Deuteronomy was composed earlier in the northern kingdom. With the fall of the northern kingdom in 722, the document may have been brought with priests fleeing to Jerusalem, where it was stored in the Temple until its discovery in 622. Josiah undertook a radical reformation in 622 and succeeded where Hezekiah had had less success. He purged the pagan cults, destroyed the outlying altars, and brought their priests to Jerusalem, centralizing all worship in the Temple there. Josiah convened the elders of the people, read them the book of the Torah, and renewed the covenant with Yahweh.

## CHAPTER 15
## Israelite Prophecy

1. Sarna, *Exploring Exodus,* p. 49.

2. For further discussion, see Chapter 16.

3. Yehezkel Kaufmann, *The Religion of Israel,* trans. Moshe Greenberg (New York: Schocken Books, 1972), p. 214. See further the discussion of the message of the prophets in Part III of Kaufmann.

## CHAPTER 16
## The Prophetic Response to the Events of History

1. Yehezkel Kaufmann, *The Religion of Israel,* trans. Moshe Greenberg (New York: Schocken Books, 1972), p. 347.

2. Archaeologists have indeed uncovered couches made of ivory in the area of ancient Samaria.

3. A unit of measure.

4. Kaufmann, *The Religion of Israel,* p. 345.

5. Kaufmann, *The Religion of Israel,* p. 367.

6. Kaufmann, *The Religion of Israel,* p. 365.

## CHAPTER 17
## Prophets of the Assyrian Crisis

1. There is a pun here. The words "Ishi" and "Baali" both can designate a husband, but the latter has obvious connections with the god Baal. The prophecy points forward

to a time when Israel will speak of Yahweh as her husband in terms that are free of Baal associations (Ishi rather than Baali).

2. The identification is based on the Greek translation of Hebrew "young woman" as *parthenos,* meaning "virgin." However, the original Hebrew term does not indicate virginity, and the passage does not refer to a virgin birth.

3. The last line contains an example of chiasm (a literary pattern that features inverted order, resemblingthe Greek letter *chi,* or "X"): mind, ears, and eyes are repeated in reverse order (abc-cba).

## CHAPTER 18
## Judean Prophets

1. Hayes's translation.

2. On an archaeological note, scholars have identified two bullae as seals of Jeremiah's amanuensis, Baruch son of Neriah. Discovered in Jerusalem in 1975 and 1996, the inscriptions on these bullae read "Of Baruch, son of Neriah, the scribe." See Figure 9.

## CHAPTER 19
## Responses to the Destruction: Ezekiel and 2–3 Isaiah

1. This idea is not unique to Israel. In the Moabite Stone inscription, Chemosh is said to punish his city by allowing it to be humbled by Omri of Israel. See Pritchard, *ANET,* p. 320.

2. Some of the most vivid and bizarre visions and actions of prophets are prefaced with an announcement that "the hand of Yahweh was/fell upon" the prophet. So, for example, Ezek 1:3; 3:14–15, 22–24; 8:1–2; 33:21–23; 37:1–2; 40:1–4; and in connection with other prophets 1 Kgs 18:4; 2 Kgs 3:15; Jer 15:17. According to J. J. M. Roberts, arguing on the basis of various parallels within Akkadian, Canaanite, and Egyptian literature, the semantic development of the prophetic use of the phrase "the hand of Yahweh [upon him/me]" depends on "a similarity between the prophetic phenomenon designated by the expression and certain symptoms of a pathological nature"—either disease or insanity. See Roberts, "The Hand of Yahweh," *Vetus Testamentum* 21, no. 2 (1971): 244–251, p. 251. Reprinted in J. J. M. Roberts, *The Bible and the Ancient Near East: Collected Essays* (Winona Lake, IN: Eisenbrauns, 2002), pp. 95–101.

3. "I Yahweh your god am an impassioned god, visiting the guilt of the parents upon the children, upon the third and upon the fourth generations of those who reject me, but showing kindness to the thousandth generation of those who love me and keep my commandments."

4. Even the repetition of the Decalogue in Deuteronomy 7 rejects the idea and states that Yahweh punishes the sinner instantly.

5. The recently discovered Isaiah scroll among the Dead Sea Scrolls starts a new column with chapter 40, which many scholars interpret as an implicit recognition of the distinct provenance of chapters 1–39 and the remaining chapters.

6. For example, Matthew 8:17; Luke 22:28; Acts 8:32–35; Romans 10:16; 1 Peter 2:21–5.

7. In other words, the covenant and loyalty that was promised to David, Yahweh now transfers to Israel.

CHAPTER 20
## Responses to the Destruction: Lamentations and Wisdom

1. Mesopotamian city laments, or dirges intoned by a city's tutelary goddess over the city's ruins, exist for Sumer, Ur, Nippur, Eridu, and Uruk.
2. Wisdom material is not confined to these books. In the Torah and Prophets, we find individual proverbs and wise sayings—testimony to the antiquity of this genre in Israel. There are also extrabiblical examples of Israelite wisdom texts dating to the Second Temple period, including the Wisdom of Solomon and Ecclesiasticus (or Ben Sira), which have been preserved primarily in Greek.
3. The universal and humanistic features of Israelite literature have been taken as a sign of lateness by scholars who see universalism as a "moral advance" and therefore assume that it was something toward which Israel evolved in her maturity, under the influence of the classical prophets and the experience of exile. This view reflects a modern bias that favors universalistic thinking. Individual and universal morality both have ancient roots, making this view somewhat difficult to maintain as a criterion for dating these works.
4. Compare in particular the third-millennium B.C.E. Egyptian "Teaching of Amen-emopet" (Pritchard, *ANET*, pp. 421–424) and the Babylonian "Counsels of Wisdom" (Pritchard, *ANET*, pp. 426–427).
5. The two component literary units in the book of Job employ different terms to refer to the deity, suggesting diverse sources. The prose framework predominantly employs the tetragrammaton Yahweh, with occasional occurrences of Elohim, while the lengthy poetic dialogue uses only El/Eloah forms.
6. The term appears in 1 Chr 21:1 without the definite article, but even this relatively late occurrence is understood by most scholars as a reference to a human accuser and not the "Devil" of Hellenistic Jewish literature and Christian literature.
7. The Hebrew text euphemistically reads "bless Yahweh" in order to avoid writing "curse Yahweh." Translations vary: Some replicate the euphemisms, while others give the intended sense of "curse Yahweh."
8. The translations of Job in this chapter are an eclectic mix based on the translations of Moshe Greenberg, "Job," in *The Literary Guide to the Bible*, edited by Robert Alter and Frank Kermode (Cambridge, MA: Belknap Press of Harvard University Press, 1987), pp. 283–304 (indicated by a "Gr"); Edwin M. Good, *In Turns of Tempest: A Reading of Job, with a Translation* (Stanford, CA: Stanford University Press, 1990), pp. 49–173 (indicated by a "G"); and the *JPS* translation (unmarked). All translations are adjusted to reflect the original text's designation of the deity as Yahweh, Elohim, El, or Eloah.
9. Good, *In Turns of Tempest*. The interpretation offered in this chapter follows Good closely and is also deeply influenced by Moshe Greenberg, "Job."
10. Y. Kaufmann, *The Religion of Israel*, p. 335.
11. Moshe Greenberg, "Job," p. 295.
12. That is, the god of the monotheizing sources of the Bible, as opposed to the god of Israelite-Judean religion, who, as we have seen, shared many characteristics with gods like El and Baal.

## CHAPTER 21
## Canonical Criticism

1. Sheol refers to a shadowy place beneath the earth where the shades of the dead reside, an ancient notion in Israel. However, Sheol is in no way connected with the idea of just rewards and punishments after death.
2. See also 2:24–25, 8:15.
3. There is much ambiguity in this Hebrew preposition, which can mean "for David," "to David," or "of/by David."
4. See Hermann Gunkel and Joachim Begrich, *Introduction to the Psalms: The Genres of the Religious Lyrics of Israel,* trans. James D. Nogalski (Macon, GA: Mercer University Press, 1998), and Sigmund Mowinckel, *The Psalms in Israel's Worship* (Nashville, TN: Abingdon Press, 1962).
5. Adapted from C. E. Walsh, *Exquisite Desire: Religion, the Erotic and the Song of Songs* (Minneapolis, MN: Fortress Press, 2000), pp. 111–112, as presented in Michael Coogan, *The Old Testament: A Historical and Literary Introduction to the Hebrew Scriptures* (New York: Oxford University Press, 2006), p. 496.
6. Mishnah Yadayim 3:5.

## CHAPTER 22
## The Restoration

1. The books of 1 and 2 Chronicles provide a second account of the history of Israel (indeed, 1 Chr begins with Adam) up to the Babylonian exile, echoing much of what is contained in the books of Samuel and Kings but with a priestly bias and eliminating some materials that shed a poor light on Israel's kings (e.g., the story of David and Bathsheba). The Chronicler is less interested in David's political genius than in his role in establishing Jerusalem as the religious capital, in conceiving of the building of the Temple, and in organizing the music of the Temple.
2. The Masoretic tradition presents Ezra and Nehemiah as a single unified work, but differences in theme and language use suggest that the works were originally independent.
3. See Victor H. Matthews, *A Brief History of Ancient Israel* (Louisville, KY: Westminster John Knox Press, 2002), pp. 117–119.
4. It is not clear that Ezra had the Torah as we have it today, but he seems to have had something very close since his prohibitions are closely allied with (and possibly creative exegesis of) some Pentateuchal passages. On the other hand, there are significant differences and expansions. It is possible that Ezra is simply transmitting older customary traditions directly or (more likely) in modified form.
5. See Isa 7:20 for "feet" as a euphemism for genitals. "To lie down" may also be a euphemism for sexual intercourse.
6. See Christine Hayes, *Gentile Impurities and Jewish Identities: Intermarriage and Conversion from the Bible to the Talmud* (New York: Oxford University Press, 2002), Chapters 4 and 5.

CHAPTER 23
## Postexilic Prophets and the Rise of Apocalyptic

1. The math is not perfect, as the author of Daniel did not have an accurate sense of the passage of time since Jeremiah, but it was close enough.

CHAPTER 24
## Israel and the Nations

1. There is a pun on Jonah's name. Amittai is from the same root as *emet* (truth). Jonah ben Amittai is thus the champion of truth, upbraiding Yahweh for his lack of truthfulness in executing justice.

# Index